What's So Important About Music Education?

Routledge Research in Education

What's So Important About Music Education?

J. Scott Goble

Routledge
Taylor & Francis Group
New York   London

First published 2010
by Routledge
711 Third Avenue, New York, NY 10017

Simultaneously published in the UK
by Routledge
2 Park Square, Milton Park, Abingdon, Oxfordshire OX14 4RN

Routledge is an imprint of the Taylor & Francis Group, an informa business

First issued in paperback 2011

Typeset in Sabon by IBT Global.

Library of Congress Cataloging in Publication Data
Goble, J. Scott.
   What's so important about music education? / by J. Scott Goble.
      p. cm.—(Routledge research in education ; 32)
   Includes bibliographical references and index.
   1. Music—Instruction and study—United States—Philosophy.   2. Music—
Instruction and study—United States—History.   I. Title.
   MT1.G58 2009
   780.71'073—dc22
                                                    2009031842

ISBN13: 978-0-415-80054-9 (hbk)
ISBN13: 978-0-415-53368-3 (pbk)
ISBN13: 978-0-203-85322-1 (ebk)

To my parents James and Betty Goble, my wife Sumarme Goble, and my daughters Susanna and Jennifer

Contents

Figures

Acknowledgments

With gratitude to Judith Becker, Catherine Carignan, Jere Humphreys, Carol Scott Kassner, Paul Lehman, Sandra Goble Peabody, Barton Polot, James Standifer, Dennis Sumara, and Terrence Tice for critical commentary and support.

Portions of this book include material reprinted from the following sources:

J. Scott Goble, "Cultural Iconicities and Indexicalities: Parallel Patterns of Cognition in 'Music' and 'Visual Arts.'" In *Music and the Arts: Acta Semiotica Fennica* 23 (Proceedings of the Seventh International Congress on Musical Signification). Imatra, Finland: International Semiotics Institute, June 7, 2001. Book edited by Eero Tarasti. Helsinki, Finland: International Semiotics Institute, 2006.

J. Scott Goble, "Nationalism in United States Music Education during World War II." *Journal of Historical Research in Music Education* 30 (April 2009): 103–17.

J. Scott Goble, "Perspectives on Practice: A Pragmatic Comparison of the Praxial Philosophies of David Elliott and Thomas Regelski." *Philosophy of Music Education Review* 11 (Spring 2003): 23–44. Published by Indiana University Press.

J. Scott Goble, "A Pragmatist Perspective on the Historical Roles of Music Education in the United States." *Diskussion Musikpädagogik*, January 2010.

1 Music as an Academic Subject in the Public Schools of the United States
An Inherent Cultural Tension

The United States themselves are essentially the greatest poem. . . .
Here is not merely a nation but a teeming nation of nations.[1]

Walt Whitman

During the summer of 1967, fifty musicians, educators, scientists, philosophers, theologians, heads of labor organizations, representatives from corporations, foundations, communications, government, and other concerned leaders from throughout the United States participated in a symposium at Tanglewood, the annual summer concert venue of the Boston Symphony Orchestra. They met for the purpose of appraising the future roles of music professionals, particularly music educators, in the United States, a nation they characterized as "an emerging post-industrial society."[2] They collectively recognized that the purposes and practices of the music education profession at that time were rapidly becoming outmoded as the social and cultural characteristics, technological orientation, and musical predilections of the nation were changing. In a document they produced at the end of this conference, the "Tanglewood Declaration," they affirmed their collective belief in the importance of the study of music to public education in the U.S., and they advocated a change in the curricular focus of the subject, asserting that school music programs should be global in scope:

> Music of all periods, styles, forms, and cultures belongs in the curriculum.
> The musical repertory should be expanded to involve music of our time
> in its rich variety, including currently popular teen-age music and avant-
> garde music, American folk music and the music of other cultures.[3]

Since the time of the Tanglewood Symposium, many music educators have expanded their curricula to include not only the art music and sacred music of Europe and the U.S., as they had in the past, but also popular, folk, and contemporary music as well as the music of numerous world cultures. Recent years have seen the introduction of African drumming ensembles,

Caribbean steel bands, and Javanese gamelan ensembles into the schools, as well as other musical groups not previously associated with America's dominant musical traditions. Some of the music published for the "traditional" school music ensembles—bands, orchestras, and choruses—now utilizes sounds, melodies, and principles of construction drawn from the musical traditions of different world peoples. The leading organization of U.S. music educators, the Music Educators National Conference (MENC), has published increasing numbers of books, audio- and videotapes, and journal articles for the purpose of supporting teachers in their introduction of these various musical traditions into the schools.

At the same time, school populations have become more ethnically and culturally diverse, reflecting the increasing variation in the ancestries of the nation's citizenry due to changes in immigration patterns. The first immigrants to arrive upon the North American continent were primarily white Europeans,[4] but by the time of the 2000 census the more than 281 million citizens of the U.S. included approximately 34.7 million Blacks or African Americans, 35.3 million Hispanics, and 10.2 million Asians.[5] The ethnicity of the nation's population continues to diversify; of the 974,000 people who immigrated to the U.S. in 1992, nearly 44 percent came from Mexico, Central-, and South America, 37 percent were from Asia, and only 15 percent arrived from Europe.[6] Not surprisingly, some of the nation's music educators now utilize music of cultural groups of different ethnicities and from different geographical areas in their instruction, in an effort to make their programs more culturally inclusive. However, the increasing ethnic and cultural diversity of the U.S. and its public schools and the introduction of non-Western musical traditions into the music education curriculum have combined to create two difficult problems for music educators: One problem concerns the instructional content of music courses; the other, public questioning of the very inclusion of music classes in schools.

THE *CURRICULUM CONTENT* PROBLEM

Stated in the simplest terms, the first problem U.S. music educators are presently facing concerns this question: *Whose music should be included in the curriculum?* Some teachers presently working in the public schools have been disinclined or slow to introduce music from non-Western traditions into their classes, despite the increase in the ethnic and cultural diversity of the students comprising them. With regard to first-generation immigrant students, these teachers hold the opinion that "Since they have come to *our* country, they should learn *our* musical traditions," and, given the international ubiquity of American popular music and the attractiveness it holds for people—especially young people—in many countries, many recent immigrants may prefer to go along with them and leave their past traditions behind. Other teachers have pointed out that they personally don't know how to teach music from non-Western traditions, since they have little knowledge of the vocal styles or the instruments involved, and there is no way that they could develop adequate knowledge about *all* cultural traditions. Still others hold that introducing music from non-Western traditions falls more appropriately into the domain of *social studies* classes than that of music classes. They stress that educating students *about* the diverse musical traditions of the world may indeed make them knowledgeable listeners, but that the primary purpose and value of music education lies in *bringing students into the traditions* of music in the U.S. that have historically been important to the nation by *teaching them to perform vocally or instrumentally* within these traditions. Furthermore, they maintain, since the time students spend in music classes is quite limited, learning about the music of "other cultures" should not be a priority.

Other teachers feel strongly that teaching the music of different cultural groups is indeed important. Some believe that if young people are to develop an understanding of music and its place in human life, then music education classes must include *all* music, not just music of one or a small number of cultural traditions. Some argue that if they continue the practice of teaching only Western music to classes that include increasing numbers of students whose cultural origins are in countries outside of Europe, they will effectively be communicating to those students that their own musical heritages are comparatively unimportant. Furthermore, these teachers say, instruction in the music of different cultural traditions is likely to raise students' awareness and knowledge of the people with whom they originated and is thus likely to diminish students' potential resistance to and hostility toward them. Most citizens would agree that any enterprise that has the effect of promoting ethnic and cultural harmony and thereby encouraging domestic peace is in itself a highly desirable undertaking.

But the problem of including the music of different cultural traditions is even more complex than it may seem at first glance. Many U.S. citizens—including music teachers—are likely unaware of the degree to which the conceptions of different world peoples of what most Americans would call "music" differ from their own. In some of the world's cultural communities, musical practices are highly personal, they are closely related to spiritual or religious beliefs, and the social customs with which they are involved are an important, even sacred part of the community's collective identity. As a result, recent immigrant students' participation in U.S. music classes—in which all music is typically treated as "art" or "entertainment"—may require that they suspend, if not surrender, their past beliefs about music as they become socialized into the American way of life. Indeed, most school-aged children do not have sufficient perspective to evaluate whether the musical values held tacitly in school music classes might be somehow superior or inferior to the unique cultural beliefs and values concerning music that they held before entering the class. Spiritual concerns are not usually even discussed in the secular, rationalist context of U.S. public schools.

A small sampling of some of the widely differing beliefs about music held by various cultural groups will provide some indication of the great differences in the ways the world's peoples conceptualize "music." Social concerns arising from the coming together of people with such differences in beliefs will likely become more evident as the nation continues to increase in ethnic and cultural diversity.

- For some of the cultural groups grounded in Islam, considerable reservation surrounds performances of all music (or *al-musiqi*) due to the potential they believe it has for sensually distracting and thereby misleading believers. Notably, however, members of these groups do not regard as "music" the melodious vocalizing of passages from the Qur'an and Islamic religious poetry that is a part of their worship, although it would most probably be regarded as "musical" by a non-Muslim European or American observer. Not surprisingly, members of these Islamic groups would likely object to any attempt to formulate a pan-cultural, "neutral," or "objective" definition of music that included the audible, vocal dimension of their sacred practices. Their attitude is not, however, shared by all Muslims; Islamic mystics (Sufis), for instance, typically value music making very highly, believing that musical experience can contribute to one's spiritual fulfillment.[7]
- For some cultural groups of Indonesia, such as the Balinese, collective life is permeated by activities that most Americans would call "musical," yet until recently the Balinese language included no word directly equivalent in meaning to the English-language term "music." Those Americans who have studied the language, musical practices, and other cultural traditions of Indonesia describe a radical difference between Indonesian ways of conceptualizing "reality" and those that predominate in the U.S.; naturally, these groups also conceive of their "musical" activities in a very different way.[8]
- Native American peoples typically make music in their collective ritualized activities. Certain communities believe that some of their songs are not to be shared with people who are not members of their community, and that it is wrong to sing these songs at times and in places other than those for which they were intended.[9] It is important to realize that, unlike a number of Americans of European origin, they make no distinction between secular and sacred (or "spiritual") life.
- A perspective similar in certain respects to that held by some Muslims exists among Jehovah's Witnesses, a Christian group present in the U.S. While many parents who are Jehovah's Witnesses are glad to allow their children to participate in school musical activities, they stipulate specifically that their children must be exempted from participating in those activities that involve sacred music of any kind. The children are not to be exposed to music that might lead to their worshipping of "false gods."[10]

By contrast with the perspectives of these groups, a majority of citizens in the U.S. experience music primarily through broadcast communications, recordings, and concerts, so they typically conceptualize music much differently. Because of the ways they have collectively learned to think about it, most citizens would define music either as an "art"—a manifestation of someone's personal self-expression—or perhaps as "entertainment"— something done just for the pleasure of an audience and a performer, not necessarily having any wider social significance. Citizens who have not had much experience making music of their own are especially likely to include notions of music as a purchasable product (e.g., MP3 files, or CDs) or a hirable service (e.g., entertainment at wedding receptions) in their overall conception of "music." A smaller group regards music as consequential religious activity, while still others regard such activity as something they should take steps to avoid. Indeed, discussion of beliefs about music that are associated with concepts of the "sacred" held by different cultural groups have been minimized throughout the history of the nation in the science-based, "secular," and thus ostensibly value-free context of the public schools. Notably, most U.S. citizens are generally accepting of the musical practices and beliefs of people whose cultural backgrounds are different from their own, although they may have little knowledge of them. What has largely gone without consideration until recently, however, is that the beliefs about music that predominate in the popular culture of the U.S. and the beliefs upon which the enterprise of public school music education is based are themselves culturally and historically unique conceptions. Since music teachers could thus be said to be teaching something that they do not openly intend (or that they are not even aware of), they could be said to be implementing a hidden curriculum in their teaching.

Problems concerning the differences in beliefs that surround musical practices are most evident in U.S. public-school music classes in which the music of different cultural traditions are included without an accompanying presentation of information describing their social context and cultural meanings. Displacing a song, chant, or other musical practice from its usual social context and the people to whom it belongs and into a public school classroom can obscure the intended meaning of the music for students who are expected to learn it—and perhaps perform it—for the first time, just as isolating a sentence in a "foreign" language from the paragraph of which it is a part and introducing it in a different context may have the effect of severing it from the original personal and social import of its deployment. Instead of coming to understand the music on its own terms, class members may misinterpret the meaning of a lyric or find something about the music to be objectionable, distasteful, boring, or even ridiculous because it seems contrary to their own values.

Also, the focused consideration or analysis of certain formal, technical, or aesthetic qualities of music that generally takes place in music education classes but does not reflect the interests of the originating cultural group may represent a reduction in or lack of concern with the originally intended meaning of the music or the purposes it was first intended to serve. In this sense, music educators and their students may be "missing the point" for which the music was created. In addition, including such music in a class rehearsal or public concert with music of numerous other traditions may represent an appropriation of the music for purposes much different from those for which it was originally intended. This may, in some cases, constitute exploitation of the cultural group involved. Indeed, the practice adopted by some U.S. musicians of making arrangements of "sacred" or socially important music of different cultural groups to be sold for use in school classrooms (without accompanying materials explaining their social meanings) raises issues concerning the appropriation of the musical products of these cultural groups for the personal, financial gain of opportunists in the U.S. marketplace.

In those classroom situations in which music educators *do* strive to illuminate cultural traditions and the social meanings of music, problems similar to those described previously may arise due to limitations of the teachers' knowledge about and experience with these disparate traditions, many of which are relatively unknown in the mainstream of American society. The musical traditions of some cultural groups are very elaborate and intricate, some involving notation systems wholly different from that of European and American music—or no notation at all. No teacher is adequately familiar with the languages, social and religious customs, and political dimensions of the musical traditions of all world cultures, let alone their complex technical aspects, to teach them all with comprehensive understanding. In fact, rather than receiving a culturally diversified music education that might modestly prepare them to begin such an undertaking, most U.S. music teachers instead complete a college or university degree program that requires them to focus on becoming Western art musicians, at least in some measure. The study of "world" or "non-Western" musics is only a minute part of most of these degree programs. Inevitably, time constraints on degree completion seem to ensure that nascent music educators will study non-Western musical traditions only superficially prior to their being certified as teachers.

Increasing recognition of music education's *curriculum content* problem has motivated university music professors charged with the preparation of school music teachers to focus increasingly on the philosophical foundations of their profession in recent years. The questions "What *should* be the societal role of music education in the United States?," "What *is* the value of music education in the development of children?," and even "*What is music?*" are presently under discussion by leaders in the profession. The past two decades have seen multiple revisions of an influential and long-standing philosophical statement on music education,[11] the publication of a new philosophical statement for music educators to consider,[12] and the release of new journals focusing on the philosophy of music education.[13] U.S. music educators clearly have their purposes under review at present.

THE *PLACE OF MUSIC IN SCHOOLS* PROBLEM

Just as U.S. music educators are finding it necessary to consider these questions and conflicts of purpose, they are continuing to face another problem that has dogged the enterprise of public-school music education ever since its inception in the early nineteenth century: Despite their continuing efforts (such as the Tanglewood Symposium) to keep the subject matter of music education generally relevant to the mainstream concerns of the nation, music classes are periodically and not infrequently cut from the curriculum of the public schools. This often occurs with little advance warning from the school administrators who eliminate them. Music classes are removed from schools usually not for reasons stemming from the cultural and religious differences described earlier, but more typically on the basis that music is not a "sufficiently important" subject (as compared with other subjects) to warrant sustained support.

Music classes are most often eliminated when a school district is suffering financial difficulties or when questions are being raised about a school's effectiveness in teaching the so-called basic subjects (e.g., mathematics and reading). They also may be cut when a school or district undergoes a change in its chief administrators and thus in its guiding educational philosophy. The continuing presence of music education in the schools can be attributed to several factors: to its long, past history of inclusion in the schools, to the positive experiences many parents have had with their children's performance programs and their subsequent enthusiastic lobbying, to the past positive experiences in music education of some school administrators during their own public-school education, and perhaps also to the persistent, publicly visible advocacy of music educators, which stems from their steadfast conviction that the study of music and musical involvement play an important role in the developing lives of young people. The typically strong supporting statements from groups of community members and the often moderate acceptance of many school administrators and government officials even in times of financial crises confirm that some Americans believe music education in the schools to be societally important.

Despite these bases of support, the profession encounters one of its greatest challenges at those times when the role of music in the schools must be explained and its place there justified. When the question is asked, "What place does music have in the education of young people in the United States?", the spectrum of answers given by parents, music teachers, and seasoned scholars in music and education have seemed to many administrators and other listeners to range from such emotion-laden arguments to such disparately biased philosophical positions that they find them difficult to consider seriously. To accomplished amateur or professional musicians, just raising the question of music's importance in education seems odd; the answer seems quite evident to them, though difficult to articulate. Even among the numerous nonmusicians who concede the importance of the various arts to society for one reason or another, the role of music in education seems debatable. Some educational writers have pointed out that music is present in nearly all world cultures and that it has been included in the Western educational forum since the time of the ancient Greeks, but arguments that present curricula should necessarily follow practices of the past that have evolved in different social conditions are difficult to accept, though they seem worthy of consideration.

While the importance that citizens of the U.S. ascribe to music education differs widely among individuals and communities, the importance they collectively give to music seems beyond question. It is difficult to find a social situation that does not include "background" music provided by radio or television; food and department stores, restaurants, elevators, offices, and many homes are rarely silent during waking hours. Many citizens participate in musical activities in clubs, theaters, temples, churches, and in their own homes. Sales of musical recordings, while variable over time, are generally very high: In 2008, more than 384.7 million CD album recordings were sold nationally, 568.9 million albums were downloaded, over 1.022 trillion singles were downloaded, and total domestic revenue for the U.S. music industry was over $8.48 billion.[14]

Given the ubiquity of and the widespread interest in music in the U.S., the question inevitably arises as to why music education is not more consistently supported. If one believes that the essential purpose of public education is to help young people learn how to live as successful participants in and contributors to their society, then it must be conceded that most Americans do not now regard musical learning as being as important in the education of their children as study in mathematical, literacy, and vocational-technological areas. While a comparatively small number of children do grow up to pursue music-related occupations, most individuals do not regard musical skill and understanding as being as central to their lives as their skills in these other areas. Still, music's notable presence as a human activity observable in nearly all human societies, its consistent inclusion in Western educational curricula since at least the time of ancient Greece, and the pervasiveness of music listening, record buying, and amateur music making in the lives of U.S. citizens—considered collectively—suggest that music is an important aspect of human life, including the lives of Americans. After so many years of striving to justify and explain the importance of music's inclusion in U.S. schools, the supporters of public-school music education are frustrated with not being able to articulate a single, timeless, unifying theme underlying all of the explanations that would secure a continuing place for it in school curricula.

A WAY FORWARD

Both of the broad problems described earlier—the apparent collective ambivalence of music educators regarding the content of their instruction and the societal ambivalence concerning the importance of music instruction in the public schools—may be attributed to the wide differences in beliefs that exist in the U.S. about what music *is* and about its role and importance in the life of human communities and in the education of children. Scholars in anthropology and sociology often use the term *worldview* to refer to the tacitly held conception of "reality," the "coherence system," or the distinctive body of beliefs shared as factual truth by the members of a given cultural group, but not by all human beings.[15] Such holistic conceptions are uniquely manifested in the distinctive and collectively shared practices of every cultural group, and particular worldviews contribute to defining the members of each group as its members. In societies that are culturally homogeneous, that is, in which all people largely share a common heritage of similar beliefs and similarly evolving conceptions about the world and their place in it, there is also an unspoken but largely shared understanding of the practices of the community (such as music and music teaching), the reasons for undertaking them, and their societal importance. In societies that are not culturally homogeneous, such as the U.S., such a consensus is less likely to occur.

Throughout the history of U.S. public-school education, the schools have often been regarded, at least theoretically, as a culturally neutral context, a forum within which persons from different cultural traditions can have an equal voice. In recent years, however, cultural anthropologists and social historians have demonstrated that there is no such thing as a culturally neutral context; in fact, culturally unique and historically grounded beliefs and values are implicit in all social situations. In addition, research into the cultural practices of different world peoples has demonstrated that musical practices are also not culturally neutral, and that they can be understood as socially important and meaningful in their original sense only to individuals who embody or who have come to understand the worldview with which they originate.

The Tanglewood Declaration, the document that publicly opened music education curricula in the U.S. to include "music of all periods, styles, forms, and cultures," was written by individuals living during a period in the history of Europe and the U.S. now described by some historians of Western philosophy as the end of the modern era. Modernity originated in the European Renaissance of the fourteenth, fifteenth, and sixteenth centuries, a time when autocratic systems of government were replaced by new forms of government emerging in the city-states, when the Protestant Reformation shattered the supremacy of the Catholic church, and when the "scientific revolution" displaced Biblical conceptions of the earth as the center of the universe. The worldviews sustained in Europe (and the U.S.) throughout the modern period increasingly grounded human actions in reason rather than religious faith, placing great confidence in the ability of scientific inquiry to provide final and universal answers to all questions, and in the expectation that social and technological progress would eventually solve all major human problems. For some, the notion of "the modern" carries with it an implicit assumption of the superiority of industrialized societies.

By contrast with the modern era, the present age has been characterized by some philosophers and historians of philosophy as an era of postmodernity.[16] While the writings of postmodern scholars do not, in most cases, represent a revolt against the ideas of modernity, they do suggest that modernity's confidence in the rational pursuit of universal truths and its belief in scientific, social, and technological progress may have been too limiting, since many of the practices that have stemmed from the modern worldview have come to affect individuals, societies, and the earth itself in decidedly detrimental ways. These scholars have suggested that because the confidence in rationalism that prevailed throughout the modern era was generally untempered by globally conscious, moral, or religious sensibilities, it led inevitably to such practices as colonialism, slavery, and fascism. In addition, they have observed that the modern belief in the certain value of scientific, social, and technological progress not only brought great social benefits for certain members of the societies that embraced this belief, but also led to the creation of weapons of mass destruction, the psychological and social disorientation of individuals and communities that had previously been comparatively well-balanced, and great damage to the earth as a whole.

To show how the foundations of the modern worldview are inherently problematic, postmodern philosophers have pointed out that the differing conceptions of *truth* that exist among the members of different cultural groups—and even among different groups of scientists—stem from ways of thinking that are unique to their different ways of life and are not universal among all human beings. The implication of this is that these differing conceptions of "truth" must be considered as potentially valid, insofar as they represent sincere, well-formulated efforts to provide answers to problems that have arisen in particular environmental, cultural, and historical contexts.[17] Following from this realization, the high value given to scientific discoveries and concepts that characterized the modern era has been tempered in recent years by greater acceptance of and interest in the dissimilar perspectives—the diverse ways of knowing and being—of people of different ethnic, cultural, and religious origins. Not surprisingly, many of these individuals are now advocating that decisions that make use of the results of scientific inquiry must take into account their long-term effects on the quality of life experienced by individuals and communities.

As persons living during the mid-twentieth century—near the culmination of the modern era—the Tanglewood Symposium participants likely felt confident in assuming an eventual universal coalescence of perspectives would emerge in the American public forum concerning the role and importance of music in human life. Thus there is nothing in the Tanglewood Declaration to suggest that they perceived a need to take into account the radical differences in beliefs about music (such as those described previously) that would eventually coexist among the various cultural groups comprising the citizenry of the U.S. Though their enthusiastic recommendation that the "music of all periods, styles, forms, and cultures" be included in school curricula seems admirable, the members of the symposium regrettably did not have foresight adequate to suggest just how the music educators who followed them might deal with the curricular quandaries that would become evident as larger numbers of people from disparate cultural groups entered the public and academic forums of the nation.

As noted earlier, the United States of America was established as a nation during the Enlightenment period of the eighteenth century. During that era, the modern confidence in the rational pursuit of universal truth, individual freedom, and social and technological progress was gaining particularly great momentum. In the midst of the social changes that followed during the early nineteenth century, music education was established in the public schools of the nation. Many citizens, including school officials of that time, believed that music was an important part of a child's overall education, and their beliefs provided the basis for the first inclusion of music as an academic subject in U.S. public schools. Today, as postmodern perspectives are tempering the tenets of modernism and the population of the public schools is increasing in cultural diversity, music education is one of many U.S. institutions finding it necessary to reconsider its basic premises. Clearly, if music education is to continue in the nation's public schools, its practices must be both viable and valuable to the various cultural groups comprising the society. If a majority of U.S. citizens cannot collectively affirm that the inclusion of music in school curricula fulfills an important need, its place in the schools will remain tenuous. Faced with this possibility, a variation on the question originally addressed by the Tanglewood participants presents itself as being unavoidable:

> What is the role or social importance of public school music education in the United States as a postmodern society?

Any effort to provide an answer to this question worthy of consideration by the profession would require a strong conceptual base in three areas. First, the preconceptions upon which an inquiry into these dilemmas or any recommendations for their resolution were to be based would need to be stated outright and rooted in a philosophical foundation adequate for embracing the different perspectives of the myriad cultural groups that comprise the nation. Second, an understanding of the diverse nature of "music" as it is manifested in the lives of people of the world's varied cultural groups would need to be established, in order that all recommendations for the future practice of the profession could adequately reflect consideration of the great diversity of human beliefs about it. Finally, the establishment of a historical perspective on the stated premises upon which

U.S. music education has been based would be necessary, in order to ensure that recommendations for future directions could be informed by its past and present tenets.

This book thus has three purposes:

1. To provide a philosophical foundation capable of accommodating the beliefs and practices of diverse cultural groups;

2. To demonstrate how this conceptual foundation embraces different cultural beliefs and practices, especially those concerning "music"; and

3. To survey the various rationales and philosophical statements that have been used to defend and explain music education in the public schools of the U.S. for the purpose of understanding how they reflect the beliefs and practices of the nation at the time of their composition.

With this foundation, we will be able to suggest criteria upon which music might best be included in the curricula of U.S. schools in the present "postmodern" age. The book is organized in the following way:

Chapter 2 briefly describes approaches to the study of "culture" that have been taken by cultural anthropologists in the past, explains their limitations, and sets forth the pragmatist philosophy of Charles Sanders Peirce as a practicable alternative by demonstrating its usefulness as a model for understanding the diverse practices of different world peoples (such as music making) as manifestations of the worldviews collectively shared by those who undertake them. Despite the fact that Peirce lived nearly a century ago, his philosophy, as revealed in his writings, is remarkably consistent with the views of many postmodern scholars in cultural anthropology and social history. In particular, Peirce's theory of signs, or *semiotic*, provides a powerful conceptual vocabulary for describing cultural and historical differences; it is presently being used by scholars in various fields of inquiry for this purpose.

Chapter 3 demonstrates how Peirce's philosophy is uniquely well suited for accommodating various conceptions of music as they are manifested among peoples of different cultural backgrounds and historical eras. His pragmatism will provide a basis for conceptualizing the nature of musical practices in human communities in a way different from that of most scholarship of the modern era.

With this background on musical practices as a diverse cluster of human behaviors, it will be possible to identify factors that have contributed to determining the conceptions of music that have predominated historically in the U.S. public forum; these factors are described in Chapter 4. With this foundation, Chapter 5 chronicles significant rationale statements and philosophical explanations that have been used historically to justify music education in the U.S., identifying the societal purposes that music educators have seen their profession as fulfilling since Colonial times. The chapter shows how the publicly professed beliefs of music educators evolved over four specific eras, although concepts held during each of these eras have overlapped historically and all are still present in the nation's public forum today.

Finally, Chapter 6 presents a reconceptualization of the role or purpose of music education in U.S. schools that seems congruent with recent scholarship on music as a diverse cultural phenomenon and that also seems an appropriate outgrowth of its historical antecedents. This new culturally informed and historically grounded conception—with its attendant curricular recommendations—is intended to provide a sound foundation for the continuing inclusion of music classes in the curricula of U.S. public schools.

PRAGMATIST: "I'M LOOKING FOR WHATEVER WORKS."
(WHAT MUSED JUSTIFICATIONS HAVE WORKED ACROSS AMER. HISTORY?
ACROSS OTHER CULTURES/NATIONS?) WHAT HAS WORKED?

PHILOSOPHY: STUDY OF HOW PEOPLE JUSTIFY THEIR
BELIEFS, THOUGHTS, ACTIONS

"PHIL. IS THE STUDY OF JUSTIFICATIONS"
JOHN HOSPERS

PHIL FOR DUMMIES, I.E., STUDY OF THE REASONS PEOPLE HAVE FOR
THINKING AS THEY DO.

MARTIN COHEN

A TECHNIQUE, A WAY OF TEASING APART
AND EXAMINING REALITY.

DEVELOP EMOTIONAL INTELLIGENCE
LISTEN W/ UNDERSTANDING

MUSIC BELONGS IN THE SCHOOL CURRICULUM BECAUSE EDUCATION
IN THE ARTS DEVELOPS EMOTIONAL INTELLIGENCE. IN PARTICULAR,
MUSIC STUDY DEEPENS THE STUDENT'S ABILITY TO LISTEN TO THEIR WORLD
W/ AWARENESS + UNDERSTANDING.

TRANSFER OF LEARNING - IF IT HAPPENS AT ALL, ITS AT THIS LEVEL,
WELL BELOW THE SURFACE OF MEASURABLE STANDARDS, OBJECTIVES,
AND SKILLS.

2 "Culture," "Worldview," and Pragmatism

The Philosophy and Semiotic of Charles Sanders Peirce

A human being is part of the whole, called by us the universe. A part limited in time and space. He experiences himself, his thoughts and feelings, as something separate from the rest, a kind of optical delusion of his consciousness. This delusion is part of a prison for us, restricting us to our personal desires and to affection for a few persons nearest to us. Our task must be to free ourselves from this prison by widening our circle of compassion to embrace all living creatures.[1]

Albert Einstein

As noted in the previous chapter, two of the problems presently facing the profession of public-school music education in the U.S. stem from the great differences in beliefs among the people of this nation about what music *is* and about its importance in human life. The first problem arises from the marked increase in the cultural diversity of the student population of U.S. public schools over the past thirty years, the concomitant efforts of some music educators to include the music of diverse world peoples in the curriculum, and the ensuing ambivalence of other music educators concerning the purposes of their profession in light of this curricular expansion. The second problem concerns the apparent disagreement among the American public on the importance of music instruction in the public schools. Before it will be possible for us to come to terms with these problems, it will be necessary to establish a philosophical foundation, a position from which widely differing beliefs about music can be considered systematically.

While philosophers throughout history have sought to establish a descriptive framework comprehensive enough to account for all human behavior and thought, the science of anthropology represents the most long-continuing, cooperative effort to verify empirically such generalizations about human beings as well as develop a full understanding of human diversity. *Cultural* anthropology is the branch of the science that is concerned specifically with the ways of life in different societies. Since musical activity and beliefs about it differ widely among human societies, it seems appropriate that this inquiry should be based on a philosophical foundation congruent with the perspectives of contemporary cultural anthropology.

Like music education, however, the science of cultural anthropology has itself been characterized historically by great differences of opinion concerning its central concepts, many of which are still being debated. In this chapter we will briefly consider the historical development of the term *culture*, the central concept of cultural anthropology, and then describe and explore the implications of the philosophical conceptions of "culture" and "worldview" we will adopt for considering the various conceptions of "music" contained in the rationales proffered for the inclusion of music education in the public schools throughout the history of the U.S.

A BRIEF HISTORY OF ANTHROPOLOGICAL CONCEPTIONS OF "CULTURE"

"Culture" is the central concept around which the field of cultural anthropology arose, and most anthropologists acknowledge that the introduction of the concept in the late nineteenth century did much to resolve the problem of explaining the wide differences in behavior and thought among human societies. Victorians were particularly curious to know how the so-called primitive or simple peoples of the world had acquired their "mistaken" ideas and seemingly bizarre practices, and "culture" would not have been a word that most would have associated with these differences. The English word *culture* originally stemmed from the Latin *cultura*, which was derived from the verb *colere*, meaning to till or to cultivate. The term was used for hundreds of years among Europeans as a metaphor for the refinement of human civilization toward perfection. "Primitive" societies would not have been thought to reflect "culture."

The technical, anthropological use of the word *culture* originated with the Englishman Edward Tylor (1832–1917), who is often regarded as the founder of cultural anthropology. Tylor published his two-volume work *Primitive Culture* in 1871, following an extended journey in North America during which he had experienced great differences as well as similarities among the various human societies he encountered. On the first page of his book, Tylor presented the following definition: "Culture or Civilization is that complex whole which includes knowledge, belief, art, morals, law, custom, and any other capabilities and habits acquired by man as a member of society."[2] Tylor's book represents an effort to list and compare similar practices among different groups, with a bent toward demonstrating that religious beliefs and culture in general are products of human evolution.

Tylor's defining conception of culture differed from previous conceptions of societal differences in two important ways. First, his use of the word *acquired* implied that the differences in behavior and thought among human beings should, in some measure, be attributed to the social and environmental differences of the groups in which they had been raised. Thus the behavior and thought of any person would be different if he or she was raised in a different society. However, for Tylor, who was strongly influenced by Charles Darwin's evolutionary ideas, a corollary of this idea was that European societies represented a more highly evolved state; he maintained that human social development progressed from savagery through barbarism to culminate in civilization . . . with European civilization representing the apex.

A second aspect of Tylor's conception that set his views apart from his contemporaries was his notion that culture is manifested as a complex whole existing in *all* human societies. An important but not obvious implication of this notion is the idea that the diverse customs and traditions of different world peoples all stem from a reasoning faculty common to all human beings. Thus all human behavior, no matter how seemingly bizarre to an "outsider," would make sense if one could understand the reasoning with which it originated. Tylor's conception that culture had simply evolved differently and more completely in different situations had the effect of making the "primitives" seem more comprehensible and thus less strange to his English readers. As Rodney Needham has observed, many Victorians believed that the purpose of anthropology was to explain how the primitive people of the world had acquired their mistaken conceptions. However, Needham noted, "it was at the same time desired to demonstrate that the errors were reasonable ones, understandable in the circumstances, such as evolution naturally tended to correct and which could more speedily be eradicated as the savages copied European standards of observation and discourse."[3]

In direct opposition to Tylor's unifying and evolution-based views, the French philosopher and armchair anthropologist Lucien Lévy-Bruhl (1857–1939) proposed that the mind of the primitive is characterized by a "pre-logical" mentality, fundamentally different from the "logical mentality" of the modern European. He insisted that this pre-logical mentality had to be understood on its own terms, and he maintained that the primitive mind has its own unique organization, which he termed the *law of participation*. As an example, Lévy-Bruhl explained that when a primitive man claims to be an animal (such as a bird or a fish), he actually regards the animal external to himself as being both consubstantial with himself and separate from himself. He maintained that this sense of participation was not merely metaphorical, but instead implied both a physical and mystical union of the man with the external entity in question.[4]

Lévy-Bruhl's insistence on a radical difference in mentation between the so-called primitive and the modern European was certainly important, as it focused many future studies of culture specifically on the *mental* representations held collectively by different human populations, rather than on their physical artifacts and social practices. By the end of his career, however, Lévy-Bruhl found that he could no longer hold his notion of a "pre-logical" mentality, and he agreed with his contemporaries who viewed all human minds as having fundamentally the same features: "[L]et us expressly rectify what I believed correct in 1910: there is not a primitive mentality distinguishable from the other . . . There is a mystical mentality . . . more easily observable among 'primitive peoples' . . . but it is present in every human mind."[5]

Disagreeing with Tylor's evolutionary conception of European culture as superior and Lévy-Bruhl's notions of "different mentalities," Franz Boas (1858–1942) emphasized that the key to understanding the cultural differences of different societies lay in focusing on the environmental conditions and historical causes that led to the formation of their customs, as well as the psychological processes involved in their development. He opposed the notion of European—or any other—society as representing a pinnacle of cultural development. Boas challenged the evolutionary idea that "there is one grand system according to which mankind has developed everywhere," and he redirected inquiry in the field, stating that "if anthropology desires to establish the laws governing the growth of culture it must not confine itself to comparing the results of the growth alone, but . . . it must compare the processes of growth . . ."[6] of different groups in different situations. Incidentally, Boas also made the important inference that the recording and systematizing of philosophical knowledge that had taken place over several generations in modern literate societies had done the most to distinguish them from those they regarded as primitive.

Trained as a physicist in Germany, Boas moved to the U.S. as a young man to conduct his doctoral research. While undertaking a geographical study in the Arctic as part of his dissertation research, he met a group of Eskimos and became so interested in their language and customs that he changed his career focus toward anthropology. Boas's fascination with cultural difference coalesced with his natural facility for language-learning, eventually leading him to conduct descriptive studies of the languages of various Native American groups. His recognition that every language is an organized whole, and that each language plays a major part in the thought and activities of those who speak it, forged the first alliance between cultural anthropology and linguistics, an affiliation that continues to the present.

Influenced by Boas's work, French cultural anthropologist Claude Levi-Strauss (b. 1908) based much of his life's work on the premises that culture is an inherently mental phenomenon and that it is integrally associated with language—a universal, uniquely human capacity. Levi-Strauss held that the systematic analysis of the relationships among the components of a language—which he termed structural linguistics—would provide the most fruitful basis for studying culture as a phenomenon. One of Boas's associates, the Czech linguist Roman Jakobson, had suggested that the ways languages operate were determined by certain inherent properties of the human mind. Levi-Strauss inferred from the ideas of Boas and Jakobson that all cultures must also have certain structural similarities and that analysis of the formal relationships within them and comparison of these analyses would yield insight into innate, universal structures of human thought or cognition.

Levi-Strauss began his career focusing on kinship relationships among different cultural groups; he identified what he held to be culturally universal "laws" of relationship types within families (e.g., the incidence of formality or informality of the relationships among particular family members). Later he initiated a method for studying the structure of myths in all cultures, in order to identify what the meaning of the myth "really is."[7] For example, he would identify common relationships between the logic and values inherent in the myths of a particular cultural group (such as the Oedipus myth) to those inherent in the social (kinship) structures of that group.[8] Levi-Strauss's agenda, now known as structural anthropology or "structuralism," was to reduce all of the information he could acquire about different cultural groups to what he understood to be the elemental, formal relationships among their essential parts, to construct models with which they could be interpreted, and to make inferences from the results of these efforts about the nature of human cognition.

Levi-Strauss did much to bring the discipline of cultural anthropology toward considering culture as a manifestation of human cognition, as well as opening it to consideration of different and innovative methods of analysis. As can easily be imagined, however, many scholars have criticized his work. They have charged that his theories can be neither tested nor proven, that he has not provided sufficiently rigorous descriptions of his self-fabricated analytic methods that others could utilize them, and that the intricate workings-out of his culturally "reductive" agenda, while impressive, focus too heavily on the intellectual aspects of the human mind, neglecting emotion and omitting the important historical aspects of myth and social organization. Nevertheless, his influence on the field continues to be felt.

One continuing branch of anthropology that owes a considerable debt to the ideas of Levi-Strauss is *ethnoscience*, a field dedicated to the study of different cultural groups as unique systems of thought. Its basic premise is that cultures are cognitive organizations of material phenomena. As ethnoscientist Ward Goodenough defines it, "A society's culture consists of whatever it is one has to know or believe in order to operate in a manner acceptable to its members."[9] This linguistics-based, analytical approach to the study of cultures involves observations and interviews with the members of a cultural group, inferring the group's organizing principles in particular domains (e.g., kinship or color) from the speech and behavior of its members, and then systematically mapping out these relationships in a comprehensive but simplifying outline (e.g., in a grid, taxonomy, or diagram).

At first consideration, the research program practiced by ethnoscientists would apparently have much to recommend it, as the continued creation and compilation of such analyses would seem to result in a set of skeleton keys for the unlocking of different cultural groups as different "systems of understanding." However, this approach has also been the subject of considerable criticism. Some critics have focused on the difficulties that inhere in determining the accuracy of different, conflicting ethnoscientific analyses of the same domains in the same cultural contexts, while others have pointed out that the huge problems inherent in translating terms and categories between different languages without adequate contextual background may substantially diminish the value of the analyses. Perhaps the most damning critique is voiced by those who realize that the logic inherent in the speech of a cultural group is not always reflected in the actual behavior of its members in all situations. As Clifford Geertz has noted with regard to the products of ethnoscience, "Nothing has done more . . . to discredit cultural analysis than the construction of impeccable descriptions of formal order in whose actual existence nobody can quite believe."[10]

Geertz (1923–2006), a highly influential figure in contemporary cultural anthropology, largely embraced the general program suggested by Boas and has challenged the culturally reductionist approaches taken by Levi-Strauss and the ethnoscientists. In his view, cultural anthropology should not be a science searching for foundational laws of human cognition, or one that seeks to assemble sets of systematically constructed representations drawn from the thought systems of different populations. Geertz advocated instead what he called an "interpretive anthropology." He offered the following definition of culture, as he described the direction he advocated for anthropological inquiry:

> The concept of culture I espouse . . . is essentially a semiotic one. Believing . . . that man is an animal suspended in webs of significance he himself has spun, I take culture to be those webs, and the analysis of it to be therefore not an experimental science in search of law but an interpretive one in search of meaning.[11]

The word *semiotic* is a term that has been used since antiquity within healing traditions, philosophy, and other domains to refer to the nature and relationship of *signs*. In Geertz's conception, all human actions and the results of those actions are signs, the meanings of which are shared by those who share a common "imaginative universe." He conceptualized culture as being manifested in the various, interworked systems of interpretable signs used by human beings. In Geertz's view, a *particular* culture is grounded in and dependent on a social context within which a group of individuals shares a common understanding of signs. Geertz held that the work of cultural anthropologists is best carried out in the intellectual effort of what the philosopher Gilbert Ryle termed "thick description"—the process of carefully recording and explicating the inferences and implications that inhere in the data they cull from their investigations in different cultural contexts, much in the manner of a literary critic. Beyond this, he explained, cultural anthropologists have two tasks: "to uncover the conceptual structures" that inform human acts in a given cultural context, and "to construct a system of analysis in whose terms what is generic to those structures . . . will stand out against the other determinants of human behavior."[12]

Geertz recognized that it is inevitable that all anthropological writings are inherently culturally biased due to the fact that they are written in the native languages of anthropologists and are grounded in their social systems. However, he pointed out, this does not necessarily diminish their value: In his view, all such studies are valuable scientific efforts insofar as they help readers to understand the perspectives and concerns of people of another cultural group, thereby enlarging "the universe of human discourse." He drove this point home, saying "the essential vocation of interpretive anthropology is not to answer our deepest questions, but to make available to us answers that others . . . have given, and thus to include them in the consultable record of what man has said."[13]

Geertz's conception of culture as the "semiotic webs" within which all human beings are suspended and that we ourselves create has been criticized by ethnoscientists and others seeking to establish a cognition-based and therefore universal "theory of culture." Nevertheless, his well-supported arguments for an interpretive approach to the study of cultural groups as semiotic systems—that is, as collectively shared and interworking imaginative universes of signs, the anthropological study of which necessitates "thick description"—have found considerable agreement in the community of cultural anthropologists and sociologists.

Geertz's semiotic conception of culture is applicable not only to the study of different cultural groups, but also to historical studies of an aspect of a single society, such as the present inquiry. Understanding how such an application might be made will require familiarity with an additional concept borrowed from the field of linguistics. Lecturing around 1906, linguist and semiologist Ferdinand de Saussure drew a distinction between *synchronic* and *diachronic* linguistic studies. According to his terminology, synchronic studies focus on the characteristics of a language system at a single point in time, while diachronic studies explore changes in a language over time.[14] Saussure compared language to a game of chess, pointing out that while the configuration of players on the board changes throughout a game, the position of the pieces may be regarded as fixed in any given moment. Similarly, a cultural system—considered as a loosely bounded semiotic "web"—may also be explored synchronically and diachronically. While the meanings of the signs shared by the members of a cultural group are always in a state of change, the meaning of any sign (such as a word or action) can be regarded as fixed at a given instant. A diachronic study of the differences in meaning of the signs shared by the members of a cultural system at successive points in time would illustrate how the collectively shared conceptions of these signs have changed over time in the thought of those who share that cultural context. In addition, such a study might also reveal the factors that have led to changes in these conceptions.

This book presents just such a synchronic and diachronic inquiry into the historical changes in the meaning of a particular *sign* within a defined societal context. In Chapter 3, we will first consider the word *music* as a sign, showing how the personal and social activities of different cultural groups that are often regarded as "musical" by many U.S. citizens actually have differing meanings in the "imaginative universes" of the people with whom they originate. Later, in Chapter 5, we will explore the changing meanings of the sign *music* as it has been conceptualized (or at least described) by music educators collectively in the rationales they have provided for the inclusion of music education in the public schools of the U.S. during four consecutive eras of the nation's history.

Geertz's definition of culture as the "webs of significance" within which human beings are suspended and that we ourselves have spun will serve as a good conceptual foundation for our inquiry. However, since neither Geertz nor any of his contemporaries in cultural anthropology has provided a semiotic theory and conceptual vocabulary comprehensive and precise enough for our purposes here, we must postpone the statement of our final, working definition of "culture" until we have established such a theoretical and conceptual vocabulary.

Within the past two decades, a number of "interpretive" anthropologists have discovered and begun to utilize the semiotic theory of Charles Sanders Peirce (1839–1914), an American philosopher who pioneered the development of semiotic theory; his work represents the most comprehensive classification of *signs* to date. As these anthropologists have explored Peirce's writings, they have discovered that many of the concepts central to his "pragmatic" philosophy are both radically different from those of his late-nineteenth-century contemporaries and remarkably consistent with their own. Unlike Geertz and other cultural anthropologists, however, Peirce had no interest in exploring differences between persons having origins in different places and societies. Peirce's focus was more akin to that of contemporary cognitive scientists and cognition-oriented cultural anthropologists: His primary interest in philosophy was *mind*, and he was particularly interested in explaining the logic with which human minds symbolically construct their "imaginative universes." As we shall see, Peirce's pragmatism actually foreshadowed many of the ideas more recently described by scholars in the cognitive science–related fields of neuroscience, linguistics, psychology, philosophy, and cultural anthropology. Owing to the comprehensiveness of his ideas, Peirce's philosophy represents a unique coalescence of the culturally interpretive concerns of Geertz and the mind/brain inquiries of cognitive scientists. Peirce's unified concept of "mind," his philosophy of science, and his semiotic terminology, taken collectively, make his pragmatism an especially well-integrated, powerful, and useful foundation for this inquiry into music and differing beliefs.

PRAGMATISM: THE PHILOSOPHY OF C. S. PEIRCE

The broad applicability of Peirce's philosophy to different cultural view-points is attributable to a fundamental premise upon which it is based. Like Einstein and many later twentieth-century scholars (particularly those in the presently burgeoning ecological sciences), Peirce maintained that all phenomena are interconnected or "continuous," and he held that all philosophical or scientific endeavor should be guided by this principle. He named the principle "synechism."

> I do not merely use it [i.e., synechism or continuity] subjectively as a way of looking at things, but objectively put it forward to account for all interaction between mind and body, mind and mind, body and body.[15]

Each of these areas of interaction will be considered in turn.

First, in his conception of the relationship between mind and body, Peirce's synechism challenges the foundational bases of many of the long-standing European philosophical perspectives still tacitly held by many in Europe and the U.S., while it has some similarity with those of Asia and elsewhere.[16] Many European philosophers have followed the conception that mind and body are inherently separate entities. This "dualism," or premise of separateness, is attributed by some scholars to the seventeenth-century philosopher René Descartes, who based his widely influential philosophical reasoning on it. Other scholars have argued that mind-body dualism stems from the theological doctrines set forth in the religious institutions prevalent in Europe and the Middle East (Judaism, Christianity, and Islam). These institutions hold that the spirit, soul, or "mind" of every individual human being is unique, separate from the body, and eternal in life and in death.[17] Still other scholars assert that such a dualism has been evident in Western thought since the time of the ancient Greeks.

Arguments for the opposite notion, that mind and body are in continuous relationship with one another (i.e., are "of one substance"), have been supported with medical evidence. For example, a remarkable number of physical illnesses have been recognized as being psychosomatic (i.e., originating in or aggravated by psychological or emotional processes). Similarly, placebos (i.e., chemically inert substances given as medicine) have been shown to have positive physical effects on the body if the subjects to whom they are administered believe that such an effect may occur. Strongly enthusiastic or abusive language (ostensibly a strictly aural and "mental" phenomenon) has been seen to effect actual physiological changes in the bodies of individuals involved in conflict. Conversely, it is tacitly understood by most adults that climatic changes and ingested foods and drugs can affect the human body, thereby impacting mental functioning. Damage to the brain has also been shown to dramatically alter human personality.

Second, Peirce denied not only mind-body dualism but also the conception that human minds are absolutely separate from one another. Mind-body dualism and the insularity of human minds are notions that were tacitly embraced by most of Peirce's contemporaries, and they represent his main differences with the views of William James. James's early and important influence on psychological theorizing and research in the U.S. likely contributed to the shaping of psychological theories innovated subsequently by his successors in the field. In James's writings, human consciousness is conceptualized as being personal, and it thus necessitates irreducible social pluralism. According to Vincent Colapietro, "this difference between James and Peirce is to note that, for the former, the most fundamental feature of personal consciousness is the irreducible fact of privacy whereas, for the latter, its most basic characteristic is the ubiquitous possibility of communication."[18] Peirce provided a systematic explanation of the cognition of individual minds as well as the interaction of "mind and mind"—individuals in social contexts. Peirce's concept of a community as a "collective mind" forms the basis of his semiotic theory, which we will explore in depth following.

Finally, in his allusion to the "synechistic" interrelationship of "body and body," Peirce was reflecting a conception some readers may recognize as being much like that of G. W. F. Hegel's objective idealism; Peirce considered mind and matter to be but different aspects of the same totality.[19] Peirce intended it to be understood that what we commonly call matter is only an aspect of mind (and vice versa), and that we are all inextricably a part of the organic whole of the universe—part of "absolute mind." In his view, matter is "not completely dead, but merely mind hidebound with habits."[20] All matter is thus physically and mentally interconnected.

> [I]f matter has no existence except as a specialization of mind, it follows that whatever affects matter according to regular laws is itself matter. But all mind is directly or indirectly connected with all matter, and acts in a more or less regular way; so that all mind more or less partakes of the nature of matter. Hence, it would be a mistake to conceive of the psychical and the physical aspects of matter as two aspects absolutely distinct. Viewing a thing from the outside . . . it appears as matter. Viewing it from the inside . . . it appears as consciousness. . . . [R]emember that mechanical laws are nothing but acquired habits, like all the regularities of mind, including the tendency to take habits, itself.[21]

In order to grasp Peirce's conception of the ways in which human minds are synechistic, a concept central to this inquiry, it will be helpful first to understand his concept of the mind of an individual human being. A brief discussion of his learning theory will facilitate this, while also introducing more of Peirce's conceptual vocabulary.

INDIVIDUAL MIND

Peirce recognized that the survival of every individual organism depends on its development of habits of behavior that will satisfy its needs. He observed that every human being develops a general pattern of coping actions out of the actual series of struggles undergone throughout life, and he asserted that " . . . the whole function of thought is to produce habits of action."[22] Peirce noted that human beings exhibit coping actions that are species-similar and, while individually somewhat different, relatively consistent in each person over time. This recognition led to his conception of human beings as "bundles of habits."[23]

Through the development of these coping actions, human beings concomitantly acquire "habits of mind" or *beliefs* that guide their actions. According to Peirce, "Belief is not a momentary mode of consciousness; it is a habit of mind essentially enduring for some time, and mostly (at least) unconscious . . ."[24] Often, however, something happens to interrupt the habituated actions of every human being. At those times of interruption, when the human being has no inveterate response, he or she experiences *doubt*. Doubt, in Peirce's view, "is not a habit, but the privation of a habit."[25] Doubt activates *thought*, which Peirce held to be best conceptualized as the formation of one or more hypotheses that could account for the interruption. In thought, the human being seeks for a new understanding of the situation that will allow her or him either to return to previously habituated action or to establish newly habituated actions. Thought ceases again when a hypothesis is validated by experience, thus resolving the doubt. A new set of habits with which equilibrium can be maintained—a new *belief*—is attained in this way " . . . so that the production of belief is the sole function of thought."[26]

Readers may recognize a certain similarity between Peirce's theory of cognition and that of twentieth-century cognitive scientist Jean Piaget (1896–1980). For Piaget also, thought begins when something new is presented to consciousness. At this point, either the new element is quickly *assimilated* into the mind or "cognitive structure" of the learner (because it is familiar), or the learner's cognitive structure must be altered to *accommodate* the new information (because it is unusual). Piaget called this the process of *equilibrating*, implying that, in this way, the individual maintains psychological equilibrium through cognition.[27] Piaget and Peirce differ, however, in that Peirce posited no mental "cognitive structure" into which a new element is assimilated, but rather suggested only that a new set of habits of mind are established.

Holding his synechistic view, Peirce conceptualized learning as involving body and mind alike. This view is consistent with the "neural Darwinist" position set forth by Gerald Edelman, recipient of the Nobel Prize in Physiology or Medicine in 1972. Edelman's work demonstrated how strong reactions in the brain to certain stimuli result in the formation of neuronal groups out of the individual nerve cells involved with such reactions. These neuronal groups become organized into sheets or "maps" that interact with each other. When a radical, "learned" change takes place, the brain exhibits a different pattern of neuronal firings, thus revealing that it has actually become altered physiologically. (Researchers have conducted related studies dealing with electrical energy in the brain during musical activity; these will be discussed briefly in Chapter 3.)

In characterizing thought as "hypothesis-making" (which leads to relative stasis in habitual mental action or *belief*), Peirce was identifying a special type of logical reasoning. As we have already noted, logic was one of Peirce's philosophical specialties, and he classified "hypothesis-making" as a special form of inference, different from induction (reasoning from particular facts or individual cases to a general conclusion) and deduction (reasoning from general propositions to a particular conclusion). He recognized that in the process of making some inductions there is a certain amount of guesswork. Peirce called this "abductive induction" or *abduction*.

> The first starting of a hypothesis and the entertaining of it, whether as a simple interrogation or with any degree of confidence, is an inferential step which I propose to call abduction.
> . . . The form of inference . . . is this:
>> The surprising fact, C is observed;
>> But if A were true, C would be a matter of course,
>> Hence, there is reason to suspect that A is true.[28]

Insofar as none of us is able to answer every conceivable question that could arise concerning "the way the universe is," we all actively engage in the process of abduction whenever we experience doubt—an inability to account for an interruption of our beliefs. Peirce recognized that abduction is largely an automatic response.

> The abductive suggestion comes to us like a flash. It is an act of *insight*, although of extremely fallible insight. It is true that the different elements of the hypothesis were in our minds before; but it is the idea of putting together what we had never before dreamed of putting together which flashes the new suggestion before our contemplation.[29]

Through such mental activity, we come to conceptualize the world in a new way, and our habitual actions and thoughts are thus modified. For Peirce, conception-making is a uniquely important human activity, since, in his view, "the function of conceptions is to reduce the manifold of sensuous impressions to unity."[30] Moreover, such unified conceptions are not held solely by individuals, but are shared collectively by members of communities.

COLLECTIVE MIND

On the basis of his synechistic perspective, Peirce regarded communities not merely as collectives of discrete minds but as living unions of individual minds, characterizable by their unique and habitualized behavior and thought. While he did not use the term *collective mind* to describe this concept of human community, the idea is clearly implicit in his descriptions of pragmatism and semiotic. Colapietro has noted, "[Peirce's] union of selves that constitutes a community is analogous to the coordination of ideas that constitutes a personality; indeed, the community is in some measure a person."[31]

The concept of "collective mind" represents the main intersection of Peirce's thought with the anthropological concept *culture*. Peirce's statement on abduction, quoted earlier, that "the function of conceptions is to reduce the manifold of sensuous impressions to unity"[32] has particular importance for the concept of community utilized in this inquiry, as the unity of conceptions shared by the members of a community amounts to a collectively shared understanding of the "way things are," consistent with Geertz's notion of an "imaginative universe" shared by the members of a cultural group.

Peirce came to infer that the minds of the members of a community are essentially interpenetrating and largely isomorphic from having recognized that they collectively share common *signs* as vehicles of thought and communication; he asserted that without such organization in common they would not be able to communicate. In his words, "two minds can communicate only by becoming in so far one mind."[33] He developed his extensive semiotic theory to account for communication across all conceivable communicative domains. We will explore this theory in depth at the end of this chapter.

From Peirce's concept of collective mind stemmed his conception of *meaning*. Peirce recognized that since members of a community share common struggles and questions, the meaning of their actions and thoughts must inevitably be predicated on the collective "habits of mind" of the community. Thus, for the members of a community, " . . . what a thing means is simply what habits it involves."[34] He further clarified his conception of meaning in this way:

> We are too apt to think that what one *means* to do and the *meaning* of a word are quite unrelated meanings of the word "meaning," or that they are only connected by both referring to some actual operation of the mind. . . . In truth the only difference is that when a person *means* to do anything he is in some state in consequence of which the brute reactions between things will be moulded to conformity to the form to which the man's mind is itself moulded, while the meaning of a word really lies in the way in which it might in a proper position believed, tend to mould the conduct of a person into conformity to that to which

it is itself moulded. Not only will meaning always, more or less, in the long run, mould reactions to itself, but it is only in doing so that its own being consists.[35]

Therefore, Peirce maintained, for the members of a community, shared meanings are dependent on—and, reciprocally, create—the habits of the community.

Peirce further noted that the conceptions of *truth* that people hold individually are largely dependent on the habitually held conceptions of their communities. In the following passage he makes an important distinction, central to his philosophy, between "what we do not typically doubt" (i.e., tacitly held, provisional truth as it is habitually conceptualized by the members of a community) and absolute Truth (the ultimate, final answers to which all inquirers into a matter will eventually give assent). In making this distinction, he in essence made his philosophy capable of accounting for the possibility of cultural differences. In this statement Peirce implied that truth for an individual is in some measure determined by her or his "circle of society," and that it is thus likely an incomplete, relative truth.

> Two things . . . are all-important to assure oneself of and to remember. The first is that a person is not absolutely an individual . . . When one reasons, it is [one's] critical self that one is trying to persuade . . . The second thing to remember is that the man's circle of society (however widely or narrowly this phrase may be understood), is a sort of loosely compacted person, in some respects of higher rank than the person of an individual organism. It is these two things alone that render it possible for you . . . to distinguish between absolute truth and what you do not doubt.[36]

We will return to Peirce's distinction between absolute truth and the conceptions of truth held by the members of a community in our discussion of his philosophy of science, also following.

As noted previously, Peirce's concept of a "union of individual minds" characterized by its collective "habits of mind" or its shared "abductions" as providing the ground or basis of meaning for human action in community is generally consistent with Geertz's concept of culture as an "imaginative universe" within which the actions and thought of the members of a cultural group have meaning. Twentieth-century scholars have used concepts similar to this one in several areas of discourse, although the terminology and the ways of employing the concept differ somewhat among them. Culture, ideology, *habitus*, cosmology, paradigm, tacit dimension, and myth are all roughly synonymous terms that have been used by social theorists to describe what Peirce would describe as the "habits of mind" or "abductions" collectively shared within a community that provide its internal coherence, but which differ among communities.[37]

In his own writings, Peirce used the word *Argument* as a specialized term to describe the concept to which we have been referring as "collective mind," "shared abduction," or "culture." His unique use of the word *Argument* is so far removed from the common meaning of this word in contemporary academic discourse, however, that it seems particularly inappropriate and awkward for our use in exploring the differing beliefs about music that inhere in different cultural groups. The term *culture*, as Geertz and other "interpretive" anthropologists use it, may seem a better choice, yet it also may not be the best alternative. In recent years global communications and migrations have changed the nature of relationships among peoples having differing cultural origins in an important way: No longer do people of radically differing cultural origins necessarily live at such great distances from one another that differences among them can be regarded as being of primarily scientific interest by cultural anthropologists. (Such foundationally different cultural groups live in particularly close proximity—even intermingled with others— in the U.S.) It may thus be more appropriate to adopt the term *worldview* for our descriptions of the differences in "habits of mind" often regarded as "cultural" among different groups for our purposes in this inquiry. Furthermore, the word *group* seems to imply close physical proximity, while Peirce's word *community* suggests a cultural association that may continue to exist despite physical dispersion. The following two terms are thus presented with definitions for use in this inquiry:

> The term *worldview* is defined as the unique constellation of habitual signs and meanings shared by the members of a cultural community that distinguishes their ultimate values and beliefs from those of other communities and which gradually become evident to a researcher through the process of inquiry.

> The term *cultural community* is defined as a group of people sharing a common worldview as is evidenced in their social practices and their ultimate values and beliefs.

Consistent with this terminology, an individual's membership in a cultural community is conceived as largely defining her or his worldview, and, reciprocally, a number of individuals who share the same worldview are conceived as defining a cultural community. These designations of the terms *cultural community* and *worldview* are generally consistent with their uses in current scholarly discourse.

Before beginning our exploration of Peirce's semiotic, which will assist us in considering the beliefs of different cultural communities as manifestations of their respective worldviews, it will be helpful first to explore further his conceptions of "truth" and "reality" in order to grasp the ways in which he understood these concepts to be related to the ultimate values and beliefs shared by the members of a community. These concepts are at the root of his philosophy of science.

"TRUTH," "REALITY," AND THE PRAGMATIC PHILOSOPHY OF SCIENCE

As we have already noted, Peirce recognized that within any community people tend to hold tightly to the beliefs—the coherent "habits of mind"— that they share in common, and they generally tend to avoid doubt. He further observed that human beings avoid doubt in a number of predictable ways, and he listed and expressed his views on each of the several "methods" by which individuals in community "settle" their doubts: According to Peirce, the *method of tenacity* is used by those who have an instinctive dislike of being undecided, but such persons eventually discover that they cannot hold their ground in practice because interaction with other individuals eventually shakes their confidence. Peirce viewed the *method of authority* as the main means of sustaining theological and political doctrines in all states in which there is an aristocracy. He opined that this method governs the mass of mankind, but that there are always individuals in such states who have a wider social awareness than others and who will, upon coming to doubt the "authoritative" views sustained by such social forces, begin to challenge them. The *a priori method,* which is an appeal to an existing metaphysical system tacitly held by a community, is usually sustained by people who have suspended inquiry because the fundamental propositions of the metaphysical systems they espouse seem so agreeable to reason. The main shortcoming of this method is that it is not based on consistently verifiable experience. (Peirce noted that theologians are the main proponents of such views.[38]) Since all of these methods can be shown to have shortcomings, Peirce concluded, the *scientific method* (i.e., hypothesis testing by experiment) is the only means by which beliefs may be settled to satisfy doubt. Peirce expressed what he called the "fundamental hypothesis of science" in the following way:

> There are Real things whose characters are entirely independent of our opinions about them; those Reals affect our senses according to regular laws, and though our sensations are as different as are our relations to the objects, yet, by taking advantage of the laws of perception, we can ascertain by reasoning how things really and truly are; and any man, if he have sufficient experience and he reason enough about it will be led to the one True conclusion. The new conception here involved is that of Reality.[39]

In his view, the scientific method of settling belief is "far more wholesome" because it allows "integrity of belief"—that is, development of a *conception* of Reality that is potentially more well integrated with *true* Reality.[40]

However, Peirce was actually far ahead of many of his contemporaries in that he also recognized a distinction between the conceptions of Reality held by scientists (i.e., a worldview or *reality*), and true *Reality*—of which he held any human conceptualization to be inevitably imperfect and incomplete.

[A]ll the followers of science are animated by a cheerful hope that the processes of investigation, if only pushed far enough, will give one certain solution to each question to which they apply it. . . . The opinion which is fated to be ultimately agreed to by all who investigate, is what we mean by the truth, and the object represented in this opinion is the real. That is the way I would explain reality.

But it may be said that this view is directly opposed to the abstract definition which we have given of reality, inasmuch as it makes the characters of the real depend on what is ultimately thought about them. But the answer to this is that reality is independent, not necessarily of thought in general, but only of what you or I or any finite number of men may think about it; and . . . on the other hand, though the object of the final opinion depends on what that opinion is, yet what that opinion is does not depend on what you or I or any man thinks.[41]

Since human conceptions are not necessarily revelatory of final Truth or Reality, Peirce concluded, it follows that all conceptions are best held provisionally. Also, he held, it is important to remember that all presently held concepts of truth shared by the members of a community have been established from doubt and the assimilation of a hypothesis (or abduction) into their collective beliefs. In a journal article describing how to make concepts or ideas—scientific and otherwise—"clear," that is, free from being consistently doubted and disagreed upon, Peirce explained that all ideas could best be clarified by considering them in relation to the *effects* they are conceived as having by the members of the community with which they originate—their pragmatic *meaning*. Asserting that "our idea of anything *is* our idea of its sensible effects,"[42] he coined the following "pragmatic maxim" as a guiding principle; it is widely regarded as a central idea of his pragmatism.

Consider what effects, that might conceivably have practical bearings, we conceive the object of our conception to have. Then, our conception of these effects is the whole of our conception of the object.[43]

It is important to note that in coining this maxim Peirce was *not* implying that an idea should be evaluated on the basis of its practical value to the life of a community. This view is a common misinterpretation of what Peirce meant by pragmatism. Instead, Peirce intended his pragmatic maxim to imply that since human beings live in communities that are defined by common belief, the "clear" meaning of an idea held by a member of the community will almost inevitably stem from the beliefs—or ways of understanding—held by members of that community. After all, he reasoned, "we perceive what we are adjusted for interpreting . . ."[44]

Recognizing that the results of inquiry may yield useful information, but that they do not yield a comprehensive understanding of Reality because they are inevitably partial, humanly constructed, contextually grounded ways of understanding, Peirce adopted a position that he called *fallibilism*, a position of acknowledgment that any and all *conceptions* of Reality will inevitably be incomplete. He saw fallibilism as consistent with synechism—his doctrine of the interconnectedness of all phenomena.

> The principle of continuity [i.e., synechism] is the idea of fallibilism objectified. For fallibilism is the doctrine that our knowledge is never absolute but always swims, as it were, in a continuum of uncertainty and of indeterminacy. Now the doctrine of continuity is that *all things* so swim in continua.[45]

Since one can never be certain that one's own or one's community's conception of Reality is perfectly "true" to absolute Reality, all inquirers must be willing to admit to their fallibility and to the tentative nature of their conclusions. He proclaimed, "The scientific spirit requires a man to be at all times ready to dump his whole cartload of beliefs, the moment experience is against them."[46] After all, he maintained, it is always possible that new information may be found to challenge the beliefs one presently holds incontrovertible.

As we have already noted, Peirce had no interest in focusing his studies on the differing beliefs—or worldviews—of different communities as collective "abductions of reality." However, his pragmatic philosophy has largely been adopted and his semiotic has been applied by cultural anthropologists as a tool for understanding and explicating aspects of the worldviews of different cultural groups. In addition, his philosophy provides a useful and conceptually powerful lens through which to view *signs* in the "same" society at various historical points in time. In this inquiry, such an application will demonstrate the ways in which the worldview of a community, specifically the community of U.S. music educators, has changed historically with respect to the *sign* "music." This will be our focus in Chapter 5.

SEMIOTIC—PEIRCE'S THEORY OF *SIGNS*

Although Peirce never intended that his conception would be employed for such purposes, his semiotic—or theory of *signs*—has been used by "interpretive" cultural anthropologists as a heuristic conception of the "cells" or basal units of the webs of meaning of different cultural communities. In order to grasp Peirce's semiotic and appreciate its unique applicability, it will be necessary first to develop a general understanding of his phenomenology.

As a demonstration of the consistency of synechism—his conception of the continuous, conscious relationship of everything in the universe—with his ideas on human behavior and communication, Peirce set forth a hierarchy of phenomenal categories—a taxonomy of "all that is in any way or in any sense present to the mind"—as the foundation of his logic.[47] His semiotic theory is based on this foundation. Peirce identified three unique elements of consciousness—the realms of (1) *pure quality* or *sensory feeling*, (2) *brute fact* or *physical otherness*, and (3) *thought* or *synthetic consciousness*—as being the ultimate categories into which *everything* that is present to the human mind could be assigned. "If we accept these [as] the fundamental elementary modes of consciousness, they afford a psychological explanation of the three logical conceptions of quality, relation, and synthesis or mediation."[48] He assigned the categories the rather cumbersome names of Firstness, Secondness, and Thirdness, respectively.

These categories demand precise description, and, in fact, Peirce struggled to explain them adequately throughout his life, defining them again and again in various ways, consistently striving to overcome the limitations of language. Peirce scholar Michael Shapiro attempted to clarify the categories by compiling and summarizing a number of Peirce's descriptions of them; useful excerpts and clarifications from his compilation are presented following.

> *Firstness*: a *quality* or character that can be regarded in itself as an undifferentiated unity. "Firstness is the mode of being of that which is such as it is, positively and without reference to anything else." Firstness is found in freshness, life, freedom, immediacy, feeling, quality, vivacity, independence, being-in-itself, and potentiality.

> *Secondness*: a *brute fact*; the experience of effort, resistance, or force— one thing acting upon another. "Secondness is the mode of being of that which is such as it is, with respect to a second but regardless of any third." Secondness is found in action, resistance, facticity, dependence, relation, compulsion, effect, reality, and result.

> *Thirdness*: the *mental* element; the status of two things when they are combined or mediated by some third thing. "Thirdness is the mode of being of that which is such as it is, in bringing a second and third into relation to each other." Thirdness is found in habit, mediation, rule, growth, synthesis, living, continuity, process, moderation, learning, memory, inference, representation, intelligence, intelligibility, generality, infinity, diffusion, growth, and conduct.[49]

Even in this condensed form, the categories may be difficult for the reader to grasp. However, when one understands Peirce's conception of the *sign* as the central concept in his semiotic explanation of cognition, the categories can be seen as a logically necessary foundation for the theory. As such, they can be grasped intuitively.

THE *SIGN*

Peirce developed his semiotic as an explanation of cognition, according to which a *sign*—a single element of thought—is conceptualized as an indivisible triadic relationship, the three aspects of which include: (1) the *Sign* (sometimes also termed a *Representamen*)—as a "Firstness" or "First" and (2) the *Object* to which it is understood to refer—as a "Second." The *Sign* is understood to refer to the *Object* according to (3) the *Interpretant*—a "Third"—as an effect in the mind of the perceiver.[50] In Peirce's words, "A Sign is anything which is so determined by something else, called its Object, and so determines an effect upon a person, which effect I call its Interpretant, that the latter is thereby mediately determined by the former." Figure 2.1 illustrates the triad of Peirce's sign relationship for a single individual as it is described earlier.

Another way of describing the relationship between the categories might be to say that we perceive the world as a diverse array of pure *qualities* or sensory impressions. (Peirce would regard each of these qualitative entities of perception as a First, or *Sign*.) Each such perception is construed as "something" (a Second, or *Object*). Finally, each individual perceiver conceives the perceived Sign as an Object according to her or his own personal "habit of mind"—(a Third, or *Interpretant*). The following statement of Peirce's may help to illuminate the way in which he understood the mind of a perceiver to construct conceptions from her or his perceptions:

> All our knowledge may be said to rest upon *observed facts*. It is true that there are psychological states which antecede our observing facts as such. Thus it is a fact that I see an inkstand before me; but before

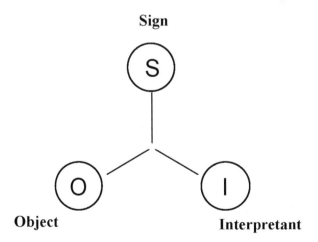

Figure 2.1   Peirce's triadic conception of the *sign*.

I can say that, I am obliged to have impressions of sense [Firsts] into which no idea of an inkstand, or of any separate object, or of an "I," or of seeing, enter at all; and it is true that my judging that I see an inkstand [Second] before me is the product of mental operations [Thirds] upon these impressions of sense. But it is only when the cognition has become worked up into a proposition, or judgment of a fact, that I can exercise any direct control over the process. . . . [51]

In other words, the First or Sign is a perception, the Second or Object is the conception of that perception, and the Third or Interpretant is the "habit of mind" of the perceiver according to which the perception is construed as a conception. With his concept of the sign relationship, Peirce intended to draw a distinction between "what we are immediately conscious of" (the Sign) and "what we are mediately conscious of" (the Object).[52]

Readers initially may be more inclined to think of the Object as the First, and the Sign as the "mind's conception," rather than the other way around. Indeed, Peirce's use of the Sign rather than the Object—as the First in his triadic conception—seems counterintuitive and difficult to grasp, but it also makes his semiotic uniquely powerful: It prevents his philosophy and any analytic conceptions drawn from it from tending toward realism (which would be subject to positivistic reduction) on the one hand, or toward an ungrounded, purely subjective idealism (which would be inaccessible to any empirical verification and agreement) on the other.

It must also be noted that the triadic conception of the *sign* in Peirce's semiotic differs in a way important for the heuristic discussion of different cultural viewpoints from the *semiology* of linguist Ferdinand de Saussure, which heavily influenced Claude Levi-Strauss, the central theorist in structural anthropology discussed earlier.[53] Saussure had posited that a *dyadic* relationship inheres between "signifier" and "signified" for all the members of a single cultural group. Levi-Strauss extrapolated from this notion (and others) the idea that analysis of the dialogues and myths of a given cultural group would reveal not only aspects of the structure of the cultural group, but also aspects of the structure of the human mind as they are manifested in that group. As noted earlier, this conception of Levi-Strauss's had a profound impact on the discipline of cultural anthropology, and many studies have been predicated on it. The problem with Saussure's conception is that no cultural community's language can truly be characterized as, in Paul Ricoeur's words, an "autonomous entity of internal dependencies"[54] since, in fact, members of all cultural communities have some intercourse with the members of others. Peirce's notion of individuals as "bundles of habits" and his *triadic* conception of the sign are, by contrast, not so culturally restrictive; Peirce's semiotic acknowledges that the individual's potential interpretations are largely determined by her or his "habits of mind," but it does not necessarily assume cultural closure.

A visual representation of Peirce's conception of the *sign* relationship that involves different perceivers will serve to demonstrate how human disagreements might arise from different individual conceptions. The following diagram illustrates how any given perception (as a Sign) may be conceived differently (as an Object) by individuals (manifesting unique Interpretants) who may differ not only in their cultural origins, but also in other ways. Their social traditions, religions, families, friends, occupations, unique physiological characteristics, the time during which they live, and other relevant experiential (i.e., cultural) background characteristics are all factors that contribute to the formation of their "habits of mind" or Thirdness, and thus to the ways they conceptualize that which they perceive.

Two examples will serve to demonstrate the way in which a single perceived *sign* (at the center of the diagram in Figure 2.2) might be conceptualized differently by the three different individuals also represented in the diagram. If the Sign were a single sound—the sound phonetically spelled "rān" in English—which is the only sound heard clearly from a conversation in an adjoining room, our three hypothetical English-speaking individuals may conceive that the conversation is about three different topics. If Individual 1 were a member of a royal family, she may conceive the sound

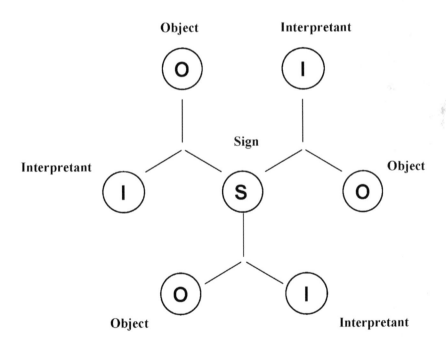

Figure 2.2   A Sign perceived and conceptualized differently by three culturally dissimilar individuals.

as "reign"; if Individual 2 were a horseman, he may conceive the sound as "rein"; and if Individual 3 were a meteorologist, she may conceive the sound as "rain." Similarly, an adult male human being, perceived as a Sign, may be conceptualized as a friend, a criminal, or a plumber by the same three individuals depending on their prior experiences with that man or with men qualitatively similar to him. A fourth individual coming from a radically different cultural community in another part of the world may not be able to conceptualize meaningfully the sounded Sign "rān" or correctly identify *any* social attributes of that male human being. Conversely, this individual might conceptualize the sound and the individual in a fourth, unique, and possibly mistaken way. This example demonstrates that in no case can the Sign be truly conceptualized as what it *is* in an ontological sense, since any such description would inherently limit the sign to the way in which it is conceptualized as an Object according to an Interpretant.

Another illustration will show how a musical event (as a *sign*) might be understood differently by individuals of differing cultural backgrounds. Listeners from three different cultural communities may conceptualize the sound of a solo voice singing an indistinguishable text (unaccompanied) in *at least* three different ways: A Muslim listener may hear the sound as a prayer and *not* as music, a Tibetan listener may hear it as a sound intoned in meditation, and an American of European descent might hear it as an entertainingly good tune. Such culturally grounded differences lie at the root of the problems of music education in the U.S. described in Chapter 1. We will return to this example in Chapter 3 in a discussion of "music" as a *sign*.

We should note before proceeding any further that though certain aspects of Peirce's semiotic—as a model of cognition—are not strictly pragmatic (in the sense that they might eventually be universally agreed to by all members of the human community of inquirers), they do serve as good *provisional* descriptors of how knowing (and thus meaning) occurs. Most notably, his triadic conception of the *sign*—as comprised of Sign, Object, and Interpretant—might well receive assent eventually from the members of all cultural communities, but his attendant phenomenological concepts of Firstness, Secondness, and Thirdness and their manifestations as particular kinds of *signs* are less likely to receive such agreement, though they do serve pragmatic purposes. Nevertheless, the lack of some such provisional conceptualization would make it difficult to achieve the degree of understanding sought after in the present inquiry, hence accurately to describe and interpret the history of music education in the U.S., to assess it, and to consider its future directions.

TYPES OF *SIGNS*

As explained earlier, Peirce asserted that *anything* that is registered in consciousness will be "cognized" as a Sign of Firstness (quality), Secondness (brute fact), or Thirdness (the mental aspect). In his view, "it is not right to call these categories conceptions; . . . they are rather tones or tints upon conceptions."[55] Peirce firmly maintained the basal or nonderived nature of the categories.

> [T]he ideas of First, Second, Third [are] ideas so broad that they may be looked upon rather as moods or tones of thought, than as definite notions, but which have definite significance for all that. . . . That there are such ideas of the really First, Second, and Third, we shall presently find reason to admit.[56]

From these three basal, phenomenal categories of "all that is in any way or in any sense present to the mind," Peirce developed taxonomies of ten, twenty-eight, and sixty-six classes of signs, ultimately deriving 59,049 possible varieties of sign relationships. Since these classes will not be employed in the context of this inquiry, we will not explore them here.[57]

In the body of this inquiry, we will focus primarily on signs that designate the potential relationship of a Sign to an Object. An *Icon* (as a First) shares a qualitative similarity with its Object. Peirce notes that "[a]nything whatever, be it quality, existent individual, or law, is an Icon of anything, in so far as it is like that thing and used as a sign of it."[58] Peirce's definition of Icon is thus related to the standard English dictionary definition of an icon as a "likeness." An *Index*, as a Second, is a sign that is somehow in contiguous, physical relationship with its Object. In Peirce's words, it is "really affected" by that Object.[59] A *Symbol*, as a Third, is a sign that is associated with its object by virtue of a law, usually a tacitly held human convention. It is thus usually of a general type, such as the name of a town or person. The following definitions and examples may help to make the classification clearer.

- Icon (a First)—A Sign that refers to the Object that it denotes merely by virtue of qualities of its own, whether any such Object exists or not. (Examples include a map and the terrain it represents; an instance of onomatopoeia and the sound to which it refers.)
- Index (a Second)—A Sign that refers to the Object that it denotes by virtue of its being "really affected" by that Object. (Examples include smoke and fire; red litmus and acidity.)
- Symbol (a Third)—A Sign that refers to the Object that it denotes by virtue of a law, usually an association of general ideas or a convention, which operates to cause the symbol to be interpreted as referring to that Object. (Examples include a word or a sign language gesture and the concept each denotes.)

Peirce explained that only one dimension of a perceived Sign is conceptualized (as an Object) according to the "habit of mind" of an individual person

(Interpretant) at a given moment, although every sign has the potential of being simultaneously perceived and conceptualized in many different ways by different individuals. Anthropologist E. Valentine Daniel has offered a striking metaphor to describe the multifarious nature of Peirce's sign:

> A . . . sign can be likened to a jewel . . . In the experience of human interpretants, often only one facet will tilt toward the observer-interpreter, catch light, and throw it back; the other facets merely refract light. The reflecting facet, then, becomes the dominant mode. This does not, however, deny the existence of other modes of signification; modes that are sometimes expressed subjunctively and at other times remain potentialities. Different contexts help bring to light different aspects or modes of the sign.[60]

SEMIOSIS—THE INTERPLAY AND TRANSFORMATION OF SIGNS

Peirce maintained that Signs—and our conceptions of them—are continuously in motion and constantly changing. It is through the process of *semiosis*, which Peirce described as the "action, or influence"[61] of signs upon one another, that signs typically change. Another visual representation will illustrate the way in which an individual's conception of a Sign may change over time. Figure 2.3 is intended to illustrate how any given perception (as a Sign) may be conceptualized differently (as an Object) by a single, continually changing individual (an Interpretant) over the course of that individual's lifetime.

Upon an individual's first conscious perception of a given Sign, the Sign may be regarded as new *information*, as it has much new data to yield.

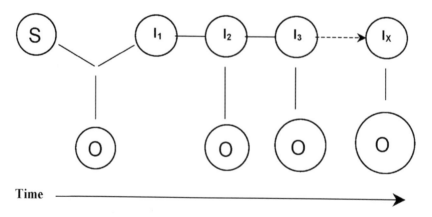

Figure 2.3 Changes in the Interpretant over time, resulting in changes in the conception of the Sign as Object.

However, as he or she encounters and reflects on the same Sign over a period of time, meeting it perhaps in a variety of social contexts, the sign may be said to become more *meaningful*—more well-understood and more well-integrated into habitual patterns of belief, while yielding less and less new *information* with each encounter (illustrated here by I_1, I_2, I_3 . . . I_X). For example, a favorite story, a religious ritual, or another person will gradually yield less and less information to an individual, but will become a more meaningful part of life over time as her or his habits of thought and action grow and change. The way that the individual conceptualizes the perceived Sign as Object is thus likely to change over time. We should note also that as the individual him- or herself (considered as a Sign) changes throughout this process of semiosis, the way in which he or she is likely conceptualized (as an Object) by another Interpretant (such as a friend or spouse) is also likely to change.

Similarly, this aspect of Peirce's semiotic provides a particularly good means for describing how a musical piece or practice can be regarded as meaningful for a listener or participant. A given musical work or form of musical activity can be said to be *meaningful* for those in the community from which it stems if it is somehow related to the "habits of mind" of the members of that cultural community. By contrast, the same musical piece or practice may be regarded as too different, too highly *informational*, when it is experienced by persons who are *not* a part of that community. Since such individuals lack the necessary background to grasp its connection to the life of the community, the musical piece or practice may not be meaningful to them at all. On the other hand, in those instances in which two communities have widely differing or conflicting worldviews, the music of one community may have meaning for the members of both communities, but the second community may conceive the music of the first to be objectionable, regarding it as noise. Numerous possibilities for differences and similarities of conception exist, depending on the prior experience and cultural (*habitual*) differences of the listeners.

In the same way, a word considered as a Sign (i.e., a Symbol, a Third) may also change in meaning over time, as it is conceptualized differently by different Interpretants at different points in history. The concept that the word is intended to designate may be given a different name in different cultural contexts, as well.[62] We will encounter these notions again in Chapter 3, when we develop our pragmatic conception of "music."

ONTOLOGICAL RELATIONSHIP OF ONE INDIVIDUAL TO THE WORLDVIEW OF ANOTHER

It is important to note that Peirce not only accounted for our logical, mental conceptions of the perceived Sign in his notion of the Interpretant, but that he included emotional and other aspects of the human psyche as well.

Peirce extended his conceptions of Firstness, Secondness, and Thirdness to class Interpretants according to an interlocking set of trichotomies. The First trichotomy includes the Immediate Interpretant—"an abstraction, consisting in a possibility"; the Dynamic Interpretant—"the actual semiotic effect of a sign"; and the Final Interpretant—"The one Interpretative result to which every Interpreter is destined to come if the Sign is sufficiently considered." Each of these classes of Interpretants was further divided into a sub-trichotomy, the second of which, the Dynamic Interpretant, is essential to our inquiry.[63]

The Dynamic Interpretant, as the "actual semiotic effect of a sign," he subclassified according to whether it is Emotional—having the qualitative effect of the sign; Energetic—having the mode of interpretation of a sign stimulating an *act* in which some energy is expended; or Logical—having the nature of a general rule or hypothesis. The important idea to keep in mind from this is that Peirce clearly recognized that, concomitant with the perception of a Sign, the effect on the perceiver would be emotional, energetic (involving physical action), and/or logical.

Given this conceptual vocabulary, we can use Peirce's terminology to describe how an individual person or a community (as an Interpretant) may undergo cultural change over time. As a person learns new ways of conceptualizing the same Sign as an Object due to prolonged exposure and communication with individuals embodying another worldview, he or she may come to accept partially or entirely that worldview as her or his own. Those who live for a time in a foreign country, who earn an advanced degree in a technical discipline, who marry a spouse having different cultural origins, or whose communities undergo major changes often find that their perceptions of various Signs have changed radically since the days of their youth.

A good example of the possible relationships an individual may have to the signs of a cultural community embodying a worldview different from her or his own comes from the terminology used by cultural anthropologists to describe the ontological relationship existing between a researcher and the cultural community he or she is studying. *Observer* is the term applied to a researcher who relates to the cultural community on the level of the intellect, perhaps partially understanding the views of the group, but not physically (i.e., experientially) sharing in their activities and emotions. *Observer-participant* is the term used to describe one who explores intellectually and participates physically in the life activities of the group, but still maintains (or emotionally reserves) her or his own worldview as an observer. Finally, *"gone native"* is an expression used to describe humorously those who have found the worldview of the group being studied to be a better-fitting or more psychologically satisfying apprehension of reality than her or his own worldview, thus adopting fully the concepts, behaviors, and emotions associated with the new worldview, and renouncing the worldview they originally embodied as well as their status as observers.

Peirce likely would have described the relationship of the anthropologist's mind (as an Interpretant, or Thirdness) to the "collective mind" or worldview of the cultural community being studied in each of the foregoing cases in the following ways: The relationship of the *observer's* worldview to the worldview of the "other" being studied would be described as a "Thirdness of Thirdness." In such a relationship, the "mind" of the observer (as a Logical Interpretant or Third) in some measure *understands* intellectually the different worldview of the "others" as that of a unique "cultural community" (another Third), but he or she has not adopted the worldview of the "others" in any other way. The relationship of the *observer-participant's* worldview to the "others" would be described as a "Thirdness and Secondness of Thirdness." In such a relationship, the researcher shares experiences both intellectually (as a Logical Interpretant or Third) *and physically* (as an Energetic Interpretant or Second) and thus has become in some measure intellectually and physically unified with the group—perhaps as an "acquaintance" or "friend." Such a researcher has thus *experienced* life with the "other" group and has come to experience physically what they experience. Finally, the relationship of the person *"gone native"* might best be described as a "Thirdness, Secondness, and Firstness of Thirdness." In such a relationship, the "mind" of the researcher (a Third) has become unified with the group intellectually (as a Logical Interpretant or Third), physically (as an Energetic Interpretant, or Second) and emotionally (as an Emotional Interpretant, or First). He or she has become "one of them," intellectually, physically, and emotionally unified with them, finally sharing the worldview previously experienced as "other."[64]

Other possibilities stemming from this example can also be considered. For example, an anthropologist may participate in the activities of a dissimilar cultural community, having no conceptual understanding of or emotional connection to the proceedings. (Comedians in theatre and film often exploit such situations, as when an individual enters a room and participates in the activities going on around her or him, but has no idea of how to think or feel about what is experienced.) Peirce would classify such an experience as a "Secondness of Thirdness"; it involves the Energetic (physical) aspect of the Interpretant, but neither the Emotional nor the Logical aspects. The reader can probably conceive of the other types of relationships.

In communicating, every individual may to some degree be a "cultural anthropologist" insofar as he or she defers, reflects, and strives to learn more before attempting to formulate a translation of another's meanings—a description of the other's imaginative universe or worldview. The anthropologist defers in order to construct a more accurate description—based on her or his acquired conception. Such an inquirer's exploration into the conceptual world of another becomes more accurate and comprehensive depending on the thoroughness and depth of the personal inquiry and her or his experience of the background and perspectives of the other, plus the degree to which the inquirer defers and reflects on what is learned through such inquiry. Through this dialogue and social intercourse the inquirer may come to more or less clearly grasp the "reality" of the informant, and eventually the inquirer and informant may become more or less "of one mind," thus partially sharing the same worldview.

Colapietro has drawn both the limit and the extreme to which Peirce's philosophy accounts for this unification of minds:

> Of course, two individually distinct minds never *completely* fuse into a formally identical mind; nonetheless, there are moments when the barrier that sunders one consciousness from another disappears. Thus, not insularity but interpenetrability is the law that most truly governs the relations between two minds. It is perhaps no exaggeration to say that Peirce desired above all else to present an account of mind that did justice to sympathy, our feeling *one with another*.[65]

As we shall see in the next chapter, the cultural congruity that stems from this unification of individual minds is integrally associated with all musical activity that can be described as socially *meaningful* according to Peirce's definition.

Before leaving this idea, we should note a few other points concerning cultural status and transformation. When the members of two dissimilar cultural communities coexist in close proximity, the two communities (as "collective minds" or Interpretants) may go to war. They may also gradually adopt from one another information previously regarded as "objectionable" into their respective imaginative universes, thereby partially assimilating or fusing their worldviews. Furthermore, because individual human beings are abductive and creative, Peirce recognized, we may also, over time, come together to create new communities around new conceptions of Reality.

REVIEW AND APPLICATION

We began this chapter by reviewing critically the approaches to the study of "culture" that have been taken historically within cultural anthropology, the field of scientific inquiry dedicated to understanding both the common and diverse characteristics of human beings and their behavior, before finally adopting the concept of "culture" or "worldview" implicit in the pragmatic philosophy of turn-of-the-twentieth-century scholar Charles Sanders Peirce as the conceptual foundation for our inquiry. We saw that Peirce's philosophy is generally congruent with the foundational premises of current scholarship in cultural anthropology and cognitive psychology, among other fields, making it particularly well-suited for our inquiry, which involves the musical practices and beliefs of diverse cultural communities.

Perhaps the most important aspect of Peirce's philosophy is the fundamental premise of *synechism* (i.e., the interconnectedness of all phenomena) upon which the philosophy is based. Among the notable elements of Peirce's philosophy that follow from this premise are his recognition that behavioral and conceptual differences among individual human beings stem from the differing "habits of mind" they have acquired as survival strategies in the communities (or "collective minds") to which they belong; his acknowledgment that the conception of Reality held by any community will inevitably be partial and biased due to having its origins in its members' distinctive, collective efforts toward survival; his recognition that the *meaning* any person conceives his actions to have is inevitably related to the recognized, efficacious coping actions of the community within which they are undertaken; and his assertion that the scientific method (i.e., hypothesis-testing by experiment) represents the only effective means for determining ultimate Truth (i.e., truth beyond that tacitly recognized by the community), but that even scientific conclusions may be superseded by further inquiry. Finally, we saw that Peirce's *semiotic*—as a provisional theory of cognition—represents a uniquely effective vocabulary for describing systematically both intra- and intercultural meanings, and that his *phenomenological* terminology provides us with a means of describing the ontological relationship one individual may have to the culturally distinctive worldview of another.

In the following chapter we will explore the ways in which a culturally particular form of "music" (as a sound-producing human practice) can be considered efficacious within a community and thus as a *sign* of that community's worldview. Following a brief, critical review of conceptions of "music" held historically within the field of ethnomusicology, we will develop a pragmatic conception of musical *meaning*—how a musical practice can be understood to be pragmatically meaningful for the members of a given cultural community at a given time. Our exploration will demonstrate how a musical "artifact" or a given instance of "music" can be understood as a *sign* of the worldview of the cultural community from which it stems due to its sharing of inherent qualities with that worldview (*iconic* relationship), its physical connection with members of the cultural community (*indexical* relationship), and its association with the worldview of the cultural community due to its use of conventional signs (*symbolic* relationship). Finally, Peirce's categorical terms Firstness, Secondness, and Thirdness will provide us with a vocabulary for discussing the ontological relationship of an individual student or teacher to the varieties of "music" recommended for inclusion in the curriculum. This conception of "music" as a *sign* of worldview will serve as a foundation for our consideration of the ways in which "music" has been conceptualized, and the bases upon which instruction in "music" has been justified for inclusion in the public schools of the U.S. throughout the history of the nation.

At the conclusion of our historical overview in Chapter 5, Peirce's semiotic vocabulary will facilitate our explanation of approaches that might be taken to resolve the two problems presented in the previous chapter that are presently facing the profession of public-school music education in the U.S. Specifically, as Peirce's pragmatism enables us to come to a clearer understanding of the great differences in beliefs about what "music" *is* and about its importance in human life, it will help us to reconcile more effectively the purposes of the profession to the present cultural characteristics of the U.S., thus establishing for teachers and the general public a more sound conceptual grounding for the present and future practice of public-school music education.

3   A Pragmatic Conception
of Musical Practices
"Music" as a *Sign* of Worldview

I asked Einstein one day, "Do you believe that absolutely everything can be expressed scientifically?" "Yes," he replied, "it would be possible but it would make no sense. It would be a description without meaning—as if you described a Beethoven symphony as a variation of wave pressure."[1]

Hedwig Born, as quoted by Ronald W. Clark

As we saw in Chapter 1, both the disparity of opinions presently held by United States citizens on the importance of public-school music education and the curricular dilemmas presently facing American music educators concerning the inclusion of music of various cultural communities from around the world in their classes have their bases in the myriad conceptions of music now evident among the diverse citizenry of the U.S. Before we begin to explore the concepts of music that have been held historically by music educators or make any recommendations about future practices of the profession, we need to establish our own foundational understanding of the importance of music in the lives of human beings from which we can consider these different concepts. Because of the increasingly varied cultural backgrounds of the students attending public schools in the U.S., it seems necessary that this conception reflect some understanding of the great diversity of musical practices and beliefs of the world's different cultural communities. In the previous chapter, we traced changes in the concepts of "culture" held by anthropologists over the past century before establishing the pragmatic conception of C. S. Peirce as providing our philosophical foundation for this inquiry. In this chapter, we will similarly acquaint ourselves with the differing concepts of "music" held by ethnomusicologists over the past century, and then investigate both the differing views they presently hold on the related practices of different world peoples *and* the implications these views have for music educators. Finally, we will explore ways in which Peirce's pragmatism might embrace and offer a new perspective on these differing views of "music."

HISTORICAL PERSPECTIVES ON "MUSIC" AS AN ETHNOMUSICOLOGICAL CONSTRUCT

As one might expect, changes in the conceptions of "music" held by ethnomusicologists over the history of their inquiry have in some ways paralleled the changes in the concept of "culture" held by anthropologists over the same period. Specifically, concepts of both have been refined and expanded over time to reflect scholars' increased understanding of the differences and similarities among cultural communities. However, concepts of "music" within ethnomusicology have also been influenced by an inherent difference between musicological and anthropological orientations to the study of "music" in different cultural contexts; this difference is largely attributable to the different educational backgrounds and research interests of practitioners in the field.[2]

Austrian musicologist Guido Adler is usually given credit for assigning the name "comparative musicology" in 1885 to the field of inquiry defined by the "comparison of the musical works—especially the folksongs—of the various peoples of the earth for ethnographical purposes, and the classification of them according to their various forms,"[3] but the inauguration of the modern, scientific study of music as a world phenomenon is more commonly attributed to Alexander J. Ellis, Carl Stumpf, and Erich Moritz von Hornbostel. All three of these early scholars sought to apply methods from the natural sciences to their studies of music as it appeared around the world. Ellis (1814–1890), an Englishman, undertook to establish differences and similarities in the musical scales of different world peoples primarily by studying the pitches produced on their instruments. His work resulted in the development of a method, still in use today, for converting the ratios between pitches into numerical values that can be compared easily (*cents*), but his efforts at associating scale types with cultural communities in particular geographical areas were ultimately not very fruitful.[4] Stumpf (1848–1936) and Hornbostel (1877–1935), both German "armchair anthropologists" who also did no field studies of their own, listened to and analyzed recordings of music made by ethnologists who had studied various peoples. From their analyses of these samples of "primitive music," they developed theories about the evolution and the common aesthetic foundations of music in general.

One theory under discussion at the time originated with Charles Darwin, who hypothesized that, since music is found "prefigured" in birds (among which males strive to please females), the human being likewise becomes a singer under the stress of sexual excitation.[5] Another theory was that music and speech are the expression of two "allied orders of feeling" both of which "find voice" through the same muscular apparatus.[6] Stumpf theorized that music had its origins in other human activities; he noted, for example, that when one person calls to another over a considerable distance, the voice is raised spontaneously and a musical tone and musical motive are engendered.[7] Hornbostel articulated several other theories more tentatively, holding strongly to the position that the continued study of music would allow for parallels to be drawn between the condition of "primitive" peoples and earlier stages of "our own" culture. He enthusiastically proclaimed, "[t]he more extensive the data that we submit for comparison, the sooner we may hope to be able to explain *a posteriori* the archetypal beginnings of music from the course of its development."[8]

The theoretical efforts just described were all founded on the ethnocentric assumption tacitly held in European and American intellectual society of the time that European music was a manifestation of the superiority of European cultural development. In fact, historical musicologists of the period saw the studies of comparative musicologists as confirming the superiority of European art music. It must be noted, however, that the theoretical efforts of these three influential Europeans are not representative of the work of all "comparative musicologists" of the early twentieth century. A number of studies of this time were more descriptive in character, primarily involving collection of data, and many utilized recording equipment for the purpose of preserving the sounds produced by the cultural community under study. Not surprisingly, some of these studies stemmed from the influence of anthropologist Franz Boas (who was introduced in Chapter 2). Boas advocated inquiry into the processes by which different cultures had developed their musical customs. Some scholars now hold that his studies and recordings of music of the Kwakiutl Indians, and the similar work of J. Walter Fewkes with the Passamaquoddy and Zuni Indians, are among the most important research efforts of the era.

In the years following World War II, when commercially available airplane travel made distant parts of the world more accessible to Europeans and Americans, the study of the musical practices of different world peoples in their originating social contexts became more feasible for many scholars. At about the same time, they gradually became dissatisfied with using the title "comparative musicology" to delineate their area of inquiry, and began to substitute the name "ethnomusicology" to describe their work. In 1961, Curt Sachs gave one explanation for the change:

> [T]oday 'comparative musicology' has lost its usefulness. For at the bottom every branch of knowledge is comparative; all our descriptions, in the humanities no less than in the sciences, state similarities and divergences.[9]

In reflecting on the name change years later, Alan Merriam identified the reason for it more specifically. He explained that, over time, more and more definitions of the field of study offered under the new title pointed to its practitioners' emphasis on *processes* and on conceptualizing musical sound as a part of the totality of society and culture, rather than on studying musical form as it appeared in different parts of the world.[10] In discussing the more culturally holistic orientation of "ethnomusicology," scholar Charles Seeger lamented that the more inclusive name, musicology, was taken by historians of European art music to describe their more culturally insular pursuits.[11]

By the mid-twentieth century, ethnomusicologists could be separated into two groups, each of which embraced in its own way the shift in emphasis toward understanding the musical practices of different world peoples on their own terms. Many ethnomusicologists having backgrounds in musicology conducted extended field studies to develop mastery of a "foreign" musical system, largely with the intent of using what they learned to compare the musical traditions of different cultural communities. Mantle Hood, arguably the most influential scholar in this group, maintained that, despite the name change, comparison was still an appropriate undertaking for ethnomusicologists and that the search for universals—common aspects of different cultural communities' musical practices—was still a "proper concern."[12] The second group of ethnomusicologists, those with primarily anthropological background, was largely opposed to the creation of "general theories" of music, primarily on the basis that not enough information was available for the results of such efforts to be veracious. Alan Merriam, a leading scholar in this second group, held that efforts at generalizing between cultural communities should be undertaken only if they are directed at solving a particular research problem; he stressed that "comparison for its own sake is not the goal to be sought."[13]

The difference in the perspectives of these two groups may seem to some readers outside of ethnomusicology to be so subtle as to render them inconsequential. However, those who have some experience with the radically differing conceptual systems, or worldviews, of different cultural communities also realize how inherently problematical efforts at comparison between and generalization among them can be. Any English-speaking person who has attempted to learn another language, particularly a non-European language, has likely become aware that some of the concepts inherent in one language cannot be translated directly into the other because of the different worldview that is implicit in it. Something is always lost in the translation; specifically, it is the *way* of knowing or understanding (i.e., the worldview) that frames the information that cannot be fully communicated. Ethnomusicologists have had to confront this issue directly in their field studies upon realizing that the members of all cultural communities do not share the Euro-American concept "music," and that the concept apparently differs even among those groups that share use of the word.

The word *music* originally stemmed from classical Greek mythology, in which it was used to describe broadly "the art of the Muses." The Muses were the nine daughters of Zeus, the principal god of the Greek pantheon, and each of them was supposed to preside over a different art or science: epic poetry, history, love poetry, lyric poetry, sacred poetry, tragedy, choral dance and song, comedy, and astronomy. Thus, for the Greeks, "music" included all of these endeavors. The ancient Greeks had no word equivalent to what is presently called "music" in the U.S. public forum, and, obviously, the word "music" only rarely carries its original Greek meaning in contemporary American discourse. Today, most citizens of Greece, along with other Europeans,

Americans, and many others, customarily use the word "music" to describe collectively the "sound artifacts" produced during diverse human practices involving the patterned production of sounds (which they typically conceptualize as "music making"). However, as we noted in Chapter 1, persons from some cultural communities conceptualize their actions involving the patterned production of sounds in ways wholly different from the ways they are conceptualized in Europe and the U.S. "Meditation" and "prayer" are but two easily graspable examples that we have already cited; others are more abstruse, but are also more revealing of the wide chasm of cultural differences separating different cultural communities' views of their uses of sound.

Steven Feld's book *Sound and Sentiment: Birds, Weeping, Poetics and Song in Kaluli Expression*, a report of his field study of the Kaluli people living in the rain forest of Papua New Guinea, provides a good example of how an ethnomusicologist might effectively deal with describing in the American-English language the apparently "musical" behavior of a cultural community whose worldview radically differs from that of most Europeans and Americans. Feld's study is clearly ethnomusicological, in that it focuses on the meaningful production of sounds by the members of a cultural community, but the concept "music" is necessarily omitted from it because the Kaluli have no directly equivalent concept. Because of the conceptual difference at the root of his study, Feld describes his report as "an ethnographic account of sound as a cultural system."[14]

In his book, Feld explains that as he lived and worked with the Kaluli he began to recognize the "pattern" of knowledge (i.e., worldview) that metaphorically links the sounds of birds, poetics, weeping, and song, among the other sounds he encountered in the rain forest and among the people, to the "sentiments" of their social ethos. He discovered that "becoming a bird" is the core metaphor for the Kaluli, tacitly used to mediate the social expression of emotion through sound forms in different contexts. For example, the Kaluli believe the melodic "sung-weeping" performed improvisationally by women at funerals to be the human sound expression closest to that of a bird, and they feel that the women's "bird-nature" is revealed as they sing. Recognizing the importance of the bird metaphor for his understanding of the "soundscape" of the community, Feld undertook to learn their "folk ornithology" from a Kaluli man named Jubi, and in doing so he came to grasp something of their unique worldview:

[Jubi's comment] pointed out that I was equating contextless texts, disembodied words, and taxonomic modes with knowledge and reality, as if knowledge was simply a sum of taxa, a mirror of content. Knowledge is something more: a method for putting a construction on the perceived, a means for scaffolding belief systems, a guide to actions and feelings.

"To you they are birds" meant that I was forcing a method of knowledge construction—isolation and reduction—onto a domain of experience that Kaluli do not isolate or reduce. "To me they are voices in the forest" meant that there are many ways to think about birds, depending on the context in which knowledge is activated and social needs are served. Birds are "voices" because Kaluli recognize and acknowledge their existence primarily through sound, and because they are the spirit reflections . . . of deceased men and women. Bird sounds simultaneously have an "outside," from which Kaluli attribute a bird's identification, and an "inside," from which they interpret the underlying meaning as a spirit communication.[15]

The uniqueness of the Kaluli's ornithological metaphor clearly illustrates how radically different the conceptions of music making held by a given cultural community can be from those of most U.S. citizens, and Feld's report is admirable for its effective description in American English of a cultural perspective incommensurable with that of most Europeans and Americans.

Despite their awareness of its "nonuniversality" as a concept, most ethnomusicologists still tacitly employ the term "music" in discussing and writing reports of their field studies, but it is important to note that they use the word as an anthropological construct. A *construct* is a term introduced by an anthropologist for the purpose of integrating provisionally the diverse data on an apparent phenomenon that appears to take different forms, but which may not, in fact, be shared as a concept by all cultural communities. ("Culture" is an example of such a construct.) Unlike Feld, many ethnomusicologists use the word "music" as a construct in their writings to describe both the human "behavior" of patterned sound production and the "sound artifacts" (i.e., sonic events of a determinable duration) produced as part of the various human practices in which this behavior is manifested within different cultural communities; they use the word primarily to facilitate communication about their studies with members of their own society.[16] Often, in their field reports, ethnomusicologists must go to great lengths to explain how the cultural communities that do not share the concept "music" conceptualize such behavior within their unique worldview. Feld's writings are but one example.

In keeping with practices of contemporary ethnomusicology, we will use the terms "musical practice" and "music" as constructs throughout this inquiry. Specifically, "musical practices" will be used to denote the disparate practices involving sound production undertaken by different cultural communities (which are typically conceptualized by Europeans and Americans as "musical"),[17] and the term "music" will specifically denote the actual sound artifacts (sonic events of a determinable duration) that are produced as they undertake these diverse practices. Nevertheless, the reader should constantly keep in mind while reading that the terms "musical practices" and "music" (without quotation marks) are being used provisionally to describe a wide variety of different cultural activities that may or may not bear much conceptual or auditory resemblance to one another (or to musical practices in the U.S.). Later in this chapter we will formulate another conception of these terms based on pragmatist philosophy; the resulting "pragmatic" definition will serve as our conceptual foundation for the remainder of this inquiry.

Since the change of name from "comparative musicology" to "ethnomusicology" in the mid-twentieth century, researchers have focused increasingly on the unique ways in which the members of different cultural communities collectively understand their own musical practices in their respective cultural contexts, and most have come to eschew extensive comparison between the musics (or sound artifacts) of different traditions. In recent years, ethnomusicology as a field of study has expanded to encompass a remarkably broad variety of research efforts, all of which generally share in common the orientation toward understanding musical sound as a part of the totality of the cultural community that produces it. Recent research approaches have involved innovative studies of relationships between music and language, music and gender, and the ways in which the musical practices of certain cultural communities have affected those of others, among many other efforts.[18] Nevertheless, ethnomusicologist Bruno Nettl has observed a continuing lack of agreement about the philosophical center of the field's inquiry:

> There is little consensus about the attitudes of ethnomusicological research in the early 1990s. One trend is a gradual abandonment of the division of the field into "musical" and "anthropological." It is widely accepted that a scholar needs to be at least competent and interested in both. . . . There is a widespread tendency to move ethnomusicology where many feel it has belonged all along, into the mainstream of musicology (bringing with it, not at all abandoning, the interest in culture). For good reason, this is debated by those whose principal allegiance is anthropology.[19]

To Nettl, at least, it seems evident that ambivalence still persists among scholars concerning musicological and anthropological orientations to the study of musical practices in different cultural contexts.

"RELATIVISM," "UNIVERSALISM," AND MUSIC EDUCATION

The preceding short history has identified two general orientations that comparative musicologists and ethnomusicologists have taken to the study of music in different world cultures throughout the history of their inquiry. A distinction could be drawn between the two by saying that the efforts of the musicologically oriented ethnomusicologists have generally been more *universalizing* (i.e., characterized by an interest in comparing among and drawing connections between the musical practices of different cultural communities), whereas the efforts of the anthropologically oriented ethnomusicologists have generally been more *relativizing* (i.e., characterized by an emphasis on understanding the musical practices of different cultural communities in terms of their inherent cultural uniqueness). Naturally, it must be admitted that this division in some measure oversimplifies the situation, as the universalist position is not held by *all* ethnomusicologists who have their primary background in musicology, nor is the relativist position held by *all* ethnomusicologists having their primary background in anthropology. Furthermore, neither of these positions is necessarily representative of any single individual; most scholars have more complex views on this issue, some are ambivalent, and some have changed their views over time. Nevertheless, the "universalist/relativist" distinction does describe a real difference in orientation that has persisted throughout the history of ethnomusicological inquiry, and each of these positions has in some measure been associated with the musicological and anthropological backgrounds of its proponents.

The essential difference defining the two orientations concerns the question of whether there is something (besides *sound* itself) shared in common among all of the musical practices of different cultural communities or there is little or nothing shared in common among them, in which case they are more or less completely unique culturally. We will consider the unequivocal case of each of these orientations, or positions, in turn.

The *universalist* maintains that the musical practices of different cultural communities are all related manifestations of the same innate human characteristic (thought by some to be *communication*, by others to be *expression*, and by still others to be something else) that has developed differently in different cultural circumstances. Figure 3.1 provides a semiotic

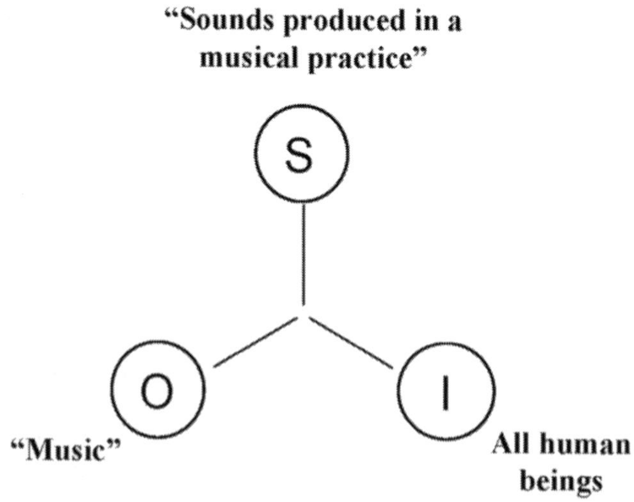

"Sounds produced in a musical practice"

S

O   **I**

"Music"   **All human beings**

Figure 3.1   The Sign "Sounds produced in a musical practice" conceptualized as "Music" on presupposition of a universal "musical" human attribute; a universalizing, "musicological" conception.

representation of the Sign "sounds produced in musical practices" (i.e., such humanly patterned sounds) according to the way a universalist would conceptualize them.

In the universalist's view, the different varieties of musical practices undertaken by different cultural communities are assumed to be something like the different food preparation and consumption practices manifested among different peoples. Certain animals and vegetables are condoned as appropriate for consumption in some cultural contexts and not in others, and cooking methods and eating utensils vary from one cultural community to another. Similarly, certain sounds, instruments, and methods vary among cultural communities, and these are condoned or condemned in different cultural contexts. Also, some individuals and communities abstain from eating at times for varying culturally based (e.g., religious) reasons; likewise, some individuals and communities choose not to engage in music making for such reasons. Nevertheless, all food preparation and consumption is related to a universal human need for physical nourishment. According to the universalist, the *sounds produced in musical practices* (as the Sign) are not unlike "edible material prepared as food" in that they take different forms in different cultural communities, but there is a dimension beyond mere sound—that they recognize as *music* (as an Object)—that is inherently common to its different manifestations among *all human beings* (as Interpretant). Thus, music is a universal human attribute that transcends cultural difference.

Conversely, the *relativist* holds that the musical practices of different cultures are more accurately regarded as generally unrelated behaviors that have been developed in some contexts (and not in others) for reasons unique to their environmental and historical circumstances. Figure 3.2 presents the semiotic representation discussed in Chapter 2 of the Sign "Sound of a vocalized melody, sung solo" according to the way a relativist might conceptualize it.

In the relativist's view, an analogy could be drawn between different musical practices and the body-decorating practices undertaken by different cultural communities. Body painting, makeup, tattooing, and the wearing of jewelry on particular body parts are all practices undertaken by the members of different communities for various reasons shared by members of that community having to do with initiation, camouflage, courtship, sunscreen, religious devotion, or other unrelated motivation. Similarly, musical practices are undertaken for such diverse purposes as artistic expression, entertainment, worship, advertising, and meditation in different cultural contexts. Some communities strictly prohibit certain of these body-decorating practices, and others condone all or none of them; the same could be said of musical practices. According to the relativist, the *sounds involved in music making* (as the Sign) are thus analogous to body decorations: Their creation occurs among many *different* cultural communities (as embodied Interpretants), but, as they take different forms and are

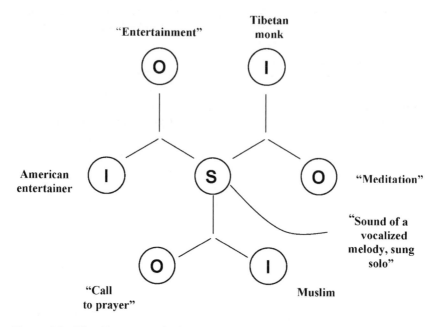

Figure 3.2   The Sign "Sound of a vocalized melody, sung solo" conceptualized according to cultural perspective; a "relativizing," anthropological representation.

undertaken for different reasons in each cultural context, they are inevitably conceptualized differently (as an Object) in each of them. Thus, music cannot be considered a cultural universal.

Each of these orientations represents a conceptual problem for those holding the opposite view. The relativist might accuse the universalist of ethnocentrically misapplying the European American concept "music" to the various undertakings of different world peoples that are related only by the attribute of involving "sounds produced in a cultural practice." Furthermore, the relativist might say, despite the fact that all human beings have a natural human tendency to compare what they experience in different cultural contexts with their own background experiences and to make generalizations from these comparisons, the ethnomusicologist, as a scientist, is professionally responsible for understanding diverse cultural phenomena completely on their own terms and for suspending the concepts of her or his own cultural community until the collection of data is sufficient to warrant such comparison. The universalist might respond that, as all individuals involved in music making share the experience of physically creating and responding to *sounds*, this alone should establish a universal dimension to music making. Furthermore, the universalist might say, ethnomusicology is predicated on music making as a common basis for all studies in the field, and there are sufficient data to suggest that there are attributes common to its different manifestations besides sound. Finally, if there is no such universal attribute, then the entire field of inquiry is just cultural anthropology with an emphasis on *sound*, and ethno*music*ology is not at all an appropriate name for the field.

This tension between universalist and relativist viewpoints has taken different forms over the years, but it has been inherent in ethnomusicological discourse almost since its inception. Of course, as we noted in Chapter 2, tensions stemming from conceptual differences between scholars inhere in all fields of scientific inquiry, and these tensions are likely to persist until sufficient research and thought eventually provide a satisfactory resolution to them or they are passed over as no longer being worthy of attention. The difference in universalists' and relativists' views has historically stimulated lively discussion among ethnomusicologists, but a final resolution to the question of what is universal and what is unique among the various practices of different cultural communities has not consistently been of primary interest to the profession. As we have seen, most ethnomusicological inquiry since the mid-twentieth century has emphasized the study and understanding of the musical practices of different world peoples on their own terms.

While this lack of resolution to the universal/relative question is not a great concern for ethnomusicologists, it does present a problem for music educators in the U.S., as it is the locus of the curricular quandaries described in Chapter 1 that are now facing the profession. Unlike ethnomusicologists, who are inquirers by definition and thus comparatively comfortable with suspending indefinitely the resolution of such questions, music educators have the opposite task: They are charged with the music education and development of increasingly culturally diverse groups of students, and, as we have seen, the profession's collective confusion over what constitutes "music" has rendered its members ambivalent about the expansion of curricula to include the traditions of different cultural communities around the world. A pragmatic, "clear" conception of what is universal and what is unique among the musical practices of different cultural communities (besides *sound* itself) is becoming increasingly necessary for the profession, as school populations continue to become more and more culturally diverse.

In Chapter 1, we explored the great variety of views held by members of the U.S. music education profession on the inclusion of the music of different cultural communities in the curriculum, and we saw that music educators presently appear to have a wide variety of opinions about and options for including non-Western musical traditions in their curricula. However, all of their recommendations for curricular modification can be seen to fall into one of three general categories, each of which we will consider in turn. Regrettably, based on what we have learned about musical practices as they are conceptualized differently by different cultural communities and by ethnomusicologists, none of these options is satisfactory. We will briefly review these options for the purpose of clarifying their respective limitations before exploring a possible resolution to the cultural quandaries they each fail to resolve.

PRESENT, "CULTURALLY BIASED" CURRICULAR OPTIONS FOR MUSIC EDUCATION

One possible curricular orientation, which some might regard as overly conservative, is the approach taken by most teachers prior to 1960 and still employed by some teachers today. This approach involves focusing classes primarily on the *performance and historical study of Western art music.* The great advantage with this approach, it is argued, is that its adoption would allow students to develop a high level of knowledge about and performance proficiency in one historical tradition. Development of strong performance skills has been a hallmark of music education in the U.S. ever since its inception, as most music educators (and, historically, parents and students) have attributed great value to performance. A second advantage with this approach is that it would avoid such problems as miseducation about and exploitation and misappropriation of non-Western cultural traditions. Also, the past practices of preparing U.S. music teachers with university degree programs that focus primarily on Western art music could be continued under this orientation.

However, the great problem with adopting this approach is its apparent failure to include and recognize on their own terms many "other" world traditions that involve music. Since some students (particularly Native Americans and numerous recent immigrants) hold unique and widely differing perspectives, they may suffer under the impression that the views and practices of their cultural community are comparatively unimportant in the context of the American public forum. This approach does not seek to inform students of the different ways in which sound is conceptualized and employed in the contexts of different cultural communities, nor does it emphasize the value of these other traditions for the people with whom they originated. For these reasons, this approach may not be suitable for the culturally inclusive goals of a U.S. public school. We might describe this orientation as *ethnocentric*, since it apparently does not adequately acknowledge or provide a means by which students could come to an understanding of the various perspectives of different cultural communities concerning their musical practices.

A second possible curricular orientation, which some might regard as overly liberal or academic, would involve taking an *anthropological study* approach to the music of many different traditions, while minimizing or eliminating performance due to a lack of sufficient time for students to develop passable performance skills in each of the traditions studied. The great advantage with this orientation is that its adoption would provide time for students to focus on developing an understanding of the contexts and beliefs from which the diverse musical practices of different cultural communities stem; music classes could thus be more culturally inclusive and egalitarian.

However, this approach has three major disadvantages: First, and most importantly, without an emphasis on the development of performance skills, students would develop an understanding of the musical practices of different cultural communities without having opportunity to experience music making and develop performance skills of their own. (As we noted earlier, music educators and many others have historically attributed great value to performance.) Second, this instructional approach would be ill suited for elementary-school children, since most are typically not developmentally ready for in-depth exploration of the differences in worldviews among cultural communities. Third, adoption of this approach would present major curricular difficulties for the academic preparation of teachers, since it carries with it the expectation that they would complete a course of study much different from the music teacher degree courses presently offered by the nation's universities, one that would focus directly on the practices and beliefs of different cultural communities. As noted in Chapter 1, such an approach would require extensive study of more cultural communities than could be covered effectively in a four-year degree program. For these reasons, this approach may also be deemed unsuitable. The concept of music implicit in this orientation is generally congruent with the *relativist* position represented in Figure 3.2.

A third option, which might at first seem to embrace or circumvent and thus solve the problems of the ethnocentric and relativist orientations, would be to adopt the approach presently taken by many teachers of *studying and performing music from all cultural communities* for which there are instructional materials available (published arrangements, background information, recordings, etc.) for the purpose of developing musical skills. This apparently "culturally inclusive" approach would seem to incorporate the benefits of both of the approaches described earlier, in that it includes some performance and some academic study of different traditions, but it also may diminish the benefits of each of the other two approaches. In fact, when the two approaches are combined, they might be considered mutually contradictory. Courses in which students are encouraged to develop skills in performing music from one or more traditions could carry the implicit message that "music" is a culturally universal concept.

Furthermore, the concept of music tacitly underlying such courses is typically consistent with Western notions of "art" or "entertainment." While considerable evidence is available to suggest that all human beings can develop skill at manipulating sound and sound patterns, such skills are not valued equally highly by all peoples; indeed, skillful sound manipulation is not a central concern for "successful" performance in many traditions.[20] The question of just *which* cultural communities' traditions should be included in such classes presents a significant quandary. Selecting and preparing lessons to represent fairly and accurately *all* world traditions or even just the traditions of the students in a culturally diverse classroom would be a daunting if not impossible task for most teachers, particularly given the complex associations between the musical practices of many cultural communities and their respective religious beliefs and practices. Thus, the application of this approach almost inevitably raises the issues of cultural appropriation and exploitation discussed in Chapter 1, and, like the first two approaches, it is also unsuitable. The concept of music implicit in this orientation is generally congruent with the *universalist* position represented in Figure 3.1.

While numerous other curricular orientations have been suggested, all typically represent variations on one of the three approaches described earlier. Some teachers emphasize the values of performance, while others value more highly the academic study of the beliefs of the cultural communities from which the various practices stem. Some suggest limiting the curricular focus to one or two cultural traditions; others advocate "multicultural" music education. We have seen that an argument can be made for each of the approaches just described, and that important objections can also be raised to each of them.

Notably, each of the curricular orientations previously described carries with it a set of tacit assumptions about the value and importance of music instruction in the schools. "Ethnocentric" music educators, those who place emphasis on teaching performance skills associated with Western art music and popular music, value most highly the traditional European American concepts of *music* associated with "art" and "entertainment"; they evidently believe that music education that centers on "traditional" musical practices and values in the U.S. will benefit children most greatly. "Relativist" music educators, those who place emphasis on teaching the practices and beliefs of different cultural communities on their own terms, value most highly the fostering of respect for all the diverse cultural communities that comprise the populace; they apparently believe that music education that fosters the valuing and understanding of the musical practices of the different cultural communities that comprise the U.S. will be of the greatest benefit to children. "Universalist" music educators, those whose teaching includes Western art and popular music as well as non-Western traditions, value most highly the development of refined music performance skills, which they conceive to be a universal human characteristic common to all musical practice. They evidently believe that music education that develops these skills will benefit children most of all.

Each of these curricular orientations conflicts with the others, in some measure, as the values implicit in each of them are not universally shared by all members of the profession, let alone all citizens of the U.S. Thus, it is apparent that none of them is grounded in a conception of music or a philosophy of music education suitable to provide a solid basis for the continuing inclusion of music education programs in the schools of this culturally diverse nation. As we noted in Chapter 1, this lack of a shared conceptual foundation has contributed to putting music education in the position of not seeming necessarily relevant to all persons, and, as a result, its place in the curriculum has been tenuous. Without such a foundation, music educators have been unable to provide an explanation of and rationale for the social relevance of music education in the schools sufficiently strong to sustain its continuing place in the curriculum. As long as members of the profession remain unclear about what is universal and what is unique in the various manifestations of musical practice among the diverse cultural communities that comprise the country, it seems fairly certain that the public will remain ambivalent about the importance of music education in the public schools. As a result, support for music education in U.S. public schools will continue to be uncertain.

When the pragmatist philosophy of Charles Sanders Peirce is used as a framework for considering recent research into the musical practices of different world peoples, it provides a perspective with which these curricular dilemmas may be reconceptualized and, in some measure, resolved.

A PEIRCIAN PRAGMATIC APPROACH TO MUSICAL PRACTICES

Peirce based his pragmatic philosophy upon a fundamental principle that makes it especially useful for our present inquiry into the musical practices of different human societies. *Synechism*, the notion that everything is continuous, or interconnected, renders Peirce's pragmatism a powerful tool for reconceptualizing the interrelationships during music making of the "bodies and minds" of single individuals, as well as those of the "individual minds and the collective mind" of communities. By contrast, most European and American scholarly writings on music of the past two centuries have focused more directly on musical artifacts (the patterned sounds produced) as "music" than on the interrelationship of human beings and their musical practices. As we shall see, the socially disjunct conceptions of music at the root of past modes of scholarship have impacted the practice of music education in many ways during this time, not the least of which was that they led to the raising of questions about the relevance of music study in U.S. public schools. Developing a pragmatic understanding of how a musical practice can be said to be *important to* or interconnected with the lives of individuals and communities may help in rectifying this situation.

Our purpose is to utilize Peirce's pragmatism first to determine what is unique (or "relative") and what is shared in common (or "universal") among the musical practices of all cultural communities, and then, on this basis, to develop a conception of how musical practices can be said to be pragmatically important to (or have *meaning* in) the lives of individuals in all societies. Such a conception will provide us with a more solid basis for the future practice of music education in the U.S.

In our exploration of the pragmatist philosophy of Peirce in the last chapter, we learned that Peirce stated what he held to be the "fundamental hypothesis of science" in the following way:

> There are Real things whose characters are entirely independent of our opinions about them; those Reals affect our senses according to regular laws, and though our sensations are as different as are our relations to the objects, yet, by taking advantage of the laws of perception, we can ascertain by reasoning how things really and truly are; and any man, if he have sufficient experience and he reason enough about it will be led to the one True conclusion. The new conception here involved is that of Reality.[21]

In the terms of our present discussion, we are seeking to establish a conception of music on the basis what is "Real," or universal, among the diverse musical practices of all cultural communities. As we have already seen, most ethnomusicologists now agree that there is very little (if anything at all) shared in common among them besides the actual patterned production of *sound* itself, and that these differences are attributable to the vastly different ways in which different cultural communities conceptualize Reality. Therefore, we must be aware at the outset that any "Real" or universal aspects of music we encounter will inevitably be described differently, according to the beliefs shared collectively by the individuals comprising different cultural communities. Furthermore, any "universal" description we might offer will inevitably be biased in being communicated, since it must, of necessity, be articulated in the American-English language using the terminology of Peircian pragmatism and science.

These points notwithstanding, Peirce offered his "pragmatic maxim" as a means by which we might make the meaning of our concepts free from being consistently doubted and disagreed upon; thus, applying it to our present quandary should provide us with a comparatively culturally open conception of musical practice. In order to clarify any concept, Peirce recommended that it should be considered in relation to its practical *effects* on the members of a community. As we saw in Chapter 2, he articulated his "pragmatic maxim" in the following way:

> Consider what effects, that might conceivably have practical bearings, we conceive the object of our conception to have. Then, our conception of these effects is the whole of our conception of the object.[22]

What we are seeking is to understand how the musical practices of different cultural communities can be said to be meaningful to individual human beings, and to the communities of which they are a part, as part of the universal *human* community. It is our intention that by coming to an understanding of the *effects* of different musical practices on the culturally diverse individuals and communities who undertake them, we may be able to identify that which is universal in the musical practices of all cultural communities.

APPARENT UNIVERSALS

In 1970, the Society for Ethnomusicology, an association of ethnomusicologists founded in the U.S., held a plenary session during their annual meeting for the purpose of discussing the topic "Music in Universal Perspective." The various views presented in this session were subsequently published, and they represent one of the few recorded scholarly dialogues focusing specifically on the subject of musical universals in the second half of the twentieth century. During the meeting, David McAllester expressed his belief that, while there are probably no absolute universals in music, there may be some "near-universals." Among them, he said, he found most interesting the apparent "transformation of experience" that seems to accompany many musical practices. In his words, "music may heighten excitement or it may soothe tensions, but in either case it takes one away into another state of being."[23] Klaus Wachsmann acknowledged McAllester's suggestion, but noted as an example of the nonuniversality of "heightened experience" the disequilibrium in states of mind clearly apparent among a number of the scholars who had attended a musical event together earlier in the conference. Wachsmann reaffirmed the nonuniversality of music as a concept, and he went on to suggest that musical universals likely have more to do with the awareness of a "special kind of time" during musical engagement.[24] George List remarked that the "heightened experience" noted by McAllester was not unique to music, but that it also applied to other arts. He suggested instead that the most universal characteristic of music is its *non*universality as a means of communication; in his view, whatever music communicates is evidently communicated to an "in-group" only. List also noted that whatever music communicates to an individual, it must change over the years, as he no longer experienced "electric tingles" to musical works that once affected him strongly. He concluded by suggesting that "the only universal aspect of music seems to be that most people make it" and that the profession was unlikely ever to find "true" universals.[25]

While these scholars did not provide a satisfactory, final resolution to the universalist/relativist conflict, their comments do implicitly suggest two points of agreement on musical practices as a pan-cultural cluster or category of human behaviors which, considered in the framework of Peircian pragmatism, may contribute to our understanding and resolution of the dilemmas facing U.S. music education that we have been exploring: First, their comments suggest that a given example of musical practice communicates or has meaning in its original sense only for those individuals who share a cultural perspective or worldview in common. Second, and perhaps more directly on the question of "universals," their comments suggest that all of the diverse musical practices practiced among different cultural communities share in common the attribute of at least sometimes having an *effect* or *effects* on the human beings involved in them that could be described in the language of science as *psychological*, or perhaps *psychophysiological*. We will consider each of these points in turn.

The first point, that a given example or type of musical practice may well carry its original meaning only for those who share a cultural perspective or worldview in common, appears fairly evident when considered in light of our discussion earlier in this chapter. It seems highly unlikely that any citizens of the U.S. would conceive of any form of musical practice as being revelatory of their "bird nature," as it is for the Kaluli people of Papua New Guinea, discussed earlier. As a further example, the central musical practice of Tibetan monks, specifically their meditational chanting, would likely not be understood by an American jazz aficionado, an Australian rock and roll fan, or a European art musician in the same sense that the monks collectively understand it.[26] Without the necessary experiential background, any listener will be incapable of fully understanding the originally intended meaning of the musical practices of an unfamiliar community, much in the same way as one who has no experience with a given foreign language is incapable of fully understanding the import of a spoken utterance in that language.[27] The popular notion that "music is a universal language" is indeed a fallacy.

The second point, that musical practices often evoke a psychophysiological *effect*, such as a "heightening of experience" in some or all of the individuals participating in them, has been noted so frequently and by so many that it is almost axiomatic. After all, it must be acknowledged that only a small number of people would be likely to find listening to or participating in musical practices to be valuable if they appealed only to the intellect, without any accompanying affective or emotional effect. However, the idea that a certain *kind* of effect or that a certain *aspect* of the effects of musical engagement might be universal to all cultural communities could only be suggested authoritatively by someone with as broad a perspective on human musical practices as an ethnomusicologist. Notably, McAllester's suggestion of the universality of "heightened experience" has received assent from various other distinguished scholars in the field since the time of the meeting described earlier.[28] Ethnomusicologist Judith Becker also recognized and eloquently described this effect of musical engagement as a possible cultural universal:

> [T]here seems to be a particular state of mind, a state of surrender to, and self-identification with, the musical performance which is described often enough in the literature about musical experience to be called a kind of universal. From our own personal experience, to the descriptions of experience of those far removed in time or space from

us, we know that the giving-up of the strong sense of selfhood during a musical event is exhilarating and liberating, though transitory. The dissolution of one's personal self into the fabric of tone and timbre brings with it an elation, a feeling of oneness with the world outside ourselves. An euphoric state such as I am describing circumvents or transcends self-conscious critical intelligence.[29]

Indeed, some mention of an apparent "heightening of experience" does arise frequently in the descriptions of musical practices provided by people of different cultural origins, and ethnomusicological researchers have often noted such effects in their studies of different peoples as well. However, we must keep in mind that the ways of describing this effect of different musical practices are invariably unique to the cultural communities with which they originate.

Mention of such an experience in association with musical practices appears with particularly great frequency in the discourse of different cultural communities on what we might describe as their religious practices; in fact, religiously oriented cultural communities typically give this "heightened experience" centrality and high value in their discourse. For example, in Sufism, the mystical tradition of Islam, worshippers acknowledge that they are intentionally seeking such an experience when they engage in the *sama*, a musically accompanied ritual dance, and they conceptualize this experience as the attainment of union with their supreme god (Allah).[30] As described by Jalal ad-Din Rumi, originator of the Mevlevi order of Sufis, " . . . [Sama] is the food of the lovers, for within it they find the Image of the meeting with the Beloved [God]."[31] Similarly, in describing the theory of beauty in the classical aesthetics of the Japanese, Toyo Izutsu has noted the importance of the experience of *yugen*, one of their highest aesthetic values. According to Izutsu, *yugen* denotes the "dissolution of the subject-object relationship" that they experience in the contemplation of art, drama, or music.[32] Also, etymological exploration has revealed that the associational structure of the Chinese language includes a consistent relationship between sound (*sheng*) and a condition of superior awareness (*sheng*), and the Chinese concept of *ch'i* has historically associated musical engagement with notions of spirit and inspiration, suggesting that Chinese people may recognize a similar experience.[33] In addition, both the Old and New Testaments of the Bible include various allusions to music that describe the enhancement of the worship of God by the singing and playing of instruments; musical practices have been associated with the worship of many Jewish and Christian communities since the beginning of each tradition.[34] Pentecostal Christians in particular frequently acknowledge that they feel themselves to be "touched by God" while engaging in their musical practices.[35] Examples from numerous other traditions could be cited.

It is not certain, and at first glance it seems unlikely, that the experiences associated with *all* these various musical practices are the *same* experience.

After all, most Europeans and Americans typically describe their experience of many *different* emotions while listening, singing, playing, or dancing to different musical pieces. While these disparate but similarly consequential descriptions may not, in fact, allude to a psychophysiological effect experienced in association with the respective varieties of musical practices that is indeed the *same* in all respects, taken together they do suggest the possibility that they all may share a *common aspect*—that is, the "heightening of experience" or a profound absorption or "loss of self" into the experience.

When the various descriptions of the experiences associated with different musical practices are considered collectively, and particularly when the centrality of this experience in the musical practices associated with various religious traditions is recognized, one question almost inevitably presents itself: Might the sort of "heightened experience" associated with the various musical practices of different peoples actually have the resultant effect of psychologically or experientially confirming the worldview of the community for those who experience it? This notion requires further exploration.

In Chapter 2 we learned that Peirce drew a distinction between *belief,* as the "habits of mind" that typically guide our actions, and *thought,* as the "hypothesis making," or *abduction,* in which all human beings tend to engage whenever we experience doubt—an inability to account for an interruption of our beliefs. Furthermore, Peirce held that the scientific method of hypothesis-testing is the only satisfactory way to satisfy our doubts— that is, to bring them into accord with true Reality. He described abduction in the following way:

> The first starting of a hypothesis and the entertaining of it, whether as a simple interrogation or with any degree of confidence, is an inferential step which I propose to call abduction.
>
> . . . The form of inference . . . is this:
>> The surprising fact, C is observed;
>> But if A were true, C would be a matter of course,
>> Hence, there is reason to suspect that A is true.[36]

In our present discussion, the "surprising fact" ("C") that we have observed is that different cultural communities practice different musical practices for different reasons in their respective contexts, and it is apparent that each of them at least at times involves a "heightened" psychophysiological effect as a result of participating in these musical practices. But if it were true that ("A") each of these disparate practices had the effect of joining the psychophysical processes of the individuals who were members of a given cultural community with the worldview of their community, then "C" would be a matter of course. Hence, there is reason to suspect that A is true.

In fact, there is considerable evidence to suggest that ("A") "psychological unification with and confirmation of worldview" is precisely what is taking place to some degree in many, if not all, of the musical practices undertaken by the members of different cultural communities. However, understanding just *how* musical practices and the psychophysiological experiences associated with them might be said to have such an effect will require our familiarity with an additional construct from the specialized vocabulary of cultural anthropology.

The word *ritual* is employed in common American-English usage to refer to two types of habitual actions: the commonplace behaviors customarily repeated in the daily lives of individuals and the more socially significant practices undertaken collectively on a regular basis by the members of communities. The word is used in its first sense to refer to such behaviors as an individual's habit of hanging a cherished hat on the same hook upon arriving home each evening, or of setting the table in a particular way before every meal that is to be shared with a certain friend. In its second sense, the word's meaning is generally consistent with its use as an anthropological construct; cultural anthropologists employ the term to describe certain socially important collective practices that take different forms in different societies. The word *ritual* is synonymous in the minds of some Americans with the ceremonial practices of organized religious communities, while others use it pejoratively to refer to what they regard as the "primitive" practices of "other" communities. Both associations unnecessarily limit the term, as many of the practices undertaken collectively at regular intervals by the members of every human community can be considered rituals in some sense. Both meanings of the term are synonymous with Peirce's conception of *habit*; the first refers to the inveterate behaviors of individuals, while the second, in which we are interested primarily, refers to those of communities.

Many of the world's musical practices are closely associated with the habitual social gatherings of people living in community (i.e., rituals), although this close association is not always readily apparent to those living in the present social context of the U.S. It is important to remember that prior to the advent of recording and broadcast technology in the twentieth century, nearly all musical practices were undertaken in conjunction with or in settings such as communal celebrations, social dances, and religious exercises, much as they still are in nonindustrialized societies of the world. In contemporary U.S. society, by contrast, many individuals now experience music by watching television, listening to the radio, attending to recorded films and audio recordings, and engaging in various other comparatively solitary practices.

While it can easily be seen that not all musical practices are connected with events acknowledged by the members of a society to be rituals, understanding how musical practices have historically been and are often presently *associated with* or *a part of* established communal rituals will provide a means by which the individual and societal importance of all musical practices may be understood. Musical practices have been associated with ritual in scholarly writings of the past, some of which have had a notable impact on the practice of music education in the U.S.,[37] but certain insights of scholars in various disciplines in the fairly recent past have shed new light on this relationship that will illuminate our present discussion and provide a perspective unlike those that have been described in previous music education scholarship. Thus, we will explore writings on musical practices and ritual that have more recently been offered by scholars in three broad areas—clinical psychiatry (and, by association, neurobiology), ethnomusicology, and cultural anthropology—for the purpose of developing a greater understanding of the nature of this relationship. The scholars whose writings we will consider in each of these areas have reached conclusions that are generally congruent with Peircian pragmatism, but each of them has framed the subject in a manner unique to her or his particular area of scholarship, which we will call the psychophysiological, psychosocial, and sociopolitical perspectives, respectively.

One additional point must be noted. Cultural anthropologists customarily utilize a taxonomy by which human societies or cultures are classified according to their form of sociopolitical organization. They identify them as being one of four types: a band, a tribe, a chiefdom, or a state. While there are many differences among these types of societies that are important for certain types of analysis, the crucial distinction for our purposes in this inquiry lies between the characteristics of the three "nonstate" or *traditional* types of societies (which are all characterized by relative homogeneity in worldview) and those of *state* societies (which are characterized by cultural pluralism and which involve the leading and controlling of certain segments of the population by others that carry political power). For purposes of clarity, we will first focus on the interrelationship of musical practice and ritual in *traditional*, or relatively culturally homogeneous, communities before addressing directly their implications for music education in culturally pluralistic, *state* societies. Then we shall see that musical practices in the U.S. manifest somewhat different characteristics, due to the unique, defining features of the nation's public forum.

MUSICAL PRACTICES AND RITUAL IN TRADITIONAL SOCIETIES: A PSYCHOPHYSIOLOGICAL DESCRIPTION

Clinical psychiatrists Eugene d'Aquili and Charles Laughlin, Jr. have taken a pragmatic approach that draws on scholarship in neurobiology and phylogeny (i.e., evolutionary biology) to explain the relationship between the practices undertaken in human rituals and the culturally homogeneous social contexts within which they are embedded. They observe that *any* organism whose successful adaptation for survival depends on its cooperation with one or more of its own kind must develop some means by which it can decrease the distance between itself and others in order that this cooperation can be achieved. They note that the periodic performance of *rituals* by the members of a group of like organisms provides a means by which this lessening of distance and collective cooperation can be effected. In d'Aquili and Laughlin's conception, *ritual* is behavior that is sequentially patterned; is to some degree repetitive and rhythmic; tends to recur in the same or nearly the same form with some regularity; acts to coordinate affective, cognitive, and motor processes within the central nervous systems of the participants; and, most importantly, coordinates and synchronizes these processes among the various individual participants.[38] In their view, the repetitive or rhythmic emanation of signals during human rituals such as the "chanting of prayers"[39] (or, presumably, other musical practices) has the effect of generating a high degree of "limbic arousal" (i.e., emotional affect) in the brains of the participating individuals, an arousal that, when effected, ultimately results in decreased distancing and increased social cohesion within the group. They observe that this effect (specifically, limbic or affective coordination leading to group cohesion among individual organisms of the same kind) is at the root of the ritual behaviors exhibited by human beings as well as various other animals.[40]

However, D'Aquili and Laughlin note, human beings appear to be different from other animals in that their rituals are invariably associated with a "web of meaning" (i.e., a worldview) that allows members of the community to conceptualize similarly the significance of the ritualized behavior. The reason for this, they explain, is that human beings have a unique characteristic: specifically, a neurobiological drive to organize unexplained external stimuli (i.e., forces beyond their personal control) into a coherent cognitive matrix for the purpose of understanding them and controlling their effects. The authors attribute this drive to the regular operation of an inherent feature of the human brain that they term the "causal operator." (We will return to explore the concept of the "causal operator" further, following.) They observe that in different societies the cognitive matrix (or worldview) collectively shared by the members of a community takes different forms largely due to differences in their environments and histories; in some societies the worldview involves an elaborate myth that describes various powers, demons, gods, or a supreme god to whom the unexplained external stimuli can be attributed, while in other societies the worldview is more scientific (i.e., causes for such interruptions are more likely to be explained by theories that have been verified empirically which attribute them to phenomena in the physical environment that may not be readily detectable).

At those times when members of the group find themselves to be beset with various forces beyond their physical control, they seek and often find resolution for their resulting, irresolvable psychological conflicts in the community-unifying, ritual practices of the group. D'Aquili and Laughlin note that when conflicts cannot be resolved cognitively within the capabilities of the myth or worldview itself (i.e., by finding a satisfactory logical explanation or actively solving the problem), a psychological resolution can be effected by a psychophysiological *joining* of the individual with the worldview of the group via such practices as ritual or meditation, behaviors that profoundly affect the limbic and autonomic nervous systems of the individuals involved. Ultimately, when the ritual is successful, the psychological conflict is resolved for these individuals in an intensely pleasurable but difficult-to-describe experience that the authors observe is conceptualized by some participants as an apparent "union of contingent and vulnerable man with a powerful, possibly omnipotent force."[41] In this psychological state, not only does the "heightened experience" have the effect of confirming the worldview for the individual, but it effectively, psychologically *unites* her or him with it. However, d'Aquili and Laughlin comment, it is evident that such practices have this power to affect individuals and groups psychophysiologically only when the participants in some measure believe the worldview or myth to *be* existential reality. They also note that when the adult members of a group undertake such ritual acts, they have the secondary effect of socializing the young into the collectively shared worldview of the community.[42]

From our pragmatic philosophical perspective, three points in d'Aquili and Laughlin's description of ritual seem particularly remarkable: First, their definition of ritual seems general enough to encompass all types of community musical practices, irrespective of a particular cultural context. Indeed, all musical practices invariably involve the "repetitive or rhythmic emanation of signals" (such as sounds) that d'Aquili and Laughlin describe. Most such practices are undertaken in communal contexts, and those that do not take place in such contexts do occur in a form consistent with or related in some way to the traditions of a community. Second, their description is foundationally congruent with the principle of synechism, or interconnectedness, at the root of Peirce's pragmatic philosophy, in that it provides a satisfactory explanation of the psychological effects of ritual predicated on psychophysiological processes undertaken by individuals in community and not on the influence of forces outside of nature (such as gods or spirits). Third, in supporting their description of ritual behavior with results of research on the neurobiological substrates of human social behavior, they have added an important corollary to pragmatic philosophy: specifically, the notion that ritual might be best conceptualized as an adaptive means by which individuals may effect psychological stability through social reconciliation or unification with the worldview of their community.

Also, underlying their description is Peirce's concept that the survival of any biological organism, including a human being, depends on its acquisition of *habits* of behavior to satisfy its needs; this point of agreement is, of course, not surprising, as it is now a basic precept of biological science. A more important point of accord, however, is their observation that human beings are apparently unique from other animals in having a neurobiological drive to organize their conceptions of Reality in ways that take into account unexplained external stimuli; they term this drive the "causal operator." As we have seen, Peirce characterized *thought* as "hypothesis-making" or abduction, and he recognized it as a distinctive attribute of the human organism. From this principle and his concept of the "union of individual minds," we developed our concept of *worldview* for this inquiry. D'Aquili and Laughlin have thus provided a biological explanation of Peirce's conception of "abduction" (and our concept of worldview) with their notion of the "causal operator," and they go so far as to locate its neural substratum in the "anterior convexity of the frontal lobe, the inferior parietal lobule, and the reciprocal interconnections" of the human brain. They describe its operation in the following way:

> The causal operator treats any given strip of reality in the same way that a mathematical operator functions. It organizes that strip of reality into what is subjectively perceived as causal sequences, back to the initial terminus of that strip or forward toward some desired final terminus. In view of the apparently universal human trait, under ordinary circumstances, of positing causes for any given strip of reality, we postulate that, if the initial terminus is not given by sense data, then the causal operator grinds out an initial terminus automatically.[43]

In their view, therefore, the minds of all human beings are inherently adapted for the "abductive" generation of worldviews as comprehensive conceptions of Reality, and the formulation of some of these worldviews may involve gods, spirits, or other first causes and final termini when other satisfactory explanatory conceptions are not available.[44]

D'Aquili and Laughlin predicate their further assertion, that the rituals of a community (which typically involve musical practices) have the effect of joining or reconciling an individual participant with the cognitive matrix (or worldview) of the community of which he or she is a part, upon the results of experimental research conducted by numerous scholars in the biological and social sciences. However, their views depend primarily on a synthesis of these studies offered by neuroscientist Barbara Lex. Lex attributes the psychological efficacy of ritual largely to what she terms the "ergotropic-trophotropic rebound" effects brought on by the "driving practices" associated with ritual behavior, and she characterizes the outwardly observable, physical manifestations of these effects as "ritual trance."[45]

Lex presents an argument on the basis of "general principles of neurophysiological function" that the various "driving practices" undertaken in rituals, such as chanting, singing, hand clapping, or other rhythmic forms of synchronized mass movement, serve to generate a "stimulus bombardment" of the human nervous system, potentially stimulating a reciprocal "tuning" among specialized brain systems in the individuals involved. According to the model of brain function that Lex has adopted and utilized for her explanation,[46] these "driving practices" tend to stimulate a high level of activity in the right hemisphere of the brain (which emphasizes holistic, synthetic, atemporal thought) while simultaneously tending to block activity in the left hemisphere of the brain (which tends to be more specialized for linear, analytic, time-bound thought).[47] These "driving practices" simultaneously impact the autonomic nervous system, effecting responses that she identifies as ergotropic and trophotropic. *Ergotropic* responses involve the sympathetic nervous system, which governs arousal states and "fight or flight" responses, as well as certain other energy-expending systems within the nervous system. *Trophotropic* responses, by contrast, involve the parasympathetic nervous system, which governs basic homeostatic functions of the central nervous system as well as certain other processes that serve to maintain an organism's baseline stability. Lex observes that every person typically maintains a normative balance or integration between ergotropic and trophotropic processes, but that life circumstances involving personal and collective conflicts and their accompanying stresses may disturb this balance, leading to "dysphasic biological rhythms" that are often manifested in maladaptive behavior.[48]

In Lex's view, the "driving practices" of ritual facilitate right-hemisphere dominance, simultaneously causing "rebound," or a shifting of trophotropic-ergotropic balance, toward homeostasis, or psychophysiological equilibrium. She asserts that this effect concomitantly aligns the individual's holistic conception of reality with the worldview shared collectively by the members of the group:

> If the ritual is conducted correctly, the result is easing of tension or strain. Significantly, another relevant aspect of ritual is the shift to the mode of consciousness characteristic of the right cerebral hemisphere, associated . . . with perceptions of unity and holism. Hence, individuals, eager or reluctant, are integrated into a group, not only by the sharing of pleasurable emotions through participation in formalized, repetitive, precisely performed interaction forms, but also by a mode of thought that reinforces feelings of solidarity.[49]

Lex points out that, like many other human practices associated with the satisfaction of biological necessities (such as eating and reproduction), rituals are invariably embellished with symbolic behaviors unique to each cultural community. Thus, she asserts, any thoroughgoing interpretation of the psychological effects of a particular ritual must be grounded in an understanding of the cultural milieu within which it is undertaken. In sum, Lex concludes that the *raison d'être* of rituals is "the readjustment of dysphasic biological and social rhythms by manipulation of neurophysiological structures under controlled conditions." We might add that it is the group undertaking the "ritual practice" that controls the conditions, and that they invariably control it in a manner consistent with their collective worldview.

MUSICAL PRACTICES AND RITUAL IN TRADITIONAL SOCIETIES: A PSYCHOSOCIAL DESCRIPTION

Unlike d'Aquili, Laughlin, and Lex, who have emphasized the psycho*physiological* effects of ritualized behavior (such as a musical practice) on individuals, ethnomusicologist Gilbert Rouget has focused more specifically on the varying psycho*social* manifestations of musical practice among different cultural communities. At first encounter, some readers may find Rouget's descriptions of the social dimensions of the psychological or reportedly "spiritual" effects of musical practice inapplicable to contemporary Western contexts, but this can be attributed largely to the fact that discussion of different "states of consciousness" has been tacitly proscribed in most Western academic discourse; such references have more conventionally been applied to the musical practices of non-Western cultural communities. Even with this recognition, some readers may still be put off by applications of Rouget's terminology to the "heightened experience" associated with musical practices in the U.S. Nevertheless, certain striking parallels can indeed be drawn between the examples Rouget has selected from the practices of diverse world cultural communities and the musical practices manifested in the different cultural communities in contemporary societies. Also, upon exploring Rouget's culturally expansive and synoptic work, it becomes evident that the pragmatic conception at the core of his work is generally consistent with that of d'Aquili, Laughlin, and Lex (with the addition of an important distinction). Thus, it seems worthwhile to consider the possibility that, broadly conceived, Rouget's terminology may indeed be applied appropriately to *all* musical practices.

Rouget observes that the belief that certain human problems and illnesses (particularly those of a mental or emotional nature) can be attributed to "malevolent spirits" or "wrathful divinities" is extremely common, if not universal, among the world's diverse cultural groups,[50] and he notes that two different approaches stand out among these groups as means for putting an end to this condition.[51] In both courses of action, individuals undertake an experience involving a musical practice by which their relationship with the "spirits" seen as responsible for their disturbance may be transformed. He identifies these means as possession rituals and shamanism.

In a *possession ritual*, a "possessee" is *visited by* inhabitants of the "spirit" world or "other" world while other members of her or his cultural community perform musically, and the transformation is thereby effected. In *shamanism*, by contrast, an individual *journeys to* the realm of the "spirits" or "gods" to transform her or his relationship with them; the shaman's relation to the musical practice is usually active, most often involving singing or drumming. Rouget explains that when these ritual procedures are successful, each involves the individual in experiencing a "trance" state, whereby her or his structure of consciousness is transformed, and a particular and exceptional type of relationship between her or his "self" and the world is created. Like d'Aquili and Laughlin, Rouget observes that these practices are effective in bringing about this result only when they are undertaken by the individual members of a group who collectively share a common "system of representations" (i.e., worldview). He explores both possession and shamanism in considerable detail in his intricately documented book *Music and Trance: A Theory of the Relations between Music and Possession*, though he focuses most of the book on possession. We will consider each of these categories of "psychosocial" effects of musical practice in turn.

Rouget bases his characterization of *possession ritual* on an extraordinarily large number of ethnographic studies describing the practices and beliefs of different cultural communities from around the world. He observes that the aim of possession rituals is to transform the individual's relationship to the world through identification with a "god" or "spirit." While the "entranced" individual is sometimes passive during such rituals, the event is usually actively accompanied by the musical practice of a community of individuals who "share a common code"[52] (or musical system consistent with their worldview), and the sounds produced in the attendant musical practice are almost always held to be responsible for bringing about the onset of the trance. Rouget observes that the music of possession rituals varies considerably among different cultural communities but that it may involve both vocal and instrumental performance, as well as dance. Like d'Aquili and Laughlin, Rouget concludes that the net result of the trance is the joining or "coming together" of individuals with the worldview of the community within which the precipitating practice is undertaken, and that it is this union that effects the "cure" for the individual afflicted by the "malevolent spirits."

In an extended chapter, Rouget explores musical practices and trance among the ancient Greeks, focusing especially on the theory of their psychosocial effects articulated by Plato. Rouget notes that Plato's thoughts on music and ritual have been difficult for many readers of his writings to grasp, primarily because of the conceptual differences involving the word *music* that are inherent in the ancient Greek language (which we noted earlier), and also because Plato's writings on music and ritual are scattered throughout his dialogues (primarily the *Laws*, *Timaeus*, *Phaedrus*, and *Ion*).[53] Nevertheless, Rouget affirms, when Plato's various writings specifically on the psychological effects of musical engagement are collated, they do form a cohesive theory.

According to Rouget's interpretation, Plato derived his theory from having observed successful methods used in raising infants. In the *Laws*, Plato noted that the mothers of small children typically help them to sleep by rocking them in their arms and singing to them. He surmised that the reason this was so effective was that the external movement of rocking and the sounds of singing served to overcome the sufferings of frights stemming from the infants' "defective dispositions." Rouget translates Plato's inference from this observation as follows.

> So whenever one applies an external shaking to the sufferings of this kind, the external movement overpowers the internal movement of fear and madness, and by thus overpowering it, it brings about a manifest calm in the soul and a cessation of the grievous palpitations of the heart, which had existed in each case.[54]

Thus, in Plato's view, the rocking of the child by the mother (typically accompanied by her singing) has the effect of "calming an infant's soul" sufficiently to allow the infant to sleep.

Similarly, Rouget notes, in the *Timaeus* Plato described the diseases of the body and soul to which human beings are prone. In order to maintain health (that is, to avoid illness and madness), Plato suggested that "nothing is more important" than to preserve the correct relationship between the soul and the body. In his view, the means to this end is to *move*, and one must "never move the soul without the body or the body without the soul, so that, each defending itself against the other, the two sides will retain their balance and their health." While physical activity and dance have great benefits of this kind, one should also provide the "most lordly" part of one's soul with movement by cultivating music and philosophy and thus bringing it into accord with the harmonies and revolutions of the universe.[55]

Next, Rouget summarizes a passage of the *Phaedrus*, in which Plato noted that many "people suffer from diseases and woes that are the consequence of certain offenses" they have committed. Plato attributes these diseases and woes not only to their personal offenses but to their inherent "weaknesses of the soul" that stem from "ancient faults committed by their ancestors." In Plato's view, certain types of trance (which, Rouget notes, are evoked in ritual by music and dance) have the effect of delivering these persons from their problems by providing them with recourse to the gods, thereby purifying them and bringing them recovery, or release from their troubles.[56]

Rouget concludes that it was on the basis of the information set forth in these dialogues that Plato developed his theory. Rouget articulates Plato's theory of the relations between trance and music in the following way:

> People who are psychologically somewhat fragile, and who as the result of god's anger suffer from divine madness, cure themselves by practicing ritual trance, which is triggered by a musical motto and takes the form of a dance; music and dance, by the effect of their movement,

reintegrate the sick person into the general movement of the cosmos, and this healing is brought about thanks to the benevolence of gods who have been rendered propitious by sacrifices.[57]

We should note that, unlike Plato, Rouget does not attribute the "trance" effects of music to movement or dance (or to the "driving practices" indicated by d'Aquili, Laughlin, and Lex), though he acknowledges that they often accompany each other. In Rouget's view, musical engagement induces trance via a "strange mechanism" that is not yet fully understood. He believes that the sound of certain music acts as an aural cue or trigger for effecting a *learned* change in an individual's state of mind (the music and the change of state having been associated in the socializing, ritual practices of an individual's society over time), and this cue prompts the individual to identify herself or himself publicly with the possessing "god." When the event has a therapeutic effect of any importance, it is this public identification that is the principal agent of the cure. Rouget clarifies the difference between his theory and Plato's as one of orientation:

> If I had to draw a parallel between Plato's theory and my own, I would say that, for him, the healing process is achieved by reinsertion of the individual in the cosmos as a result of the movement of dance and music, which reestablishes harmony with the universe, whereas for me healing is achieved by the reinsertion of the individual in society as a result of the movement of music and dance, which provokes identification with the god.
>   . . . Plato's theory is both physical and metaphysical, whereas mine is both psychological and sociological; both are equally physiological.[58]

It seems altogether likely that Plato's view of musical practice as being effective in aiding the individual to establish harmony with the *universe*— rather than harmony with a "god" unique to the worldview of a particular cultural community—is attributable to his holding of a conception of musical engagement far more limited in pan-cultural perspective than that of Rouget. For all Plato knew, the world within his scope of knowledge was representative of the entire universe. It seems evident that a similar perspective is held today by the members of different cultural communities who adamantly maintain that their group's conception of reality represents "true" Reality.

Incidentally, we should note that it is not our primary concern in this inquiry to come to a resolution of the apparent disagreement between d'Aquili, Laughlin, Lex, Plato, and Rouget on precisely *how* musical engagement has the effect of unifying or reconciling the private psychophysiological processes of the individual (such problems or psychological illnesses) with the worldview of her or his community. Our focus, rather, is on demonstrating *that* musical practices have been identified by these and other scholars as having this effect, each on the basis of her or his own research and reasoning. Having made this clear, however, we should also note that the differing theories presented by these thinkers on *how* musical practices have this effect are not necessarily mutually contradictory. It seems altogether possible that the historical interrelationship of musical engagement, dance, and ritual ceremonies in the collective, phylogenetic past of human beings may have left our species with an inherited propensity for responding psychophysiologically to the sounds of music by going into a form of "trance" even when musical practices are separated from these historically "natural" concomitants, and that the socializing practices of all musical cultural communities now merely reconfirm for each individual what he or she biologically "knows."[59] At present, data are not available to provide a firm basis for resolving this issue.

Rouget's treatment of *shamanism* is less extensive than his work on possession, yet it too rests on the foundation of his broad knowledge of relevant ethnographic research. Notably, Rouget's characterization of shamanism is like his writings on possession rituals in that it also suggests several points of similarity (particularly concerning psychosocial processes) with certain musical practices in U.S. society. Rouget emphasizes the distinction that whereas possession rituals have the positive social effect of transforming the individual's relationship to the worldview of the community via her or his identification with a "god" or "spirit," the shaman claims to transform "the world" on the basis of what he or she experiences while visiting the "other" world. Thus, he says, possession trance is best conceptualized as having been *undergone*, whereas the trance in shamanism is *acted*.[60]

Rouget explains that while sustaining the "dramatic" trance involved in many traditions and thus journeying into "another" world, the shaman typically describes what he or she sees, recounting personal adventures in a "truly theatrical performance."[61] Such "performances" may involve chants, songs, recitatives, invocations, and spoken monologues and dialogues, among other colorful forms of behavior, and these divinatory activities of the shaman may have a profound effect on the community. Rouget quotes Levi-Strauss in explaining the social effect of the shaman's behavior, noting that the music of the shaman "seeks to intervene in natural determinism in order to modify its course."[62] For this reason, says Rouget, shamanic music is often believed to be endowed with magical power.

Rouget's characterization of *shamanism* as a ritual that has the potential to change the society in some way resonates strongly with descriptions of what has been called the "prophetic function" or herald-like nature of the unconventional or *avant-garde* musicians composing, improvising, and performing new, often societally objectionable music in the contemporary public forums of Europe and the U.S. In his book *Noise: The Political Economy of Music*, French economist Jacques Attali has argued persuasively that the music heard as "noise" (i.e., objectionable sound) within a given society at any point in time might be best regarded as an aural harbinger of the new social order simultaneously emerging in that society. He suggests that a connection can be recognized between the musical practices evolving in a community at a given point in time and the community's simultaneously emerging worldview.

> Music is prophecy. Its styles and economic organization are ahead of the rest of society because it explores, much faster than material reality can, the entire range of possibilities in a given code. It makes audible the new world that will gradually become visible, that will impose itself and regulate the order of things; it is not only the image of things, but the transcending of the everyday, the herald of the future. For this reason musicians, even when officially recognized, are dangerous, disturbing, and subversive; for this reason it is impossible to separate their history from that of repression and surveillance.
>
> Musician, priest, and officiant were in fact a single function among ancient peoples.
>
> . . . A creator, [the musician] changes the world's reality.[63]

Attali's book-length articulation of this conception, while highly abstract, nevertheless points to certain ways in which the social and formal characteristics of Western music have prophetically foreshadowed changes in the economic and political history of Europe. Attali defends his position with historical references, which he sketches briefly in his introductory chapter as follows.

> [E]very major social rupture has been preceded by an essential mutation in the codes of music, in its mode of audition, and in its economy. For example, in Europe, during three different periods with three different styles (the liturgical music of the tenth century, the polyphonic music of the sixteenth century, and the harmony of the eighteenth and twentieth centuries), music found expression within a single, stable code and had stable modes of economic organization; correlatively, these societies were very clearly dominated by a single worldview. In the intervening periods, times of disorder and disarray prepared the way for what was to follow.[64]

Attali's claim that *every* major social change is preceded by a change "in the codes of music, in its mode of audition, and in its economy" may be a bit extreme, as it would seem to be true of only certain social changes and not others. Nevertheless, his argument is highly compelling, because of the many connections he draws between the musical practices of a given era and the social, political, and economic developments in the same era. Also, it seems important to note that not *every* instance of musical practice that manifests mutations in musical codes necessarily presages social change in the wider society; some do and some don't. Clearly, not *all* musicians (or composers) are equally adept at "listening for" or presaging in their music the new social orders latent in the collective psyches of their respective communities.

British philosopher of music Christopher Small has also recognized what he describes as a "prophetic function" inherent in the music practices evidenced in different world societies. Like Peirce, Small acknowledges that human beings are largely conditioned by the assumptions of the cultural community in which they live, he observes that the music of a community typically reflects characteristics of the collective worldview of the people in that group in a concrete way, and, like Attali, he asserts that changes in the music of the group often signal in advance changes in its social order. He supports this thesis—among others—by describing the musical *processes* of various different societies in his stimulating book *Music—Society—Education.*

In an extended discussion of different forms of music undertaken outside of Europe, Small recounts the research of Hugh Tracey, an ethnomusicologist who studied the music of the Chopi people living near the coast of the African nation of Mozambique in the 1940s.[65] In each of the Chopi villages he studied, Tracey reportedly found an *ngodo*—a large musical ensemble—comprised of musicians who play *timbila* (xylophone-like instruments), a group of singer-dancers, and a leader, who serves as the village's resident "composer and musical director." The leader is responsible for creating musical works for the collective participation of the villagers, and the works he creates are typically of "symphonic size" and duration, featuring multiple "movements." The "composer-director" of each village (who, Tracey insisted, was not influenced by European musical traditions) typically builds the text of a new "movement" (also called a *ngodo*) by listening to and reflecting on what he overhears in the dialogues of those living in the community. These texts are "cunning mixtures of mirth and sadness, political comment and protest and just plain gossip, outbursts of vitality which remain indissolubly linked to the concrete lives of the people from whom they arose and yet at the same time [bear] a universally human and spiritual message."[66]

Tracey explained that once the texts are established, the "composer-director" begins mentally to create musical settings for them, develops them more fully on his own *timbila*, and then calls on his fellow musicians to participate with him in the last stages of creation, though he remains the final judge of what musical materials are included in the final *ngodo*. At that point, a dance leader joins the group to create movements suitable for the music. Small stresses Tracey's explanation that these extended, complex works are not written down, but are created and performed entirely by memory. Most importantly, he notes, the performance of these works serves "a highly social and cathartic function in a society which has no daily press, no publications, and no stage other than the village yard in which publicly to express its feelings or voice its protests against the rub of the times."[67] Remarkably, as each new *ngodo* is created, it is inserted into the existing work, while older *ngodo* are dropped, the whole eventually being replaced entirely by the new "movements." The old works are then forgotten, as they are no longer socially relevant. Small asserts his view in later chapters that a similarly socially effective, even *prophetic* "function" can be discerned in the historical changes of the music of Europe, but that unlike the more or less *consistently* socially effective, yet transitory musical efforts of the Chopi, the concert life of European society has become "choked with past works," many of which, he asserts, should have been allowed to die long ago, since they have exceeded their "natural life span" of social effectiveness. Small's analysis of Western society is clearly debatable, but his observation that the musical practices undertaken by the Chopi and others reflect and often presage changes in the organization of the societies in which they appear is certainly consistent with the views of the other scholars whose works we have explored.

On the basis of Rouget's, Attali's, and Small's writings, we can see that when *shamanic* rituals and *possession* rituals (as Rouget has characterized them) are considered in terms of their social effects, they may indeed have correlates in the respective *creative* versus *re-creative* musical practices undertaken among the different groups that comprise European and American social forums. We thus might extend the designation *possession* to describe any musical practice in which performers iconically (qualitatively) "embody" roles of preexisting characters (such as "gods," "stars," or other beings) that are recognized by the members of a community to have (or to have had) great social significance or importance, *and* in which the musical practice has the effect of resocializing those involved into a preexisting worldview. Such events generally confirm the existing worldview of the community for its members. Similarly, we might extend the appellation *shamanism* to describe as well any musical practice in which one or more performers "prophesy" and thus potentially make manifest a different, ostensibly "better" worldview from the one presently held by the individuals who may come to adopt it. Such events tend to challenge the existing worldview of a community and may manifest a new, more inherently satisfying holistic conception for its members. In this view, we can see that *any* musical practice having high psychophysiological and psychosocial value for a group of people can be regarded as representative of one of these two categories.[68] While Rouget makes no mention of the possibility, it also seems apparent that, over time, a given musical practice might gradually take on a different role in a society (as a result of changes in that society) and thus change categories; what was once a shamanic ritual might become a possession ritual.[69]

Before we conclude our discussion of Rouget's writings, we should briefly review the points he has raised that contribute to our pragmatic conception of musical practices. In identifying two types of rituals that involve practices on the basis of their psychosocial *effects* upon the individuals and societies within which they take place, Rouget has identified his views with the pragmatist perspective. While Rouget does not assert that *all* musical practices are of the nature of either possession or shamanism, we have seen that the social effects of both are indeed paralleled in the diverse musical practices of different cultural communities: Specifically, some musical practices facilitate the union of individuals with the *presently* shared worldview of the community (as in possession rituals), while other musical practices challenges the present worldview of the community with a *new* worldview or vision according to which the community may be unified (as in shamanic rituals). In either case, the ultimate effect of what is construed by the community involved to be a successful musical event is the psychosocial union of "individual minds" with the "collective mind" (or worldview) of the community via the experience of "trance."[70]

MUSICAL PRACTICES AND RITUAL IN TRADITIONAL SOCIETIES: A SOCIOPOLITICAL DESCRIPTION

Certain writings of the late anthropologist Victor Turner continue to be cited in the recent work of contemporary cultural anthropologists, since the conceptual vocabulary he adopted to discuss his ethnographic observations and impart his many insights remains useful. Turner placed rituals in a broader social frame than d'Aquili, Laughlin, Lex, and Rouget, and his writings represent a logical extension of their pragmatic observations into the political realm. While he had relatively little to say specifically about the different musical practices involved in ritual, Turner took as a commonplace the notion that ritual behavior expresses and manifests the worldview of a community for the individuals that comprise it, and he emphasized that the ritual practices of a community serve to implement its social solidarity and sanction its social order. Thus, Turner's views on the place of ritual in society will provide us with a broader political perspective on such behaviors than the theorists we have discussed thus far. In addition, his characterization of the place of ritual behavior in what he termed the "processual" life of a community will aid us in expanding our conception of the socially dynamic nature of ritualized behavior (including musical practices) in different types of societies.

According to Turner's conception, ritual has its roots in the day-to-day conflicts unfolding in the lives of the individuals and groups that comprise human societies; he established the term *social drama* to characterize the workings-out of these conflicts. Turner observed that the social drama taking place in any given society at any point in time is invariably similar in certain respects to the dramas perennially unfolding in all societies, and he set forth a scheme according to which such dramas could be divided into four phases of process. In the first phase, *breach* occurs where interpersonal and intergroup stresses or conflicting interests result in a disruption of the shared values and integrity of a society. The second phase, *crisis*, is characterized by the growth of awareness among members of the society that these conflicts threaten social relations or the existing social structure. In Turner's third phase, *redress*, members of the society work together using various processes such as ritual or legal means to effect resolution and set the situation right; such periods are experienced as times of transition for those undergoing them. The fourth phase involves either *reconciliation and reintegration* of the social group or the *agreement to differ*.[71]

In his early writings, Turner focused a good deal on the second and third phases of this processual scheme, exploring various types of personal and social transitions, their accompanying rituals, and their effects on those involved in them in different cultural contexts. Turner borrowed from cultural anthropologist Arnold Van Gennep the term *liminal* (from the Latin word *limen,* meaning "threshold"). which he employed to identify the unclassified and uncertain state in which those who are at the crux of transition find themselves. Turner used the term to describe both the "in-between" state of individuals who are undergoing "rite-of-passage" types of transitions (such as initiations into adulthood or marriage) as well as the state experienced by larger collectives in transition (such as social "movements," or political dissensions). In both types of cases, individuals undergoing the transition are necessarily marginalized by the society. Turner observed that "[d]uring the . . . 'liminal' period, the characteristics of the ritual subject (the 'passenger') are ambiguous; he passes through a cultural realm that has few or none of the attributes of the past or coming state."[72] Also, "liminal" situations and persons are often vested with magical or religious qualities, primarily because they fall between the normal social classifications recognized collectively by the society. Individuals experiencing the state of "liminality" feel it to be a moment both "in and out of time."[73]

Notably, those who undergo together the "ambiguity of social status" that defines a liminal state typically experience the time to be one of what Turner called *communitas*—great comradeship—characterized by "an even communion of equal individuals."[74] He likened the social relationships inherent in communitas to those described by Jewish theologian Martin Buber in his definition of community: "Community is the being no longer side by side (and one might add, above and below) but *with* one another of a multitude of persons."[75] This description seems consistent with the strong sense of a "loss of self" and the feeling of social unity that we noted is often experienced by persons collectively engaging in a musical practice. Turner noted that many of these new, unifying movements cut across tribal and national divisions during their initial momentum, gathering adherents from a variety of backgrounds.

As we have noted, Turner mentioned music only briefly in his discussion of liminality and communitas, but he did recognize that myths, symbols, and various art forms (such as music) arise out of such "liminal" movements, and he emphasized that they have the social effect of validating and furthering the conception of Reality collectively held by the liminal individuals; their shared "vision" generally differs in significant ways from that of the society from which it stems.

> Liminality, marginality, and [inferior societal status] are conditions in which are frequently generated myths, symbols, rituals, philosophical systems, and works of art. These cultural forms provide men with a set of templates or models which are, at one level, periodical reclassifications of reality and man's relationship to society, nature, and culture. But they are more than classifications, since they incite men to action as well as to thought.[76]

As they inevitably manifest differences from the conceptions of Reality (i.e., worldviews) held within the society or societies from which they emerge, we can see that they typically have political implications. Unlike d'Aquili and Laughlin, Lex, Rouget, and Plato, Turner did not identify musical practice as a locus of societal transition, but he did acknowledge that such transitions are typically manifested in ritual behavior. Since we have seen that musical practices involve social processes similar to those described by Turner, we can be fairly safe in saying that Turner *generally* agreed with the conclusions of the scholars whose writings we have explored thus far.

Turner observed that in the time following the liminal period, its passage is consummated. Individuals who have undergone the experience find themselves in a relatively stable state once more, either reassimilated into the community of which they had previously been a part (sometimes with new social status) or else collectively institutionalized as an independent community and acknowledged as being worthy of recognition along with other like communities. He also noted that such communities are often more fanatically dedicated to the truths that its members believe they uniquely hold, and they often borrow much of their mythology and symbolism from the traditional rites of passage of the societies from which they have emerged.[77]

While Turner's research did not focus primarily on musical practices, as we have done throughout this inquiry, his recognition that societally "reclassifying" cultural forms tend to emerge from the shared vision of marginalized individuals and communities is consistent in many ways with the characterization of shamanism we set forth in the last section. Indeed, in many communities the "musician" (or "shaman") is a marginal character, often living a liminal life in response to what he or she perceives to be certain problems with the society's present form, and certain disparate members of the community may be "inspired" by her or his "alternative" vision. However, for our purposes it is most important to note that by attributing the processual dynamics of social change to the intergroup stresses and conflicting interests that are latent in a society and by noting that new cultural forms tend to emerge from the conceptions of those marginalized in such conflicts, Turner has provided us with a means of understanding how the emergence of various new cultural forms (including, presumably, forms of music and musical practices) may be attributed to potential or unconscious forces existing in the individuals and social contexts from which they emerge. His conception is thus consistent with the pragmatic conception we have set forth here in that it attributes the emergence and the form of a musical practice in a community to forces latent in that society, rather than to the inspiration of external "gods" or "spirits."

A PRAGMATIC CONCEPTION OF MUSICAL PRACTICES IN TRADITIONAL SOCIETIES

Earlier in this chapter we adopted Peirce's recommendation that to "clarify" any concept, that is, to free it from being consistently doubted and disagreed upon, we should consider it in relation to its practical *effects* upon the members of a community. On this basis, we noted that the diverse musical practices manifested among the world's various cultural communities are at least at times associated in some way with an accompanying "heightened" experience or psychophysiological *effect* on the individuals involved, and that this experience is conceptualized in different ways according to the worldview of each community within which the musical practice takes place. Using these observations as our base of departure, we set out to explore the work of scholars in clinical psychiatry, ethnomusicology, and cultural anthropology for the purpose of coming to an understanding of how the psychophysiological effect associated with musical practices can be said to be meaningful to individual human beings, and to the different cultural communities of which they are a part, as part of the universal *human* community.

The views of these scholars have collectively provided us with a conception of music in traditional societies that is consistent with our pragmatist philosophical perspective, in that they all generally agree upon certain collective social effects that typically accompany the psychophysiological experience which often result from participation in a musical practice. On the basis of the information provided by these scholars, our pragmatic conception of musical practices can be formally described as follows:

> The diverse musical practices of the world's many and varied culturally homogeneous communities are each undertaken for what are conceived to be—and are—different pragmatic personal and social purposes unique to their respective social contexts, but each of these practices, when experienced as "successful" by the individuals engaged in them, necessarily draws much of its personal and social value from an accompanying, pleasurable, psychophysiological *effect*. Such an effect upon

an individual engaged in a musical practice operatively unifies her or his mind with the "collective mind"—or worldview—of the community embodying that worldview.[78] Thus, in the pragmatist's view, all such musical practices that are personally and/or socially valued *are* so valued because they are inherently psychosocially unifying and confirming of worldview.

Stated differently, we have discovered that for the *individual* one relative benefit or value of engagement in a musical practice stems from the psychophysiological and psychosocial effect it has for her or him. The occurrence of this effect depends on whether or not the musical practice confirms in some way the conception of Reality that the individual psychophysiologically embodies, thereby providing a means by which the individual's personal conflicts can be reconciled via a psychological union with the worldview that person shares with the community. At the same time, the relative benefit or value of a musical practice for the *community* stems from its promotion of social solidarity via a collective confirmation of the community's worldview. Thus, in the pragmatist's view, every musical practice that is held to be personally and socially meaningful derives its value at least in part from its inherently culturally unifying or reconciling effect, as it simultaneously provides "psychophysiological" and "psychosocial" benefit to individuals, and "psychosocial" and "sociopolitical" benefit to the culturally homogeneous community of individuals who find this value in it.

Nevertheless, Rouget and Turner would remind us, while all musical practices undertaken in culturally homogeneous communities may indeed serve to bring about the psychophysiological reconciliation of individuals to the conception of Reality collectively shared by the community of which they are a part (as in cases of possession), some musical practices may manifest the embodiment in a group of individuals of a worldview that is different from that of the larger society to which they belong (as in cases of shamanism). In such a circumstance, one of two possibilities may occur following the musical event: Either the worldview of the larger society will change to assimilate the new "vision" manifested in the smaller community, or the smaller community may break away from or otherwise defy the larger society.[79]

In either of these cases, however, the musical practice that the individuals involved come to experience as "successful" or "good" will inevitably validate the conception of Reality that they collectively find most satisfying or appropriate. On this basis, the pragmatist affirms that musical practices may be regarded as mediums by which individuals of a community collectively attain psychophysiological equilibrium (or *balance*) and social solidarity according to the worldview they collectively share. Figure 3.3 presents a semiotic representation of the Sign "musical practice" according to the way in which a pragmatist would conceptualize such an undertaking.

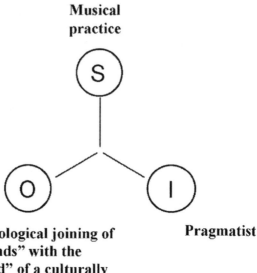

Musical practice

A psychophysiological joining of "individual minds" with the "collective mind" of a culturally homogenous community

Pragmatist

Figure 3.3   The Sign "Musical practice" conceptualized as collective, psychosocially equilibrating and thus culturally integrative behavior; a pragmatic conception.

This pragmatic conception of musical practice both embraces and represents a substantial difference in orientation from the "universalist" and "relativist" perspectives described earlier in this chapter. As we have seen, *universalists* have tended historically to conceptualize the Sign "sounds produced in a musical practice" as the universal Object "music," while placing comparatively less emphasis on the context-specific social forces from which its various manifestations stem and the human psychophysiological drives that motivate the diverse instances of "musical practice" as behaviors. On the other hand, *relativists* have tended historically to conceptualize the Sign "sounds produced in a musical practice" as culturally unique sound artifacts (i.e., Objects) manifested in particular cultural contexts for reasons unique to those contexts, and they have placed less emphasis on the psychophysiological drives common to all human beings that underlie or motivate their creation.

In contrast with the views of both universalists and relativists, this Peircian *pragmatic* conception recognizes different musical practices as culturally unique, conventional behaviors involving sound by which individuals of a community individually and collectively come to terms psychophysiologically, psychosocially, and/or sociopolitically with various forces affecting them. In the pragmatist view we have established here, each musical practice, when thought by a community to be "successful," has the concomitant effect of validating the worldview of the group participating in it. Thus, according to our pragmatic conception, the diverse musical practices of different cultural communities (conceptualized in their various ways) may be regarded as culturally unique behaviors that share in common the human patterning of sound, each of which supports *both* the psychophysiological and psychosocial equilibrium of individuals in community *and* the psychosocial and sociopolitical solidarity of their community as a whole. Unlike the universalist and the relativist, this pragmatist view does not focus on the Sign "sounds produced in musical practice" as the Object "music," but instead recognizes the Sign "musical practice" as the Object "psychosocially equilibrating and culturally integrative behavior." Thus, participating in a musical practice that manifests the worldview of a community invariably serves the individuals in that community as a means of validating their personal and collective identity and for sustaining their psychosocial health via the confirmation of their shared worldview.

While he did not formally identify his perspective as having been derived from pragmatist philosophy, ethnomusicologist John Blacking nevertheless eloquently affirmed just such a pragmatic conception of musical practices in his 1976 book *How Musical Is Man?* His words underscore the importance both of understanding every instance of musical practice on "its own cultural terms" *and* of recognizing that all musical behavior is rooted in aspects of experience common to all human beings.

> The rules of musical behavior are not arbitrary cultural conventions, and techniques of music are not like developments in technology. Musical behavior reflects varying degrees of consciousness of social forces, and the structures and functions of music are related to basic human drives and the biological need to maintain a balance between them.[80]

Some readers may object to this pragmatic view of music on the basis that it does not seem to account for musical practices that individuals might undertake alone, in private moments. According to the pragmatist conception we have sketched here, solitary musical practices can indeed be regarded as psychosocially equilibrating and culturally validating behaviors, on the basis that when undertaking a musical practice alone, an individual is almost invariably relating to aspects of her or his psyche that have been influenced and in some measure formed by participation in communal activity. This is the case regardless of whether the musical practice is of a more re-creative (possession-like) or more creative (shamanic) nature. Every musical innovator (or shaman) who is taken seriously by a community is aware on some level that her or his efforts are invariably, somehow related to the past actions of the community—even if they represent only a "psychotic" response. Thus, we can see that every new form of musical practice acknowledged by a community stems in *some* way from the form of musical practice formerly undertaken by that community. Furthermore, in all solitary musical practices an individual invariably deals consciously and unconsciously with thoughts stimulated by experiences in community. Anthropologist Roy Rappaport's explanation of mental activity in solitary rituals is suggestive of how a musical practice can be psychophysiologically, culturally related even in moments when one is practicing or improvising alone.

> [G]iven the extent to which in solitary rituals various parts of the psyche may be brought in touch with each other it is reasonable to take ritual to be auto-communicative as well as allo-communicative. Auto-communication is important even in public rituals. In fact, the transmitters of ritual messages are often, if not always, their most significant receivers.[81]

Peirce, too, implied that in one's private thoughts one is invariably relating to both the different parts of one's own psyche as well as to those of his community.

> [It is] all-important . . . to remember . . . that a person is not absolutely an individual. His thoughts are what he is "saying to himself," that is, is saying to that other self that is just coming into life in the flow of time. . . . The second thing to remember is that the man's circle of society (however widely or narrowly this phrase may be understood), is a sort of loosely compacted person, in some respects of higher rank than the person of an individual organism.[82]

On this basis, we can see that every musical practice undertaken by an "individual mind" when alone is nevertheless related to the worldview of the "collective mind" of a community, regardless of whether it is more of the nature of a psychophysiological reconciliation to societal ideals (as in *possession* or re-creation) or motivated by a presently conscious or latent impetus to effect societal change (as in *shamanism* or "inspired" creation).

Some readers may find resonance with the pragmatic conception of musical practices in traditional societies presented here, recognizing consistencies between these descriptions and the ways that musical practices have psychophysiologically, psychosocially, and sociopolitically equilibrating effects for individuals in contemporary, culturally pluralistic societies. Other readers, however, may object to it on the basis that the musical practices in their experience don't necessarily seem to be associated with a recognized communal ritual. In some measure this objection misses the central idea of our argument. In describing our pragmatic perspective we explored ways in which musical practices in culturally homogeneous societies could be considered synonymous with the anthropological construct *ritual* in order to demonstrate heuristically how different musical practices could be seen as inherently culturally equilibrating, unifying, and validating behavior. Certainly, we must acknowledge that not *all* musical practices can be said to have a culturally unifying effect for *every* individual. In pluralistic societies, individuals are exposed to a tremendous variety of music every day and in innumerable contexts. Thus, it would be a great exaggeration to suggest that anyone could possibly experience *all* of the different instances of music they encounter as personally, culturally confirming. Nevertheless, on the basis of our recent discussion we can now affirm that any musical practice that *does* have high personal and social value for an individual or community derives some of its value from the culturally validating or transformative psychophysiological effect we have described. In other words, we could say that—in general—human beings respond psychophysiologically in the most profound and positive way to those instances of music to which they have a cultural predilection. Thus, we can also say that while not all musical practices take place in a ritual context, all musical practices that are experienced as profoundly, personally, and socially *meaningful* are invariably *of the nature of* ritual, in that they are inherently validating or transformative of worldview.

Now that we have come to an understanding of the ways in which all personally and collectively motivated music making can be likened to or is associated with ritual, we can understand how musical practices came to be associated historically with the organized practice of religion. In Chapter 2 we noted that the term *worldview* not only describes the beliefs held tacitly by individuals in community but also includes those beliefs they overtly regard as "religious." Peirce, it is important to remember, recognized no real distinction between tacitly held knowledge and "belief," religious or otherwise.[83] Since it is from the experience of intellectual, physical, and emotional unity with a worldview that musical practices derive profound personal and social importance, it should not surprise us that engagement in some form of musical practice would be a part of the collective practices of many religions. Indeed, for many individuals living in traditional societies, a form of musical practice is central to their collective life, and the psychophysiological effect they experience in their respective forms of musical practice typically contributes to validating their conception of Reality as "sacred."

As we noted earlier, the members of some traditional communities now living in state societies, such as the Mevlevi Sufis and Pentecostal Christians, regard the experience associated with the unique forms of music they have respectively practiced for years as contributing strongly to the confirmation of their community's unique worldview as Reality. Since we have seen that any musical practice that an individual experiences as personally valuable typically has the effect of validating psychophysiologically the conception of Reality that he or she embodies (or transforming that worldview to one more inherently satisfying), we can also see that from the pragmatist's perspective all such musical practice could be said to be religious.

This notion is likely to raise objections from some readers, as the notion that all musical practices are associated with worldview (or "religion") has not often been acknowledged historically in the U.S. public forum, where individuals' personal differences in musical practice are not always associated conceptually with their connection with a community, and are now typically regarded as matters of "personal taste." Indeed, modernism and its effects have done much to fragment, reorder, and obscure the cultural associations of many people in modern societies (such as the U.S.), but the fact remains that they—like all human beings—still cluster into communities of "like mind" and these connections are generally reflected in their engagement with particular musical practices (and not others). Moreover, the close connection between music and ritual may be difficult for people who presently live in modern, pluralistic societies to grasp because the widespread use of media and sound technologies in such societies has eliminated for many people the *necessity* to meet physically and collectively with communities of "like mind." Yet the culturally rooted, identity-validating effects of particular musical practices undertaken in modern nations have been recognized by several scholars.[84] We will explore more thoroughly in Chapter 4 the factors that have contributed to obscuring the culturally validating nature of musical practices in the public forum of the U.S.

However, before we can demonstrate this and thus conclude our pragmatically "clear" account of culturally different musical practices, we must come to some understanding of how certain unique musical practices and conceptions of them have emerged historically in *state* societies in general. This necessitates that we briefly acquaint ourselves with an anthropological explanation of how some of the societally beneficial effects of *ritual* in traditional societies have come to be provided by *theatre* in emerging state societies. On the basis of this and other historical evidence, we shall examine further how musical practices are often manifested in culturally pluralistic, state societies; this will serve as a conceptual foundation for considering how concepts of music in the U.S. and other such modern societies differ from those held in traditional and some other state societies.

MUSICAL PRACTICES IN CULTURALLY PLURALISTIC, STATE SOCIETIES

In his book *From Ritual to Theatre*, Victor Turner observed that when independent, culturally homogeneous communities come together to form complex state-level societies, *stage drama* simultaneously emerges as a means preferable to ritual for resolving the conflicts of the new, larger society's "social dramas." Thus, in Turner's view, theatre is like ritual, in that its roots are embedded in the third "redressive" phase of social drama (which we explored earlier). However, while ritual and stage drama do share in common the element of "performance," Turner does not suggest that they are essentially the same. To him, the two merely share common features and have a similar socially educative effect in those societies in which they are found.[85]

William Morgan and Per Brask expanded on Turner's thesis, arguing that the emergence of theatre in state societies is actually an adaptive response to changing social, political, and historical circumstances in newly developing, culturally pluralistic social arenas. In their view, as traditional societies come together in one society, ritual is no longer adequate by itself to meet effectively the critical social needs of a statehood. While traditional communal rituals are to some degree capable of incorporating innovation and improvisation, no ritual is sufficiently malleable or comprehensive in its conceptual scheme to address fully all of the potentially disruptive issues arising in state societies. In large measure, this is because none of the communal rituals of the culturally homogeneous segments of the populace represents or provides a worldview acceptable to all of the groups comprising the society. Morgan and Brask observe that, unlike ritual, theatrical performance is not bound to a particular worldview but rather has the innovative capacity to incorporate different cultural views into its structure, giving all or many of them a "voice" in the drama. However, beyond its entertainment value, the newly emerged phenomenon of theatre invariably does have the important, socially educative effect of communicating that the worldview that supports the authority structure of the state is indeed a fair representation of how things "are" and how they "ought" to be. These authors note that when theatre emerges to meet the societal demands that communal ritual cannot, ritual does not die out in state societies. Instead, communal ritual continues to support the internal unity of constituent segments of the society. We might add that as theatre rarely addresses, let alone begins to provide, any means for grappling with the great ontological questions of life, as most organized religions do, it should not surprise us that traditional rituals and "religious" or culturally unified institutions would endure. Also, since theatrical playwrights do not necessarily have much respect for preserving the unique identities of the historically associated, constituent groups that collectively comprise the new state society (as the established religions of these groups do), it seems consistent with expectations that ritual would continue in pluralistic, state societies to meet such social needs.

Morgan and Brask draw support for their argument from the history of ancient Greece and the sixteenth century Aztec state, citing evidence that theatre emerged coincident with the rise of state society in both circumstances as a nonphysically coercive means for the state to exercise social control (i.e., cultural conditioning) over the various class and ethnic population segments that comprised it. They explain that in early Greece, Dionysian cult ritual attracted the largest groups of people from different geographical and socially diverse communities, and that leaders in the authority structure of the state saw in these large assemblies an opportunity to inculcate in the audience a cosmology and belief system sanctioning the extant social order. Wealthy citizens and the state itself sponsored large-scale theatrical performances, complete with scripted dialogue, characterization, and symbolic paraphernalia drawing on myths from the distant past that could be used to reflect contemporary reality. Morgan and Brask explain that the plays portrayed a coherent universe in which the audience could see "universally valid principles in action" that were concordant with the state's interests. They summarize their argument as follows:

> In ancient Greece . . . theatre emerges from specified circumstances of communal ritual . . . It served as a mode of creating and maintaining the social order desired by state authorities in their wish that unity and integrity of the body politic, and not individuation and segmentary autonomy, be the order of the day.[86]

They document a similar pattern in the emergence of theatre in the pre-Hispanic Aztec state, emphasizing that "the spectator received a new perception of personal truth or reality" in accordance with that of the state in both contexts.

We can extrapolate from the argument made by Morgan and Brask and observe that as theatre has emerged in various places and times throughout history to accommodate the social needs of newly formed complex state societies, new musical practices have also emerged, separate from the rituals practiced in formally religious contexts by the culturally homogeneous groups comprising the population. Historical evidence bears this out, but it also reveals that in some cases new musical practices have accompanied theatre in its emergence (as they did in the cases of Greek theatre and opera, for example).[87] However, the other musical practices that have arisen apart from the central religious rituals of communities are unlike theatre in that they do not *easily* allow for the integrated representation of more than one unified segment of a culturally diverse society (in, say, a tonal dialogue).[88] Thus, the new musical practices emerging in state societies that are not associated with theatre are likely to retain more of the culturally distinctive, community-unifying nature of ritual than does theatre, as they provide an experience of psychosocial reconciliation for only one culturally homogeneous segment of the population. We have seen that when a new form of music first emerges in a traditional society (as in shamanism), it typically manifests a worldview significantly different from that of the society from which it stems. When this occurs in culturally pluralistic, state societies, the new forms of music emerging in them often manifest the cultural unification of individuals previously belonging to different, culturally homogeneous segments of the population who have come, by association with one another, to embody collectively a new worldview that includes some attributes of each of their previous worldviews. This can certainly be seen to have been the case in the emergence of jazz, which began as a cultural fusion of European-American and African-American traditions.[89]

Historically speaking, many state societies have been strongly nationalistic in their musical practices, and efforts at musical nationalism have arisen both spontaneously among the people and by government edict. Historian Henry Raynor has observed that in many of the state societies of Europe (such as Germany and Italy) during the nineteenth century music was more or less universally regarded as having a special position in the life of the society since its stylistic unity provided a sense of national unity even where the state was not otherwise unified by a common language or by a cohesive governmental system. Raynor notes that during this era, "Italian music insisted, as did German music, upon a fundamental unity of style and spirit inevitably clamouring to become political unity."[90] Elsewhere during the same era, by contrast, other state governments held firm control over certain musical practices for reasons of maintaining cultural unity.

Incidentally, we should note that to this day many culturally pluralistic, state societies have in place various formal and informal strategies for censoring musical practices that threaten to subvert radically the existing worldview of the state; they deem such measures necessary for maintenance of the status quo. Indeed, some state leaders who have recognized the inherently culturally unifying nature of music have even sought to bring about and maintain cultural unity within their societies by controlling quite narrowly the options for musical engagement within them.

While political history is rife with such instances, one event of the fairly recent past seems particularly outstanding. Shortly after assuming leadership of the country of Iran in 1979, the religious and political leader Ayatollah Ruhollah Khomeini took the culturally conservative act of banning all music from his country's radio and television broadcasts. Prior to the issuance of this edict, Iranian programming had included Western popular and art music recordings, as well as traditional Persian music. In the view of the ayatollah, however, music is "no different from opium . . . [A] youth who spends his time listening to music can no longer appreciate realities, just as a drug addict cannot."[91] Notably, the ayatollah's ban did not affect the melodious vocalizing of passages from the Qur'an and Islamic religious poetry typically included in Muslim worship that many U.S. citizens would likely regard as a musical practice; as we noted in Chapter 1, most Muslims do not regard the sounds produced in that practice as music. Thus, the ayatollah's ban affected only those musical practices that manifested a worldview different from his own (such as those included in the radio broadcasts). Most positively construed, Khomeini's action could be said to have been motivated by a concern to protect the citizens of his country from being dissuaded from their worshipful relationship with their god, Allah, and thus to foster their spiritual health. Construed in another way, the action could be said to have been motivated by the religious and political leader's wish to maintain the cultural solidarity of the nation by reducing options for "psychosocial unification" among the country's citizenry. The positive or negative value of the ayatollah's action depends on one's own cultural perspective.

A similar effort was made in 1934 by the first All-Union Congress of Soviet Writers when they collectively proclaimed that all artistic work (and by extension all musical practices) undertaken in the Soviet Union "ought to contribute to the ideological transformation and education of the workers in the spirit of socialism."[92] Perhaps the most extreme case is that of Adolf Hitler, the German head of state from 1934 to 1945 whose Nazi party carried out the systematic "extermination" of approximately six million Jews for the purpose of promoting what he held to be a "master race" of humanity. Hitler insisted that the arts of Germany (including music) must "serve for the maintenance of the eternal values present in the essential character of our people."[93]

While the foregoing explanation represents a somewhat oversimplified view of the social dynamics involved in the emergence of new musics and different musical practices in different types of societies, it nevertheless provides us with a rough, pragmatic conception of a psychophysiologically and psychosocially based motor that has historically driven changes in music and, correspondingly, worldviews.

ONTOLOGICAL RELATIONSHIP OF AN INDIVIDUAL PERSON TO A PARTICULAR MUSICAL PRACTICE

Before turning our discussion to explore the factors that have contributed to diminishing conscious awareness of the culturally unifying nature—and thus the social value—of musical practices among the population of the U.S., a nation that differs radically in many ways from traditional societies and some other culturally pluralistic state societies, it will be helpful for us to see how Peirce's phenomenological vocabulary can aid us in identifying the different types of relationships an individual person may have with respect to the worldview of a particular community as it is manifested in a given instance of music.

In many societal contexts, but especially in culturally pluralistic, state societies, people are likely to come into contact with a number of different musical practices which they do *not* personally experience as culturally validating or meaningfully transformative, yet the nature of the relationship a single individual may have to a given musical practice (and the worldview it manifests) can actually take many different forms. In Chapter 2, we saw that Peirce's phenomenological terminology could be used to describe the different types of ontological relationships that may exist between a cultural anthropologist and the worldview of a cultural community he or she is studying (that is, the degree to which the individual and the community are "of one mind"). Using Peirce's terms *Firstness, Secondness,* and *Thirdness* to denote the qualitative or *emotional, physical,* and *mental* aspects of cultural relationships, respectively, we made note of the following relationships:

- A relationship of *Thirdness of Thirdness* is characterized by *rational understanding* of the "other's" worldview (but not necessarily physical experience of or emotional union with it).
- A relationship of *Secondness of Thirdness* is characterized by *physical experience* of the "other's" worldview (but not necessarily rational understanding of it or emotional union with it).
- A relationship of *Firstness of Thirdness* is characterized by *emotional union* with the "other's" worldview (but not necessarily rational understanding of it or physical experience with it).

On the basis of the pragmatist conception of music we have presented in this chapter, we can now see that these terms may be utilized to describe the experiential relationship of a given individual to the worldview of another cultural community as it is manifested in a particular musical practice.

For example, Peirce would term the relationship of an individual who participates *physically* in the musical practice of a culturally dissimilar cultural community (i.e., on the level of Secondness), but has little or no conceptual understanding of (i.e., Thirdness) or emotional connection to (i.e., Firstness) the worldview of the community with which it originated, a "Secondness of Thirdness." This may occur at times when an individual is invited to sing along with others in a musical tradition (and perhaps in a language) foreign to her or him, and neither understands the meaning of the practice nor experiences emotional unity with the others in doing so.

In the same way, an individual may understand *rationally* and participate *physically* in the musical practice of a culturally dissimilar cultural community (i.e., on the levels of Thirdness and Secondness) but have little or no emotional connection (i.e., Firstness) to the worldview of the community with which it originated. This may come about when the player of a musical instrument rationally grasps and correctly performs "all the right notes" in a composition, but is not committed to it emotionally, as when a well-educated and technically proficient but culturally unrelated musician is hired to perform in a religious service with which he or she has no personal, emotional connection or cultural affiliation. Since a person who relates to a particular musical practice only on the levels of Thirdness and Secondness does not fully embody the worldview of the community from which it stems (i.e., experience union with the community on the level of Firstness as well), he or she may not be fully committed to that community, and her or his experience of the event involving the musical practice is likely to be described as being "merely superficial."

Similarly, we can see that it is possible for an individual to have great rational understanding of and emotional resonance with the musical practice of a community, while having little physical involvement with it. This describes the experience of a great number of Europeans and Americans who understand intellectually and respond emotionally to the musical practices of their particular communities (or to recordings of them) but do not physically involve themselves in the event by singing, playing, dancing, or perhaps even being present. Peirce would designate such a relationship a "Thirdness and Firstness of Thirdness." Of course, other relationships between an individual and the worldview of a community may also be observed in the world's myriad musical practices and described with Peirce's terminology.

It is most important for us to note, however, that Peirce would term the relationship between an individual and a community in which a particular musical practice manifests more or less completely her or his own conception of Reality *intellectually*, *physically*, and *emotionally* a "Thirdness, Secondness, and Firstness of Thirdness." Such a person can be said to experience *ontological unity* or "identity" with the worldview of the community from which the music stems, as he or she *understands*, *participates*, and *resonates emotionally* and thus fully embodies—or "is at one" with—the worldview of that community. Such is the case in all musical practices that a given individual or community regard as "deeply meaningful" or "religious." We must keep in mind that while all of the different relationships we have described earlier (and others) are possible and clearly in evidence among the world's diverse cultural communities, the primary personal and social *value* of the different cultural manifestations of music for all individuals and communities stems from the experience of "Firstness"—or emotional union—that it brings about with the worldview or "collective mind" of one's community.

On the basis of this sketch of the types of ontological relationships that may exist between the "habits of mind" of an individual and those of a community, it is not difficult for us to imagine how a person may come to recognize greater intellectual congruity, physical well-being, and/or emotional consonance with a community different from the one with which he or she is associated at present, and thus be motivated to shift her or his allegiance (i.e., "cheat," "defect," or "convert") to the "other" community. Human lives are filled with experiences and stories of illicit love, religious conversion, and political intrigue, involving anguished individuals who find themselves drawn toward a community that embodies a worldview somehow more consistent with their own "habits of mind," and which they thus believe to be "better" than the community of which they are presently a part. At the same time, these individuals may feel a tremendous need to leave the community of which they are presently a part because they do not experience identity on one or more levels. Indeed, one may commit oneself intellectually or physically to an individual or community culturally dissimilar to oneself for an indefinite period of time, but one only feels oneself to be truly "at home" when one experiences sufficient levels of intellectual congruity, physical well-being, and emotional resonance with one's community that one can feel "safe" and believe the relationship to be "meaningful." As we have seen, the different musical practices undertaken by individuals in nearly all world societies serve as means by which such cultural unity can be effected.

MUSICAL SEMIOTIC: MUSIC AS A *SIGN* OF WORLDVIEW

We have seen considerable evidence from the disciplines of clinical psychiatry, ethnomusicology, and cultural anthropology to support our thesis that the personal and social value of disparate musical practices to the individual members of different cultural communities who undertake them is attributable in some measure to the capacity of these practices to unify "individual minds" with the conception of reality shared by the "collective mind" or community of which they are a part. Thus, we should not be surprised to find that the actual sounds produced in musical practices—that is, the particular "sound artifacts" or specimens of music themselves—invariably reflect the worldview of the cultural communities that produce them. Peirce's semiotic provides a means by which we can grasp how every sound artifact, or "music," can be recognized as a *sign* of a particular worldview.

In Chapter 2 we learned that Peirce believed his phenomenology to be exhaustive, that is, to account for "all that is in any way present to the mind."[94] In his scheme, anything that is registered in consciousness may be "cognized" as a Sign of Firstness (quality), Secondness (brute fact), or Thirdness (the mental aspect). He recognized that *anything* that is presented to the mind may be conceptualized in a great number of ways, but that only one aspect of a perceived Sign would be conceptualized (as an Object) according to the "habit of mind" of an individual person (or Interpretant) at a given moment. Recall anthropologist Valentine Daniel's description of this evidently multifarious nature of the sign:

> A ... sign can be likened to a jewel. ... In the experience of human interpretants, often only one facet will tilt toward the observer-interpreter, catch light, and throw it back; the other facets merely refract light. The reflecting facet, then, becomes the dominant mode. This does not, however, deny the existence of other modes of signification; modes that are sometimes expressed subjunctively and at other times remain potentialities. Different contexts help bring to light different aspects or modes of the sign.[95]

Peirce used the terms *Icon, Index*, and *Symbol* to denote the "dominant modes" by which a given Sign may refer to an Object according to the "habits of mind" of an Interpretant. Our task now is to consider some of the various ways in which different music or "sound artifacts" can be said to be iconic, indexical, and symbolic of the worldviews of the cultural communities that created them.

MUSIC AS AN *ICON* OF WORLDVIEW

According to Peirce's semiotic terminology, an *Icon* is a First: a Sign that has a qualitative similarity to its Object. In his words, "[a]nything whatever, be it quality, existent individual, or law, is an Icon of anything, in so far as it is like that thing and used as a sign of it."[96] Coming to an understanding of precisely how human musical practices and the patterned sound artifacts (or music) human beings produce while engaging in them might be said to be *iconic* of, or qualitatively comparable to, the worldview of their respective cultural communities is a daunting task, primarily because the qualities of a worldview are so much a part of—and in fact *define*—the identity of a group. The worldview of a group of people is so much a part of them that they typically assume it simply must be universal (or, when they are confronted with a conflicting worldview, they assume theirs must certainly be the best among all options). The expression "You can't talk to a fish about water" serves as a good metaphor for illustrating the difficulty any individual is likely to have in attempting to gain a perspective sufficiently detached from the worldview that he or she embodies to be able to discuss the qualities that make it unique. Since fish ostensibly cannot imagine existing in an environment in which water is not a part of what they *are*, so most human beings cannot imagine the possibility of becoming personally identified with a worldview radically different from their own. Two extended examples will serve to demonstrate just *how* the musical practices of particular cultural communities can be said to be iconic of their worldviews.

In a collaborative study on the Javanese gamelan, ethnomusicologist Judith Becker and linguist Alton Becker have provided a convincing illustration of how the musical practices of a cultural community may be conceptualized by the individuals comprising that group as being innate or "natural" because of the iconicity of these musical practices with the "coherence system" (or worldview) that organizes their thought and behavior. The Beckers observe that the most prominent, sensorially afferent, and thus psychosocially powerful attribute of the music produced by the Javanese gamelan ensemble is *cyclic coincidence*, and they assert that the gamelan's iconicity with Javanese worldview can be seen in the cyclic coincidence inherent in Javanese conceptions of *time* that are also manifested in their language and calendar system.

The Javanese language differs from English in several ways: the language is tenseless, it features reversed deixis (i.e., "here" is near the hearer, rather than the speaker), and the language lacks a copula (i.e., the verb *to be*). The Beckers note, "translating from a tenseless, hearer-centered, copulaless language (like Javanese or classical Malay) into English would *require* adding things like *tense*, English *locationals*, the copula . . . and *omitting* things like intricate interpersonal levels, particular sound symbolisms, hearer deixis, classifiers, degree of intentionality for each act, etc. as non-essential."[97] While a well-composed English text typically organizes time in terms of a narrative order, a Javanese text does not; rather, it includes "a series of overlays and simultaneous actions, in which a word has multiple and simultaneous etymologies, an event has multiple and simultaneous motives."[98]

Similarly, the organization of the Javanese calendar designates a single day according to its occurrence within a number of simultaneous cycles, each of which is of a different length. For example, the Javanese would designate a given day (in this case Wednesday, April 5, 1978), in the following way:

Rebo	=	the fourth day of a seven-day cycle
Kliwon	=	the first day of a five-day cycle
Pahang	=	the sixteenth week of a thirty-week cycle (each year has 210 days within this cycle)
Kasepuluh	=	the tenth month of a twelve-month cycle (each of the twelve months varies in length with a total of 360 days per year)
Panglong	=	the descending half of the lunar-month cycle
1910	=	linear reckoning of years according to the Caka era, a Hindu system introduced into Java in the seventh century A.D.[99]

The various days of coincidence of the calendar cycles have important cosmological and social meanings for the Javanese, and, as a result, they recognize knowledge of these meanings as a field of expertise. Almanacs called *primbon* are published to help individuals chart the course of their lives so that they may benefit from days of advantageous coincidence and avoid perilous others. In setting a wedding date, for example, a Javanese couple will typically seek the counsel of an astrologer for the purpose of finding a day with as many positively meaningful cyclic coincidences as possible. Dates of personal importance for the couple, such as birthdays, will be taken into account.

Just as the Javanese language involves simultaneous actions, etymologies, and motives, and the Javanese way of planning life events involves using the correspondences of multiple simultaneous cycles in their calendar system, the music of the gamelan derives its power from the coincidences occurring in its cyclic organization of melodies. *Gongan* is the name given to a melodic sequence that forms the basic unit of a gamelan piece. It may be repeated as many times as desired in a performance, and the gong stroke on the largest gong of the ensemble that begins a gongan sequence also serves as the last gong stroke when all cycles, or repetitions, of the sequence are complete. The *kenongan*, the primary subcycle of the gongan, is played on the horizontal pot gongs called the *kenong*, and it may be repeated two or four times per cycle, marking the halfway point or the four quarters of the cycle. In the most archaic gamelan pieces, the gongan and kenongan constitute an entire composition, but in pieces more recent and complex numerous other instruments will also play their own melodic sequences. All of the gamelan instruments must conclude (or *coincide*) at the final stroke of each cyclic repetition of the kenong, also called the *kenongan,* and they do so on the same pitch as the kenong.

The Beckers point out that the word *kenong* comes from the root *kena,* which means not only "to strike" or "to touch," but also "to coincide" or "to come together." To support their assertion of an iconic relationship between the music of the gamelan and the cosmological basis of the Javanese calendar, they offer an additional possible connection with the origin of the term:

> The word *kenong* itself may in Javanese have formerly referred to the coincidence of a particular constellation with the moon which was the beginning of the agricultural cycle. At least that is the case today in North Sumatra where the seasons are regulated by the conjunction of the constellation Scorpio with the moon and the divisions between two such encounters, called *kenong* periods.[100]

Furthermore, an Indonesian word for coincidence, *kebetulan,* and the corresponding Javanese word *kebeneran* are both derived from the root words *betul* and *bener,* each of which mean "truth" in their respective languages. The Beckers assert the importance of this point for the Javanese in the following way:

> As pitches coincide at important structural points in gamelan music, so certain days coincide to mark important moments in one's personal life. One might say that gamelan music is an idea made audible and tactile (one hears with one's skin as well as one's ears). Tonal coincidings are no more random than calendrical coincidings, but occur at the severely constrained cycle subdivisions marked by *kenong,* the word itself suggesting its musical import.[101]

Thus, for the Javanese, the aesthetic power or "naturalness" of the gamelan stems from its iconicity with their culturally unique conception of time, which is also manifested in their language.

The Beckers' illustration of how the collectively shared worldview of the Javanese is iconically manifested in their music raises the question of how the music of Western traditions might iconically embody the historically shared worldview of individuals of European and European-American descent. Although he did not use Peirce's semiotic term "icon" to describe the relationship, musicologist Christopher Small has presented a persuasive argument for just such a qualitative similarity between symphonic music and the values shared by symphony orchestra audiences in Europe and the U.S. In Small's view, symphony concerts are rituals that celebrate the "sacred history" of the Western middle classes, and, like all rituals, they represent an affirmation of faith in the values of the group "as the abiding stuff of life."[102] More specifically, Small argues that in attending a concert of symphonic music written prior to the twentieth century, individual audience members invariably, tacitly identify with the composer, participating in a "drama of the individual soul which is the symphonic work" through the medium of tonal functional harmony.

> [T]he music is highly dramatic in character, full of strong, even violent, contrasts of mood and emotion; its central technique, to which all others are subordinate, and which unifies all the music written between about 1600 and 1900, is that of tonal functional harmony, the arranging of chords in meaningful sequences by means of which the listener is led forward in time, his expectations being frustrated and teased but ultimately satisfied by the final perfect cadence in the home key (it is remarkable that there is scarcely a single piece written in the period that does not end in this fashion).[103]

Small explains that symphonic music derives its emotional value from the dramatic force of the struggle it signifies, and that it is intended to reflect a wide range of human experiences, including joy, pain, happiness in and loss of love, loyalty and treachery, heroism and patriotism—almost invariably concluding with the "triumph of the human spirit." However, he observes, in keeping with Western societal conventions that typically emphasize the importance of the minds or souls of individuals while denying the physical body, the symphonic drama is purely *abstract*, taking place solely in the minds of the participants, without their physical involvement (i.e., omitting the level of Secondness):

> To the majority of the audience the drama . . . holds no real surprises, but the excitement generated by the music seems to be no less real than if it were the very first time that the work had been played. Because of the abstract nature of the music [the audience] is not permitted to give physical expression to that excitement during the performance, and the whole response to the drama must be bottled up until the end, when it is likely to explode with a lack of moderation that would sometimes put a football crowd to shame.[104]

Thus, in Small's interpretation, a symphony concert is best regarded as a ritual in which the audience individually and collectively celebrates the autonomy and solitude of the individual's successful life struggle in Western society.

On the basis of the Beckers' demonstration of iconicity between the music of the gamelan and the language structure of the Javanese, we can infer that the dramatic progression Small recognizes as being the essential basis of Western "tonal functional harmony" might in fact be an iconic manifestation of the organization of *time* inherent in English and other European languages, particularly the subject/predicate syntactical form at the root of these languages and the sequential, temporal order of narrative inherent in them. Unlike the tenseless Javanese language, which, as we noted earlier, lacks the copula (the verb *to be*), the English language centrally involves verb tenses, allowing a speaker or writer to account in linear discourse for her or his progression between different physical and mental "states" at different times.

Furthermore, while Small does not draw the connection, the struggle and ultimate "apotheosis of the soul" he identified as characteristic of symphonic music can also be iconically associated with the life struggle depicted for all humankind in the conceptions of both Judaism and Christianity, the historically related, dominant religions of Europe and the U.S. Jews hold as a central tenet of their religion that their God judges them on the basis of their personal works. This is evident throughout their sacred texts; in the Psalms, for example, David sings, " . . . [S]teadfast love belongs to you, O Lord. For you repay to all according to their work."[105] Similarly, most Christians believe that by keeping faith in Christ throughout the struggles of their lives on earth they will eventually be personally delivered into a heavenly, eternal life with God after death. The Christian apostle Paul expressed this doctrine in the book of Romans as follows:

> Therefore, since we are justified by faith, we have peace with God through our Lord Jesus Christ, through whom we have obtained access to this grace in which we stand; and we boast in our hope of sharing the glory of God. And not only that, but we also boast in our sufferings, knowing that suffering produces endurance, and endurance produces character, and character produces hope, and hope does not disappoint us, because God's love has been poured into our hearts through the Holy Spirit that has been given to us.[106]

Paul's words underscore the centrality of the struggle to each Christian's life, as well as the ultimately redeeming glory that is believed to lie at the end of such a life. Small's description of the music of the West, which derives its dramatic import from the struggle depicted via the "tonal functional harmony" upon which it is based, seems strongly suggestive of the idea that symphonic music iconically manifests this promise for the Western listener. Given the close relationship between the history of Western music and the history of the Christian church, it stands to reason that this aspect of symphonic music would most likely seem "natural" to the majority of Europeans and European-Americans who tacitly embody Jewish and Christian worldviews.

In addition, Small's writings suggest that, like music itself, a musical *ensemble* may also iconically manifest the worldview of the cultural community from which it stems. The symphony orchestra emerged as the predominant European musical ensemble of Europe in the years leading up to the industrial revolution of the eighteenth and nineteenth centuries, a time during which a substantial part of the populace gradually gave up their live-lihoods as farmers, merchants, and craftsmen to take jobs in the new "man-ufactories"; Small has likened the symphony orchestra to an "industrial enterprise." His comparison illuminates points of remarkable qualitative likeness (i.e., iconicity) between the orchestral ensemble and the emerging industrial worldview of the society within which it developed:

> The modern professional symphony orchestra is the very model of an industrial enterprise, a highly efficient body permeated through and through with the industrial philosophy, directed like all industrial en-terprises towards the making of a product, namely a performance. Its social relations are those of the industrial workplace, being entirely functional and depending only upon the job to be done; players may know and care nothing about colleagues' lives apart from the job, and if, as in other jobs, friendships do develop, these are irrelevant to the task to be performed. The written notes control the actions of the players and mediate their relationship. As in any other job, too, the rank and file are rarely consulted about the nature of the product to be made, but are required simply to play whatever notes are set be-fore them, under the direction of as dynamic a managerial type as it is possible to engage. Time is money; the workers are highly unionized and generally unwilling to work extra time without extra pay, while the foreman (known as the leader) acts as middleman between rank and file and higher management. There is a distinct social hierarchy within the organization, with the string players accorded the highest status (white-collar, one might almost say), the brass and percussion having on the other hand a distinct blue-collar image, being generally regarded as jolly fellows, not over-sensitive and given to the consump-tion of large quantities of beer.[107]

Given the implications of Small's analysis, that symphony concerts are ritu-als that iconically manifest the Western, Judeo-Christian, industrial world-view, it does not seem surprising that a large number of leadership positions on the governing boards of symphony orchestras in the U.S. are presently held by the chief executive officers of major corporations or their spouses.

It seems important to note, before leaving our discussion of how music can be understood as iconically embodying the worldview of a community, that as we have noted the most highly visible and uniquely American musi-cal ensemble at present is the rock band. Perhaps it is only "natural" that the ritualized musical practices of a nation whose collective worldview is so consistently changing (insofar as it can be determined at all) and which is often recognized internationally by the "rugged" personal individualism and political skepticism of many of its citizens would be produced by a variety of small, individually unconventional musical ensembles of dissent-ing voices accompanying themselves with societally obstreperous sounds.

Indeed, most every "cutting edge" rock musician in the U.S. views herself or himself as something like a shaman.

MUSIC AS AN *INDEX* OF WORLDVIEW

The ways in which a given sound artifact or music is indexically connected with the worldview of the cultural community from which it stems are more overt and thus less difficult to conceptualize than the ways in which music iconically embodies worldview. In Peirce's semiotic terminology, an *Index*, as a Second, is a sign that is somehow in contiguous, physical relationship with its Object. In his words, it is "really affected" by that Object.[108] Of course, the most obvious sense in which music is indexical of (or connected with) worldview is that the sounds produced in musical practices normally emanate from persons who embody that worldview. Also, we should note that the most radical sense in which a musical practice indexes individuals and the worldview of their group is that which was provided by d'Aquili, Laughlin, and the other theorists in their descriptions of the ways in which communities are psychophysiologically unified with their collective worldview through collective participation. However, we are interested here in noting other important ways in which a sound artifact or music itself, rather than a musical practice, can be understood as being indexically related to the worldview of a given cultural community.

In the previous chapter we noted that one major point of agreement between the perspectives of Boas and Peirce was their recognition that the worldview of every cultural community is largely, if not entirely, an outgrowth of the group's collectively shared environment and common history. That is, the "habits of mind" shared by the members of a given cultural community are inevitably rooted in the coping actions developed and acquired throughout the struggles of their collective history. Likewise, the sounds produced in a musical practice by the members of a particular cultural community invariably stem from the indexical or *physical* relationship they have had to their environment in their present and past history. In fact, music is invariably indexical of the historical, physical environment and the adaptive "habits of mind" of a cultural community in both obvious and subtle ways.

It is perhaps obvious that prior to the emergence of global trade before the Middle Ages, the members of all cultural communities made their instruments from materials they found available in their physical environment. Thus the sounds of their instruments were originally, necessarily connected with their respective physical environments. For example, the *keren* and the *shofar*, the trumpet-like instruments used by the nomadic shepherd Jews of the Old Testament on solemn occasions and for military purposes, were made from the horns of the sheep they raised for their livelihood;[109] these instruments are still in use in Jewish temples today. Steven Feld, whose research we explored earlier, has mentioned that the *sob*, a rattle used by the Kaluli people in the performance of their *gisalo* ceremonies, is made from mussel shells they have gathered in their native habitat.[110] While it might be difficult to determine the precise nature of the original, physical relationship between the instruments (with their attendant sounds) and the environments of all cultural communities from whence stemmed their unique worldviews, it must be acknowledged that such an indexical association inevitably exists. One makes music with the materials one has available to produce it.[111]

Perhaps equally obvious is the notion that the musical instruments of every cultural community have necessarily stemmed from the technological knowledge that each group has developed over time or has acquired from other cultural communities they have encountered in their historical past. For example, the production of early metal instruments (forerunners of the modern brass family) would not have been possible for any group that had not developed or acquired from others the technology for refining and forming metal. Thus, the sounds of such instruments were not available to groups lacking this technology. A good example involving a more recently developed music was provided by critic Jon Parales, who observed that *rap* originated in the "poverty, violence, lack of education, frustration and rage of the ghetto" where young people who couldn't afford musical instruments or lessons and who weren't receiving music education in the schools created their own music with the record turntables and old records they had available. They utilized the turntables and the previously recorded music as a foundation for their own rhythmic, verbal innovations, thereby "changing the passive act of playing records into the active creation of new songs."[112] Again, such a relationship invariably exists between the technology required for the creation of instruments of all cultural communities and their respective worldviews.

It seems less obvious, however, that in undertaking the prolonged, habitual practice necessary to learn to produce the musical sounds traditionally created and valued by a given cultural community, human beings must actually form some of the physical characteristics of their bodies to match an established, culturally unique norm. Clearly, the voice of an Italian opera singer has invariably been trained or "cultivated" to become something quite different from that which a Native American would want to hear in a powwow or a Tibetan monk would find suitable for meditational chanting. Through continued musical involvement with the traditions of one cultural community, human bodies gradually and invariably come to manifest certain physical aspects characteristic of other persons (particularly other musicians) embodying one worldview and not another. The same can be said of the neural connections in the human brain ("habits of mind") that are formed during repeated musical practice.

Yoshiaki Kikuchi has brought to light another, less obvious and perhaps more psychophysically essential sense in which music might be said to be indexical of worldview. In a 1985 study, Kikuchi used the technology of brain-wave topography to demonstrate visibly that the distribution of electrical potentials generated by certain types of auditory stimuli (such as violin and flute sounds) are distributed differently between the two hemispheres of the human brain in European-American versus Japanese listeners, although it is generally consistent within each of these groups. His study helped to confirm the findings of earlier studies by Tadanobu Tsunoda, which had also suggested differences in hemispheric dominance patterns between Westerners and Japanese persons in the aural perception of various sounds. These studies suggest by extension that the cultural differences manifested in culturally unique musical practices might be said to stem from differences in the neural formations of culturally different human brains.[113] Most importantly, these studies provide evidence to support further Peirce's tenet of synechism, specifically the interconnection of mental phenomena or minds (Thirds) with physical phenomena (such as cultural products) and brains (Seconds).

MUSIC AS A *SYMBOL* OF WORLDVIEW

In Peirce's conception, a *Symbol*, as a Third, is associated with its Object primarily by social convention or habit. In his words, "a Symbol is a Sign which refers to the Object that it denotes by virtue of a law, usually an association of general ideas, which operates to cause the Symbol to be interpreted as referring to that Object."[114] One example of a Symbol is an individual's *name*. In most cases, a personal name (as a Sign) has neither an iconic (or qualitative) relationship nor an inherent indexical (or physical) connection with the physical *person* (as the Object) who bears it; the name is, rather, associated with that individual by virtue of the social agreement (or "law") established by her *family or larger community* (as the Interpretant) that she should be called by that name.[115] Similarly, there is no readily evident iconic or indexical association between an eight-sided, red-and-white *piece of metal* on a post (as a Sign) and the *requirement to stop* one's automobile (as an Object); instead, the sign (and the word "Stop" printed on it) are only conventionally or symbolically associated with the legal mandate established and shared by the *community* (as the Interpretant) to preserve safety and order. Incidentally, this explanation should make it clear that individual *words* are among the best examples of symbols, as most words (other than those that are onomatopoeic) are associated with the objects they denote primarily by social convention.

Cultural communities vary widely in the ways they experience their own musical practices, and some of the differences can be accounted for by the relative degree of emphasis they place on symbolic aspects. People participating in musical practices that we might call primarily *meditative* in intent (such as the chanting of various declared "religious" traditions) tend to place greater emphasis on those aspects of their practice that iconically manifest and indexically connect them with the collectively shared world-view of their communities. Indeed, communities that undertake medita-tive musical practices generally do so with the primary, conscious intent of effecting psychosocial reconciliation within their communities. Musical practices of meditation tend to be highly repetitive, and the sounds incorpo-rated in them frequently stem directly from the aural environment of which the community is a part, thus reconciling them to the environment.[116] By contrast, people participating in those musical practices that we might call more *communicative* in intent (such as those associated with much of the popular music of the U.S.) tend to place greater emphasis on the symbolic communication that takes place within or along with them. In such circum-stances, the symbolic aspect of the musical practice is often the aspect of the music that is given the greatest conscious attention by the community; the iconic and indexical realms, while still inherent in the practice, tend to be less emphasized and, in some cases, go unrecognized.

Of course, much *vocal* music reflects symbolically the worldview of the group from which it stems owing to its inclusion of a text set in the lan-guage of that community. It seems quite apparent that a German art song, an Irish folk song, or a Mexican pop song will carry its full symbolic mean-ing only for those who are capable of understanding the language in which it is set. A listener or participant who does not understand the language cannot fully participate in the performance, since he or she is not able to understand fully what is being communicated as the community is collec-tively unified in the musical practice.

While we can readily recognize that the words (i.e., linguistic symbols) that are used in a particular cultural community's musical practice are associated by convention with their worldview, the ways in which a musi-cal practice itself may carry symbolic meaning in ways unique to a par-ticular worldview are more germane to our present discussion. We will explore two examples. The reader will note that in both cases, the symbols included in the musical practice that are unique to the tradition under dis-cussion necessarily carry meaning in their original sense only for those persons (embodied Interpretants) who have had sufficient experience with the conventions of that tradition to have grasped all or most of the possible referents (or Objects) that the music (as a Symbol) might signify.

First, within European and American traditions, the sound of a "IV–I" or "plagal" cadence, performed with appropriate voicing and tempo and placed in an appropriate context, typically evokes for a large number of European and American listeners the "Amen" ending conventionally sung and played to conclude the sacred hymns of Christianity, and it thus can be included in a musical composition to symbolize that worldview for listeners familiar with that tradition. Listeners who will find this sequence of sounds meaningful in this way are likely to have attended or at least experienced parts of a Chris-tian service of worship; thus they will recognize the indexical connection between the music and Christian worldview. When a "IV–I" cadence is used symbolically in a new composition with either ironic intent (as a "religious" cliché) or serious intent (to evoke in the listener the reverential response associated with an "Amen"), it has the effect of symbolizing "Christian worship" for those listeners (as embodied Interpretants) who have sufficient knowledge (Thirdness) of that tradition to recognize it as a symbol. For a listener outside the European and American social forum who has not had such experience, such a cadence would be heard as "just another series of sounds" (and therefore not be particularly meaningful) or it might be tacitly assigned a new meaning consistent with the perceiver's cultural background.[117]

Similarly, the sounds of music played in a certain way on the *shakuhachi*, the bamboo flute that originated in China, may evoke specific intracultural meanings for persons familiar with the history of the instrument. During the Edo period of Japan's history (1603–1868), the Zen Buddhist monks known as *komusô* use the *shakuhachi* as a *hoki* or "spiritual tool" for attaining enlightenment. While the *shakuhachi* has since been used in Japan in a number of ways, including Western-influenced contemporary compositions, certain sounds produced on the instrument, particularly those using the method of breathing employed when the instrument is being used as a *hoki*, have the effect of evoking in a knowledgeable listener the instrument's association with Zen. In both of the preceding cases, the Christian "Amen" cadence and the Zen Buddhist approach to breathing in *shakuhachi* performance, the sounds produced in the musical practice in question are recognizable and thus meaningful as symbols only to those who are familiar with the conventions unique to that community's worldview.

It is important to realize that many contemporary composers of Western music often "borrow" the sounds of the music of different cultural communities and use them in their works as symbols to represent these groups aurally. For example, composers writing accompaniment scores for film and television productions often "set the stage" aurally for dramatic action ostensibly taking place somewhere in Asia by utilizing a certain pentatonic scale as the basis for their melodic composition of the music that accompanies the scene. Since much of the music of China, Japan, and other Asian countries has historically utilized such scales—and much of the American public is able to recognize this aurally—the composer is able to use these scales to evoke symbolically mental associations of such cultural settings in the listener. Art music composers, too, regularly use iconic imitation or "borrowing" of the timbres and patterns of the Balinese gamelan or an Indian *raga* to symbolically evoke such cultural associations for their listeners.

Earlier in this chapter we noted Morgan and Brask's observation that theatrical performance is not bound to a particular worldview but rather has the innovative capacity to incorporate different cultural views into its structure, giving them a "voice" in the drama. However, they noted, theatre does have the important, socially educative effect of communicating that the worldview that supports the authority structure of the state is indeed a fair representation of how things "are" and how they "ought" to be. We can now see that some instances of more highly communicative musical practices (such as film scores and art music) are much like theatre in that they too are capable of including the differing musical practices of different communities as voices in the "social drama" they manifest. However, those musical "dramas" of U.S. and European composers that are formally grounded—and reach their conclusions—in Western tonal functional harmony may ultimately have the effect of validating the Judeo-Christian, industrial worldview of the composer as how things "really are," and they may thus be regarded by some listeners as disparaging the other worldviews they symbolically include.

The liberties composers of film scores and art music take with symbolically representing the worldviews of different cultures in their music has likely contributed to the view shared by many citizens of the Europe and U.S. that all music is *merely* symbolic and is thus not a highly consequential part of human life. However, musical practices and music should never be regarded as "merely" symbolic. The personal, social, and political importance of musical practices and music become most evident in those volatile situations when the iconic and indexical relationships between music and worldview are brought to consciousness.

MUSIC MISTAKEN FOR A *MERE* SYMBOL

Perhaps the most famous story in the annals of Western music of a "clash of worldviews" stemming from the error of conceptualizing a musical practice as "merely" symbolic concerns the premiere performance of Igor Stravinsky's *Rite of Spring* in 1913. Following on the success of two of his compositions staged as ballets, *The Firebird* (1910) and *Petrushka* (1911), the young Russian composer Igor Stravinsky was commissioned by the impresario Sergei Diaghilev to compose a new work for the Ballets Russes of Paris. The Paris audience had a particularly high regard for Stravinsky's work at that time, perhaps since French society was then taken with exoticism (the practice of reaching out to foreign cultures for artistic inspiration) and Stravinsky was incorporating Russian folk themes while continuing to embrace many nineteenth-century, central European musical traditions in his work. Meanwhile, the Russian artistic community (including Stravinsky) was fascinated with exploring primitivist art, primarily influenced by recent research into early icon painting and other areas of folk art. Through Diaghilev, Stravinsky met Nicholas Roerich, an artist, amateur archaeologist, and theatrical set designer with considerable knowledge of various types of preliterate Russian theater. Roerich and Stravinsky explored pagan rituals, village weddings, minstrel animal impersonations, and peasant stories before finally collaborating on the new ballet, the *Rite of Spring: Scenes of Pagan Russia,* a work with no plot, comprised only of a "ritual" celebration of spring and the sacrifice of a virgin.

In composing music for the *Rite*, Stravinsky continued his use of diatonic Russian folk melodies and late-romantic chromaticism, but he also dramatically extended his previous melodic and harmonic innovations, inventing new orchestrational and rhythmic techniques that seemed to contribute to the "primitive" theme. Roerich fashioned the costumes and sets, which were simple and crude in comparison with any contemporaneous designs, and Nijinsky choreographed the ballet, using angular, aggressive movements and gestures.

The *Rite of Spring* premiered in the Theatre des Champs-Elysees, Paris, on May 29, 1913. The audience's violent reaction to the performance has become legendary. They whistled, stamped their feet, and, upon leaving the theatre before the conclusion of the ballet, honked their automobile horns continuously. Stravinsky fled the theatre in confusion: "I knew the music so well and it was so dear to me that I couldn't understand why people were protesting against it prematurely without even hearing it through."[118] According to Stravinsky's later description, " . . . Diaghilev's only comment was: 'Exactly what I wanted.'"[119]

It seems evident that the violent reaction accorded the *Rite* in its first performance stemmed from its failure to provide the audience with the experience of "Firstness" they had come to expect from a night at the ballet. Instead, it must have seemed to the audience as if Stravinsky was introducing into the ballet—as their sacred ritual—the sounds of an opposing tradition, and thus mocking or desecrating their own. In semiotic terms, the *Rite*'s dissimilarity with previous works (i.e., other ballets by Stravinsky and others) had the effect of forcing the audience to perceive it only on the level of Secondness. That is, as they were unable to relate to the ballet affectively according to the mental habits of their own musical meaning systems (Thirdness), members of the audience were forced to sit and listen only to brute sound, the "facticity" of the work. Stravinsky's abrasive and percussive use of unfamiliar timbres, the employment of irregular rhythms, the uncharacteristic sets, costumes, mode of dance, and the lack of plot evidently placed the work too far beyond the audience's worldview for them to apprehend it rationally. To some members of the audience, the *Rite* must have sounded like noise—a violent desecration of their tradition—but to those who were familiar with the Russian primitivist movement, the work probably seemed to threaten their musical and artistic convention with replacement by another; thus they likely felt that their worldview was being challenged. The events of the premiere performance can thus be best understood as a collision of two worldviews, one of which was incapable of meaningfully grasping the other: one, that of the French, late-romantic exoticists (the audience), and the other, that of Stravinsky and the Russian primitivists. Reportedly, similarly violent reactions were provoked by the premieres of Hugo's *Hernani* in 1830, Wagner's *Lohengrin* in 1887, and Debussy's *Pelleas et Melisande* in 1913 for reasons also related to cultural difference.[120]

A highly visible result of cultural conflict stemming from the error of conceptualizing music as being "merely" symbolic and ignoring its iconic and indexical association with the worldview of a particular cultural community was the public outcry that ensued in Israel in late 1991, when the Israel Philharmonic Orchestra announced plans to perform a program featuring works by the nineteenth-century German composer Richard Wagner.[121] Wagner was the favorite composer of the notorious German leader Adolf Hitler, mentioned earlier, who is known to have condemned approximately six million Jews to death in the Holocaust of World War II. Although Wagner died in 1883, fifty years before Hitler rose to power, many Jews associate Wagner's music with the Nazi regime, not only because of Hitler's affinity for it but also because of the composer's anti-Semitism and the similarity of certain aspects of the mythology idealized in some of his operas with social ideals held by the Nazis (e.g., the notion of a "superior race"). Israel is a largely Jewish state, and, in 1991, Holocaust survivors represented 6 percent of its population; thus it does not seem surprising that these individuals and their families, friends, and religious organizations would react negatively and passionately to their national orchestra's programming of Wagner's music.

The fact that some U.S. citizens do recognize on some level the inherently iconic and indexically powerful nature of musical practice becomes most evident on those occasions when music is utilized for culturally associational, psychological effect. Notably, music has been used in this way for both positive and negative purposes. For example, the advertising industry of the U.S. customarily utilizes the music of particular segments of the population as a symbol for its positive, iconic, and indexical associational effect. Advertisers routinely select music for radio and television commercials on the basis of what they recognize as a symbolic association between the type of music and a given product for the particular segment of the populace they believe likely to purchase it. "Classical" or symphonic art music is often used in advertisements for items accessible to wealthy individuals (such as diamonds, wines, and luxury cars), while "rock and roll" more typically underlies advertisements for products of greater interest to the middle classes (such as fast food, beer, and pickup trucks). The assumption is, of course, that those who are members of the group to which the advertisement is designed to appeal (i.e., middle-class vs. upper-class buyers) will be enticed to buy the product because it reinforces their unity with the group to which they conceive themselves as belonging. Given the ubiquity of this practice, one could almost guess that it has been shown statistically to be effective.[122]

Conversely, the U.S. military has used music for its negative, iconic, and indexical associational effect. During the Gulf War of 1991, the U.S. Marine Corps broadcast American heavy metal rock and roll through concert-sized speakers at Iraqi troops fighting on the Kuwaiti border as part of a psychological warfare campaign. These musical assaults were interspersed with Arabic-language messages encouraging the Iraqis to surrender, for the expressed purpose of undermining Iraqi morale and encouraging defections.[123] As Iraq is an Islamic country, and, as noted above, some Islamic groups prohibit music making on the basis of what they hold to be its sinful nature, this effort quite likely had a powerfully unnerving effect on the Iraqis. Notably, during the same war, U.S. pilots reportedly also used American rock and roll for its positive, culturally associational effect to boost their own morale during bombing missions.[124]

In this chapter, we have explored perspectives from a great number of fields of inquiry to demonstrate how different, historical musical practices can be understood as inherently culturally rooted behaviors, each valued intraculturally for its psychophysiologically, psychosocially, and sociopolitically equilibrating effects. We have seen how particular instances of music, as sound artifacts produced in culture-specific musical practices, can be understood or "read" as *signs* of the individuals or communities with which they originated. In the next chapter we will turn our attention to considering the factors that have contributed historically to obscuring the socially important and thus politically charged nature of different cultural forms of music in the public forum of the U.S. With this foundation, we will be ready to consider in Chapter 5 the rationales that have been proffered for the inclusion of music education in the public schools of the U.S. over the history of the nation.

4 Conceptions of Music in the United States

> The condition upon which God hath given liberty to man is eternal vigilance; which condition if he break, servitude is at once the consequence of his crime and the punishment of his guilt.[1]
>
> John Philpot Curran

In the previous chapter we explored the ethnocentric, universalizing, and relativizing conceptions of music that have been held in the Western academic forum during the nineteenth and twentieth centuries and then demonstrated that a Peircian pragmatic conception of musical practices as *a diverse cluster of culturally relative, psychosocially equilibrating behaviors* both embraces and reconciles certain dilemmas to which each of these other conceptions gives rise. We saw that this Peircian pragmatic conception is supported by scholarship in clinical psychiatry, ethnomusicology, and cultural anthropology. In addition, we observed that, in traditional societies, a musical practice undertaken collectively by the members of the community has the effect of unifying them psychosocially and concomitantly validating their religious worldview and that, in many culturally pluralistic, state societies, a central form of musical practice is tacitly valued by citizens and supported by the state's leaders for its validation of the worldview they regard as being most amenable to the state's continued stability. Finally, we further substantiated our pragmatic conception of musical practice by demonstrating how any instance of music—as a sound artifact—can be heard as a multidimensional *sign* of the culturally distinctive worldview of the community with which it originated.

While persons living in most traditional societies and some culturally pluralistic state societies tacitly recognize and value most highly a societally central musical practice for its psychosocially equilibrating effects (which each community characteristically describes using a vocabulary unique to its own worldview), this is not necessarily the case for persons living in the United States, a culturally pluralistic nation founded on philosophical precepts that differ from those of other world societies formed prior to the eighteenth century.[2] The nation's orientation toward principles of democracy, scientific progress, and capitalist economics have afforded citizens a level of personal freedom, a degree of technological facility, and an economic standard of living largely unequaled in recorded history. However, these orienting principles have also had the effect of obscuring citizens' collective awareness of the important psychosocially equilibrating and identity validating effects the different musical practices alive in the nation have had for the health of the nation; in addition, they have diminished citizens' recognition of their political significance. Furthermore, since the founding of the U.S., many other world nations have come to emulate in varying degrees the form of government and the guiding principles upon which the U.S. was based, some of them motivated by political pressure stemming from the comparatively great benefits the nation has provided its citizens.[3] As a result, conceptions of music and musical practices have undergone— and are continuing to undergo—similar changes in these nations.

Our task now is to briefly explore certain social circumstances pertaining to the origin of the U.S. in order to understand how the philosophical precepts upon which the nation was established and certain historical consequences of their adoption have led to the present state of affairs. While the historical foundation of our account will likely be familiar to many readers, our Peircian pragmatic focus will serve to illuminate effects these events have had on citizens' conceptions of music that may not have been evident previously. Later, in Chapter 5, we will explore ways these changes in conceptions have been reflected in rationales given by music educators for the inclusion of music education in the public schools.

WELLSPRINGS OF UNITED STATES SOCIETY IN THE EUROPEAN ENLIGHTENMENT

As we noted briefly at the beginning of this inquiry, the U.S. was formed as a nation during the period of European history that historians now call the "Enlightenment" era of the late seventeenth and eighteenth centuries, an epoch marked by tumultuous changes in all aspects of human life. The Enlightenment began as an intellectual movement in France involving the synthesis of certain ideas about God, reason, nature, and the human being into a new, more broadly inclusive worldview. This worldview emphasized above all the application of human reason (rather than religious revelation) to understanding the universe and to improving the human condition. The change in thinking that characterized this time is thought by many scholars to have had its origins in the European "Renaissance" era of the fourteenth through sixteenth centuries, as it drew much of its power from the humanistic, secular bent of many of that period's greatest achievements. However, the possibility of a humanist worldview grounded in reason became even more feasible during the sixteenth century, after the German priest Martin Luther began applying methods of reason to Christian theology, challenging the authority of church leaders (including the pope) and setting off a corresponding religious and political rebellion. This rebellion, soon joined from other quarters, led to the formation of the "Protestant" churches, and it served to seriously undermine the political and intellectual authority of the previously all-powerful Roman Catholic Church over many Europeans. In the following century, the success of scientific experimentation by such pioneers as Francis Bacon, Galileo Galilei, Nicolaus Copernicus, and Isaac Newton strongly confirmed the power of human reason, and their discoveries eventually came to be interpreted widely as suggesting that the universe might well be better regarded as a mechanism that operated by discernible laws rather than as a mysterious physical manifestation of a "spiritual" domain. Their efforts had the effect of further subverting the church's power and authority by raising doubts about its long-held concepts of a personal God and individual salvation, thus all but confirming the era as the "age of reason."

During the years leading up to the eighteenth century, small European communities gradually came together to assume the form of what has been termed state societies, though many still reflected their traditional roots. Many were governed by kings like Louis XIV of France and James II of England, both of whom legitimized their rule as a "divine right," stemming from God. This arrangement reflected earlier, still enduring feudal conceptions of the state as an earthly approximation of the eternal city of heaven. However, as the position of the church as the supreme political authority was weakened and confidence in human reason was strengthened, a new interest in the sphere of political philosophy began to emerge. Thus, such thinkers as Thomas Hobbes, John Locke, and Jean-Jacques Rousseau were emboldened to criticize existing authoritarian forms of society and to propose new forms of government based on a reasoned understanding of human social behavior.

Each of these philosophers contributed something important to the formation of modern democratic theory, and each can be said to have based his conceptions on what he believed to be the "natural rights" of human beings. Perhaps the most central conception to emerge from these scholars' efforts was the notion that a society could be based upon a social contract: a collective agreement instituted by the members of a community to create a system of government to which all could consent. English scholar Hobbes's main contribution, proffered in his work *Leviathan* of 1651, was the view that political power actually rests in the people—in accordance with natural laws derived from the basic one of self-preservation—rather than in God. Pessimistically, he held the opinion that societal rule alienated to a sovereign would probably always be necessary to restrain human evil. Most significantly, his writings divorced the state from any "ultimate" external source of morality, such as a particular conception of God. By contrast, English philosopher Locke's *Essay Concerning Human Understanding* and his *Essays on Civil Government*, both written in 1690, described a society in which government would serve as an agency for the dispensation of justice among the people. Locke's more optimistic opinion of humanity led him to believe that the sole purpose of government should be to support the rights of the individual, as the evils of a corrupt society might otherwise corrupt the minds of the people. French writer Rousseau described his ideal state in *The Social Contract* of 1762, portraying a society in which each person would be directed by the collective, "general will" of the full "organism" of society. He conceptualized this general will as a combination of the wills of all of the persons comprising the society. Recognizing the human tendency to find comfort in autocratic systems of government, Rousseau went so far as to assert that the democratic society he envisioned might entail the additional responsibility of compelling its citizens to exercise their liberty. In his words, "[W]hoever refuses to obey the general will shall be constrained by the whole body [of his fellow citizens] to do so; which means nothing else than that he shall be forced to be free. . . ."[4]

While many Europeans of the time doubted that democracy could work as a system of government, others went on to explore its possible implications in other realms of life. In his monumental treatise of 1776, *An Inquiry into the Nature and Causes of the Wealth of Nations*, the Scottish political economist Adam Smith presented his case that the collective good of a society would be best served when individuals were allowed to work to serve their own self-interest, thus pioneering the modern field of economics and laying the theoretical foundations for capitalism. While he recognized that some legal and moral restrictions would likely be necessary in such a free society, Smith strongly advocated a *laissez-faire* economy, believing that free trade would stimulate production and thus best serve a society's interests overall. Smith's ideas bore a great influence in Europe, where they strikingly addressed arising issues of industrialization. At that time a large majority of the populace were leaving their livelihoods as farmers, merchants, and craftsmen to take new positions in the various emerging large-scale industries, which were applying new technologies to the mass production of goods.

As is well known to students of the history of Western civilization, these profound transformations in the intellectual, political, and economic spheres of life in Europe during the years leading up to the full-scale Enlightenment directly influenced the formation of the U.S. as a democratic capitalist nation. Less widely understood, however, is the tremendous impact these changes had not only on the social conventions and circumstances involving musical practices in European society thereafter, but also on the ways in which music generally came to be conceptualized in the eighteenth century. Since the U.S. was established as a nation at that time, these events contributed directly to determining the ways in which music was to be conceptualized in the new nation's public forum. Accordingly, we now turn our attention to understanding the effects of these events on conceptions of music in Europe and the U.S.

SOCIAL FACTORS EFFECTING CHANGES IN CONCEPTIONS OF MUSIC IN EUROPE DURING THE YEARS LEADING TO THE ENLIGHTENMENT

Most of the different musical practices undertaken in Europe prior to the eighteenth century that were societally sanctioned for their psychosocially equilibrating and culturally integrative effects on large numbers of people took place in the churches and under the patronage of the ruling royal families.[5] As the small city-states of Europe were gradually brought together under monarchical governments in the years leading to the seventeenth century, the royal courts typically sponsored musicians to support worship in their own chapels as well as for their own courtly events, and most of their musical practices were undertaken for purposes of religious worship. A majority of the musicians of this era, including such well-known composers as Georg Philipp Telemann, Antonio Vivaldi, and Johann Sebastian Bach, all made their livelihoods largely if not entirely in the service of churches or of wealthy patrons associated with the ruling aristocracies. From the Peircian pragmatic perspective we established in the last chapter, we can see that European nations of the eighteenth century were in various states of evolution during this time, moving from what we have identified as traditional societies to culturally pluralistic, state societies.

Notably, opera also emerged as a new musical form in the courts during the years leading up to the Enlightenment, and by the 1630s opera performances were beginning to be presented for profit in public opera houses. As we noted in Chapter 3, opera served European society as a musical form of theatre, providing a social medium for reconciling the views of the culturally diverse groups that made up the society, a practice separate from existing religious and state institutions. Thus, we should not be surprised to discover that the first such public opera house, in Venice, was underwritten by members of the nobility, as were all subsequent houses, assuring that the culturally reconciling effects of this new musical form would be in accord with the worldview sanctioned by the state.[6] However, in the years following the emergence of opera, George Frideric Handel and various other composers began presenting performances of oratorios, concertos, and other secular works to large audiences for profit independent of both church and court. The introduction of these large-scale "entertainments" had the effect of weakening, in some measure, the conceptual connection between certain musical practices, church, and state among Europeans, fostering the notion that such musical practices could be societally acceptable as well as economically and politically "free." Nevertheless, most of the musical practices that were regarded by the populace as being of substantive societal significance continued to be those that were undertaken in the churches and under the auspices of the royal courts.

Perhaps not surprisingly, the introduction of large-scale, secular entertainment pieces stimulated some resistance among devoutly religious persons who were accustomed to long-standing Christian religious conceptions of music. Handel himself received particularly harsh criticism for using biblical stories and texts as the bases of his secular entertainment pieces. The London *Universal Spectator* published a protest prior to the first performance of his 1741 oratorio *Messiah* from a reader who, despite his admiration of Handel's music in general, objected to his having created and presented a secular entertainment piece on the most sacred of Biblical stories.

> How will this appear to After-Ages, when it shall be read in History, that in such an Age the People of England were arriv'd to such a Height of Impiety and Prophaneness, that the most sacred Things were suffer'd to be us'd as publick Diversions, and that in a Place, and by Persons, appropriated to the Performance not only of light and vain, but too often prophane and dissolute pieces?[7]

While other examples could be cited, this statement serves as a particularly good illustration of the disquieting effect the presentation of large-scale musical entertainments had on religious sensibilities in England in 1741, particularly concerning the reception of musical pieces on religious themes as mere "entertainments."

The practices of writing, printing, and marketing written scores of music also emerged gradually during the centuries leading up to the Enlightenment, facilitating the shift of focus in European society away from notions of musical engagement as psychosocially equilibrating (or "spiritual") behavior and toward concepts of music as a material object or commodity. As is well known, the historical precursors of the modern system of Western musical notation originated in the monasteries of the ninth century, where they were developed for the purpose of recording and standardizing the melodies of liturgical chant. The resulting scores were used exclusively in the "spiritual" service of worship, as was the case with all music of the church composed up to the sixteenth century. However, the introduction of a method by which the sounds produced in musical practices could be transcribed onto paper also marked the first time in European history that music could be considered as a physical object, thus paving the way for later conceptions of it as a salable commodity. When Franco of Cologne systematized mensural notation (i.e., musical notation that precisely represents the relative duration of tones) in the early thirteenth century, he did so for the purpose of facilitating the performance of polyphonic, polyrhythmic forms of music. At the same time, his efforts contributed to transforming the societal conception of the composer. Whereas previously composers had been primarily performing musicians, they were thenceforth regarded as something more like intellectual craftspersons who created "works"—musical objects—while laboring at a desk.

The development of printing technology contributed to the reifying conceptual shift as well. Music publishing was established in France near the turn of the sixteenth century, and by 1527 the French *Parlement* had accorded publishers exclusive rights over the reproduction and sale of scores. Copyists, who had held a monopoly over the reproduction of all musical manuscripts throughout the middle ages and the early Renaissance, were successful in opposing printing for a time, but by the mid-seventeenth century, when public concerts separate from church and court were fairly commonplace, music publishing was well established as a profitable business. Publishers held the rights to the reproduction of scores until 1786, when the French *Conseil du Roi* instituted the first copyright law, marking the first time in European history that composers had control over the production and sale of their works in multiple copies. This event, and similar events occurring in other nations, seated yet more firmly in the "collective mind" of eighteenth century European society a concept of music as an object: a marketable commodity created by a composer.

The emergence of music publishing and copyright are indicative of the widespread social changes unfolding in Western Europe during the eighteenth century, leading directly to the industrialization of European society. Various scholars have observed that wherever industrialization has occurred, its advent and the subsequent emergence of a "music industry" have changed radically the relationship between musical practices and the rest of life. Reebee Garofalo stated the matter succinctly:

> [I]t is in the establishment of a commercial music industry that the social relations of culture are irrevocably altered . . . Commodification . . . begins to separate culture from everyday life.[8]

Indeed, as music became a tangible *object* in European society it began to take on a life of its own, and the populace's conceptualization of musical engagement as a form of religious practice (i.e., as a psychosocially unifying and equilibrating vehicle for a community) began to be attenuated.

The change in the orientation of European society away from recognizing musical engagement as a means of psychosocial or "spiritual" equilibration in community and toward conceptualizing music as a material object can perhaps be seen most clearly in the scholarly writings composed about music during the years leading to the Enlightenment era, as these writings reflect the gradual marginalization of music from the central concerns of society in the "collective mind" of Europeans. Prior to the Renaissance, most written accounts of music offered in Europe were drawn in relation to the theologically grounded conceptions of the church, though they do reveal some differences of opinion as to the place and value of music in Christian life. An associated ambivalence is epitomized in the writings of Augustine (354–430 C.E.), the noted Catholic theologian and saint. Like some of the scholars of ancient Greece who preceded him (such as Plato),

Augustine held that good music reflected the laws of divine or cosmic order, though he derived this notion from rhetoric, emphasizing the importance of the mathematical basis of poetic meter. In Augustine's view, the music of a composer who was truly devoted to the service of God would invariably reflect the composer's accord with God in its ordered manifestation of sublime beauty. While he was somewhat suspicious of music because he saw that it could evoke sensual pleasure and draw people in the wrong directions, Augustine ultimately affirmed that music making (especially congregational singing) could be good for the soul, since it evoked feelings of ecstasy and promoted Christian brotherhood.[9] On this basis, we can say that his conception of music as a social practice is generally in line with the Peircian pragmatist conception of it as "psychosocially equilibrating" behavior, with the qualification that, like most persons with minimal intercultural experience, Augustine evaluated all musical practices on the basis of their congruence with—or validation of—his own worldview.

During the European "Renaissance" era of the fourteenth through sixteenth centuries, scholars such as Marsilio Ficino (1433–1499) sought to integrate perspectives from ancient Greece and the Middle Ages with Christian religious conceptions to arrive at a humanist synthesis of philosophy and faith. A remarkable polymath, Ficino served both as head of the secular Platonic academy in Florence and as canon of the city's cathedral. Writing in 1476, he observed that participation in music making could aid and restore harmony between the parts of the soul, thus supporting the health of the body. His writings suggest that he also recognized that the audible music of his society shared much in common with the worldview manifested in other ways in his community.

> The primary music is in the mind, the secondary in the phantasy, the tertiary in the text, then follows song, then the movement of the fingers to produce sound, and finally the motion of the whole body dancing. We see therefore the music of the soul gradually descending to all parts of the body. This music is also imitated by orators, poets, painters, sculptors, and architects in their works.[10]

Ficino's views too can be taken to share something in common with the pragmatist perspective set forth in previous chapters' inquiry if our word *worldview* is substituted for his word *music*. Indeed, he seems to have recognized that the commonality of form evident in the works of the various artisans who surrounded him stemmed from a similarity in their patterns of thought (i.e., worldview), and that engagement in a given musical practice could have the effect of unifying the parts of the soul.

The conception of a musical practice as behavior by which one may be psychosocially reconciled to God (i.e., the community-held conception of ultimate Reality) evidently remained an unspoken assumption well into the seventeenth century, as it is still implicit in the writings on music of

Johannes Kepler (1571–1630), the German astronomer best known for having deduced that the planets move in elliptical rather than circular orbits around the sun. Kepler set forth his thoughts and "deductions" on music in his *Harmonia Mundi*, a work well known for its introduction of his "harmony of the spheres" theory. Remarkably, Kepler attributed the psychosocially reconciling effects of musical practice to a correspondence he claimed to have discovered between the proportional relationships inherent in consonant musical harmonies and the proportional relationships evident in the movements of the planets revolving around the sun. Using the movement of Saturn to represent the pitch G, Kepler believed he had found Mars to be "of the same magnitude" four octaves higher, Jupiter higher by one octave, and additional proportional relationships in the movements of the other planets. On this basis, he noted, "all of the notes of the major scale within one octave . . . are marked in the extreme movements of the planets" . . . with certain reconcilable exceptions.[11] Kepler maintained that his findings revealed a divine correspondence between planetary movements and music. "One should not be astonished," he wrote, "that man has established such an excellent order of tones or steps in the musical system or scale, since they are but aping God the Creator and, as it were, acting out the drama of the arrangement of celestial movements."[12] While Kepler's other astronomical discoveries served to vindicate Copernicus's earlier conceptions and served to support indirectly Isaac Newton's epoch-making work later on, his theory of a direct mathematical correspondence between musical and planetary movements now seems quite ludicrous. Nevertheless, the notion of a musical practice as behavior by which one may be psychosocially reconciled to Reality is clearly implicit in his theory, however far-fetched the "discoveries" he used to support it.

However, writings on music took a decidedly different turn during the eighteenth century "Enlightenment" era, particularly as Isaac Newton's conception of a mechanical universe began to take hold for thinkers in different intellectual fields. Indeed, the explosion of revolutionary writings in all fields during this period reveals the energy with which scholars sought to apply the methods of reason to every aspect of life. In response to the momentous conceptual change, some European philosophers of the time sought to fill the vacuum created by the unseating of the biblically grounded conception of Reality as the predominant worldview, applying the methods of reason to create their own grand, comprehensive "philosophies of everything," while others took reasoned approaches to specialized areas of knowledge, unconcerned with producing large, general theories. It was during this era that a distinctly new branch of philosophy now known as "aesthetics" first appeared, an endeavor that assumed as its purpose the placement and understanding of "the arts" (including music) in the emerging reason-based conceptions of the world.

The modern use of the term *aesthetics* originated with German philosopher Alexander Baumgarten (1714–1762), who introduced it in 1750 as the title of a work in which he sought to draw a distinction between knowledge acquired immediately via the senses ("aesthetic" knowledge) and that acquired via reasoning ("logical" knowledge). While Baumgarten envisioned in his original formulation that all future studies in the area of aesthetics would involve perception generally, his own study focused primarily on what he understood to be the perception of "beauty" or "the beautiful," and, despite his initial intentions, the term was adopted by later writers for their own logical inquiries into the nature of "art." In titling his work *Aesthetica*, Baumgarten thus unwittingly established the modern use of the word as designating the branch of philosophy concerned with "the arts." Baumgarten, like many philosophers who followed him, sought to provide a rationalized account of the functional effects of art. He regarded the creation of art as the rendering of images that have not yet undergone conceptualization; in his view, works of art manifest "clear but confused" ideas stemming from sensory data. Once ideas are thus formally fixed (e.g., in a poem or painting), the reverse process allows the perceiver to "reconstruct" the experience. While Baumgarten's arguments have been largely regarded as being of minor importance in the history of philosophy and his writings focused on poetry rather than art or music, his designation of aesthetics as a separate and distinct branch of philosophy reflected the great emphasis on reason and the attendant marginalization of the "sensate dimension" or "felt world" that characterized much intellectual thought during the Enlightenment. As some scholars have noted, this marginalization has remained as a characteristic of the conceptualizations of many writers throughout the modern era.[13]

The influential Scottish philosopher David Hume (1711–1776) shared Baumgarten's concern with explaining the apparent perception of "beauty," though in his famous essay of 1757 he framed the question as being one "of the standard of taste." Hume, an avowed atheist, set out to find the "rule by which the various sentiments of men may be reconciled, [or] at least a decision afforded, confirming one sentiment and condemning another."[14] After acknowledging the various complications he encountered in coming to his conclusion, such as the existence of persons whose strong sense, delicate sentiment, and broad knowledge might render them closer to being "true judges" of artistic matters, Hume ultimately concluded that beauty and deformity do not exist as qualities in objects but are rather sentiments in the perceiver, and that they are therefore *not* universal. In his words: "Beauty is no quality in things themselves; it exists merely in the mind which contemplates them, and each mind perceives a different beauty."[15] As to the origins of the differences in taste among human beings, Hume identified two:

> But notwithstanding all our endeavors to fix a standard of taste and reconcile the discordant apprehensions of men, there still remain two sources of variation, which are not sufficient indeed to confound all the

boundaries of beauty and deformity, but will often serve to produce a difference in the degrees of our approbation or blame. The one is the different humors of particular men; the other, the particular manners and opinions of our age and country.[16]

While Hume's theory accounted for personal and cultural differences in taste over time, as our Peircian pragmatic conception does, he was not writing on music in particular, and he thus did not consider the important psychophysiologically equilibrating effects of musical practices that have given them value historically, nor did he consider the sociopolitical implications of different forms of musical practices. Instead, Hume's views fall in line with other philosophers of the time in denying the place of art (and, by extension, music) in the psychosocial equilibration of community, and regarding them primarily as mere objects of beauty.

In contrast with Hume's resolutely atheistic empirical approach, German philosopher Immanuel Kant (1724–1804) sought to preserve what he held to be the foundations of Christian belief in his idealist philosophy. Kant's religious predisposition is evident in his idealistic writings on art and music, making his argument more akin to that of Baumgarten than of Hume. The *Critique of Aesthetical Judgement* of 1790 represents Kant's effort to establish his own account of "taste." In this work, Kant drew a distinction between most aesthetic judgments—which he identified as simple acknowledgments of pleasure or satisfaction—and true judgments of taste—which he held to involve "the faculty of judging the beautiful."

Kant asserted that the satisfaction one experiences when one judges something to be beautiful is "disinterested" (i.e., unrelated to human desires and prejudices) and is thus strictly contemplative. In Kant's view, judgments of beauty do not have the objective universality of logical judgments, but they can be said to have subjective universality or interpersonal validity. He argued that this universal validity arises from the harmonious interplay of what he held to be two "universal faculties" of the human mind: the *imagination* (i.e., the means by which sensory input is gathered into mental representations) and the *understanding* (which unifies these mental representations into concepts).

More specifically, Kant observed that most human cognition involves the determined association of particular representations (i.e., perceptions) with particular concepts.[17] However, he asserted, when people are not in direct pursuit of knowledge, their cognitive faculties of imagination and understanding can "play freely." He asserted that the pleasurable, satisfied state of mind that arises when one beholds an object that stimulates "a feeling of the free play of the representative powers in a given representation with reference to a cognition in general" *is* the experience of beauty.[18] In other words, Kant believed that when one judges an object to be beautiful, the experience from which this judgment stems is attributable to one's having recognized the object as being perfectly formed; the perception of such a "perfect" object has stimulated the harmonious interplay of one's imagination and understanding. Because this unique state of mind is attainable by all rational beings, Kant reasoned, beauty must be a subjective universal. Therefore, in Kant's view, when two people have a difference of opinion about the beauty of an object, one of them must be wrong.[19]

Kant asserted further that when one considers the relation between the perceiver and such a "beautiful" object, by which the object can be said to provide this disinterested and universal pleasure, it can be understood as stemming from the object's "purposiveness without purpose." That is, while the judgment of taste is connected with purposiveness (i.e., the creation of an object according to a preexisting concept), it is not concerned with *particular* purposes, as it would then be conceptual and not "disinterested." Nevertheless, Kant emphasized, it is the sense of a formal purpose in an object that stimulates the interplay of the imagination and understanding.

For Kant, music differs from the other forms of art (e.g., painting) in that a given work of music has no relation to an extrinsic concept, but rather derives its beauty from the mere arrangement of tones. He opined that it may thus represent the thought process itself in some measure. However, Kant maintained, the fact that music has no relation to anything outside itself does not make it unimportant; the very relationship between music and the senses maintains its importance.

We can see that Kant's conception differs in at least two important ways from the Peircian pragmatic perspective on musical practices developed in the previous chapter. These differences should be noted not only because Kant's views were so widely influential in his own time but also because views like his continue to be held today by persons with little substantive intercultural experience or political awareness. As we can see, Kant's notion of "beauty" as a subjective universal and his relegation of art to a realm of "disinterested contemplation" effectively negate the validity and importance of different personal and cultural perspectives, thereby depoliticizing art (including music) and rendering it socially inert, as it focuses on the evaluation of certain objects according to ostensibly universal standards or norms of "beauty." Kant's tacit focus on created of works of art as objects (presumably including different forms of music as objects also) thus negates the importance of musical engagement (i.e., actual physical involvement) to the psychophysiological equilibration of individuals and the psychosocial equilibration of human societies. Indeed, his focus on created works of art themselves (e.g., the sound artifacts produced in musical practices) fails to acknowledge adequately the human psychophysiological motivations for musical practices. In developing his view, Kant's tacit intention was to establish the social importance and centrality of art, but, as we shall see, his conception of art (and, by extension, music) as belonging to a disinterested realm of contemplation ultimately contributed to its marginalization from the rest of human life in the thinking of the modern world.

The social significance of art was, however, addressed in some measure by the German philosopher Georg Wilhelm Friedrich Hegel (1770–1831) in his extended philosophical writings in the field of aesthetics. Directly or indirectly influenced by Hegel's writings, many scholars in Europe and the U.S. have subsequently come to adopt his modern conception of different works of art (and music) as being artifactual manifestations or "expressions" of "the Absolute" (i.e., renderings of Reality) as created by different persons living in different historical eras. We will explore Hegel's aesthetic philosophy at somewhat greater length for reasons owing not only to its complexity but also to its considerable influence on concepts of art (and, thus, music) held historically in the U.S. Furthermore, Hegel's aesthetic philosophy is similar in certain ways to the Peircian pragmatic conception of music that we established and adopted as our own in the previous chapter and it is certainly not similar in other ways, so the differences between the two conceptions will be of great interest for us.

Hegel's entire architectonic philosophical system consists of three main parts: logic, philosophy of nature, and philosophy of mind or spirit (*Geist*). He divided the latter part, in which we are primarily interested, into three main areas as well: subjective spirit (dealing primarily with individual psychology, but also anthropology and phenomenology), objective spirit (involving morality, social and economic ethics, the state, and political history), and absolute spirit (embracing art, religion, and philosophy). In Hegel's view, art (including music and other forms), religion, and philosophy represent the various means by which human beings come to be aware of and contribute to the nature of the universe (or, better, "the Absolute") and their place in it.

Hegel utilized the notions of *concept*, *reality*, and *Idea* to identify aspects of the phenomenal universe. For Hegel an *Idea* is a *concept* manifested in a physical *reality* (or tangible form). That is, the *concept* and the *reality* are constituent parts—or different aspects—of an *Idea* as a whole. A particular human being, for instance, has both inner and outer aspects: the inner aspect (unique personal substance or content) and the outer (or physical body) together make up the whole person (as an Idea). Similarly, a work of art *is* an Idea, comprising both content (the artist's intention) and form (the physical reality of the work). Moreover, in Hegel's Christianity-influenced view, the universe as a whole (i.e., God's creation) is itself an Idea, a unity of concept and reality, simultaneously comprising many constituent Ideas. The great purpose of the universe, according to Hegel, is for it to realize or become conscious of itself. In revealing the Absolute through one's artwork, he believed, the individual artist in essence *realizes* (i.e., makes real) the Absolute and thus contributes to the self-realizing nature of the universe *as* the Absolute Idea.

Hegel drew distinctions between art, religion, and philosophy, explaining that while all three represent means to the realization of Absolute spirit, art reveals the Absolute in a unique way. Specifically, the different forms of art (architecture, sculpture, painting, music, poetry) express sensory construals of the Absolute, manifesting the worldviews of their creators in physically tangible media, while religion and philosophy are only conceptual in their renderings. However, Hegel asserted, when one considers art historically, one comes to realize that art has gradually become less and less important throughout history, as its place has been superseded in later eras by religion and philosophy. In fact, he argued, art reached its pinnacle in ancient Greece and then declined in the years leading to the modern era. He made this argument on the basis of what he considered to be the evident "ideal harmony of content and form" of the works of art composed by the Greeks and the apparent lack of this harmony in subsequent eras.[20]

In addition, Hegel believed that any thoughtful reflection on art (such as his own musings) would not only develop the artist's vision beyond what is sensorially expressible, but would also undermine the artist's attachment to any definite view of the world (i.e., the worldview of the artist's own community). He expressed doubts as to whether a reflectively detached artist—one whose attachment to a particular vision had been undermined—could ever produce art to approach the quality of past, less reflective ages. Furthermore, he doubted whether art itself could ever come to express such ironic detachment effectively, noting that all past efforts to produce ironic art had generally resulted in feeble art. Hegel worried in his writings over the question of whether all historically significant artistic and philosophical possibilities might already have been actualized, leaving no possibility for future progress. At other times, however, he suggested that only the possibilities he and his contemporaries could conceive of, from their historical standpoint, had been exhausted, and that new, as yet inconceivable possibilities might someday be manifested. Never did he conclude that art had come to an end.

We can now see that Hegel's perspective shares both similarities and differences with the Peircian pragmatic perspective established in the last chapter. Certainly the most important similarity is Hegel's recognition that different forms of music (as works of art) manifest different worldviews or conceptions of the Absolute (i.e., Reality). However, there are at least three important differences between Hegel's conception of music and our pragmatic view. First of all, like his predecessors Baumgarten, Hume, Kant, and most if not all of the other Enlightenment "aesthetic" philosophers, Hegel focused too heavily on the individual work or *artifact* in his philosophical scheme, giving insufficient attention to the dynamic effect and the psychosocial importance of musical practices in the lives of human individuals and communities. This is likely attributable to his having placed music together with architecture, sculpture, and painting in the single conceptual category of art in his philosophical conception; these "arts" are arguably less dynamic than music and poetry, in that their dimension of realization is space rather than time.[21] Second, Hegel focused on what he believed to be the progress of art in a single society (i.e., in his own European society, which he ethnocentrically construed as "the world"), and he evaluated all works of art on the basis of what he personally regarded as their "realization of the Absolute." As we can see, his decision to define things in this way prevented him from considering the different forms of music (and the important role of different musical practices) in the lives of the culturally differing individuals and communities comprising the world. Third, Hegel placed art (including music) not only in a secondary, but in a tertiary relationship to religion and philosophy, suggesting its inferiority as a means of realizing the Absolute during his own time, rather than recognizing art, religion, and philosophy as parallel, uniquely effective forms.

The conceptions of Kant, Hegel, and other Enlightenment and post-Enlightenment philosophers were "in the air" in Europe at the very time the U.S. was established as a nation, and both Kant's and Hegel's conceptions of art—or notions akin to them—have continued to have considerable influence in the nation's public forum up to the present day. Specifically, perspectives like that of Kant (i.e., the notion of beauty as a subjective universal and the attendant idea that different works of music—as works of art—can be evaluated on the basis of their attainment of the ideal of "perfect form") have continued to be held by many persons among the general public in the U.S.—particularly among those with limited intercultural experience or who have chosen to close their minds to such experience. At the same time, more expansive conceptions like that of Hegel—specifically, the notion of different works of music as different sensory realizations of the Absolute—have served to frame the very foundation for much of the composition and performance of music that has taken place subsequent to his time in Europe and the U.S.[22]

While it does not appear that the two views can be accommodated to each other as they stand, it does make sense that a particular musical practice could have the effect of *unifying* the "collective mind" of a specific community into a common conception of Reality, and, at the same time, the music—or sound artifact produced in that activity—could be regarded as *standing for* that shared conception. A given instance of music could then be said both to embody and to stand for the conception of Reality held by the person or persons with whom it originates.[23] Such an idea, in the relatively modest, interculturally mindful form of our Peircian pragmatic perspective and in the more expansive, universalizing form articulated by Hegel, is implicit in the modern notion of "art music." This notion too had its inception in the early nineteenth century, when the term *art song* began to be used to delineate songs written by a professional composer—as one supposedly more in touch with true Reality—as distinguished from folk songs and songs composed for religious purposes.[24] In creating a work of "art music," the composer—as an artist—would seek to manifest an aspect of her or his own conception of Reality for the perception and participation of others. In the decades following the emergence of "art music" in Europe, similar practices gradually began to develop in other societies as well.[25]

In the years following the broad dissemination of Hegel's ideas, the notion of "art music" developed and blossomed in what has been termed the Romantic era of European history, a time when writings on music reflected a spirited return by many to the recognition of music as important to the healthful life of the psyche. Naturally, as in all eras, the conceptions of music held by the Romantics bore the imprint of their own distinctive cultural attributes, but they also manifested a renewed recognition of the importance of feeling, emotional intuition, and the relationship of the human being to nature in the music of all eras. These perspectives of the Romantics served well to correct and offset in some measure the confining rationalism and empiricism of their recent forebears.

The conception of a work of "art music" as manifesting a composer's own conception of Reality is implicit in the writings of virtually all of the Romantics who wrote on "music," though it is more overtly stated in the writings of some of them. For instance, the poet Johann Wolfgang von Goethe (1749–1832), though not strictly a Romantic, observed that every good work "creates a little world of its own, in which all proceeds according to fixed laws, which must be judged by its own laws, felt according to its own spirit."[26] In another vein, the writer and composer E. T. A. Hoffmann (1776–1822) wrote of music that "it is the most romantic of all the arts—one might almost say, the only genuinely romantic art—for its own sole subject is the infinite."[27] The writer and critic Wilhelm Heinrich Wackenroder (1773–1798) underscored in his own way the uniquely effective manner in which a musical practice could balance and reveal the human psyche. His mannered description reveals something of the passionate way in which he and his contemporaries regarded music.

> I shall use a flowing stream as an illustration. It is beyond human art to depict in words meant for the eye the thousands of individual waves, smooth and rugged, bursting and foaming, in the flow of a mighty river—words can but meagerly recount the incessant movements and cannot visibly picture the consequent rearrangement of the drops of water. Just so it is with the mysterious stream in the depths of the human soul; words mention and name and describe its flux in a foreign medium. In music, however, the stream itself seems to be released. Music courageously smites upon the hidden harp strings and, in that inner world of mystery, strikes up in due succession certain mysterious chords—our heart-strings, and we understand the music.[28]

In addition to inspiring such ardor, the era's new focus on music as a means of emotional expression and on the shared inner or "spiritual" lives of all human beings evoked a new interest in the details of each composer's personal background. Indeed, many began to realize that the line between one's self and one's environment is not at all a clear one. Goethe sought to emphasize this point when he wrote: "The artist has a twofold relation to nature; he is at once her master and her slave."[29] While this view—which is congruent with our pragmatic conception in its acknowledgment of a relationship between one's music and the context in which one makes it—appeared in the writings of many of the Romantic writers, who were also artists of one kind or another (e.g., composers, poets), it took different, less pragmatic forms in the writings of the era's philosophers. Such a potentially promising—though inherently limited and more idealistic than Romantic—view appears, for example, in the writings of German philosopher Arthur Schopenhauer (1788–1860).

Schopenhauer postulated the existence of a great, undifferentiated *Will*—a primordial drive to endure—as the cause of all occurrences, and an assemblage of *Ideas*—somewhat akin to Plato's notion of the permanent, essential *forms* of the phenomenal world—as the middle ground between the Will and the phenomenal world. He opined that through pure contemplation a genius (an individual ostensibly capable of complete objectivity) would be capable of comprehending these Ideas and then reproducing that which was apprehended as *Art*. In Schopenhauer's view, Art "reproduces the eternal Ideas grasped through pure contemplation, the essential and abiding in all the phenomena of the world . . ."[30] He introduced the notion of Imagination as being an essential element of genius, but he stressed that Imagination and genius must not be regarded as identical. Specifically, in his view, it is Imagination that enables the genius to construct, or comprehend, the "whole" out of the little that is actually humanly perceivable. He also held that in the case of the genius such constructions are not "mere fancy" (as they are with persons with lesser minds), but that they in fact reflect true Reality. As to the place of Art (including music) in the lives of *all* humans, Schopenhauer pessimistically concluded that it exists to serve as a means of escape from the tyranny of the Will and the accompanying pain of existence.

In his hierarchy of the arts, Schopenhauer saw architecture as the lowest manifestation of the Will and tragic poetry as the highest. However, he argued, music is special: It differs from all of the other arts in that it is not a mere copy of the Ideas of the phenomenal world, but is rather a copy of the Will itself. To demonstrate this, he drew an elaborate analogy between music and the phenomenal world, both of which express the Will: According to his scheme, bass pitches correspond to inorganic bodies, while higher pitches correspond to the plant and animal worlds. Man, at the top of the hierarchy, corresponds to melody. "[Melody] . . . relates the most secret history of [the] intellectually enlightened will . . . which it cannot apprehend further through its abstract concepts."[31] Man's own striving from desire to satisfaction corresponds to melody's digressions and deviations from the tonic—or tonal center—of the music. On this foundation, Schopenhauer predicated his belief: "The composer reveals the inner nature of the world, and expresses the deepest wisdom in a language which his reason does not understand . . ."[32]

Schopenhauer shared much in common with the Romantic artists who were his nearest predecessors and contemporaries. Moreover, his writings reveal an important concurrence with the pragmatic view of music we established in the previous chapter, most notably in his recognition that different forms of music reflect the conceptions of Reality held by their creators. However, instead of recognizing the important psychosocially equilibrating effects that different musical practices have for persons of different backgrounds, Schopenhauer, like Kant and Hegel, placed undue emphasis on the music—the material artifact produced in such activity— rather than on the activity itself. In addition, he regarded the creation of music as lying most appropriately in the domain of those he held to be "true" geniuses and virtuosi, thereby maintaining the same cultural bias that for us invalidated the universalist—and ethnocentric—theories of Kant and Hegel. Finally, while his account of Art (including music) as a means of escape from the miseries of life does acknowledge that its personal importance for human beings stems from the psychophysiological effects engagement in a musical practice has on them, it too fails to address adequately its psychosocial and sociopolitical importance. Sadly, his view ultimately validates the conceptions of music as being relatively peripheral and substantively unimportant to the life of society that appeared in the writings of earlier "aesthetic" philosophers.

Despite the spirited, countervailing efforts of the artists of the Romantic era to assert the importance of music (i.e., what we have termed engagement in a musical practice) to the healthful life of the psyche, the failure of many Enlightenment and Romantic philosophers to account adequately for art and music in their architectonic philosophies in ways that demonstrated the full range of their importance to European society had the collective effect of consigning music and art to the periphery of that society.[33] As we have seen, Kant's relegation of art (including music) to a realm of "disinterested contemplation" effectively depoliticized it, rendering it socially static and placing it beyond ordinary cognitive understanding. Hegel's undue attachment to the *artifacts* of art and music (plus his failure to acknowledge the importance of such *activity*), his tacit belief that the art and music of European society (as *the* world society) were inherently central to all others, and his simultaneous consideration of art (including music) as being of tertiary importance (behind religion and philosophy) in his own historical age, effectively denied consideration of the important psychosocially equilibrating effects of different artistic or musical practices. From our pragmatic perspective we might say that, with rare exceptions, the philosophers writing in the late eighteenth and early nineteenth centuries generally failed at explaining the place of art and music in a reason-based rather than Christian religion-based society, in that they did not adequately account for its psychophysiological, psychosocial, and sociopolitical importance in the lives of all persons. Whereas Kant focused on works of music as static objects of beauty, Hegel saw works of art (and thus music) as degenerate, merely secondary realizations of Reality. Neither adequately addressed the important effects of active involvement in a musical practice on individuals and communities. Even the late German Romantic Schopenhauer contributed to the societal marginalization of music by making it the province of geniuses and virtuosi, thus tacitly devaluing the disparate musical practices undertaken by others in his own society as well as persons of different worldviews.

The German historian of music aesthetics Carl Dahlhaus commented incisively on the static, socially elitist, and object-oriented perspectives of such aesthetic philosophers, saying: "As a whole, music aesthetics represents—and this explains some of the resistance to it—the spirit of bourgeois music lovers, a spirit that arose in the eighteenth century and is threatened in the twentieth with collapse."[34] The British Marxist scholar Terry Eagleton has interpreted their impact somewhat differently, focusing on large-scale economic and political implications, but emphasizing above all that the emergence of aesthetics as a branch of philosophy was attendant upon the marginalizing and commercializing of art in European industrialized society.

> The emergence of the aesthetic as a theoretical category is closely bound up with the material process by which cultural production, at an early stage of bourgeois society, becomes "autonomous'—autonomous, that is, of the various social functions which it has traditionally served. Once artefacts become commodities in the market place, they exist for nothing and nobody in particular, and can consequently be rationalized, ideologically speaking, as existing entirely and gloriously for themselves.[35]

As Eagleton explains the matter, the "ideology of the aesthetic" (i.e., Enlightenment rationalism) effectively separated art (and thus music) from the realm of ordinary cognitive understanding, simultaneously divesting it of its previous moral and political moorings.

> The moment we are speaking of is the moment of modernity, characterized by the dissociation and specialization of . . . three crucial spheres of activity. Art is now autonomous of the cognitive, ethical, and political; but the way it came to be so is paradoxical. It became autonomous of them, curiously enough, by being *integrated* into the capitalist mode of production. When art becomes a commodity, it is released from its traditional social functions within church, court, and state into the anonymous freedom of the market place. Now it exists, not for any specific audience, but just for anybody with the taste to appreciate it and the money to buy it. And in so far as it exists for nothing and nobody in particular, it can be said to exist for itself. It is "independent" because it has been swallowed up by commodity production.[36]

Indeed, the reductive and marginalizing way in which many intellectuals in European society came to regard music in the eighteenth century is revealed in the writings of the very scholars whom we would expect not only to have valued musical practices and music most highly, but also to have recognized their psychosocial and political significance. For example, Charles Burney, the well-traveled English historian of music (and sometime composer), wrote in the preface to his 1789 book *A General History of Music*: "Music is an innocent luxury, unnecessary to our existence but a great improvement and gratification of the sense of hearing."[37] Whereas musical practices were once accorded a central place in the life of European society because of their centrality in religious worship, they had become a free entity, conceptually severed from their earlier institutional moorings in the church and cast adrift in the marketplace. The inherently limited views of these philosophers deeply influenced their contemporaries, and, as we shall see, their failure to assign a satisfactory place to music in their architectonic schemes was to have far-reaching effects on the ways in which musical practices and music came to be regarded in the public forum of the U.S.

THE EMERGENCE OF THE NEW NATION AS A CULTURALLY UNDEFINED SOCIETY

In this era of newly found confidence in human reason, as much of European intellectual society was gravitating away from the "spiritual" or religious foundations of Christianity and toward more empirically based worldviews, the U.S. emerged as a nation. During the years leading up to the colonization of North America, many European nations had become internally divided owing to the deepening of differences between their constituent communities and their rulers. In most of these cases, the reigning monarch's religion continued to serve as the official worldview of the state, and schisms were resolved by force, suppressing the voices of dissenters. Accordingly, many of the original voyagers to North America immigrated to escape from the political and religious oppression they were suffering in their homelands. Upon arriving in the "new world," most of these groups formed colonies and established their own churches as the social and political centers of their communities, each according to its own religious beliefs.[38]

It seems strange, from our early-twenty-first-century viewpoint, that more of the colonists did not adopt policies of religious tolerance upon settling in North America, considering the persecution that many had suffered in their European homelands. However, it appears that at the time the members of most of these colonies firmly believed their own religions (or worldviews) to be more well-fitting reflections of true Reality than any other. Indeed, most of the original settlers were no more tolerant of religious dissension than were the rulers of the nations they had left behind. The many stories of Colonial religious persecution include accounts of hostility by the Congregationalists of Massachusetts toward the Baptists and Quakers living in their midst, descriptions of efforts undertaken by the Anglicans of the southern coastal states to prohibit their Baptist and Presbyterian neighbors from preaching and performing marriages, and reports of the Maryland Catholics' harassment of Protestants and other Catholics who professed their faith in unconventional ways. By contrast, however, some of the colonists did practice religious tolerance. Notably, the former Congregationalist Roger Williams established the community of Providence, Rhode Island, in 1639 as a place of sanctuary for people of many religious orientations. The colony's charter, granted in 1663, was the first to include a declaration of the right to religious liberty. Similarly, the English Quaker William Penn founded Pennsylvania as a haven for adherents of all religions in 1681.

In the last years of the seventeenth century, major political changes took place in Europe, stimulating the English to challenge the French militarily for control over all of the colonies in North America. Numerous wars ensued between England and France in various parts of the world throughout the early eighteenth century, and by 1763 France had lost its holdings on the North America mainland, most of them to Great Britain.[39] Despite having essentially won these wars, the British government faced numerous problems at the end of them, including a formidable national debt as well as issues concerning how its new empire might best be controlled politically and economically. The British leaders decided to recoup their financial losses by instituting various new taxes on the American colonies, and they sought to establish greater political and economic control there by strictly enforcing navigation laws. Not surprisingly, these measures raised protests from the colonists, stimulating them collectively to oppose the British measures; this turn of events gradually brought the disparate colonies together as a political unit for the first time. Although the British Parliament eventually made some adjustments to the tax laws, skirmishes persisted in the following years, as the colonists continued to protest their "taxation without representation."

In September 1774, the First Continental Congress, an assembly of representatives from the various colonies, drafted a petition to the British sovereign, George III, for a redress of their grievances. When this petition was rejected, the colonists began to organize a militia for purposes of defense, and in the following April, after British troops were dispatched against the township of Concord, the first battle of the American Revolution occurred at Lexington, Massachusetts. When the Second Continental Congress convened at Philadelphia on May 10, 1775, the colonists made an additional appeal to the British crown for a peaceful solution to the crisis, but again their petition was rejected. On July 2, 1776, the Second Continental Congress determined to declare independence from Britain, and they adopted a formal statement written by Thomas Jefferson justifying that action two days later.

Jefferson, the foremost advocate of democracy in the Continental Congress, was, like many of his compatriots, strongly influenced by the ideas of Enlightenment philosophers, particularly the political writers Hobbes, Locke, and Rousseau, whom we discussed earlier. Jefferson's belief in the value of democracy is reflected in his authorship of the Declaration of Independence, which outlined the "injuries and usurpations" perpetrated by the British against the colonists and stated strongly the colonists' belief that government should have the consent of the governed. After its adoption by the Congress, the document was distributed to the former colonies, which had become states, and its eloquent language and cogent substance served to inspire many throughout the ensuing period of strife. After seven more years of fighting, the War of Independence was finally won by the Americans, culminating with the signing of the Treaty of Paris in 1783.

Following the war, the new nation faced the challenge of inventing a form of government that would form the states into an effective union. From 1776 to 1781, the first years free from British rule, the states had been governed by the Continental Congress, which had provisionally assumed executive powers. The Congress's powers were formally articulated shortly after the end of the war in an agreement known as the Articles of Confederation. According to this document, the individual states retained their own sovereign power, and their respective legislatures controlled such matters as taxation and the administration of justice.

In the unstable political climate of postrevolutionary America, however, limitations on the Congress's power prevented it from exercising sufficient influence to maintain domestic peace between the states or to foster recognition of the new union by other nations. Nationalists like James Madison and Alexander Hamilton raised the concern that these limitations might threaten the survival of the U.S. as a unified political entity. At their urging, Congress convened a group of delegates from all the states in 1787 for the purpose of making amendments to the Articles of Confederation. In the end, however, the convention drafted an entirely new document—the United States Constitution—that laid the foundations for the new nation as a federated union.

Madison, the primary author of the Constitution, shared with Jefferson the belief in the principle of individual liberty extolled by the political philosophers of the Enlightenment that we discussed earlier. He too considered democracy to be the best political means for maintaining such freedom in a unified state. However, Madison held a view of human nature more like that of Hobbes, one far less optimistic than that of Locke, Rousseau, or Jefferson. He believed that since human beings could often be aggressive and selfish, any system of government that lacked a satisfactory system of checks and balances would have the potential to become oppressive. Thus, he sought to construct a democratic political system that would balance the potential harshness of the government against the potential greed of the people. The organization of the U.S. government into legislative, executive, and judicial branches stemmed directly from this belief of Madison. While he strongly supported individual rights, Madison also mistrusted all groups sharing common interests, and the group he mistrusted most was the majority. For this reason, the system of government that he and others laid out in the Constitution was, while clearly democratic in supporting rule by the people, also expressly designed to protect the rights of individuals and minorities by dividing and checking the power of the majority.

The Constitution had been ratified by nine states (the required two-thirds majority) by February of 1788. The other states delayed ratifying until they were assured that a series of constitutional amendments would be added to safeguard protection of what they held to be essential human rights against undue control by the new centralized government. Among the rights these states believed most important to secure was that of religious—or cultural—liberty. Nine of the thirteen colonies had established churches in 1775, at the outbreak of the American Revolution, but in the following years several factors contributed to moving the new nation toward a spirit of religious tolerance. These factors changed the orientation of many citizens toward governmentally sanctioned religions or churches in the various states, and contributed to the disestablishment of religion there.

The main factor was the growing influence of Enlightenment conceptions on the thinking of the American populace. It is important to keep in mind that a tremendous number of religious, social, and political changes had occurred as the colonists were arriving in North America during the previous century; largely as a result of these myriad changes, many Americans were gradually becoming more accustomed to thinking in more egalitarian ways. As we have already noted, many of the new nation's leaders involved in the revolutionary movement and the establishment of the Constitution were profoundly influenced by Enlightenment political philosophers, though it must also be noted that their enthusiasm for these ideas may have stemmed from other sources. Some of the nation's early leaders—such as George Washington and Benjamin Franklin—were Freemasons, members of a secret fraternity who shared a belief in "the great Architect of the Universe" and who held universal human charity to be of prime importance, but who did not identify themselves collectively with any religious denomination. Similarly, Jefferson and others were Deists, persons who affirmed the existence of a God as the creator of the universe, but who also believed that God no longer actively participates in the universe's ongoing operations except according to certain "natural laws" and what they held to be universally discernable moral principles. In accord with their uniquely rationalistic orientations, these leaders emphasized the individual's freedom of conscience above all, and they were generally opposed to state establishments of religion. Over time, their reason-based, egalitarian philosophical conceptions came greatly to influence the wider population.

A second factor that contributed to the growth of religious tolerance was, ironically, a new religious movement that began to sweep the states in the early eighteenth century, now commonly known as the Great Awakening. Inspired by the evangelical preaching of various ministers in different colonies, the movement emphasized the religious conversion of the *individual*, the notion that every person is answerable to God alone, and the idea of the church as a more strictly spiritual rather than political institution.[40] Not surprisingly, the Awakening precipitated splits in many churches (especially in New England), increasing the strength of other churches (most notably Methodist and Baptist denominations), and it promoted Unitarianism and Universalism in some quarters. Historian George Brown Tindall has pointed out that despite the different origins of the era's two great social movements, they had a common effect on the "collective mind" of the Americans:

> [I]n some respects the counterpoint between the Awakening and the Enlightenment, between the principles of piety and reason, paradoxically led by different roads to similar ends. Both emphasized the power and right of the individual to judge things for himself, and both aroused millennial hopes that America would become the promised land in which men might attain to the perfection of piety or reason, if not of both.[41]

Indeed, these two movements did much to promote the causes of civil and religious liberty, helping to move the new nation gradually toward establishing its own unique political identity.

However, a third factor also contributed to the change in the nation's collective attitude toward religious differences, stemming from a shift in the way in which the American farmers and other common people were coming to consider monetary matters.[42] In the early years of the colonies, the farmers living in the various towns generally produced crops at a basic, subsistence level, working primarily to support their families and communities. Some historians have described the economic systems of the early Colonial towns as "moral economies," because they tended to promote social stability, self-sufficiency, and religious conformity over individual efforts to make money.[43] Other historians have emphasized the view that the reason most American farmers worked at a mere subsistence level prior to the eighteenth century was simply that they were accustomed to working that way; having lived for so long in the monarchical state societies of Europe, they saw no reason to work harder and produce more, as they did not yet regard labor as a source of wealth.[44] In any case, as trade with other nations began to increase around the time of the War of Independence, many farmers began to realize that one of the ways they could acquire greater influence and respectability in their communities was by imitating the gentry—those persons who held higher social standing than themselves, owing largely to the sizable coffers they had brought with them from Europe. Specifically, the farmers began to work more aggressively so that they could afford to buy some of the luxury items, many of them imported, that had previously been accessible only to the leisure classes. Thus, for the first time, American farmers began to produce and market crop surpluses for the purpose of acquiring greater financial wealth.[45] Not surprisingly, they gradually began to place a greater focus on the acquisition of goods, and, over time, their concern with religious matters became secondary to their interest in issues of commerce. Not only was their attention redirected in this way, but they also began to realize that the practice of religious tolerance would encourage and support further foreign and interstate trade, thus giving them greater access to the goods they desired.[46] The growing interest in personal commerce among these common citizens meshed well with the views of such Enlightenment political economists as Adam Smith, whose writings were then influencing the new nation's leaders, and gradually led the nation collectively to develop and embrace democratic capitalism as its common social system. As the nation moved toward the development of an industrial, trade-based economy, the colonies' earlier, more religiously based forms of social organization were thereby displaced.

All of these factors—the Enlightenment, the Great Awakening, and the new primacy of trade—contributed to advancing a spirit of religious toleration around the time of the revolution, and they gradually moved the various states toward the disestablishment of their existing religions. Virginia was the first state to disestablish. Upon the passage of Jefferson's "Act for Establishing Freedom of Religion" there in 1786, Madison expressed his own great confidence in reason, religious liberty, and the primacy of individual conscience when he wrote enthusiastically to Jefferson that its passage had "in this Country extinguished for ever the ambitious hope of making laws for the human mind."[47] The disestablishment of religion in New York, Maryland, and North Carolina soon followed, and by the end of the war only five states had retained their established religions.[48]

As noted earlier, several states delayed ratifying the new Constitution until they could be assured that a series of amendments would be added to protect certain human rights from the control of the new centralized government. Among their greatest concerns was religious liberty, or the freedom to hold one's own cultural worldview. Ironically, as First Amendment scholar Leonard Levy has shown, despite the many fears that were expressed by the delegates over the possible establishment of a national religion, no state or person actually favored the establishment of a state religion by Congress at the time of ratification. Nevertheless, Levy notes, the possibility that one Christian denomination might dominate over others was then "something so feared that a political necessity existed to assuage that fear by specifically making it groundless."[49] Thus, when the U.S. Congress passed into law the first ten amendments to the Constitution—collectively known as the Bill of Rights—in 1791, they included first among them an amendment directly addressing the establishment of religion by the federal government. The First Amendment reads as follows:

> Congress shall make no law respecting an establishment of religion, or prohibiting the free exercise thereof; or abridging the freedom of speech, or of the press; or the right of the people peaceably to assemble, and to petition the Government for a redress of grievances.[50]

We might even call this the "pro-diversity amendment" as it has not only served to protect the practice of religion but its various clauses have also guarded freedom of speech, press, and assembly—all inherently political acts—from the control of the state throughout the history of the nation. The clauses on religious liberty appear first in this amendment, attesting to the primacy it held for the document's creators.

On the basis of a detailed analysis of documents leading to its composition, historian Robert Cord has asserted that the First Amendment was intended to accomplish three purposes with regard to religion:

> First, it was intended to prevent the establishment of a national church or religion, or the giving of any religious sect or denomination a preferred status. Second, it was designed to safeguard the right of freedom of conscience in religious beliefs against invasion solely by the national Government. Third, it was so constructed in order to allow the States, unimpeded, to deal with religious establishments and aid to religious institutions as they saw fit.[51]

Indeed, historical evidence confirms that the First Amendment was not intended to preclude federal governmental aid to religion as long as such support was provided on a nondiscriminatory basis, nor was it intended to provide an *absolute* separation or independence of religion from the state.[52] Despite all of the factors that had contributed to moving the individual states away from maintaining established religions, the intent of the law was never to protect the nation-state (i.e., the U.S. as a whole) from the church, but was rather to protect the practice of religion from the control of the nation-state. It was also intended to assure that the new nation-state would never adopt a national religion but instead maintain religious liberty and democracy as guiding principles.

Both the aim of religious liberty and an accompanying acknowledgment of the importance of religious thinking are clearly evident in the writings of the nation's early leaders, even those whom we might have expected to discount the importance of religion in human life. For example, Madison made his position clear when he wrote his *Memorial and Remonstrance* in 1785 to defeat a bill proposed to support the churches of Virginia by taxing the state's entire population:

Whilst we assert for ourselves a freedom to embrace to profess, and to observe the Religion which we believe to be of divine origin, we cannot deny an equal freedom to those whose minds have not yet yielded to the evidence that has convinced us. If this freedom be abused, it is an offence against God, not against man.[53]

Similarly, though he holds to this day the reputation of being an extreme secularist, even Jefferson was not opposed to religion in and of itself, but rather regarded it as a matter of individual conscience. Indeed, he viewed religious liberty as "the most inalienable and sacred of all human rights."[54]

Still, despite the efforts of the founders to establish the nation as one in which religious or cultural differences would be bracketed from the public forum and addressed privately by the nation's constituent individuals and communities, legal issues concerning the nation's collective ambiguity in worldview (or cultural plurality) have remained paramount throughout the history of the nation. In particular, culturally rooted questions involving the nation's schools—concerning such issues as school prayer, government aid to parochial schools, the teaching of creationism versus evolution— have remained at the center of public debate and, in recent years, have increasingly been taken to the nation's Supreme Court for arbitration. Indeed, questions concerning the appropriate demarcation of the respective domains of religion and the state remain as complex and sensitive issues in the U.S. today.

EFFECTS OF THE ENLIGHTENMENT ON CONCEPTIONS OF MUSICAL PRACTICES IN THE NEW NATION

The preceding historical investigation into the social background of the establishment of the U.S. as a nation has shown us that the circumstances of its formation have distinguished it in three important ways from the traditional societies and the other culturally pluralistic state societies we have discussed so far. These characteristics are as follows:

1. Unlike traditional societies, the U.S. maintains a separation of religion and state.
2. Unlike many other culturally pluralistic state societies, the U.S. sanctions no official worldview, other than democracy itself.
3. In place of an official religion or worldview, the U.S. embraced democratic capitalism as its social system.

As we shall see, each of these characteristics has not only provided freedom in musical practice for the nation's citizens but has also contributed directly or indirectly to diminishing further their conscious awareness of its importance as an effective form of "psychosocially equilibrating" behavior as well as their recognition of its political significance. Obviously, these three societal attributes are interrelated, but we will consider them separately in order to demonstrate systematically how each has contributed to influencing the conceptions of musical practices and music now current in the public forum of the U.S.

SEPARATION OF RELIGION AND STATE

The establishment of the separation of religion and state in the First Amendment was intended by the writers of the Bill of Rights to have the effect of making the nation a neutral state with respect to worldview, one in which individuals and communities of diverse backgrounds could coexist peacefully, each with its attendant beliefs about the ultimate nature of Reality, but in which no cultural community would have its beliefs sanctioned as the official religion of the state.[55] We can see that in writing and adopting this amendment, the early citizens of the nation established the U.S. as a society very unlike the traditional societies and theocratic monarchies they had left behind in Europe. In their original conception, conflicts concerning the operation of the nation as a whole were to be reconciled through the legislative and juridical means established by the U.S. Constitution, the state's official "social contract," but differences in other matters—such as specifically religious questions (i.e., those concerning the ultimate meanings of life and death) and other subjective matters of the psyche—were intended to be unconstrained by government. That is, they were left to the discretion of individuals, who derived their conceptions of such matters from the various communities in which they lived.

As a result of this consensual separation, the various European cultural communities comprising the U.S. were left free to maintain their own religious beliefs without interference from the state or from one another, and their members thus continued to benefit from the psychophysiologically and psychosocially equilibrating effects of the various musical practices undertaken in their respective communities.[56] On the basis of what we have already learned about these effects, we can see that as each of the nation's constituent cultural communities undertook its own unique musical practices during the early years of the nation, this activity not only contributed directly to maintaining its own solidarity but also, because of its positive influence on the psychosocial health of its members, contributed indirectly to sustaining the health of the democracy as a whole. Indeed, most of the early citizens of the U.S., having been "psychophysiologically and psychosocially balanced" within the cultural contexts of their respective communities via their own respective musical practices (and, of course, various other ritualized and nonritualized social means), were thus enabled to live healthy, productive lives in the nation's pluralistic society.[57] Furthermore, as psychosocially well-balanced individuals, they were well suited to represent their respective communities in the discussion of issues of general concern (i.e., economic and material matters) in government and other quarters of the public forum, and they were thus able to contribute in essential ways to the maintenance of the nation's overall social and political equilibrium.[58]

However, besides providing freedom of religion, the new nation's adoption of the First Amendment simultaneously had the effect of defining it as a society in which the populace would not collectively share a common religious worldview or an attendant vocabulary for describing subjective matters of the human psyche, though such a common vocabulary is indeed an inherent part of most if not all religious traditional and nondemocratic societies. To this day, the U.S.'s lack of such a shared "subjective vocabulary" remains clearly evident in the day-to-day life of the nation, especially at those times when a culturally diverse group of citizens collectively experiences a profound trauma. At such times, each person customarily seeks a counselor, clinician, or friend of her or his own cultural community for support. Priests, ministers, rabbis, shamans, physicians, and others confirmed in various cultural traditions (many of them professedly religious) are all ostensibly qualified to administer appropriate counsel at times of distress, but each citizen typically feels comfortable receiving support from a counselor confirmed by her or his own tradition and conversant in the subjective vocabulary in which he or she places confidence. At most other times, however, an outward, objective focus tends to predominate in the nation's public forum, where subjective or particularist matters are described only rarely, and then typically using generic terms and euphemisms.[59]

As a result of the nation's having suspended discussion of religious questions from the public forum and thus sharing no single vocabulary for describing subjective matters of the psyche or of group identity, nearly all discussion of music in the nation's public forum has consistently tended toward describing the externally observable, formal aspects of particular instances of music themselves (i.e., the mere "sound artifacts"), rather than accounting for the effects of different musical practices on the psyches of individual human beings and the groups to which they belong. Over the history of the nation, discussions of music in the popular media (e.g., newspaper reviews) have typically reported in great detail the "stylistic" differences of different composers and performers, plus facts about their personal habits and idiosyncrasies, while for the most part describing the effects of culturally different musical practices on those participating in them only in terms sufficiently objective and generic that they can be grasped by most if not all citizens. Even the nation's university-educated musicians have gradually come to discuss particular works of music using primarily the objective, largely mathematical terminology of music theory, rather than employing a form of discourse that substantively accounts for the psychophysiological and psychosocial effects of given works of music on those who experience them. By contrast, as noted in Chapter 3, many of the world's different cultural communities typically conceptualize and describe their respective musical practices using the unique subjective vocabulary of their respective religious traditions, which account for its "spiritual" or psychosocial effects, thereby delineating clearly its importance to the psychosocial health of the individual and the community.

For present purposes, it is most important to realize that the nation's lack of a common vocabulary for describing subjective matters of the psyche prevented its first citizens from recognizing and discussing collectively the beneficial psychosocial effects of different musical practices present in the nation on those who participated in them.[60] Furthermore, the nation's constitutional commitment to the acceptance of cultural diversity has generally had the effect of curtailing public discussion of different religious forms of music as culturally rooted behaviors. These factors have contributed to a continuing collective difficulty among U.S. citizens in recognizing that the different musical practices undertaken independently by its constituent cultural communities (i.e., both long-standing communities and recently emerged ones) have importantly beneficial effects for the psychosocial health of the nation as a whole. Indeed, in the rationalistic, post-Enlightenment context of the U.S. public forum, the important psychophysiological and psychosocial effects of most musical practices have been discussed very little in the public forum throughout most of the nation's history, and, when they have arisen, have typically been passed off as mere matters of personal "taste."[61]

NO OFFICIAL WORLDVIEW, OTHER THAN DEMOCRACY ITSELF

Unlike many other culturally pluralistic, state societies, the U.S. sanctions no official religious or political worldview other than democracy itself. By contrast, as we have noted, some other state societies recognize no separation at all between religion and the state. We saw in Chapter 3 that in the modern Muslim nation of Iran under the Ayatollah Khomeini, for instance, the ayatollah served not only as the head of the state but also as its religious leader. The only musical practices that were unanimously, publicly condoned there were those that served to validate the state's collective religious and political worldview (i.e., those associated with Muslim worship), while engagement in all other musical practices—which would have raised the possibility of intrastate cultural differences—tended to be denied or were routinely punished. Likewise, we saw that in other culturally pluralistic societies not unified by a common religious worldview, such as the totalitarian nation-states of the former Soviet Union and the now defunct Nazi Germany, certain musical practices were sanctioned and promoted by the state's leaders because their psychosocially unifying effects supported the state's goals of homogeneity in worldview. Other practices that ran counter to the worldviews sanctioned by these nation-states were typically silenced.

Close attention to the more liberal sources of world news reveals that similar practices continues in various world nations.[62]

Due to the close relationship we have seen that exists between music, certain forms of religious practice, and the worldviews of different cultural communities in all human societies, we might expect that elected leaders of the U.S. government would have sought deliberately throughout the nation's history to avoid supporting any musical practices—just as they have avoided officially supporting any single form of religion—so as not to compromise the state's professedly democratic status. However, as we have seen, the U.S. was established as a nation at the time when Enlightenment philosophers had relegated music to the societally peripheral category of *art* in their aesthetic philosophical conceptions, considering different musical works abstractly as objects of universal beauty or as manifestations of alternate conceptions of Reality. Thus, despite the fact that most of the ongoing musical practices undertaken in the nation that have involved significantly large groups of people have been supported historically by the nation's constituent religious and cultural communities, arts patrons, and commercial entertainment companies, the U.S. government could also be considered free to support financially *some* musical practices without compromising its First Amendment doctrine of separation of religion and state. In fact, the federal government has subsidized music at various times in its history. Since the remainder of this discussion depends on a clear understanding of the nature of the involvement by the U.S. government in support of musical practices since its establishment, it seems appropriate to relate this history briefly here.[63]

George Washington, the nation's first president, affirmed his support for the arts (including music) when he wrote enthusiastically in 1781 that "the Arts and Sciences, essential to the prosperity of the State and to the ornamentation and happiness of human life, have a primary claim to the encouragement of every lover of his country and mankind."[64] While he reportedly intended that an arts center would be built for the purpose of providing a venue for music and other art forms in Washington, DC, the nation's new capital, he did not see his dream realized in his lifetime.[65] The first true instance of direct federal support for a particular musical practice did not come about until 1798, when the U.S. Marine Band was established to play for official ceremonies, but there is no evidence to suggest that the band was created to support any expressed agenda beyond rallying the troops for the protection of democracy and occasionally providing ceremonial pomp.[66] With the foundation of the Library of Congress in 1800 and the Smithsonian Institution in 1846, the federal government incidentally provided public repositories for collections of music, but, again, as no guidelines were established for including the music of particular groups, these efforts too cannot be viewed as culturally biased.[67] A congressional bill was passed in 1891 to incorporate a National Conservatory of Music, but the institution was short-lived because Congress did not make provision for its continuing financial support.[68]

The situation changed somewhat in the economic vacuum created by the stock-market crash of 1929, as a large part of the U.S. labor force—25 percent, including 70 percent of the nation's musicians—suffered unemployment for several years.[69] In order to provide temporary economic support (and to bolster public morale), the federal government established a number of work-relief programs for citizens in a variety of professional fields.[70] One such program, the Federal Music Project, provided many musicians with work for a few years beginning in 1935 by subsidizing five thousand public performances a month nationally and underwriting music education programs in twenty-six states.[71] Soon after the commencement of this project, a group of legislators considered the possible creation of a new executive department to be called the Department of Science, Art, and Literature, which would have supported music in the nation, but the idea was soon abandoned for lack of sufficient congressional support. During World War II, the federal government again briefly supported some musical practices for morale boosting, attitude development, and cultural exchange purposes. While these efforts could arguably be described as propagandistic in their support of democracy, the fact that they were quickly abandoned as unnecessary after the war suggests their benignity with respect to different cultural forms of music.[72]

The one instance of genuine, sustained commitment to music on the part of the U.S. government came about in 1965 with the establishment of the National Endowment for the Arts. Remarkably, the creation of the endowment stemmed from an expressed awareness by President John F. Kennedy and various congressional leaders that the arts (including music) *do* provide important psychosocial benefits to American society as a whole.[73] However, since the inception of the endowment, the individuals given responsibility for making decisions on the awarding of endowment funds have been charged to support the creation of new works not on the basis of their cultural content, but of the "artistic quality" of past works by the artists and composers who seek funding.[74] Thus, it is not surprising that the endowment's existence has been controversial since its inception.[75] Despite periodic public dispute over its continued existence, it nevertheless remains as a federally funded institution.

However, beyond these relatively few and largely provisional instances, federal government support for music has been strikingly minimal over the nation's history in comparison with that in other affluent nations, and in no case has the government's sponsorship of it ever been shown to have been motivated by any cultural purpose other than the support of democracy itself. We noted earlier that what we learned in Chapter 3 about the inherently culturally unifying effects of particular musical practices might lead us to wonder whether the continuing, relatively low level of governmental support of it in the U.S. might be attributable to a continuing, principled effort on the part of legislators and other state officials to maintain a separation between the affairs of the avowedly culturally neutral state and musical practices as inherently religious or potentially socially volatile behavior. While such a conception may in fact be held by some U.S. legislators, it seems clear that most of them lack interest in supporting music for reasons having to do with their proclivity to focus on what they tacitly believe to be more practical and pressing economic and political concerns.

As noted earlier, most philosophers writing at the time of the Enlightenment had relegated music to the socially peripheral category of *art* in their conceptual schemes, and the nation's founders were deeply influenced by the perspectives of these philosophers. Many of the nation's subsequent leaders have, like some other citizens, also tacitly adopted these philosophical views, their confidence in the Enlightenment philosophical conception of "the aesthetic" as a socially autonomous realm having been bolstered by the evident economic success of capitalist democracy and other social benefits stemming from that era's various intellectual insights. Thus, we should not be surprised to find that they have not considered music as being of sufficient societal importance to warrant government support. Indeed, it seems apparent that the marginalizing Enlightenment concept of music as *art* stemming from the writings of philosophers in what we have seen to be the politically nebulous field of "aesthetics" has remained rather firmly seated in the "collective mind" of the nation's leaders throughout history.

Given this state of affairs, the members of the various cultural communities (including professedly religious communities) comprising the U.S. have had considerable freedom to undertake their own musical practices as they wish, each according to their own beliefs and without government support or interference.[76] Over the years, myriad new musical practices have thus emerged independent of established religious or cultural communities, many of them involving persons from a wide variety of different cultural backgrounds, and they have flourished, serving citizens as effective means of psychosocial equilibration in various different religious, artistic, and entertainment contexts over the nation's history. However, while the nation's tacit adoption of the Enlightenment concept of music as a form of *art* and its constitutional establishment of "freedom of expression" has allowed its citizens great license in undertaking different musical practices, the U.S. government's forbearance from adopting any form of musical practice as the official practice of the state and also from substantively supporting different musics as *art* throughout most of its history has had the simultaneous effect of leading the nation's populace to conclude that music is not really substantively important to the collective psychosocial health of the nation and that it does not have any consequential political significance. Indeed, only very rarely in the nation's history have particular musical practices had sufficiently major social impact to incite censure by large segments of the populace or to stimulate governmental involvement, and, notably, most such instances have been downplayed by the nation's mass media.[77]

Incidentally, it is important to note before leaving this point that many of the world's other democratic nations do continue to support particular musical practices precisely for their psychosocial equilibrating effects and for the sense of political solidarity they provide their citizens. Indeed, most of these nations spend far more on "the arts" in general (and on music in particular) than the U.S. does at present. In 1985, the governments of Sweden, Germany, France, Canada, and Britain spent the equivalent of $45.60, $39.40, $35.10, $28.50, and $16.10 per citizen, respectively, on "the arts" and museums of their nations, while the U.S. expended only $3.30 per citizen.[78] Considering the comparatively greater support of "the arts" provided by these governments, it seems likely that citizens in these nations may have a greater awareness of the importance of music to their collective psychosocial health and their sense of a national identity than do citizens of the U.S.[79]

Of course, if we frame the issue somewhat more broadly, we can see that the U.S. government's forbearance from supporting any form of musical practice is actually quite consistent with its general policy of nonintervention into matters of the human psyche. Indeed, the federal government has historically offered few means of proactive psychological maintenance to the nation's populace throughout history, having ceded most of the responsibility for such maintenance to the individual citizen and to the nation's constituent communities. Instead, the state has elected to establish various reactive agencies and mechanisms for the purpose of responding when particular social problems stemming from citizens' psychological and psychosocial pathologies raise concern for the health of the entire society (e.g., the community mental health centers of the National Institutes of Health, drug rehabilitation programs, prisons). Notably, federal financial support of most of these measures has been much less controversial than federal support of "the arts."[80]

THE U.S. EMBRACED DEMOCRATIC CAPITALISM AS ITS SOCIAL SYSTEM

As already noted, the U.S.'s adoption of democracy as its form of government not only established it as a nation in which its constituent communities would have a voice in its governance but also defined its public forum as a theoretically neutral social context from which discussion of religion and other subjective matters of the psyche would be generally suspended, due to the populace's lack of a common "subjective vocabulary." This suspension has effectively thwarted discussion and has thus contributed to obscuring collective recognition of the importantly beneficial psychosocial effects of the various culturally unique musical practices as well as their inherently political nature. Furthermore, we have seen that the U.S. government's forbearance from condoning any religion or worldview other than democracy itself and from supporting any music as a national music has supported, if not actually fostered, a conception among the populace that most if not all musical practices represent societally insignificant behaviors.[81] However, it seems probable that the nation's ultimate adoption of capitalism as its economic system and its general orientation toward scientific and technological progress have contributed most significantly to confirming citizens' gradual shift away from recognizing different musical practices as psychosocially equilibrating and culturally significant behaviors, valuable for their unification of community, toward conceptualizing music as an ostensibly generic product of "entertainment." Indeed, over the years, the nation's democratic capitalist orientation has tended to feed the enthusiasm for scientific research that was kindled during the Enlightenment, as the technological applications of scientific discoveries have often provided great personal and financial rewards for those who have made them. At the same time, democratic capitalism and science have also had significantly disintegrative effects on many of the nation's constituent cultural communities, religious and otherwise. As a result, public recognition of musical practices as societally important, psychosocially equilibrating behaviors has been further obscured. The nation's democratic capitalist and scientific orientation has contributed to this cultural fragmentation and concomitant devaluing of musical practices in at least three ways.

First of all, the success of the nation's collective efforts at developing a more complete scientific understanding of the physical universe has for many citizens radically challenged the validity of the religious conceptions of Reality embodied in and described by the nation's different cultural communities, simultaneously obscuring the conceptual connection of musical practices with "religion" or worldview. While some citizens have throughout their lives conservatively sustained the worldviews of their youth (a great many of which are religious in the broad sense that they involve adherence to an institutionalized system of beliefs and ritual practices), others have shifted their orientation over time (especially when scientific conceptions of the universe have changed), and they have transferred their emotional allegiance to communities embodying worldviews different from those with which they were raised.[82] Still other citizens have come to embody worldviews differing greatly from those of their ancestors, having forged their own guiding doctrines more or less informally and independently from the traditions of their own cultural heritage, from perspectives they have acquired in learning about the traditions of other citizens, and from insights they have derived from recent scientific discoveries. Notably, these "homegrown" worldviews cannot be described as religious in the sense of being associated with an established religious institution, yet they typically share similarities in principle and practice with organized religion.[83] In the midst of these changes, and largely as a result of the remarkable progress made in medical and other technological areas to improving the quality of life in the U.S., many citizens have gradually renounced much of their emotional or "spiritual" commitment to the worldviews of organized religious communities and cultural communities, investing their emotional security in what might be better described as a "faith in reason and science" and in a pursuit for material gain or "worldly" satisfaction grounded in capitalist economic theory. At present, a societal ambivalence continues to exist in the U.S. public forum between commitment to religious doctrines and to post-Enlightenment philosophical conceptions.

Not surprisingly, the nation's collective religious ambivalence and cultural diversity are reflected in the diversity of musical practices undertaken within its boundaries. Actually, numerous historically grounded, traditional musical practices do continue to provide psychosocial balance for members of the nation's conservative religious communities.[84] At the same time, many of the newer, "reformed" religious groups in the U.S. now borrow sounds and concepts from the musical practices undertaken ritually by different cultural communities—as well as from "secular" entertainment practices—for the tacitly understood purpose of effecting psychosocial union within their own communities. These groups typically adapt and set the resulting music with lyrics consistent with their own beliefs, sometimes knowingly, but often ostensibly unaware of the irony of their appropriations.[85] Simultaneously, the nation's composers and performers of art music have proffered a remarkable *mélange* of sophisticated, hybrid musical practices, having both consciously and unconsciously adopted aspects of music from different cultural sources, both sacred and secular, for their own variously conceived purposes and for the intellectual consideration (and psychosocial benefit) of their audiences. Similarly, the nation's entertainment industry has popularized a tremendous diversity of ostensibly "secular" forms of popular music reflecting the religious and cultural complexity of the nation (and indeed the world), though they have routinely done so with sales rather than psychosocially beneficent purposes in mind. (Industry leaders generally justify their enterprise by saying that they are merely "giving the American people what they want.")

As a result of this diversity and the tacit dominance of economic values over those of cultural cohesion in the nation, the respective connections between ethnicity, cultural orientation, and musical practice have become much less clearly defined in the U.S. than they were historically. This cultural ambiguity has contributed to obscuring the conceptual connection between particular musical practices and the communities from which they stem in the "collective mind" of the nation's populace.

Second, the economic success of capitalist democracy and the scientific, technological bent of the nation have significantly raised the standard of living for the nation's citizens, evidently diminishing the necessity for them to be connected with the cultural community of their origins (or, for that matter, any other community) for physical survival. Over time, this too has contributed to weakening citizens' conceptual connection of music with religion or worldview. At this juncture it is important to keep in mind the point made earlier that while religious and cultural freedom—and thus freedom to choose among musical practices—is now taken for granted by a majority of U.S. citizens, such freedom has not been experienced historically by persons living in traditional and nondemocratic state societies, nor are the different musical practices undertaken in such societies conceptualized as politically neutral behaviors by persons living in them at present. Even in some present-day democratic societies, the conceptual connections between certain musical practices and the worldviews of the constituent communities that undertake them continue to be so strong that they more or less completely prevent an individual in one cultural community from participating in the musical practices of another.

For example, in the modern city of Jerusalem, Israel, where various Christian, Jewish, Muslim, and other communities embodying different worldviews strive to coexist within a relatively small land area, differences in religious practice, spoken language, race, and certain social customs remain paramount despite the confirmed democratic orientation of the government. Since land, money, and food resources are scarce in Israel, most individuals must depend heavily on the religious or cultural community to which they belong for survival. As a result, it would be *very* unusual for a member of one of Israel's constituent communities to participate in certain events involving the musical practice of a religiously or culturally dissimilar community (e.g., a religious service or other such ritual event) for fear of possibly provoking hostility by that community or arousing mistrust and perhaps being alienated by her or his own community.[86] In Jerusalem, as in all such economically and culturally strained social contexts, every adult citizen must maintain a greater awareness of the cultural significance and political importance of participation in certain musical practices than most persons living in the more economically affluent and scientifically oriented U.S. In fact, we might observe that most citizens of Jerusalem (regardless of cultural identity) regard the musical practice of their respective communities as being more *meaningful* (i.e., more integrally related to their physical and emotional well-being) than do most people of the U.S., where, by contrast, citizens may feel free to visit and even participate in the musical practices or rituals of most communities different from their own with little concern of jeopardizing their personal well-being.[87]

Third and finally, it has been scientific inquiry and the subsequent capitalist promotion of technology in one broad area of application—specifically, that of audio and video recording and transmission—that has contributed most greatly to changing the conceptions of music held among the U.S. populace, since the wide availability of products stemming from these technologies has gradually made it unnecessary for people to be physically present in community to experience its psychophysiologically and psychosocially beneficial effects. Considered in one way, recording, broadcast, and computer (Internet) technologies have provided the nation's citizens with numerous educational benefits. They have afforded them a means of "listening in on" (and seeing) musical practices of different communities in different social contexts, giving them opportunities for experiencing and learning about the musical practices undertaken by people living in distant places and times, without having to leave their homes. We can also see from our pragmatic perspective that broadcasts and recordings have served as psychosocial lifelines for persons physically unable to attend and participate in the ritual activities of their communities. Indeed, these electronic media have provided them with virtual connections to their communities, in much the same way that "letters from home" or photographs of community events have provided persons living in remote or "foreign" places with emotional sustenance by sustaining their contact with others of like mind. Furthermore, the introduction of these media has greatly facilitated the creation of new forms of music as *art*, as well as stimulating the emergence of several new art forms (e.g., cinema, television films, recording arts) as means by which socially insightful artisans might manifest their personal conceptions of Reality for the reflection and deliberation of others.

However, considered in another way, we can see that the advent of broadcast and recording technologies and the subsequent ubiquity of the sounds of music in the U.S. public forum have also contributed to diminishing the populace's awareness of the important psychosocially beneficial nature of active participation in a musical practice in community *and* to their general tendency *not* to recognize the political significance of such participation. Whereas in earlier centuries most musical practices were uniquely communal phenomena, many citizens now experience them only via secondary media—that is, through broadcasts, Webcasts, or via audio and visual recordings. Indeed, many citizens have even come to live in one of the "virtual realities" proffered by the nation's media and entertainment industries as works of *art*, mistakenly conceptualizing it as an audible manifestation of a genuine, socially well-integrated community, while actually experiencing only some of the psychological benefits of true community membership that are usually involved in a musical practice and becoming distanced from many of the greater challenges and benefits such membership naturally involves.[88] Notably, such social remove is not typically in evidence in traditional, religious societal contexts, where it would likely be regarded as deviant behavior.[89]

Concomitantly, the omnipresence, near constancy, and often seductive use of the sounds of musical practices via recordings, broadcasts, and the Internet in much of the nation's public forum has, over time, had the effect of diminishing the populace's recognition of the fact that many of the musical practices taking place around them originated in communities where they served as important participatory means of psychosocial equilibration. Furthermore, the conception of different forms of music as *art* (i.e., sound artifacts created for the purpose of manifesting unique latent worldviews for the intellectual consideration and possible incorporation of an audience) has become less and less widely acknowledged (in its original sense) in the nation's public forum.

Instead, the associational use of music for purposes of commercial enticement in advertisements, shopping malls, and other public and private contexts has proliferated, having the effect of gradually numbing the consciousness of many citizens to the important psychological benefits of musical engagement in community while at the same time luring them to buy certain products. A number of citizens have now reached the point where they tend to take *all* music for granted, often not consciously noticing it, and, at other times, regarding it as a social annoyance.[90] In some measure, these attitudes also represent reactions to the societal increase in different forms of music stemming from the increasing cultural diversity of the nation; at present, any given individual is likely to find a smaller percentage of the music he or she encounters in the public forum to be personally, substantively meaningful (i.e., profoundly psychophysiologically and psychosocially affective) than he or she would have in the past.[91] Indeed, the overwhelming presence of myriad different musical practices (of which no individual is *fully* knowledgeable) in certain contexts has contributed to the societal devaluing of *all* music (if music is considered as a generic phenomenon).

At the same time, the gradual improvement in quality of broadcast and recording technologies in the U.S. marketplace has had the effect of rendering some members of the populace musically passive by creating an expectation among them of a standard of performance quality that few nonprofessionals are able to attain. The desire for active participation of some citizens who would *like* to be actively involved for purposes related to their own psychophysiological and psychosocial equilibration has been frustrated, since they lack what they have come to believe are the requisite skills.[92]

Furthermore, the conception of music that now tends to be most widely propagated by the nation's mass media is not a religious or culture-particular notion of it as a means of psychosocial equilibrating or a vehicle for intellectual reflection, but rather the extreme commercial notion of it as a product produced merely to provide diversionary amusement and, whenever possible, to realize financial profit. Indeed, the nation's popular media tend to downplay the psychophysiological and psychosocial importance of different musical practices for the culturally dissimilar individuals or communities for whom they have meaning, and they do not acknowledge their political significance, focusing instead on promoting the music itself (as a product) to whoever will buy it and on using music (as a seductive, semiotic association device) to promote the purchase of certain products.[93] In fact, at those times when broadcast and recording companies now include in their scope the music of a "traditional" cultural community whose practices and beliefs differ widely from those already well known in the European and American public forums, they typically present it too for its entertainment value, thereby more or less completely denying the listening public the opportunity to learn about the unique cultural worldview it manifests.[94] The media industry has not only contributed to the trivialization of culturally significant musical practices in this way, but has sometimes actively disparaged some of them on the ostensibly innocent pretext of comedic irony or satire, when in fact the net effect of such clowning has been to downplay if not actually promote bias against that cultural community's worldview.[95] In fact, religious conceptions of music—and other traditional worldviews—are often disparaged by the media in relation to the commercial notion of music as mere "entertainment."

As one might expect, on those rare occasions when media leaders are questioned about the appropriateness of using "sacred" musical practices in artistic or entertainment contexts (for profit), they assert the benignity of their actions, pointing out that the groups involved have freely elected to perform and record. In their view, the political question of whether the public experiences a given instance of music as "religious behavior," "artistic engagement," or mere "entertainment" is not really their concern.[96] Rarely publicly discussed is the fact that many of these cultural communities have found themselves in something of a double bind prior to recording or broadcast. That is to say, while they recognize that in recording and broadcasting the sounds of their unique musical practice they have the potential of raising public awareness of the existence of their community and profiting financially (which is sometimes necessary for their continued solvency and existence as a community), many are also aware that in doing so they are likely allowing their music to be subsumed into popular culture as merely another form of "entertainment."[97] Indeed, in allowing their music to be recorded and sold, they are in some measure compromising their unique worldview and prostituting their unique musical practice.

Naturally, it is doubtful that anyone could effectively convict media corporations of contributing to the denigration of musical practices in the public forum. After all, most media leaders assert, it is not really their concern *why* people buy these products or *how* they regard them. Furthermore, we might ask, don't media leaders have a *right* to record, promote, and sell the music they have recorded in the "free market" of the U.S.? Certainly, citizens *are* free to "tune out" and not buy these products if they so choose.[98] This seems a valid point, but as social scholar Francis Fukuyama has pointed out, there is a problem with this kind of appeal to civil rights.

> The uncompromising character of American rights discourse is based on the belief that the end of government is to protect the sphere of autonomy in which self-sufficient individuals can enjoy their natural rights, free of pressures, constraints, or obligations to those around them. That sphere of autonomy has grown substantially over the past decades. . . . What is particularly insidious about the American culture of rights is that it dignifies with high moral purpose what often amount to low private interests or desires. . . . Rights, which should be the noble attribute of free and public-spirited citizens, [have] instead tend[ed] to

become a kind of cover for selfish individuals to pursue their private aims without any regard for the surrounding community.[99]

Indeed, notwithstanding the right of citizens *not* to attend to the broadcasts and products of the entertainment industry and the right of cultural communities *not* to record and perform, these media have become increasingly pervasive, the promotion of different forms of music as entertainment and the use of music in advertising is now almost constant, and, as a result, it is unlikely that many persons living in the U.S. could escape being affected by—if not subsumed into—the "music as entertainment" mentality.[100] Notably, different religious communities have instituted various means by which their adherents might be aided in maintaining psychological remove from such comparatively base and trivializing conceptions, but those persons (particularly young people) who have no association with a cohesive, psychologically supportive, and nonexploitive community embodying an "alternate" worldview may not have any basis for acquiring such a detached perspective, and may come to assume that *all* musical practices are inherently economically motivated "entertainment."[101]

Furthermore, it is important to recognize that, because of the dominant influence the media now have on the consciousness of many citizens, the leaders of media corporations are now in a unique position to assure that the commercial conception of music as entertainment will continue to predominate in the nation's public forum. These leaders have considerable incentive for propagating this view, since, by doing so, they also support the continuance of their own companies' economic growth, thus potentially expanding their economic and political influence over the nation. Economist Edward Herman and linguist and political scholar Noam Chomsky, among others, have pointed out that the nation now faces a potentially great danger, stemming from the fact that a relatively small number of corporations have come to control most of the U.S. information and entertainment media (e.g., radio and television stations, record and film production companies): Specifically, because of their influence over the information now disseminated to the U.S. populace as "news," these corporations are in the unique position of being able to portray world events to the U.S. populace in ways that support their own broader financial and political interests, while completely omitting other events from coverage when making such information public would contravene these interests.[102] Chomsky's main points are that since U.S. citizens have very few sources of information about world events apart from the corporately controlled mass media, it has become almost inevitable that they will tacitly accept the versions of news stories presented there as "the whole truth," and that because these corporations can limit citizens' awareness of the political factors behind world events in this way, they can thus influence citizens to act in ways which will benefit the corporations' interests. For our purposes here, it is most important to realize that as these corporations promote the concept of music as mere entertainment to the nation's populace while providing little background information about the communities who undertake it, they may discourage citizens from recognizing and addressing the inherently different cultural realities that different forms of music manifest and from understanding the important equilibrating role many musical practices play in the socially well-integrated communities in which they are undertaken. At the same time, in making decisions about what forms of music to record and broadcast, media corporations tend to favor those which will have immediate appeal to the widest audience in order to assure maximum profit, thereby strengthening their economic base and helping to assure that the concept "music as entertainment" will remain dominant.

Some readers may protest that the foregoing pragmatic analysis is ill founded, as it would seem to vilify unfairly the media corporations now operating in the nation whose intentions are not purposefully destructive of communities. In response we might note that this pragmatic analysis merely serves to point up the effects of certain historical acts and events (in this case the aggressive use of recording and broadcasting media for commercial purposes in a democratic capitalist society) on the conceptions of musical practices held by a large community of people (in this case the present populace of the U.S.), and to demonstrate the effects this commercialization is continuing to have on the conceptions of music held by much of the nation's populace.

Certainly, the mere acts of recording and broadcasting music cannot in themselves be regarded as social problems, since the mere use of these technologies is not in itself necessarily commercially manipulative. Indeed, as we have already noted, audio and video recording and broadcasting have served and continue to serve the U.S. and other modern societies as highly valuable tools for mass education and communication, and media companies certainly deserve to be compensated for providing this service. Furthermore, the mass media's representation of some musical practices as entertainment cannot be regarded as ill-founded; obviously, some of them are undertaken specifically for simple, entertaining purposes, and no broadly educated person could seriously deny that the media's presentation of them is often very socially beneficial. Neither is this argument necessarily meant to cast doubts on the comparative value of democratic capitalism as a social system, as it now seems clear that the great benefits it has provided to citizens of the U.S. (and many other world nations)—particularly in terms of personal liberty and quality of life—far outweigh those provided by any previously or subsequently developed form of society. Indeed, if Adam Smith, the best-known of the originators of capitalist theory, were to comment on this issue, he would likely point out that those individuals and communities providing significant psychophysiological and psychosocial equilibrating effects for sizable segments of the population (via music or any other means) are almost certain to survive in the nation's capitalist marketplace, regardless of how they are represented by the mass media, as long as someone continues to derive psychosocial benefit from them and provides them with due financial compensation. Finally, it must be admitted that not all individuals working with the mass media can be held responsible for contributing to the trivialization of music in the U.S., as it seems clear that most of them—having been raised in this culturally pluralistic, capitalist democracy—are merely doing what they have learned throughout their lives is appropriate for success in a capitalist economic system: maximizing profits.

However, we must surely realize that in generally subsuming *all* musical practices under the conceptual rubric of "entertainment," aggressively promoting the purchase of most recordings and other products as mere diversionary amusements, and effectively superseding for many citizens the various community-based musical practices with culturally uncommitted mass "entertainment," the nation's media have directed citizens' focus away from recognizing and acknowledging the cultural significance of most musical practices. Moreover, through their marketing efforts, these media corporations have acquired a tremendous amount of economic and political control over the "habits of mind" of the nation's populace. Historically speaking, the various musical practices undertaken by the members of the world's different cultural communities have provided uniquely powerful, culturally distinctive means of coming to terms with individual and collective conflicts of the psyche. But, regrettably, as the U.S. commercial media industry has aggressively promoted sales of all forms of music for their economic value and has increasingly used music for commercially seductive purposes in advertising, they have contributed to trivializing different conceptions of music held within the nation's populace and to diminishing public recognition of the profound importance that different musical practices have to many of the nation's—and the world's—constituent communities. Furthermore, since many of the nation's citizens do not belong to religious or cultural communities that embrace and embody a different view, these citizens now have little opportunity for gaining a perspective distinct from the commercial "music as entertainment" notions widely promoted by the media.[103]

Indeed, the unique societal characteristics just discussed have collectively contributed to defining the nation's public forum as a social context in which citizens are now more likely to regard "musicians" as a group either as hopeful opportunists (i.e., simple persons having some unique ability to provide diversionary amusement who aspire to attain great commercial success via some combination of self-promotion and luck) or as mere functionaries (i.e., artisans who work in the service of the entertainment or advertising industry), rather than considering them as societally knowledgeable and politically insightful persons who have developed certain innate and acquired capabilities through study, reflection, and practice to become effective artists, shamans, or other psychosocial conciliators and transformers of the "collective mind" of a community or a society at large. The latter, more favorable view, held (in various forms) in many of the world's traditional societies and religious or culturally oriented communities, has been increasingly eclipsed by the nation's mass media, though it does continue to inhere in some of the nation's surviving constituent communities.[104] As an additional sign that the view of musical practices as beneficial means of psychosocial equilibration in community has been obscured, U.S. citizens are now far more likely to characterize a radically new form of music—one that has significantly conciliatory or transforming psychosocial impact on a large group of people—as a potentially profitable product, rather than as a substantive contribution to the psychological health of society stemming from the reflective insight and ability of the musician who produced it. By extension, the study of music has for many citizens come to seem more like a self-indulgent, possibly lucrative hobby than as something one might undertake to benefit one's own psychological health or to enable one to contribute substantively to the psychosocial health of one's community.[105]

We might have expected the leaders of the nation's various religious communities and scholars of music to protest the progressive trivializing of music as mere entertainment. Sadly, however, the perspectives of religious leaders have often been downplayed in the public forum (on the basis that the sectarian nature of their views makes them relevant only to their own constituencies) or are misrepresented there (for reasons having to do with the media industry's incapacity or disinclination to represent them accurately).[106] At the same time, scholars in music in the nation's universities have largely focused on their own, often more culturally insular intellectual pursuits rather than concerning themselves with protesting the way their profession is generally represented in the popular media or introducing university coursework that might substantively address these issues. Even to this day, ethnomusicology and the sociology of music continue to be regarded by a number of faculty members in the nation's universities and schools of music as marginal, supplementary areas of study.[107] At the same time, the works of many twentieth-century academic composers have become increasingly difficult for most citizens to comprehend, providing little if any psychophysiological and psychosocial benefit or intellectual interest to persons outside the small groups of intellectuals who have the experiential background necessary to grasp their meanings. Not surprisingly, the media have done little to help the public understand the efforts of these introspective composers, preferring to promote primarily those forms of music that are easily accessible to larger audiences and thus more likely to stimulate sizable sales in short order.

However, despite the cultural fragmentation and commercialization now obscuring public recognition of it in the U.S., the fact remains that the vast majority of the nation's citizens do continue to undertake some form of musical practice (albeit many now only as listeners) precisely for the beneficial psychophysiologically and psychosocially equilibrating benefits it provides them (however diminished these effects may be). Furthermore, as noted in Chapter 3, when a particular musical practice has such significant effects for an individual, it does so only because the music involved embodies that person's present worldview (as in *possession*) or meaningfully transcends it (as in *shamanism*), whether that worldview is grounded in a socially well-integrated community or a virtual one and whether the individual is physically present in a public ritual context or only accessing the music via some form of media. Inevitably, these effects on individuals impact the respective communities and the larger society to which they belong. In addition, as Christopher Small, Jacques Attali, and others have demonstrated, analysis of the various forms of music that have emerged in a given society over a period of time reveals that these formal changes have typically reflected if not in fact preordained broader cultural changes throughout the history of that society.[108]

We have seen that a gradual movement away from "spiritual" or psychosocially equilibrating conceptions of music and toward more materialistic views began in Europe during the years surrounding the Enlightenment era, stemming from the advent of notation, copyright laws, and the emergence of the "professional composer," as well as from the failure of the "aesthetic" philosophers to account for the place of music in the newly emerging reason-based conceptions of society. In addition, conceptions of musical practices as societally important, psychosocially equilibrating behaviors have been further obscured in the public forum of the U.S. by the nation's adoption of laws separating religion from the state, by the nation's institutionalization of democracy in place of any particular worldview, and by the nation's establishment of democratic capitalism as its social system. Specifically, these events have contributed to forming the nation as a society in which no common vocabulary is shared for describing subjective matters of the psyche (e.g., concerning the effects of music) and where recognition of citizens' personal and cultural differences are often downplayed. As a result, commercial conceptions of all forms of music as mere entertainment products have tended to predominate in the nation's public forum.

Nevertheless, despite all the historical and societal factors now obscuring recognition of it in the nation's public forum, close study of the various musical practices presently undertaken in religious, artistic, and entertainment contexts in the U.S. reveals that most if not all of them originated in and evolved from the collective, habitual practices of unique communities where they initially served communal purposes of psychosocial equilibration. Despite the fact that no single, holistic conception of Reality is now collectively embraced by citizens living in the U.S. (beyond the ontologically shallow set of ideas describing democratic capitalism), the various musical practices presently undertaken by the nation's constituent individuals and communities continue to provide important psychological benefit and cultural orientation to those who are semiotically disposed to find them meaningful. As a result, engagement in these musical practices continues to impact and reflect the psychosocial, cultural equilibrium of the nation and, indeed, the world.

MUSIC EDUCATION IN TRADITIONAL, STATE, AND DEMOCRATIC STATE SOCIETIES

On the basis of what we have learned about how different musical practices have served historically as means of effecting psychophysiological and psychosocial balance among the members of different, culturally homogeneous communities, we would expect to find that the various forms of education in music undertaken formally or informally in the different types of societies we have delineated would reflect the unique characteristics of those societies. For example, in *traditional* societies in which a particular, culturally unique musical practice serves as a medium for the psychosocial equilibration of individuals and the community, we would expect music education to serve as the means by which the elders of the society would instill in their young the skills necessary for them to participate in and perhaps contribute to the community's unique form of musical practice for such purposes.

In fact, even a cursory survey of the different musical practices undertaken by persons living in the world's remaining traditional societies shows this to be the case. For example, the hymn, chorus, and gospel tune singing in the various Christian churches, the chanting of monks in meditation in different Buddhist traditions, the melodious, vocalized prayers of Muslim believers, and the "spiritual" songs of various Native American communities and tribes all serve as prime examples. This also describes the sound-utilizing social practices undertaken incidentally by the members of those communities whose conceptual systems embrace no concept equivalent to the Western notion of music. Numerous additional examples could be cited.

Similarly, in those culturally pluralistic *state* societies in which the government tacitly embraces or actively enforces a common worldview, state leaders have historically supported education in some form of music for the purpose of instilling in their youth a musical practice that socializes and balances them psychosocially in a way that is consistent with the worldview they collectively, tacitly believe to be optimal. Indeed, the leaders of many such nations have historically shown tremendous interest in supporting education in certain musical practices (and not others), as they recognize that by doing so they may influence the young people in their society to maintain and propagate the way of life that they have collectively come to regard as best.

Again, a brief global-historical overview of the different musical practices undertaken by persons living in the world's various nondemocratic and noncapitalist state societies reveals this to be the case. Chapter 3 described the limitations placed on musical practices in Iran under the Ayatollah Khomeini and the emphasis placed on upholding certain values in the musical practices of Nazi Germany by Adolph Hitler; in both cases the forms of education in music practiced in these nations were intended to support the state's official worldview or ideology. The same could be said of music education practices undertaken in the former Soviet bloc countries before the end of the Cold War. Similarly, during the Edo era (1603–1868) of Japan's history, the ruling Tokugawa shogunate suppressed all European musical traditions, having established the *noh* tradition as their official music and instituted schools for the various singing roles and the different instruments in that tradition.[109] In present-day England, where no division of church and state is officially recognized, music education continues to this day to be influenced by the Church of England; music educators in state-supported schools are still expected to include some of the church's sacred music in their classes and public concerts.[110]

Given this perspective, we might expect to find that much of the "music education" undertaken in the U.S., a culturally pluralistic, democratic capitalist nation, would be regarded by citizens collectively as the responsibility of the temples, churches, and other cultural institutions and communities existing within the society. In fact, this perspective is indeed held by *some* citizens, as many of the nation's various religious and cultural communities have indeed continued to provide instruction in their respective musical practices over the nation's history.[111] For example, many of the nation's private Jewish, Catholic, and Protestant schools have continually sustained educational programs in their respective musical practices, and they typically utilize music stemming from (or at least substantively consistent with) their unique religious perspectives as a major component of their curricula. African-American peoples have kept their traditions alive through traditional educational efforts involving music in their churches. Various Native American communities have also continued to induct children into the musical practices of their own "spiritual" traditions, as have many of the nations' other ethnically distinctive communities.

However, it is also evident that since the early nineteenth century many of the efforts at "music education" undertaken in the U.S. have *not* been carried out by the nation's constituent religious or culturally unique institutions, but have instead been implemented in the nation's increasingly culturally diverse, state-supported schools and universities. Thus, the following two questions arise:

- On what basis (or bases) has music education been included in the public schools of the U.S. historically?
- Should music education continue to be included in the public schools of the nation, and if so, on what basis? (More precisely, how can "music education" be included in U.S. public schools in a way that is consistent with the democratic principles on which the nation was founded and at the same time substantively meaningful and important to its constituent citizens and communities?)

The first question will be addressed in Chapter 5, and the second question will be the topic of Chapter 6.

5 A Brief Historical Survey of Concepts of Music in Music Education in the United States

[The ancient Greeks] saw the future as something that came upon them from behind their backs with the past receding away before their eyes.

When you think about it, that's a more accurate metaphor than our present one. Who really *can* face the future? All you can do is project from the past, even when the past shows that such projections are often wrong. And who really can forget the past? What else is there to know?[1]

Robert M. Pirsig

As Robert M. Pirsig suggests in the "Afterward" he appended in 1984 to his philosophical memoir of the previous decade, *Zen and the Art of Motorcycle Maintenance*, there is something more veracious about the conceptions of *past* and *future* held by the ancient Greeks than those implicit in the metaphor of time that presently predominates in the United States public forum. A metaphor compatible with the Greeks' that usefully represents the *present* is the notion of a palimpsest, an expanse of parchment or other material that has been written on several times, revealing the remnants of earlier, imperfectly erased writing still visible on its surface. Anytime we find ourselves in a situation in which we are confounded by the options before us we may be well advised to consider it as a palpable manifestation of past events—a palimpsest. By considering the historical developments that have combined to create the present confused state of affairs in music education in U.S. public schools, for example, we might be able to recognize which of its aspects should be removed or set aside—and which should be retained—in order to make most favorable the plane on which we will meet our stealthily approaching future. In fact, that is precisely our present task.

In Chapter 3 we explored the ethnocentric, universalizing, and relativizing conceptions of music that have been held historically in the Western academic forum before demonstrating that the pragmatist's conception of musical practice as *a diverse cluster of culturally relative, psychosocially equilibrating behaviors* both embraces and reconciles certain dilemmas to which each of these other conceptions gives rise. We saw that in many traditional societies, a unique and particular musical practice is typically undertaken to unify the community psychosocially, and that participation in it concomitantly validates the worldview tacitly held by the community's members. We also observed that, in many culturally pluralistic, state societies, certain musical practices are highly valued and supported by the state's leaders for validating the worldview they regard as being most amenable to the state's continued stability. In Chapter 4 we saw that the origins of the U.S. in the Enlightenment era and certain features of the nation's subsequent development as a science- and technology-based, democratic capitalist society have contributed to obscuring the fact that the different musical practices undertaken in the nation represent culturally distinctive means of effecting psychosocial equilibration relative to the worldviews held by different communities, but that citizens of the U.S. nevertheless continue to derive personal and social benefit by undertaking and participating in those musical practices they tacitly find to be inherently psychophysiologically and psychosocially effective.

In this chapter we will shift our focus to survey the various rationales and philosophical statements that have been proffered by music educators and other concerned writers over the history of the U.S. to explain and defend the enterprise of music education within the nation. Taking into account the historical forces that prompted the composition and influenced the content of these rationales, we will see how the conception of music described in each represents a *sign* of the worldview held by members of the profession at the time of its composition. Naturally, any rationale for the enterprise of music education must be based on a fairly well-defined conception of the nature and value of music in the lives of human beings, though such conceptions may not be always be articulated explicitly. Still, in our chronological review of these rationales, we will see that music has been conceptualized in a series of relatively distinct ways by music educators in each of four successive eras of the nation's history, though some conceptual ambivalence is evident during each era and, as a result, the eras overlap considerably. By comparing and contrasting these conceptions with the Peircian pragmatic conception of musical practices we developed in Chapter 3, we will become able to recognize where the music educators of today may be inappropriately sustaining conceptions from past eras and where their views are more culturally and historically well-founded. On this basis, we will be prepared to make recommendations in Chapter 6 for the present and future practice of music education in the public schools of the U.S.[2] The purpose here is not to explore exhaustively *all* of the rationales proffered for the enterprise of public school music education over the nation's history; rather, it is to identify and recount representative statements as *indexes* of the cultural orientation of the profession at various points in time. We will see that most (if not all) of the views we encounter are still alive in some measure in the present discourse of the nation's music educators.

MUSIC EDUCATION IN COLONIAL AMERICA:
MUSICAL PRACTICES AS *WORSHIP*

During the first century of the European settlement of North America, the musical practices regarded by the various colonists as being of the greatest personal and collective importance to their lives were those that they undertook in the collective worship activities of their respective communities. As we noted in Chapter 4, many of the first colonists came to North America to escape the religious and political oppression they were experiencing in their European homelands. To them, America represented a "new world," a place where they could live as they deemed best, without having to comply with the expectations of oppressive religious or state leaders whose worldviews differed from their own. While writings on music composed by the colonists during their first century on the North American continent are relatively scarce (when compared with later eras) and quite varied in content, they generally agree on one point: Musical practices were an important aspect of *worship*, and the form of musical engagement they undertook in their respective communities served as a means by which they might be reconciled with their Creator—the God or Supreme Being upon whom they depended for their existence. The religious beliefs supporting the musical practices of the early Puritan settlers, for example, are evident in the introductory remarks of the *Bay Psalm Book* of 1640, the collection of metered Calvinist song texts that they used as the guide for their singing during worship services. The Puritans sought to sing these psalms—the sacred songs of ancient Israel—in a simple and straightforward manner, in order that they would be ready to sing them in heaven (i.e., the afterlife or "Zion").

> God's altar needs not our pollishings: . . . for we have respected rather a plaine translation, then to smooth our verses with the sweetnes of any paraphrase, and soe have attended Conscience rather than Elegance, fidelity rather than poetry . . . that soe wee may sing in Sion the Lords songs of prayse according to his own will; untill hee take us from hence, and wipe away all our teares, & bid us enter into our masters joye to sing eternall Halleluiahs.[3]

A similar view can be found in the writings of Cotton Mather (1663–1728), the Boston-born Puritan minister whose prolific output as a writer yielded him great influence on the religious and political life of New England during the colonists' first century in the new world. Mather held the singing of praises to God in church to be not only a means of demonstrating one's devotion to God but also a practical exercise for setting one's soul right internally.

> It is the Concern of everyone that would enjoy *Tranquillity* in this *World*, or obtain *Felicity* in the World to come, to follow that Holy

Direction of Heaven, *Exercise thyself* in PIETY. And there is not *Exercise of* PIETY more unexceptionable than that of making *a joyful* Noise of SINGING in the Praises of our GOD; That of signifying our *Delight* in Divine *Truths* by SINGING of them; That of *Uttering* the Sentiments of Devotion, with the *Voice*, and such a *Modulation of the Voice*, as will naturally express the *Satisfaction* and *Elevation* of the *Mind*, which a Grave SONG shall be expressive of.

... The *Sacred Scriptures* with which the Holy SPIRIT of GOD has Enriched us, have directed us unto this *Way* of *Worshipping.*[4]

Mather made this statement in the introduction to *The Accomplished Singer*, his book of musical instruction, and his views are not only consistent with the beliefs about music held by his fellow Puritans during their first century in New England but they also generally confirm our Peircian pragmatic conception of musical practices as psychosocially equilibrating behaviors undertaken in community. Indeed, the Puritan settlers' collective singing of songs praising the God whom they held to be their creator and sustainer was an essential part of their collective life, it provided a vehicle for the psychological and social equilibration of their communities, and their collective musical practice reflected their shared worldview.[5]

However, by the time Mather's book was published in 1721, numerous other communities having ties to the Roman Catholic and the other Protestant churches of Europe had also been established in North America, and Mather's Calvinist notion of music making as an important *participatory* form of worship was not shared by all of them. While the various communities of the American colonies all predicated their musical practices on the accounts of music and worship described in the Bible, the sacred book of the Christian faith, each had its own understanding of the specific role and importance of music in worship and in community life. Since the distinctive beliefs held by the various Colonial communities concerning their engagement in musical practices are important to our discussion, a brief exploration of their biblical origins and certain other historical factors influencing their formation seems in order.

HISTORICAL ANTECEDENTS OF COLONIAL MUSICAL BELIEFS

Music was such a large part of the personal and collective life of the ancient Israelites—whose history is chronicled in the Old Testament of the Bible—that its absence from their daily lives likely occurred only at times when they believed themselves to have fallen out of right relationship with God; their cessation of musical engagement reflected their misery and desolation.[6] The Israelites' social gatherings typically involved singing and instrumental music, both of which were an integral part of their regular religious ceremonies as well as their weddings and funerals. In addition, the Israelites included musical instruction in the training of their prophets (i.e., persons who were charged with seeking God's guidance through prayer and then speaking to the community for God), further confirming the high value they placed on musical engagement as a means of maintaining the psycho-social balance of their communities.[7] In their collective worship, they sang Psalms—songs whose texts can now be found in the Old Testament of the Bible—in order to effect emotional, spiritual renewal among their people by bringing them into right relationship with God.

The texts of many of the Psalms represent exclamations of praise to God, the Supreme Being whom the Israelites believed to be the source of their physical and emotional sustenance, while the rest are largely prayers for strength in adversity. Nearly half of the 150 psalms included in the Old Testament book are thought to have been composed by the musician David, who later became the second king of Israel. Though David led an illustrious life filled with many notable accomplishments, it seems probable that much of his early public recognition stemmed from his musical efforts, most nota-bly from his having successfully used music to console Saul, his predecessor as king, at a time when Saul was suffering from extreme mental anguish. The story is told in the first book of Samuel in the Old Testament:

> And Saul's servants said to him, 'See now, an evil spirit from God is tormenting you. Let our lord now command the servants who attend you to look for someone who is skilful in playing the lyre; and when the evil spirit from God is upon you, he will play it, and you will feel bet-ter.' . . . And whenever the evil spirit from God came upon Saul, David took the lyre and played it with his hand, and Saul would be relieved and feel better, and the evil spirit would depart from him.[8]

David's success in consoling Saul with music has been cited by both Jews and Christians for thousands of years as affirming the psychophysiological or "spiritual" benefit of participation in music making and thus supporting its use in their respective, collective worship services.

Stories elsewhere in the Old Testament indicate that the Israelites may have regarded the strong psychophysiological *effects* of their musical prac-tices as a sign of the very presence or influence of God upon them. In an historical account in the book of Exodus, the word *cloud* is used to describe a mysterious apparition with which God leads the tribe of Israel through the wilderness.[9] Likewise, in the following passage from 2 Chronicles, the word *cloud* is used to describe an experience of God's presence shared by the Hebrew community during a musical celebration for the completion of their temple of worship in Jerusalem.

> [I]t was the duty of the trumpeters and singers to make themselves heard in unison in praise and thanksgiving to the Lord, and when the song was raised, with trumpets and cymbals and other musical

instruments, in praise to the Lord, 'For he is good, for his steadfast love endures for ever,' the house, the house of the Lord, was filled with a cloud, so that the priests could not stand to minister because of the cloud; for the glory of the Lord filled the house of God.[10]

While the writer of this passage apparently attributed the powerful *effects* of this musical practice to God's very presence among them, such an attribution is not consistent in all biblical accounts of music. Still, the ascription here and elsewhere is noteworthy, as the question of whether the strong psychophysiological effects often associated with music are merely a *gift* from God or signal God's *actual presence* (i.e., the community's *union* with God) has persisted throughout the history of both Jewish and Christian discourse on music, and, as we noted in Chapter 3, is also reflected (albeit differently) in discussions of music by persons from other cultural traditions.

From our pragmatic perspective, the Israelite priests' profound emotional response to the music made in celebration of the completion of their temple in this account—that is, their inability to "minister" to the needs of those present with them—does not seem surprising, as it is consistent with our discussion in Chapter 3 of the psychophysiological and psychosocial effects often associated with musical practices. Specifically, it seems apparent that the Israelites' experience of hearing culturally validating music performed well at the opening of a temple built to exalt the God in whom they all believed would quite likely have resulted in the experience of a "loss of self" among those gathering together and would almost certainly have been profoundly moving for them. Our Peircian pragmatic interpretation of this event is not meant to diminish the importance of their experience or to discount the view of the Israelites, who clearly interpreted the strong psychophysiological effects brought about by hearing this music as "God's presence upon them." Indeed, it is important to understand that the effects of the musical practice do not in themselves support or disaffirm the ultimacy of the truth of the collective worldview embraced by the community undertaking it, but merely confirm that the powerful effects of the musical practice in which a community is involved often serve to validate for that community the conception of Truth they collectively embody at the time.

The Israelites continued to use music making as a means for maintaining psychosocial balance within their communities during the period of their history chronicled in the New Testament of the Bible as well, engaging musically with one another not only in their formal religious ceremonies but also at other times. Understanding how they used and conceptualized the effects of musical practices at these times will require some familiarity with their further history.

The first four books of the New Testament provide four separate accounts of the life of Jesus of Nazareth, the central figure of the Christian religion, whom many of the Israelites gradually came to believe was not only a man, but the very incarnation of God—the *Messiah* (Savior) or *Christ*. According to the writers of these books, Jesus was born in Bethlehem, raised in Nazareth, and, following his baptism around the age of thirty, traveled throughout Palestine healing sick people and proclaiming that the kingdom of God was at hand. Despite reportedly having lived a sinless life, Jesus was accused of political insubordination ostensibly for having professed to be the "King of the Jews." For this crime, he was convicted and later ordered to be executed by crucifixion. According to the biblical accounts, he appeared to his disciples several times during the weeks following his execution, and, forty days after his body had first been discovered missing, he ascended into heaven to prepare a place there for all who would follow his teachings. His followers continued their efforts to share his teachings with all people, and they worshipped him as the "Son of God." The Christian religion spread slowly in the years following Jesus' death, but eventually became the dominant religion in the West.

Immediately prior to his trial and execution, Jesus and his closest disciples shared a last supper together. After the meal, one of them left the gathering to make Jesus' location known to the authorities, while Jesus and the others remained and sang a hymn together. While their singing of this hymn was probably done in accordance with Jewish custom, we can infer that they also sang it as a means of effecting psychosocial balance and union with one another, since, according to the account in the book of Matthew, "when they had sung an hymn, they went out into the mount of Olives" to spend time together and pray, at which time Jesus' followers repeatedly affirmed their solidarity with him.[11] Later that night, Jesus was seized and led away to be executed. The foregoing passage from Matthew's book is one of many scriptural passages often cited by Christians to affirm the importance they believe singing to have in their communal worship.

Several of the books comprising the remainder of the New Testament were written by the apostle Paul, an early detractor of Jesus who reportedly encountered him later in his life while walking on a road near the city of Damascus, some time *after* Jesus' execution. This astonishing experience brought about a profound personal transformation in Paul, and he dedicated the rest of his life to spreading Jesus' teachings. Paul is now widely regarded as the founder of the Christian religion, since the enthusiastic, widespread, and highly influential teaching he undertook throughout the remainder of his life led to the establishment of numerous churches, and the interpretations of Jesus' teachings that he wrote and sent in letters to them have served to illuminate those teachings to countless readers throughout history.

In the numerous letters he wrote to the various Christian churches founded over the years following the death of Jesus, Paul specifically directed them to use singing as a vehicle for effecting their own "spiritual" relationship with God and for teaching Christian principles. Writing to a community of

Christians at the church in Ephesus, Paul strongly affirmed the value of singing for keeping the community in "the Holy Spirit" described by Jesus:

> Be careful then how you live, not as unwise people but as wise, making the most of the time, because the days are evil. So do not be foolish, but understand what the will of the Lord is. Do not get drunk with wine, for that is debauchery; but be filled with the Spirit, as you sing psalms and hymns and spiritual songs among yourselves, singing and making melody to the Lord in your hearts . . . [12]

Throughout the history of the Christian church, the followers of Jesus have predicated their musical practices on the scriptural writings discussed here, as well as other biblical passages, though not without voicing a considerable variety of opinions on precisely *how* musical practices should be undertaken by a community. We noted in Chapter 4 that Augustine (354–430), one of the most influential thinkers in the history of Christianity, expressed considerable ambivalence about music in his writings; he observed that because musical engagement could evoke sensual pleasure it could also draw people in the wrong directions. While he ultimately concluded that music (especially group singing) could be good for the soul, owing to its propensity for bringing forth feelings of ecstasy and promoting Christian brotherhood, he remained cautious concerning its inclusion in worship, believing that only music which clearly reflected the musician's accord with God in its audible manifestation of divine or cosmic order was appropriate or "good." From our pragmatic perspective, this would seem to imply that Augustine was inclined to support only those forms of music that were validating or suitably transforming of his own worldview. As we have seen, such statements appear consistently in the observations of many writers on musical practices.

In the centuries following Jesus' death, Christianity was eventually adopted by the emperor Constantine I as the official religion of the Roman Empire, though its association with the powerful state was initially repugnant to many Christians who did not see the Roman Empire as a reflection of God's kingdom. Largely as a response to this action, ascetic Christian communities began to arise all over Europe in the third century following Jesus' crucifixion. In these monasteries, a variety of different but complementary liturgies began to take form, priests were trained for the spiritual leadership of "lay" congregations, and the musical practices of worship—primarily the chanting of psalms and hymns (typically in Latin, the Roman language)—came to be adopted as the responsibility of the priests. The Mass—a sacramental celebration of the last supper Jesus shared with his disciples—emerged as the central form of Christian worship. Beginning in the ninth century, the development of musical notation made it possible for the melodies on which the psalms and other scriptures were chanted in the

Mass to be recorded, and, by the twelfth century, composers had begun to use notation not only for recording and codifying the melodies on which the various scriptural texts were to be sung but also as a vehicle for creating more complex, polyphonic forms of music as musical offerings for worship. While it is known that some musical practices were undertaken outside of the churches during these centuries, much of their history has been lost, as they were not written down. It seems clear, however, that the musical practices officially regarded as societally central by the communities of Europe at this time were those of the church, and they were undertaken during worship by the priests—or by a choir selected and trained by the priests—specifically for the purpose of praising God.

The priestly dominance over music making continued in the churches of Europe for centuries, but this state of affairs was to change in the sixteenth century as a result of efforts made by the German theologian and priest Martin Luther (1483–1546) and others. Upon concluding his schooling at the University of Erfurt in 1505, Luther entered a monastery to become a priest. Shortly after arriving there, he began to experience an overwhelming depression; Luther was finding it difficult to follow Jesus' teachings and act virtuously on a consistent basis, despite his good intentions, and he thus doubted his own worthiness to enter heaven. However, not long after completing his doctorate in theology in 1513, Luther underwent a great personal transformation, having suddenly grasped the meaning of the apostle Paul's teaching that human beings attain salvation by their faith in God rather than merely by doing good works; he later attributed his long-standing depression to the defective theology in which he had been trained.

By this time, the church had gradually come to adopt a number of practices that Luther found to be inconsistent with his new understanding of the Christian faith. For example, people had come to believe that paying money to the church was a way of obtaining divine forgiveness for their sins, and the church did little to discourage them from this way of thinking, extracting sizable amounts of money from them. The origin of the practice—which came to be known as the "selling of indulgences"—is not clear, but it is thought to have stemmed from the idea that when a person confessed her or his sins to a priest, the priest would grant forgiveness on behalf of God, in return for which the individual was expected to express gratitude to God by giving gifts to charity (i.e., the church). Luther's new understanding of Paul's teaching that human beings are granted salvation—or "justified"—by their *faith* rather than merely by their good works provided him with a basis for arguing that the selling of indulgences and various other practices were evidence of the church's corruption.

On October 31, 1517, Luther sent a letter containing ninety-five "theses"—descriptions of his concerns about the issue of indulgences and various other church practices—to his bishop and another church leader, challenging them to a debate. When they failed to respond, he made his charges public. The quarrel that developed eventually led Luther to renounce his obedience to the Roman church, and he was excommunicated. However, owing largely to the support Luther's *protests* received from secular leaders, he gained many followers among both churchmen and laypeople who agreed that the practices of the church were in need of *reform*, and his new orientation toward the Christian faith was embraced by many people, eventually leading to the emergence of the *Protestant* or *Reformation* churches.

Luther had several concerns about the way worship was handled by the church. He was disturbed that neither worship services nor the Bible itself were in the language of the people, and he recognized that this had given the church's hierarchy considerable political control over them. Firmly believing that salvation was a matter held between the individual and God rather than between the individual and the institution of the church, Luther asserted that worship services should be held in the vernacular of the people (rather than in Latin, as had previously been the case) in order to help the people become more well-informed about matters of faith. Thus, he translated the Bible into German to enable them to come to their own understandings of Scripture. Most notable for our purposes, however, was Luther's accompanying belief that the people should be able not only to understand but to participate actively in worship. He thus returned the singing of hymns to the people, translating the texts of many songs and musical "works" originally set in Latin into German, carefully adapting them so that they could be sung well and understood clearly by the people in the congregation. For Luther, the active involvement of the people—rather than just the priests and the choir—in the musical practice of worship was very important, as it seemed to him that it was probably more consistent with the practices of the early church.

> I desire . . . that we have more songs which might be sung in the vernacular of the people, and which the people might sing during the celebration of the Mass after the chanting (in Latin) of the Gradual, the Sanctus and the Agnus Dei. For who doubts that these liturgical parts, which today only the choir sings and with which it responds to the bishop who pronounces the benediction, were at one time sung by all the people? In fact, the singing of these songs may be so arranged by the bishop that they are sung either immediately after the Latin chants have been sung, or interchangeably, in Latin one day (Sunday), in the vernacular the other. Finally the entire Mass will then be sung in the vernacular of the people. But we need poets; as yet we have none who are able to prepare for us pious and spiritual songs (as St. Paul calls them) which deserve being used in the church of God.[13]

Luther introduced into worship simple devotional songs based on melodies familiar to the people, and he personally wrote a number of hymns set on newly composed German texts. The emotional benefits or "spiritual" effects of musical involvement upon the people were clearly foremost in his mind.

> Next to the Word of God, Music deserves the highest praise. She is a mistress and governess of those human emotions . . . which control men or more often overwhelm them . . . Whether you wish to comfort the sad, to subdue frivolity, to encourage the despairing, to humble the proud, to calm the passionate, or to appease those full of hate . . . what more effective means than music could you find?[14]

This is not to say that Luther was not also highly discriminating about the forms of music that should be included in worship. Like Plato, Augustine, and many of the other writers we have encountered, Luther too believed that some music was to be avoided, as it could subvert the psychological or "spiritual" well-being of the individual. He thus qualified his recommendations.

> Take special care to shun perverted minds who prostitute this lovely gift of nature and of art with their erotic rantings; and be quite assured that none but the devil goads them on to defy their very nature which would and should praise God its Maker with this gift, so that these bastards purloin the gift of God and use it to worship the foe of God, the enemy of nature and of this lovely art.[15]

However, Luther also felt that all varieties of music that positively impact the human psyche were appropriate for consideration by the church for its use. He is known to have set sacred texts and his own poetic lyrics to many tunes featured in songs sung outside of the church, designating them as *hymns*, thus beginning the practice of appropriating "secular" forms of music for sacred purposes, which continues in Protestant churches to this day.[16]

Because of its profound effects on the human psyche, Luther held singing to be an important teaching tool, and he was instrumental in encouraging music education among children. Not long before the birth of his first child, Hans, in 1526, he wrote: "If I had children and would be able to carry it out, I would insist that they study not only the languages and history, but also singing, [instrumental] music and all of mathematics."[17] Sometime later, schools established under the influence of Luther's teachings began to include the study of music in their curricula.

A somewhat more restrictive view of music in Christian community was held by the influential theologian John Calvin (1509–1564), another major figure in the Protestant Reformation. Born in France, Calvin set out as a young man to pursue a career in the Roman Catholic Church, but, after a short period of studying law, he found himself convinced by many of Luther's teachings. He thus converted to Protestantism and became personally involved in the Reformation in Switzerland. In 1536, Calvin published a short version of what was to become his most important theological work, *Institutes of the Christian Religion*, a systematic articulation of his own highly rigorous and exacting (i.e., ostensibly "pure") interpretations of Christian Scripture. He revised and expanded this work throughout the rest of his life, and it came to form the foundation of a movement sometimes known as Calvinism, more generally known as Reformed Christianity. Calvin's theology differed from Luther's most notably in its doctrine of predestination (i.e., Calvin held that only those whom God chooses would be delivered from their sins), though it also differed in various other ways. Calvin's teachings had great influence on the development of the highly strict, church-centered society in Geneva, Switzerland, and they served as the theological foundation for the Puritan communities that emerged in England (where they influenced the formation of the Anglican church), those that were established in Scotland (i.e., the Presbyterian church), and those that were founded in the New England colonies in North America.

Unlike the Roman Catholics, who regarded musical practice as the responsibility of the priests and those designated by them, and unlike Luther, who elevated singing because of its emotional effects, Calvin held musical practice—specifically, congregational singing—to be an important part of worship only insofar as it provided a means for the people's heartfelt vocalizing of their praise to God.

> If the singing come not from the heart it is worth nothing, and can only awaken God's wrath. Singing in itself is good and useful; our tongues must praise God, and, as we honour Him by a common faith, we must also unite in glorifying Him before men that they may hear our confession of His name and be inspired with the desire of following our example. Singing in the church has been practised from the earliest times; the Apostle Paul recommended the use of spiritual songs. But neither the ear nor the spirit must be distracted . . . With proper moderation, therefore, the use of singing is holy and useful. Those melodies which are introduced merely to give pleasure are not agreeable to the majesty of the Church and must be infinitely displeasing to God.[18]

Calvin agreed with Luther that singing should be done in the language of the people in order that it would be meaningful to all members of the community, but, noting that music often tended to evoke pleasure rather than fulfilling the important human need of reconciling the individual with God, he gave specific recommendations for its use in worship, insisting on "simple and pure singing of the divine praises, forasmuch as where there is no meaning there is no edification."[19] While Calvin was not opposed to the occasional use of instrumental music for enjoyment, he did feel that there should be some limits on it. The following statement illuminates this circumspection.

Although the invention of the lyre and of other musical instruments serves our enjoyment and our pleasures rather than our needs, it ought not on that account to be judged of no value; still less should it be condemned. Pleasure is to be condemned only when it is not combined with reverence for God and not related to the common welfare of society. But music by its nature is adapted to rouse our devotion to God and to aid the well-being of man; we need only avoid enticements to shame, and empty entertainments which keep men from better employments and are simply a waste of time.[20]

Indeed, in Calvin's view, only those musical practices undertaken to facilitate one's right relationship with God were appropriate for the members of a Christian community.

Meanwhile, the Roman Catholic Church was finding itself deeply shaken by the Protestant revolution. Many priests and nuns had left the church in the aftermath of the emergence of such movements as Lutheranism and Calvinism, along with approximately half of the population of Europe. Finally, in 1545, Pope Paul III convened the Council of Trent to address the doctrinal abuses and shortcomings that had led to the Protestant Reformation. The council was held in three extended sessions up through the year 1563, and its deliberations resulted in numerous administrative and doctrinal changes in the church, all of which were published in the *Catechism of the Council of Trent*. The following edict set forth in this document not only reveals the church's concern of the time that only music that validated or embodied the worldview of the church should be included in worship, but it also reaffirms the notion that music making should be undertaken in worship for the listening of the congregants and for their edification rather than their pleasure.

All things should indeed be so ordered that the Masses, whether they be celebrated with or without singing, may reach tranquilly into the ears and hearts of those who hear them, when everything is executed clearly and at the right speed. In the case of those Masses which are celebrated with singing and with organ, let nothing profane be intermingled, but only hymns and divine praises. The whole plan of singing in musical modes should be constituted not to give empty pleasure to the ear but in such a way that the words may be clearly understood by all, and thus the hearts of the listeners may be drawn to the desire of heavenly harmonies, in the contemplation of the joy of the blessed.[21]

Thus, we can see that by the time the various groups of Europeans began their voyages to establish colonies in North America in the late sixteenth and early seventeenth centuries, the three most prominent churches of Europe—Roman Catholic, Lutheran, and Calvinist or Reformed—had come to hold three very different orientations toward the inclusion of music in the worship of their respective communities. The musical practices of most Roman Catholic churches were regarded as the responsibility of a specialized few, with the congregation listening passively as the priests and the church's musicians served as intermediaries between them and God.[22] Lutheran churches, by contrast, typically featured both the tradition of specialized choral singing practiced by the Roman Catholics as well as the singing of psalms and hymns by the congregation in their collective worship of God; these musical practices served them as an important participatory means of psychophysiological and psychosocial—or "spiritual"—equilibration. Finally, the Reformed, who predicated their worship practices on what they held to have been the practices of the early church, continued to sing primarily for the purpose of steeping themselves in sacred texts, thus sustaining a musical practice chiefly for the repetition and ingestion of Scripture and concerning themselves less with the quality of the musical sound itself.

MUSICAL PRACTICES AND BELIEFS DURING THE COLONIAL ERA

All of these disparate musical practices and beliefs—as well as other variants on them—were manifested in the societally central practices undertaken by the various groups of Europeans that colonized North America in the late sixteenth and early seventeenth centuries. The Catholics' distinctive beliefs about music were apparent in the intonation of chant and the polyphonic choral singing undertaken in the Masses attended by the Spanish colonists following their settlement of St. Augustine in 1565 and by the French after their settlements of Acadia and Quebec in 1605 and 1608. Calvin's strict beliefs about music were evident in the Puritans' singing of psalms in their collective worship following their settlement of the Plymouth Colony in 1620. The sounds of the more enthusiastically participatory forms of hymn and choral singing undertaken in Lutheran worship could be heard in the Swedish settlement of New Sweden along the Delaware river as early as 1638. In addition, the various groups of German Lutherans, Scottish Presbyterians, and Spanish and Portuguese Jews scattered along the Atlantic seaboard each undertook musical practices consistent with their own beliefs for purposes of psychosocial equilibration within their collective worship activities. The differences in their respective beliefs and in the musical practices they undertook were enough to keep these communities well apart from one another, culturally speaking, throughout the first century and a half of their presence in North America, with each community regarding the tenets and practices of the others as inherently misguided. However, the musical practices undertaken within each community were generally regarded by its members as important forms of psychosocially equilibrating behavior—as means of reconciling themselves spiritually with God.

Of course, we have every reason to believe that the various communities of Native Americans with whom the early settlers came into contact also undertook their own musical practices for psychosocially equilibrating purposes at this time, since the Native American communities extant today continue to sing spiritual songs and dance in the ways of their ancestors. However, as these societies had not developed the technologies of writing and reading at the time of the first European settlements, little information is available, though some details about their musical practices can be found in the writings of the early French and Spanish explorers with whom they came into contact. It is clear that the African people brought to North America as slaves during the first century of European colonization brought their own musical practices with them for psychosocial benefit as well, since numerous slave-ship captains, missionaries, and others have left behind accounts describing them.

At the same time, we must realize that the members of each of the communities present in North America during the seventeenth century tacitly regarded the form of music education they advanced (informally or formally) as a means of instilling in their members the skills necessary for them to participate in their own community's unique musical practices. For the Roman Catholics, this meant including instruction in singing in the education of priests, so that they would be able to intone the chant, and developing choirs that would be able to sing the polyphonic music used in the Mass. For the Lutherans, such education took place both formally and informally, in association with and in preparation for the regular Sunday morning hymn singing in their collective worship services and within their families. For the Calvinist Puritans of New England, however, the development of music education took quite a distinctive path of development. Since public-school music education in the U.S. has many important roots in the history of the Puritans' musical practices, it is appropriate for us to explore them at some greater length here.

Following Calvin's directives, the early Puritan settlers sang the psalms quite simply in their worship services, using their collective vocalizing as a means of steeping themselves in the sacred texts. The *Sternhold and Hopkins Psalter*, the book of psalms they brought with them from England for use in worship, contained eighty-seven psalms set to sixty tunes that were intended to be sung in unison and unaccompanied. This collection—the first book of any kind to be published in the New World—was modified to contain a more literal translation of the Hebrew psalms and reissued in 1640 as *The Whole Book of Psalmes Faithfully Translated into English Metre*; this version later became known as the *Bay Psalm Book*. Though the book contained references to forty-eight tunes on which the psalms could be sung, it included no musical notation. This lack of notation led to a decline in musical literacy among the Puritans over the following years, and, as a result, the book was modified again to include thirteen two-part tunes on which the 150 psalms could be sung, along with some simple instructions on using the "fasola" method for reading them, when it was issued fifty-eight years later in its ninth edition.[23]

The Puritans took up the English practice of "lining out"—or "deaconing," as it came to be called in America—sometime after 1644, in order to help those who had not learned to read words (or music) to participate in the singing of psalms. According to this practice, the deacon of the church would recite a line of a psalm to be sung, and the congregation would then sing it back in unison. The Puritan minister Cotton Mather, whom we encountered earlier, explained the matter thus: "For the present, where many in the congregation cannot read, it is convenient that the minister, or some other fit person . . . do read the psalm line by line before the singing thereof."[24] The melodies upon which the psalms were sung at this time were generally drawn from the collective memory of those in the congregation. It seems apparent, however, that the quality of singing among the Puritans deteriorated so much around this time that it eventually began to distract them from reflecting on the meaning of the psalms and thus from benefiting from singing them in their worship services. Thomas Mace observed the severe decline in quality in 1676, saying: "Tis sad to hear what whining, toting, yelling or screeching there is in many country congregations."[25] The problem must have persisted, as Thomas Walter described it again in the introduction to *The Grounds and Rules of Musick Explained*, an instructional text he published for the purpose of addressing the problem in 1721.

> The same Person who sets the Tune, and guides the Congregation in Singing, commonly reads the Psalm, which is a task too few are capable of performing well, that in Singing two or three Staves, the congregation falls from a cheerful pitch to downright Grumbling, and then some to relieve themselves mount an Eighth above the rest, others perhaps a Fourth or Fifth, by which Means the Singing appears to be rather a confused noise, made up of Reading, Squecking [*sic*] and Grumbling . . .
>
> In many places, one Man is upon this Note, while another is a Note before him, which produces something so hideous and disorderly, as is beyond Expression bad . . . and besides, no two Men in the Congregation quaver alike or together; which sounds in the Ears of a good Judge, like Five Hundred different Tunes roared out at the same time . . . [26]

The decline in the quality of singing eventually became extreme enough to motivate several Puritan ministers to recommend that some sort of effort be taken to address the problem. Reverend Thomas Symmes strongly advocated a possible solution in 1720:

> Would it not greatly tend to promote singing of psalms if singing schools were promoted? Would not this be conforming to the *scripture pattern*? Have we not as much need of them as God's people of old? Have we any reason to expect to be inspired with the gift of singing any more

than reading? Or to attain it without suitable means, any more than they of old, when *miracles, inspirations*, etc. were common. Where would the *difficulty* or what the disadvantage, if people who want skill in singing would procure a skillful person to instruct them, and meet two or three evenings in the week, from *five* or *six* to *eight*, and spend the time in learning to sing? Would it not be proper for *school masters* in *country parishes* to teach their scholars? Would it not be very sensible in ministers to encourage their people to learn to sing? Are they not under some obligation by virtue of their office to do so?[27]

Within the next few years, singing schools, some of them led by itinerant singing masters, began to emerge in New England as means of developing such skills among the Puritan faithful. The first known such school, the Society for Regular Singing, held its first meetings in Boston in 1722, and others were begun in South Carolina, Pennsylvania, New York, and Maryland over the next fifty years.

Of course, we would be incorrect in supposing that other musical practices—some involving making music with instruments—were not also undertaken by the Puritans outside of their collective worship activities. Indeed, advertisements appearing in the Boston *News* as early as 1716 reveal that numerous musical instruments were being imported and purchased. However, it seems quite apparent that the Puritans tended not to regard music undertaken outside of worship as societally important. In fact, for many of them quite the opposite was true: They regarded instrumental music as potentially sinful because of the pleasure it brought. At a conference in England in 1655, the issue had been discussed of "Whether a believing man or woman, being head of a family, in this day of the gospell, may keepe in his or her house an instrument of musicke, playing on them or admitting others to play thereon." At the conclusion of the discussion, the Puritan leaders adopted a cautious, but not entirely discouraging, position.

> It is the duty of the saintes to abstaine from all appearance of evil, and not to make provision for the flesh, to fulfill ye lusts thereof, to redeem the time, and to do all they do to the glory of God; and though we cannot conclude the use of such instruments to be unlawful, yet we desire the saints to be very cautious lest they transgress the aforesaid rules in the use of it, and do what may not be of good report, and so give offence to their tender brethren.[28]

We may suppose on the basis of what we learned in Chapter 3 about the iconicity of music with the coherence system of the community from which it stems that the musical practices undertaken by the Puritans outside of their central rituals probably shared many formal characteristics with those practiced in the worship of their communities. However, since the Puritans were a community that recognized no difference between their religious lives and their everyday or "secular" lives (as was the case with each of the other communities of settlers living in North America at the time), it also seems likely that this music would have been sufficiently different from that undertaken in worship to raise concerns about whether it might challenge the cultural solidarity of their community. Indeed, it seems doubtful that anyone in the community would have regarded the respectful playing of the melodies on which the psalms were sung in church as problematic.

Now, considering as a group the writings of and the reports about the various communities living in North America during the early years of colonization on their respective musical practices, it becomes evident that the members of each community regarded their own musical practices as important means of psychosocial equilibration in community. Furthermore, those who shared a common heritage in the Christian church regarded the musical practices they collectively undertook for this purpose in their socially central, ritualized activities as means of *worship*. However, because of the radically differing worldviews (or theologies) manifested in these communities, each community's members conceptualized and described their own musical practices in their own distinctive way. Likewise, those "educators" whose efforts served to inculcate skills in the musical practices of each community to its members (formally or informally) also regarded their community's unique musical practices as inherently "right," as compared to those undertaken by the members of other culturally dissimilar communities. Using the sign diagram derived from Peirce's pragmatic philosophy,

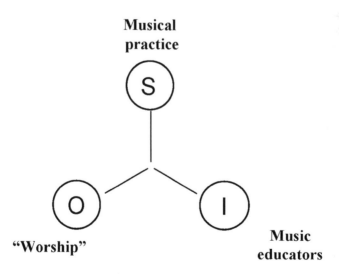

Musical practice

S

O — I

"Worship"   **Music educators**

Figure 5.1 The Sign "Musical practice" conceptualized as "Worship"; psychosocially equilibrating behavior.

we could represent the conception of musical practice held by the music educators in each of the early Colonial settlements as in Figure 5.1.

It is important to realize that the members of each of the communities present in North America in the seventeenth and early eighteenth centuries regarded their own musical practice as *true* worship (or something akin to it), and thus inherently different from and superior to that undertaken by those belonging to other communities. Indeed, the musical practices undertaken by each community of colonists (as well as the Native Americans and the African people brought to the continent as slaves) represented efforts to effect psychosocial equilibration with the conception of Reality held to be *true* by the members of each of their communities; none of them recognized any difference or separation between sacred and secular life.

MUSIC EDUCATION AND THE ENLIGHTENMENT: MUSIC AS *ART*

As we saw in Chapter 4, a confluence of forces contributed to changing the conception of societally important music in the U.S. during the late eighteenth century. We noted that the U.S. was formed as a nation at this time, during a period of European history that historians now call the "Enlightenment" era. The Enlightenment began as an intellectual movement in France that emphasized above all the application of human reason (rather than religious revelation) to understanding the universe and to improving the human condition. This movement, which had its roots in the Protestant Reformation, was brought about largely due to the influence of the writings of the rationalist philosophers of the time, and it had far-reaching effects on intellectual, political, and economic spheres of life in Europe, eventually displacing the authority of the church in many places and challenging the leadership of the autocratic governments then existing in Europe. Since the changes in the beliefs about music among those who had emigrated to North America stem largely from societal changes occurring in Europe at this time, it seems appropriate for us briefly to explore some of these events and their consequences.

CHANGES IN CONCEPTS OF MUSIC IN EUROPE

Prior to the eighteenth century, most European societies had been divided into ruling and peasant classes, with relatively few persons occupying any middle ground between them, as compared with later times. Following the French Revolution and certain other political shifts that took place in the central European nations during the late eighteenth century, a middle class gradually began to emerge. Several composers and other musicians then found themselves able to attain financial independence from their positions in church and court, and they began to draw their income both from the commissions of their aristocratic patrons and from concert subscriptions and ticket sales. The music they created reflected their greater freedom in worldview, with large-scale musical compositions of opera, oratorio, and other secular works progressively taking a more prominent role in their output than music written for church and court.

In a fascinating study on Enlightenment-era composer Ludwig van Beethoven (1770–1827), historical sociologist Tia DeNora has observed that much of the new secular music that was being composed and performed in Vienna, Austria, during the late 1780s was produced merely for entertainment, and it was not regarded as having any greater societal significance.[29] However, she observes, by the 1790s, a notion of "serious music" began to emerge among a number of Viennese aristocrats, several of whom had become regular patrons of composers, often commissioning them to compose musical works for performance in their private salons. In producing the music to be performed at these events, the composers typically drew upon musical themes and ideas from other composers and from folk traditions existing around them as well as from music of the past, translating these musical materials into new forms of *art* that reflected in their formal organization the highly ordered, rationalistic conceptions of Reality emerging in the writings of the philosophers of the era. Much of this art music was composed in a distinctive manner that featured a high level of equality, independence, and interplay among the parts, and some of it was relatively simple, making it possible for those patrons who had at least a modicum of musical skill to participate in the performances.

In a sense, the forms of music performed at these in-home concerts could be regarded as something like highly sophisticated parlor games, as the composers who wrote it were essentially borrowing and "playing" with musical ideas drawn from various sources, thus providing the Viennese elite with a sort of intellectual form of musical entertainment. At the same time, however, the events at which this musical practice took place also served as social rituals for them, unifying them as a community and validating the "superior," comparatively independent social status they enjoyed due to their relative affluence. On frequent occasions, DeNora notes, these wealthy individuals would sponsor public concerts featuring composers or works that had been premiered privately in their own chambers, thus making this music accessible to the members of the middle class via ticket purchase. In communicating the current trends emerging in the rarefied world of "serious" art music to the middle-class public in this way, these Viennese aristocrats asserted their own prestige in Viennese society. Such occasions are known to have featured the first public performances of works by Franz Josef Haydn and Wolfgang Amadeus Mozart, as well as Beethoven.

Simultaneously captivating central European society for the first time during this era was the modern notion of "genius," as a gift of nature at work within the human imagination, which was believed to guide the thoughts and efforts of exceptional individuals. Musicians (primarily composers) possessed of "genius" were thought not merely to have extraordinary intellectual ability, but also a profound or prophetic quality of mind that manifested itself in the emotionally stirring, societally impactful products of their labors, which were, in turn, assessed by the European populace of the eighteenth and nineteenth centuries as "great art."[30] Probably the concept of *genius* evolved among those of a more rationalistic bent of mind to replace the Christian concept of *prophet* (i.e., the recipient of special gifts from God) as a way of accounting for the *shamanic* quality of much of the art music produced at this time.

The respect they found themselves accorded and the ennobling treatment of their works were naturally attractive to the composers themselves, who, not surprisingly, undertook efforts to turn the situation to greater advantage and thus contribute to their own veneration. DeNora relates the revealing story of a note written in an autograph album by Count Ferdinand Waldstein, Beethoven's primary patron, just as Beethoven was leaving Bonn for Vienna.

> Dear Beethoven. You are going to Vienna in fulfillment of your long-frustrated wishes. The Genius of Mozart is still mourning and weeping the death of her pupil. She found a refuge but no occupation with the inexhaustible Haydn; through him she wishes once more to form a union with another. With the help of assiduous labor you shall receive Mozart's spirit from Haydn's hands. Your true friend, Waldstein.[31]

DeNora observes that while this note was widely regarded as "prophetic" at the time, circulation of the story of Waldstein's prophecy and other such commendatory anecdotes (some of them propagated by the composers themselves) actually helped to *create* the phenomenon of Mozart's greatness and Beethoven's promise as they were told and retold in Viennese society over the years. Furthermore, she notes, the story did as much for Haydn's reputation as it did for the young composer who was to become his heir. DeNora explains, "To tell a story about Beethoven receiving Mozart's spirit from Haydn's hands was also a way of constituting Haydn as great within the Viennese musical world. Simultaneously, it further articulated the notion of greatness itself within this world . . ."[32]

On the other hand, it was not unreasonable at all for those living in Vienna during those years to bestow this high approbation on the composers of their age, as the forms of music produced by such composers as Haydn, Mozart, and Beethoven contributed greatly to validating the new ordered and reason-based conceptions of Reality idealized—and in some measure manifested—in the minds of the citizens of central European communities who participated in them, simultaneously celebrating their relative cultural independence. Those who attended performances of the newly emerging art music of the time no doubt experienced a profound psychosocial validation of the new, rationalistic and ordered worldviews then animating European society, as such order was embodied in the formal characteristics of the music they revered. Moreover, these events validated the rationalist visions of the Enlightenment philosophers, as these composers' works manifested the insightfulness, perfectibility, and exaltation of the individual human being as an artist. Indeed, those who developed their knowledge and refined their sensibilities in such artistic endeavors as music were thought to represent a high level of refinement or "culture," owing to their relative social transcendence.

Of course, by the late eighteenth century "romantic" motifs were also beginning to emerge, in stark contrast to the contemporary "rationalist" ones. Concertgoers who listened to the emerging works of Beethoven, for example, must have had a strongly contrary experience. While some of the "educated" or "cultured" connoisseurs reacted in alarm, others embraced the new movement, which emphasized the importance of the senses, the emotions, and nature and tended to downplay the rationalistic fascination with musical structure. As we shall see, both of these tendencies would come to be reflected in concepts of music in the U.S.

Incidentally, DeNora also notes that some of these eighteenth-century musical connoisseurs began to use a culinary metaphor to describe their responses to particular musical works.[33] In 1787, a critic for the Viennese *Magazin der Musik* described some quartets of Haydn's as "too highly seasoned—and whose palate can endure this for long?" The critic apologized for his choice of language, asking his readers to "[f]orgive this simile from the cookery book." Nevertheless, the metaphor took hold in Viennese society and was gradually adopted elsewhere; the critic's comments may be one source of the modern notion of musical "taste."[34]

As the notion of "serious" art music independent of church and court became more widespread over the following century, conservatories—schools designated specifically for the training and education of musicians—began to be formed under the aegis of the governments of several European nations. These schools actually had their beginnings in Italy during the sixteenth century, where the term *conservatory* (from the Latin *conservare*, meaning to keep or preserve) was originally used to describe an orphanage, and, notably, the church supported all the orphanages of the time. Orphans living in the conservatories who showed musical promise were given special training in music so that they could be used in the church choirs and, later, employed in operatic productions. Over time, music schools developed within these institutions, and many of them began to employ composers who had attained success as teachers outside of the church. Though few Italian conservatories remained open to the end of the eighteenth century, the idea of forming schools specifically for the training of musicians had spread to other countries, where they were supported by the newly forming state governments rather than the church. We can see from our Peircian pragmatic perspective that the involvement of these governments in the creation and support of the conservatories likely stemmed from the desire of the leaders of the newly forming state governments to maintain political control over the activities of musicians as a way of sustaining the relative cultural solidarity of their nations. The government of France established the Conservatoire National de Music et de Declamation in Paris in 1795. Other nations soon followed, with conservatories of music opening in Prague in 1811, in Vienna in 1817, in London in 1822, and in Leipzig in 1843.

Arising contemporaneously with the notion of art music in central Europe during the late eighteenth and early nineteenth centuries was the philosophical field of *aesthetics*, an area of scholarly discourse that sought to explain the place of the arts, including music, in the newly emerging reason-based conceptions of Reality. As we noted in Chapter 4, the modern meaning of the word *aesthetic* had its origins in the writings of Alexander Baumgarten, a minor German philosopher, who used it to draw a distinction between knowledge acquired immediately via the senses (i.e., "aesthetic" knowledge) and that acquired via reasoning (i.e., "logical" knowledge). However, in focusing his own writings primarily on what he understood to be the innate perception of "beauty," Baumgarten unwittingly established the use of the word as designating the branch of philosophy concerned with understanding and accounting for the role of "the arts" (including music) in the emerging reason-based conceptions of the world. As we noted previously, "beauty" is not a *perception* at all, but a largely culturally determined *conception*, stemming from an individual's experience of cultural validation or meaningful cultural transcendence *associated with* a given perception (such as a particular form of music or musical practice).

Nevertheless, as we noted previously, conceptions like Immanuel Kant's idealistic notion of beauty as a subjective universal and the attendant idea that different works of music—as works of "art"—should be evaluated on the basis of their attainment of the ideal of "perfect form" have persisted in the thinking of many people to the present day. At the same time, ideas like Hegel's less culturally restrictive notion of different works of music as works of *art*—that is, as different sensory realizations (or expressions) of the Absolute—have served to frame the philosophical foundation for the composition and performance of diverse forms of art music that have emerged in Europe and the U.S. since the eighteenth century, and, retrospectively and universally, all other music.

We can see from our early twenty-first-century perspective that the emergence of this autonomous "aesthetic" realm must have had the effect of moving consideration of different forms of music into the theologically and politically inert realm of personal preference, the concomitant emergence of the concept of "taste" making it possible for the works of art music emerging at this time to be heard with a degree of psychological remove. In this context, every new musical work created by a particular composer could be considered intellectually as a "unique expression of the Absolute," and thus separated or bracketed from the cultural associations embodied in it (unlike the music of a church or state, which required both participation and commitment), thus reflecting the new more or less reason-oriented conceptions of Reality emerging at the time in yet another way. In their writings on "the arts," the philosophers of the Enlightenment had, in essence, created the notion of the aesthetic as a hypothetical, *culturally neutral mental space* in which differences in worldview could be considered rationally and explored intellectually.[35] However, the tendency of these European intellectuals to focus on the mere artifacts or objects of music rather than accounting in a more satisfactory way for the important psychophysiological, psychosocial, and sociopolitical effects of musical practices in their emerging reason-based conceptions of Reality was to have far-reaching effects on conceptions of both music and musical practices in the U.S.

CHANGES IN CONCEPTS OF MUSIC IN
THE AMERICAN COLONIES

Great social changes were taking place in the American colonies during the eighteenth century as well, many of which we discussed in Chapter 4. The influence of Enlightenment thought combined with various religious movements and a new societal penchant for the rewards of foreign trade to help advance a spirit of religious toleration among the culturally disparate populace. As the colonies came together as "states" to form the new republic, they also moved toward enacting laws disestablishing religion. Accordingly, the writings of the Enlightenment philosophers influenced the founders of the U.S. to promote the liberty of the individual over the enforced solidarity of communities when they drafted the foundational laws of the new democratic nation.

Simultaneously, a new work ethic emerged as citizens began to realize that they could acquire greater influence and respectability in their communities by imitating the gentry—persons who held higher social standing than themselves owing largely to the sizable coffers they had brought with them from Europe—by buying luxury items, many of them imported, that they had previously been unable to afford. As a result, trade with other nations and between the states increased. As the new nation moved toward the development of a trade- and industry-based capitalist economy, the colonies' earlier, more religiously based forms of social organization were gradually displaced.

At the same time, many persons of European descent living along the Atlantic seaboard were becoming enthralled with the supposed culturally transcendent art music of the European composers, and they began to undertake performances of this new "serious" form of music in their own towns. Individuals who had formerly attended the singing schools (which, as we noted earlier, had been formed expressly for the purpose of improving the quality of singing in the churches) found themselves drawn toward participation in the newly forming singing societies, some of which grew out of the singing schools; these organizations were dedicated primarily to performing the new, less-culturally constrained art music produced by the "geniuses" of Europe. The first such organization to emerge is thought to have been the Singing Society of Stoughton, Massachusetts, which was organized in 1786. One of the most well known of these organizations, the Handel and Haydn Society of Boston, dedicated primarily to the performance of choral music, was founded in 1815. The Musical Fund Society of Philadelphia, which featured instrumental works in their programs, was founded in 1820, performing a Beethoven symphony at its first concert in 1821.

From our present historical perspective, we can see that the philosophers of the Enlightenment had made a valuable contribution toward liberating citizens of the U.S. (and, eventually, of the European nations) from the confines of oppressive churches and autocratic state governments, but their failure to account adequately for certain long-standing musical practices in their conceptions of the new reason-based societies they envisioned eventually led to a societal ambivalence about them. Indeed, persons with strong emotional ties to the church retained the view that all societally important musical practices were those that took place in worship, and they were put off by the "artistic" conceptions propagated in the newly appearing singing societies and symphonies, particularly when these impacted on their worship services. For example, the Episcopal Church leaders responsible for creating the *New American Prayer Book* of 1798 strongly admonished their fellow clergy to monitor closely the nature of the music featured in their worship services.

> [I]t shall be the duty of every Minister, with such assistance as he can obtain from persons skilled in music, to give order concerning the Tunes to be sung, at any time, in his Church: And, especially, it shall be his duty, to suppress all light and unseemly music; and all indecency and irreverence in the performance; by which, vain and ungodly persons profane the service of the Sanctuary.[36]

The concern evidently persisted, as one Episcopal clergyman felt compelled to question the intent with which those who were serving as church musicians executed their duties in 1856.

> From your work of the Ministry, beloved brethren, we would ask your serious attention to the share which the Organist and the Choir are called upon to take in the public duty of devotion . . . We cannot . . . regard it as anything short of a most grievous and dangerous inconsistency, when the house of prayer is desecrated by a choice of music and a style of performance which are rather suited to the Opera than to the Church—when the organist and the choir seem to be intent only on exciting the admiration of the audience by the display of their artistic

skill; and the entertainment of the concert-room is taken as a substitute for the solemn praises of that Almighty Being "who searcheth the hearts and trieth the reins of the children of men."[37]

At the same time, those who were caught up in the new, more rationalistic, "aesthetic" philosophies came to regard the products of musical practices (i.e., music) as works of *art* that had been inspired by genius, subsequently reinterpreting the music of religious worship as manifestations of "artistic" expression. For example, Simeon Pease Cheney suggested that the music of the early American composers of psalm tunes should be reconsidered as works of *art* in his collection *The American Singing Book* of 1879.

> I have taken great interest in bringing forward our early psalm tune composers, and given some permanence, as I hope, to their true position. Their natural, and in many cases their excellent compositions, compel me to believe them to have been men of no ordinary gifts. I agree fully with the following sentiment . . ."Whatever may be said of the laws which governed our fathers in the arrangement of their musical ideas, none can reasonably deny the abounding evidence of inspiration found in their works." Their compositions *were inspirations*, hence original, hence they live.[38]

Within the ranks of those caught up in Enlightenment ideals, some held the works of the "genius" composers of Europe to be the apotheosis of "art" while others sustained more pragmatic, egalitarian perspectives, accepting different works of art music on their own terms while continuing to value also the sacred and folk music of their respective historical traditions.

Reflected in the ideas of this latter group and emerging tacitly in the society in general was the revolutionary idea of the Enlightenment discussed earlier: the modern concept of *art* or "the realm of the aesthetic" as a hypothetical politically neutral mental space in which cultural (and perhaps theological) differences manifested in different forms of music could be considered intellectually and according to which cultural differences could be bracketed or provisionally set aside in the nation's public forum. It is important to realize, however, that this perspective was not at first appreciated by all members of the nation's populace. Indeed, it has remained as a point of ambivalence throughout the history of the U.S. According to this way of thinking, musical choices were relegated to the realm of "taste," in which differences in musical preference could be discussed in the nation's public forum, unlike matters of religion.

Not long after this time, conservatories began to be established in the U.S. Modeled after the European conservatories, they too were intended to have an elevating effect on persons living in the cities in which they were established. The Oberlin Conservatory was founded in 1865, the New England

Conservatory and the Cincinnati Conservatory were formed in 1867, and the Peabody Conservatory came into existence in 1868.[39] We might note that all conservatories in the U.S. are funded by private means, unlike their counterparts in European nations, which are government funded.

However, a tension was bound to emerge eventually between those U.S. citizens having morally elevated "artistic" sensibilities and those who regarded music either as religious activity or as a mere domestic pastime. The tension between those who held such contradictory views was perhaps never so clearly manifested as it was in the early history of the Peabody Conservatory in Baltimore, Maryland. Ray Edwin Robinson has related the story of the uncertain first three years of the Peabody Institute—as it was then called—following the opening of the Academy of Music in 1868. His account of the conservatory's founding provides a good window on the ways in which European worldviews, according to which music was an *art*, were received by a city in which music was then regarded either as worship or entertainment; it thus warrants our brief consideration.

The Peabody Institute was the creation of George Peabody, a self-made businessman who had amassed a sizable fortune as a young man by importing dry goods from England to the U.S. Later in his life, Peabody became a banker, and, due to his considerable wealth, he turned to philanthropy during his last years. As a result of his numerous business trips to Europe, during which he had found himself irritated at hearing Europeans' frequent denunciations of Americans on basis of their "cultural" inferiority, Peabody sought to create an institution for the purpose of "raising the culture" of the industrial port city of Baltimore and the state of Maryland, his home during the years of his greatest business success. A great believer in education who held confidence in the potential of ambitious and intelligent poor people to better their standing, Peabody stated outright his wish to create an institution that would put the education of the masses in cultural matters over and above the training of concert artists and teachers.

> A young man of genius may have an irresistible love of science or literature, and may be without means. For him this Institute is especially designed. It affords him, in its library and lectures, means of improvement which he could not possibly obtain without its aid. So it is in music, and so in art. It is aimed at the highest and the best.[40]

At that time, the city of Baltimore had no libraries, a politically corrupt government, no sewer system, and it regularly claimed a great number of deaths stemming from infectious disease. As for its cultural life, the writer of an unsigned editorial in the Baltimore newspaper *The American* observed retrospectively in 1872: "[T]he people would hang with ecstatic delight upon the miserable melodies of [Stephen] Foster, while the florious and seraphic outbursts of Mozart and Beethoven would remain unheeded."[41] Into this dirty and apparently "culturally impoverished" city,

Peabody sought to introduce a cultural institute, one that would feature a noncirculating scholarly library, a lecture series, an academy of music, and a gallery of fine art. Peabody intended that the institute would make possible the *enlightenment* of individuals rather than catering to popular taste, and that its Academy of Music would make possible in Baltimore the kinds of experiences he had enjoyed in European concert halls.

> I wish that the Institute shall embrace within its plan an Academy of Music . . . to diffuse and cultivate a taste for that, the most refining of all arts. By providing . . . the facilities necessary to the best exhibition of the art, the means of studying its principles and practising [sic] its compositions, and . . . concerts, aided by the best talent and most eminent skill within their means to procure, the Trustees may promote the purpose to which I propose to devote this department of the Institute.[42]

Furthermore, Peabody was quite emphatic that the efforts of the Institute should always be *elevating* and not compromised by "sectarian theology or party politics . . . political dissentions . . . [or] . . . visionary theories." Instead, he asserted, those on the faculty should "teach political and religious charity, tolerance and benevolence, and prove this to be in all contingencies and conditions the true friend of our inestimable Union."[43]

Thus, it was somewhat ironic that the first director appointed to head the institute should have been Lucien H. Southard, a music educator from the North whose term of service there coincided with the end of the nation's Civil War. Southard sought to follow Peabody's wishes to "cultivate a taste for music" and build support among the people of Baltimore by promoting and presenting performances of the "very finest" musical literature at the institute. However, Southard's approach and his musical choices engendered considerable hostility among Baltimoreans, many of whom were unable to participate meaningfully in the concerts or to understand the goals of the institution. Though the Peabody Institute's first concerts were reasonably well-attended, few people in the city were then interested in listening to the "serious" music of artistically oriented, academically trained performers, most of them preferring their own, more participatory and less formal forms of musical engagement. Furthermore, the private music teachers working outside of the institute who might have been sympathetic to and supportive of its mission grew to dislike it, not on grounds of its curricular content but because it offered tuition lower than their own rates and thus drew students away from them. In addition, Southard himself was politically and socially disadvantaged by being a Northerner holding a position of leadership in a city still torn by Southern leanings and political strife left over from the Civil War. His letter of resignation of 1871 clearly reveals his frustration at having been unsuccessful in introducing "high culture" into the industrial port city of Baltimore.

I have had to encounter the bitter and unscrupulous enmity of every professional musician and teacher; the avowed and active hostility of amateur musical coteries; and worst of all, the apathy of the general Public, who seem to have no confidence in the conservatory method of class-teaching, notwithstanding the fact that this method has been practised most successfully in England, Belgium, Germany, France, and Italy for more than a hundred years; nine-tenths of all celebrated singers and instrumentalists having been educated in this manner.[44]

Asger Hamerik, Southard's successor as director of the institute, who moved there from his home in Denmark, had much more success at winning over the support and interest of Baltimoreans when he arrived in 1871. Many of the Civil War animosities alive in the city had begun to die down by that time, and its citizens had become more open to the new ideas arriving from Europe. Despite a shyness of character, Hamerik featured Peabody students in an ongoing and plentiful series of concerts, he encouraged and featured the music of American composers in Peabody concerts, he brought many important literary and musical figures of the nineteenth century to the school, and he adopted a gentle but quietly enthusiastic approach to public relations. His efforts at building cultural bridges to the community paid off, and the school's enrollment showed a steady increase throughout his tenure as director. As Robinson notes, some of the other schools of music seeking to replicate the European conservatory model that began in the U.S. during this era suffered similar challenges in their first years.

In many ways the experience of Peabody has been similar to other schools that have attempted to re-create the European conservatory idea on American soil. Ultimately they found it necessary to develop a broader base of operation and to concern themselves in some realistic way with the masses.[45]

THE ADVENT OF PUBLIC-SCHOOL MUSIC EDUCATION IN THE U.S.

Three decades prior to the founding of the Peabody Institute, two men, influenced by the influx of "aesthetic" notions of music emerging in Europe, found themselves sufficiently convinced of the value of vocal music in education that they undertook efforts to argue for its inclusion as a subject of study in the public schools of Boston. During his long career, William Channing Woodbridge served as a teacher, as a minister, and later as the publisher of *The American Annals of Education*, an educational journal that grew to have considerable importance in New England under his leadership. In the 1820s, he traveled to Europe, where he observed the teaching of Johann G. Nageli, a highly successful Swiss music educator. Nageli introduced Woodbridge to educational methods that had been developed by the noted Swiss educational theorist Heinrich Pestalozzi. Impressed by Pestalozzi's ideas that education should be based on the individual child's development and that it should be rooted in concrete experience rather than abstract study, and deeply impacted by the results apparent in Nageli's teaching of music, Woodbridge came to regard music education as an important and effective means of fostering children's intellectual and emotional development.

Though he was not a musician himself, Woodbridge was sufficiently impressed by what he had seen in Europe that when he returned home to Boston in 1830 he felt compelled to deliver a lecture before the American Institute of Instruction strongly advocating the use of vocal music in the general education of children. Though he laid the foundation of his appeal in purely practical terms, he began with a nod to the religious perspectives of his listeners.

> The Creator seems to have formed an immediate connexion between the ear and the heart. Every feeling expresses itself by a tone, and every tone awakens again the feeling from which it sprung.[46]

Woodbridge went on to recommend instruction in music for its capacity to refresh the mind (while simultaneously leaving "the intellect in repose"), to enhance the physical constitution, to foster emotional well-being, to elevate moral character, and to promote school discipline, among other things. Woodbridge's vague and passing reference to "the Creator" in the foregoing statement is notable, as it likely represents an effort to appeal to the religious sensibilities of his audience without evoking the musical associations of any particular creed or denomination. It seems apparent that, despite his background as a church minister, Woodbridge was inclined to downplay his listeners' religious associations with musical practices, promoting the study of music in the schools on a strictly practical basis in accordance with the emerging societal concept of music as a morally and intellectually elevating undertaking.

Meanwhile, a Massachusetts-born musician named Lowell Mason had recently moved back to Boston from his home in Savannah, Georgia, and had begun teaching children to sing in twice-weekly classes held at the Bowdoin Street Church. Working in a city in which most citizens thought musical talent to be relatively rare and in which few had any idea that children could develop musical skills, his classes at first involved only a few students. In a very short time, however, word of Mason's teaching skills spread throughout the town, and soon hundreds of children were participating. Woodbridge befriended Mason sometime after 1830, and, during the course of their association, he introduced him to the Pestalozzian teaching methods with which he had become familiar during his visit to Europe. Impressed with Pestalozzi's ideas, Mason began to incorporate these principles into his instruction, eventually endorsing them publicly. Mason's classes gave highly successful public concerts in 1832 and 1833, prompting a group of Boston citizens to begin promoting music education in their community; their efforts led to the founding of the Boston Academy of Music.

The following year, Mason published the *Manual of the Boston Academy of Music, for Instruction in the Elements of Vocal Music on the System of Pestalozzi*, the stated purpose of which was to put instruction in vocal music on a common level with other subjects in elementary education.[47] This book soon became very popular in Boston, and it was reprinted several times over the following eight years. Among its features was a section detailing a number of practical reasons why vocal music *should* be "cultivated" in the education of children. Among his numerous justifications, Mason noted that vocal music improves the voice, is conducive to physical health (owing primarily to its exercise of the lungs), improves the heart (i.e., the "sentiments") by softening and elevating the feelings (assuming the singer sings the right kinds of songs), and produces social order and happiness in a family (by evoking stronger attachments between family members and among schoolchildren). Furthermore, he observed, it exercises and disciplines the mind (which produces habits of physical and mental order) and it cultivates the feelings by providing a means of training them. We might note that we have accounted for many of Mason's points in our Peircian pragmatic conception of musical practices set forth in Chapter 3. Particularly remarkable among them, however, is Mason's recognition that only by introducing certain *kinds* of music would the feelings be properly softened and elevated, thus suggesting that Mason likely maintained a cultural bias in his choices of music for instruction. (Further, we should note that Mason's emphasis on the cultivation of feelings through music established a precedent for considering music education as *aesthetic education*, a concept that would be developed by others throughout the history of U.S. music education, especially in the late twentieth century.)

Possessed by the notion that nearly all children could learn to sing and that it would benefit them greatly to do so, Mason solicited the support of those whose efforts had led to the founding of the Boston Academy to promote to the general public and the Boston School Board the idea of adding classes in music to the curriculum of the city's common schools. Though the board had made an initial foray to introduce vocal music classes into the Boston schools in 1832, the effort had not been carried out successfully. Thus, following Mason's enthusiastic resubmission of the idea, the board decided to appoint a special committee to investigate the matter fully; their investigations included observation of Mason's teaching at the Bowdoin Street Church.

The committee submitted its report on August 24, 1837, unanimously agreeing that vocal music should be introduced as a regular subject into the city's common schools. The report reveals that the members of the committee had reached their decision on purely practical terms and that many of the reasons for their decision were drawn from Mason's own rationale in the *Manual*. Specifically, they argued that music is *intellectually* beneficial on the basis that it "quickens" memory, comparison, attention, and intellectual faculties; *morally* beneficial as it produces habits of feeling such as happiness, contentment, cheerfulness, and tranquillity; and *physically* beneficial as, "when not carried to an unreasonable excess," it expands the chest and thus strengthens the lungs and other vital organs.

> Judging then by this triple standard, intellectually, morally, and physically, vocal music seems to have a natural place in every system of instruction which aspires, as should every system, to develop man's whole nature . . . Now the defect of our present system, admirable as that system is, is this, that it aims to develop the intellectual part of man's nature solely, when for all the true purposes of life, it is of more importance, a hundredfold, to feel rightly, than to think profoundly. Besides, human life must and ought to have its amusements. Through vocal music you set in motion a mighty power which silently, but surely, in the end, will humanize, refine, and elevate a whole community.[48]

This argument, the original rationale for the inclusion of music to be included as a regular subject in the curriculum of public schools of the U.S., represents a justification based on strictly practical ways in which musical engagement (considered as a generic phenomenon) contributes to the intellectual, moral, and physical betterment of students. Notably, the committee clearly placed emotional or psychosocial benefits over and above those of the intellect, appealing to the emerging societal conception of music as an ennobling field of endeavor. This report had the desired effect on the Boston School Board, which resolved to introduce music as a regular subject into the city's common schools. The Board passed the matter on to the Boston City Council, but the Council failed to appropriate funds for it. Undaunted, Lowell Mason volunteered to teach music for one year in one of the city's schools without pay, for the purpose of demonstrating that music classes could indeed be successful in the public schools. At the end of this year, the council finally resolved to include music in the regular curriculum at a status commensurate with such subjects as arithmetic and reading.[49] The following years saw the introduction of vocal music into public-school curricula throughout the U.S., with the Buffalo, Chicago, Pittsburgh, and Louisville city schools being among the first to follow the lead of the Boston School Board.

It seems important to note that while the report of the special committee designated by the Boston School Board to investigate the feasibility of introducing classes in music into their schools was successful, it also faintly damned music education in its reference to music as a mere "amusement." This allusion, prominently placed in the document now regarded by many as the charter of the profession, reveals something of the societal ambivalence about music education that existed even at its first introduction into the schools; this notion has dogged the profession of music education throughout its history.

Even more significant from our present perspective, however, is the fact that no overt mention was made in this report of the religious or cultural content of the music that would be included in music classes. In accordance with the emerging egalitarian ideals of the Enlightenment philosophers in the U.S., according to which matters of cultural difference were to be bracketed from the public forum, arguments for the inclusion of music in the schools were made on the basis of the beneficial effects associated with musical engagement (considered as a generic phenomenon) and it was thus divorced from its social meanings. The origins of the music included in the schools—those from which it derived its most psychosocially beneficial effects—and other, likely religion-related reasons for its inclusion were not discussed in the report.

PURPOSES OF PUBLIC-SCHOOL MUSIC EDUCATION IN THE MID-NINETEENTH CENTURY

Judging from the descriptions of the purposes of music education set forth in the introductions to music textbooks published over the following years (as well as in other writings), public-school music educators collectively were deeply influenced by the concept of art music manifested in the works of the "great" composers of Europe by the middle of the nineteenth century. Indeed, they saw their teaching of musical skills as being grounded in three societally important purposes.

First of all, it seems apparent that they sought to immerse their students in the works of the European "masters" on the basis of their belief that exposure to and involvement in this culturally liberated and morally elevated music would have liberating and elevating effects on the students as well. For example, George B. Loomis proffered his collection of choral music, *The Progressive Glee and Chorus Book*, specifically on the basis that the music he had selected would be a morally elevating force in the lives of children.

> The musical portion of the work consists of three and four-part secular and sacred music, composed, selected, and arranged from many sources, largely from the German and English, of that which seemed to the author to be adapted to the end in view—that of educating the people through the medium of song. Of the power of music in this direction we have yet much to learn. Germany appreciates it; England is following in her wake; and may we not hope that our own favored America may soon be abreast of them in this regard. . . .

> If the book shall contribute in any degree to building up and estab-
> lishing in the rising generation greater purity and moral integrity, a
> truer and nobler manhood, the work of the author shall not have been
> in vain.[50]

He noted that his book consisted "chiefly of music elected from the best
German, English, and Italian authors," and he followed this claim with
a list of featured composers, which included Handel, Haydn, Beethoven,
Mozart, Mendelssohn, Weber, Schumann, and Schubert.[51]

Likewise, Luther Orlando Emerson and W. S. Tilden noted in the
"Preface" to *The Hour of Singing: A Book for High Schools, Seminaries,
and the Social Choir* that they had included only music of high quality
when assembling their book, and that its use should contribute to the
moral elevation of the students who would be using it. However, they
also admitted that they had to make some concessions in their choice of
materials in order to accommodate the learning of children having different levels of ability.

> The present work has been compiled to meet a want, often expressed, of
> a collection of music suitably arranged for schools of mixed voices. . . .
> The music [in this collection], while not embracing much trash, ranges
> from the somewhat difficult down to the very easy; yet all of it may be
> used in teaching, and made instructive.[52]

Henry Southwick Perkins, H. J. Danforth, and E. V. DeGraff found it
important to highlight the fact that they had focused primarily on secular music when selecting repertoire for their collection of 1883, *The Song
Wave: Designed for Schools, Teachers' Institutes, Musical Conventions,
and the Home Circle*. Their preface affirms their placement of Enlightenment ideals over religious content.

> Perhaps the most common error in the selection of music for use in
> the day-school is the exclusive use of sacred songs. While it is true that
> Music is prominent in its devotional uses, yet it is equally true that the
> continued use of sacred music is unsuited to the child's mind, because
> it gives no expression to his ordinary thought.[53]

Despite this claim, however, twenty-three of the 171 songs in their collection featured texts on sacred themes.

At the same time, the concern that the music included be of high quality impacted the selection of music for hymnals as well, revealing that the
Enlightenment notion of music as an ennobling and elevating art must have
affected the decision making of churches on musical matters. This seems
evident in the "Preface" Caryl Florio wrote in 1885 to the collection *Children's Hymns, with Tunes*:

It is, of course, as easy to spoil the taste of children as of adults, and much harm has been done in this direction by many well-intentioned but ill-judging persons; but [the editor] has found that, given the right material to work with, and the right person to work with it, children will quickly learn to recognize and to love the *best*, both in words and music, and eventually to prefer it to what is common or trashy. Speaking from his personal experience, therefore, the editor ventures to declare that nothing will be found in this book which will not, even to a vitiated taste, quickly commend itself as being good, appropriate, feasible, and enjoyable.[54]

Attendant upon the goal of morally elevating the students was the notion of elevating the taste of the students, in order that they would be able to discern good music from that of substandard quality. As Frederick H. Ripley and Thomas Tapper affirmed in the "Preface" to one of the books in their *Natural Course in Music* of 1895: " . . . The pupil will not only feel the pleasure which beautiful melody affords, but he will be conscious of a growing appreciation of good music, and feel the deep satisfaction which increasing power and skill always give."[55]

At the time, "good" music was invariably that which was drawn from the works of the European masters or from American musicians who also subscribed to artistic principles in composing their works. Frederic A. Lyman boasted that his *Normal Music Course* of 1896 was "the first to place public school music on a thoroughly pedagogical basis, and to lift it from mere song singing to its true function as a disciplinary, educational, and elevating force."[56] He compared the rewards of involvement in music to those inherent in the reading of great literature, asserting that "[n]ot to know in music some of the great themes which Beethoven, Mendelssohn, Mozart, Verdi, Rossini, Brahms, Gounod, Abt, Randegger, and Rubenstein have given to the realm of musical composition, is analogous to not knowing the great conceptions of Homer, Dante, Milton, Shakespeare, Goethe, Schiller, and other master minds in literature."[57] Lest anyone should think that such rewards are accessible only by adults, textbook author Eleanor Smith reminded teachers using her *Modern Music Series* of 1905, "With taste as well as technique cultivated, the best music may be approached at a comparatively early age. There is but a step from the classics of children's music to the simpler compositions of Beethoven and of Brahms."[58]

Also in the early years of the twentieth century, public-school music teachers and supervisors were beginning to feel that the two existing educational organizations that handled matters of music education were not adequately addressing their needs, and their writings about the creation of a new organization also reveal much about what they saw as their societal purpose. While the meetings of the Music Section of the *National Education Association* were reportedly quite well attended around the turn of the century, many educators evidently came for the musical part of the program only, leaving little time for business meetings. The other organization, the *Music Teachers National Association*, focused primarily on the needs of private teachers and music conservatories, giving scant attention to the interests and needs of those in the public schools. Thus, when a group of music supervisors from various states met together in Keokuk, Iowa, in 1907, they discussed the possibility of forming an organization of their own. Over the following months, the members of this group remained in contact with one another via the *School Music Monthly*, a publication started by one of them. When they met again in Cincinnati, Ohio, in 1910, they took action to establish themselves as a separate and independent national organization which they named the Music Supervisors National Conference (MSNC); this organization became the Music Educators National Conference (MENC) in 1934.[59] In drawing up the first constitution for the conference, they stated its objects, in Article II, as "mutual helpfulness" among the membership and "the promotion of good music through the instrumentality of the public schools."[60]

The seriousness with which the members of the organization took this goal was reinforced in a paper on "High School Music" that appeared in the first *Journal of Proceedings* published by the MSNC. In this paper, Osbourne McConathy, a founding member of the organization, wrote: "In back of all the musical activities of the high school lies the idea that a widespread, intelligent appreciation of good music is becoming more and more necessary to modern social conditions."[61]

This purpose of the organization was affirmed two decades later in a document signed by Ada Bicking, Peter Dykema, Karl W. Gehrkens, Osbourne McConathy, Ruth Haller Ottoway, Arthur G. Kahlberg, and Will Earhart, many of whom were charter members, at an MSNC planning committee meeting on the Century of Progress Exposition.

> Recognizing the failure of an industrial society to bring of itself happy living to mankind, and recognizing the inevitable changes which are bound to come in social life through economic readjustments, the Music Supervisors National Conference gladly accepts every opportunity to bring to the attention of the American people the contribution which art, and especially musical art, may make to their disinterested and enduring happiness.
>
> There will be value, rich and deep beyond computation, in the understanding of music and its place in life that will come to thousands of parents. Recognition of the worth of music by the masses has always been intuitive, yet it is this force that has maintained music in the world, and it as a school subject. The parents, by reason of limited knowledge of both music and education, may, it is true, be incapable of a reasoned judgment. But when they hear their children lifting strains of music with voice and instruments, they know, with certain knowledge and with a quick rush of feeling, that music is a blessed thing and

that their children are shielded from evil while they follow an allure-
ment so unworldly and pure.[62]

These writers' reference to the contribution that "musical art" might make
to their "disinterested and enduring happiness" provides a subtle indication
of their belief that participation in art music was believed to transcend the
more culturally restrictive forms of music manifested in the nation's constituent communities.

   The second purpose music educators saw as motivating their work at the
turn of the century was related to the first. They saw it as their responsibility to use "good" music for the purpose of cultivating the emotions—or
educating the feelings—of their students; this belief was likely a reflection
of the growing influence of romantic music in the nation's art music forums.
In a teachers' manual designed to accompany his *Normal Music Course*,
Frederic Lyman asserted: "Let us early learn to cultivate our emotions.
No better chance is offered than in the study of music. We should study
only the best music and if we are to have songs, let us search for those that
are pure in thought and expression."[63] One textbook writer, Robert Foresman, went so far as to take a systematic approach to literature selection in
assembling material for his *Books of Songs* series, intending that students
would be able to fully exercise their developing emotions through singing
the music he had chosen.

> The songs in this book have been chosen because each achieves a cer-
> tain standard of beauty and a consequent emotional reaction. The ar-
> tistic quality of each song is a challenge to the pupil's interest, and the
> varying moods expressed will adapt themselves to his ever-growing
> emotional demands. While a large proportion of the songs are new
> in their present form, they have been drawn from sources rich in tra-
> ditional charm, and their feeling-value has been tested through long
> racial and individual experience.[64]

Foresman also took a systematic, if inconclusive, approach to explaining
the source of the feelings associated with this music.

> The musical effects which stimulate musical feeling are to be found in
> all good songs. These effects can be named, recognized, analyzed, and
> shown graphically in the notation. For instance, the feeling for *unity* is
> the result of singing the entire song and perceiving musically its organic
> structure. The feeling for *continuity* is developed from the very begin-
> ning of the song, as soon as the tendency of the melodic flow makes
> itself definitely felt. The feeling for *balance* produces, as soon as the
> first tone group has been sung, the demand for a balancing tone group.
> The feeling for *proportion* must be satisfied by the singing of the larger
> tone-group entities which make up the song. The feeling for *coherence*

takes cognizance of the relation of the different tone groups through-out the song to each other and to the song as a whole.[65]

In a statement appearing in the teachers manual published in 1927 to accompany his textbook series, Foresman put forth his belief that all persons should respond to a particular piece of music in the same way, thus signaling his concurrence with Kant's ill-founded belief in the existence of subjective universals. His statement suggests that music education of the time essentially served as cultural indoctrination, socializing all children to feel the same way about the same forms of music, and it also suggests that the society in which they were teaching must have been relatively homogeneous in its confidence in Enlightenment ideals.

> Remember always that mood is something that belongs to the *music* and is quite independent of how the singer or listener feels about it. . . . *The mood is in the music.* It is the result of the special combination of tones that is found in each song.[66]

A third, though less prominent, purpose motivating music educators at this time was, somewhat paradoxically, their interest in broadening their students' cultural outlook by introducing them to "music of many lands." Members of the Music Teachers National Association had become involved with the formation of the International Musical Society in 1899, and a U.S. section of this society was formed in 1907; the work of this organization gradually began to influence a number of the nation's music teachers over the ensuing years.[67] "Patriotic songs of various peoples" were featured in Eleanor Smith's books of vocal music as early as 1905 (though most of the songs included in her collection came from Europe),[68] and Karl Gehrkens affirmed the importance of a broader vision for the nation's music educators in 1915, saying: "The ultimate aim of music teaching in the public schools is to cause children to know, to love, and to appreciate music in as many forms as possible . . ."[69]

Robert Foresman too promoted internationalism in his *Books of Songs* of 1925, boasting that in his books "the great musical heritage of the world is represented by songs which should be a part of the life and cultural background of all people." One of his aims in creating these books, he wrote, was "to assemble a group of songs which have stood the test of time, which mirror the characteristics and musical contributions of many national cultures, and which are universal in appeal."[70] (He was evidently unaware of the self-contradictory nature of such a statement.) Osbourne McConathy, John W. Beattie, and Russell V. Morgan published *Music of Many Lands and Peoples* in 1932, though their collection focused primarily on the folk and art songs of different European nations.[71]

Also seeking to promote cultural breadth among teachers and students, the Music Supervisors National Conference established a Committee on

International Affairs at their first biennial convention in Chicago in 1928. Discussions between American and British music educators at this meeting led to efforts to create an international conference, and the first such meeting, held in Lausanne, Switzerland, in 1929, was attended by over four hundred music teachers from various parts of the world. The second such conference, held in 1931 also in Lausanne, turned out to be the last, owing in some measure to the growing intensity of political tensions between nations in Europe.[72]

It is important to note that while the apparent cultural inclusiveness of these music educators may seem to be attractive from our present historical perspective, they were actually propagating a universalizing position toward the different forms of music manifested in different world societies in their teaching, generally regarding them merely as products of culturally different human minds and encouraging students to think of them as different forms of *art*. That is to say, they acknowledged, but otherwise generally ignored, the cultural differences manifested in the forms of music they were recommending for inclusion.

Considering as a group the writings on the purposes of music education set forth by music educators in the U.S. from the early nineteenth century up through the beginning of the twentieth century, we can see that all of them professed agreement with the Enlightenment ideal of music as representing an important form of *art* (i.e., as a form of personal self-expression). However, it is apparent that the way in which these music educators conceptualized "art music" differed somewhat from the concept held by the Europeans with whom it originated.

The first purpose of music education we have considered was the *moral elevation* of the individual. Insofar as the art music of Europe was composed outside of the previously existing social systems of church and court and simply for the intellectual interest and enjoyment (i.e., the psychosocial equilibration) of those individuals who freely chose to participate in it, it could be construed as socially elevated music (i.e., "above" those other systems). As an individual participated in this music, whether by listening or by performance, he or she was not involved in the music of church or court; the music thus represented a celebration of the individual's newly gained, relative independence of thought. By involving students in this new form of "art music," teachers thus had the potential of nurturing the idea of such individualism in them.

However, insofar as they failed to recognize or to impart to their students the social circumstances surrounding the creation of this music in their teaching, these educators promoted a materialistic focus on the forms of music they were introducing (i.e., the musical artifacts), denying the students an understanding of what made this new practice of creating art music meaningful to those who were engaged in it. Notably, the first pieces of the nation's capitalist economy were sliding into place at this time, contributing to a greater societal focus on the acquisition of luxury items and other objects. As teachers promoted consideration of different examples of music as works of *art* to their students, they contributed to promoting a societal conception of the great works of music as valuable objects, turning attention away from the personal and social efficacy of the musical practices of cultural communities. Supporting this social transformation was the attendant instructional goal of "improving the taste" of the students by exposing them to music of high quality so that they would be able to discern "good" music from bad.

We noted that the second purpose motivating music educators' work at the turn of the century was related to the first. They saw it as their responsibility to use "good" music in their teaching for the purpose of *cultivating the emotions* or *educating the feelings* of their students. From the perspective of contemporary cognitive science, the notion of "cultivating the emotions" is highly questionable; while an individual can learn to exercise cognitive control over her or his emotional responses, thus overriding innate reactions, and can also learn to pay attention to her or his emotions as indicators of possible action, the notion of "cultivating the emotions," as suggested by Robert Foresman and others at this time, essentially represents enculturation—teaching the students to respond favorably to music recognized as "good" by their adult contemporaries. Of course, different forms of music can be regarded as more successful or less successful than others insofar as they achieve a desired effect on those who perform or listen to them; thus, notions of "good" and "bad" truly "make sense" only within a particular cultural tradition.

The third, though less prominent, purpose motivating music educators at this time was their interest in broadening their students' cultural perspectives by introducing them to the "music of many lands and peoples." The promotion of music of many different cultural traditions along with the *art* music of the European masters (and others) in the public-school classrooms of the U.S. represents something of an irony, culturally speaking. Clearly, the music of different cultural communities that the early textbook writers selected for inclusion had to have been at least somewhat similar to the forms of music condoned in the public forum of the U.S. at the time, or it would not have been deemed suitable for inclusion in music textbooks. Certainly any music that clearly manifested a widely differing (i.e., culturally objectionable) conception of Reality would have been rejected, as would any form of music that could not be represented using conventional Western notation. Thus, music educators were not truly teaching their students anything about the musical practices manifested in different communities, but were rather encouraging students to adopt a universalizing position toward the often radically differing beliefs and practices of persons of different cultural communities. Indeed, music education—involving the re-creation of musical works of the European masters and the various forms of music produced by different world peoples—served as vehicles for the enculturation of students into the emerging democratic capitalist society in which

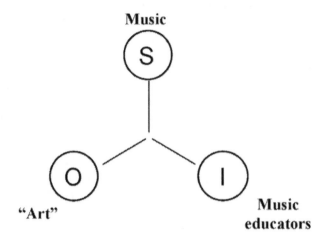

Figure 5.2 The Sign "Music" conceptualized as "Art," a physical manifestation of the *personal expression* of a great artist or genius.

different forms of music were beginning to be considered as objects (i.e., different "artistic expressions" or "sensory realizations of the Absolute.")

In sum, the primary change in this era was the shift in focus from recognizing different *musical practices* as forms of psychosocially equilibrating *behavior* (often undertaken in worship contexts) to conceptualizing works of *music* (i.e., the sound artifacts produced in a musical practice) as elevating, culturally transcendent *art* objects—personal expressions of the "master" composers of Europe. We could represent this new conception using the sign diagram derived from Peirce's pragmatic philosophy as in Figure 5.2.

Of course, as we noted earlier, not all individuals in U.S. society subscribed to this conception. Some more highly religious citizens sustained concepts of musical practices as *worship*; others continued to regard the varieties of musical practices they and their neighbors undertook in their respective communities as pleasant domestic pastimes.

MUSIC EDUCATION IN AN ERA OF SCIENCE AND TECHNOLOGY: MUSIC AS *PRODUCT*

In the decades surrounding the turn of the twentieth century, the Enlightenment conception of different forms of music as works of *art* (i.e., as an individual's *personal expression*) continued to guide the work of music educators in the U.S., and many maintained their focus on the works of the "great masters" of Europe, giving them prominence in their teaching as the epitome of musical excellence. At the same time, at least three new social trends began to emerge in U.S. society, each of which was to impact the profession of music education throughout the century. First, the nation's citizens began to develop a new appreciation for *scientific research* and to place more confidence in its results. Within the medical sciences alone, Louis Pasteur's accomplishments in microbiology, especially his development of "pasteurization" as a method of destroying harmful microorganisms in food and his introduction of "vaccination" as a means of staving off cholera and other diseases, were publicly received with great appreciation. Likewise, the application of Pierre and Marie Curie's studies of radioactivity to x-ray photography, which provided a new "window" into the human body, met with widespread public enthusiasm and gratitude. Second, the nation acquired a great fascination with applications of the scientific method to the development of *technologies* for improving the quality of human life. Thomas Edison's invention of the electric light bulb and certain other devices, the development of the automobile by various inventors in Europe and the U.S., and the invention of the airplane by Wilbur and Orville Wright are prime examples of such societally changing technological innovations. A third and equally far-reaching trend was the emerging interest in the use of *industrial methods* to make these new technologies accessible to the masses. Edison's Electric Light Company gradually brought the electric light and numerous electric appliances to homes throughout America, Henry Ford's innovation of the assembly line for the production of his "Model T" made the automobile accessible to the common person, and various related technologies gradually began to be applied to mass production of clothing and furniture as well as to agricultural products.

At the same time, music educators were beginning to take the place of music education in the schools as something of an established fact, since school music was then receiving more consistent support than ever before. This is reflected in the introductions to music textbooks of the time, where explanations of the importance of music in the life of the individual student had less prominence. The reasons set forth for including music education in the schools by Woodbridge, Mason, and others during the early nineteenth century—specifically those having to do with the benefits of music for the intellectual, moral, and physical development of children—continued to appear in one form or another in the books in which such explanations were included, though a greater emphasis tended to be placed on the morally elevating effects that participation in the study of art music was believed to have on students.

It is something of an axiom of human history that the people of one era tend to forget the concerns of their forebears as new problems and issues arise to occupy their own thinking. Indeed, the content of music textbooks at the turn of the century provides a good indication that music educators of the time were generally less concerned with explaining the importance of music education to their readers and more interested in developing a scientific approach to the practice of their profession. Their thinking at the time seems to have been that if the composition and performance of music was generally understood to be an inherently valuable *art* and the masterworks of Europe represented its highest manifestation, then efficiently teaching students how to perform or replicate these works should be their primary concern. Some teachers saw the use of "other" musical works (such as the folk songs of the U.S. and other nations) as pedagogical tools that could be used to facilitate students' skill development; once students had developed the requisite skills through performance of them, they would be able to devote their time to studying and performing the very *best* music. While this approach to music education meshed well with the increasingly scientific, technological, and industrial orientation of the nation, it also gradually moved music educators to regard music in a way somewhat different from their long held conception of music as *art*.

APPLICATIONS OF SCIENCE

The first trend we identified as emerging among the nation's citizens at the turn of the twentieth century was their new appreciation for *scientific research*, which was accompanied by an increasing confidence in its results. Accordingly, a group of researchers began seeking to use the methods of science to identify and quantify the human characteristics required for musical recreation and composition. One of them, the early psychometric researcher Carl Seashore, sought to locate musical ability in certain human aptitudes or skills. His "Measures of Musical Talents," a series of aptitude tests, included measures designed to express in quantitative terms an individual's pitch acuity, intensity discrimination, time discrimination (i.e., the ability to recognize differences in the length of tones held for different durations), consonance discrimination (i.e., tonal blend), tonal memory, and rhythmic discrimination. This deterministic approach to musical aptitude was somewhat controversial within the community of music educators, but many teachers found great value in Seashore's tests, owing largely to the fact that they provided a means of determining the strengths and weaknesses of individual students.

Jacob Kwalwasser, another psychometrically oriented researcher, sought to quantify not only the motor skills but also the human *feelings* associated with the making of music. His "Melodic Sensitivity Test" required the individual to determine whether different melodic fragments played in succession were "good" or "bad," and his "Harmonic Sensitivity Test" required similar discrimination with respect to harmonic progressions. Similarly, S. A. Courtis developed the "Courtis-Standard Research Tests," one of which measured a subject's recognition of characteristic rhythms by what sort of activity each rhythm suggested (e.g., walking, horseback riding), while another test measured recognition of *mood* from melody (e.g., going to a circus, becoming a soldier). The work of these researchers and others of the time served as a "scientific" foundation for teaching music on the basis of its importance as an inherent and cultivable human propensity. We might note, however, that in focusing on the human aptitudes and skills involved in the creation and perception of music, these researchers generally excluded its social dimension, not considering at all the broader *effects* different musical practices had on those who were involved in them.

This is not to say that all the scientifically oriented music researchers of the time subscribed to such narrowly defined notions of music. A contrasting view was held by G. Stanley Hall, a highly influential child psychology–oriented scientist of the era, who sought to understand the emergence of musical ability in relation to human developmental psychology. Hall believed that music was a universal language and an important means by which human beings could express feelings. He asserted, "[Music] is the art of arts because it is most prehumanistic and also most prophetic of the superman that is to be."[73] By observing and actively exploring the thinking of children at different ages, he came to the conclusion that human beings pass through a series of distinct phases in their maturation from childhood to adulthood. On the basis of his findings, Hall argued that the task of music education should be to provide young students with a "gymnastics of the emotions" primarily through rote singing in the early elementary grades, to nurture the development of musical skills through the use of exercise drills in older students, and ultimately to facilitate the individual's understanding of and ability with music as a language of the emotions in adulthood.

Unlike some of his other scientifically minded contemporaries, however, Hall maintained that at no point should music educators place the goal of developing musical technique over the goal of developing the students' *character* through musical experience. Indeed, in discussing the selection of musical materials for instruction, he wrote: "Every tune introduced should have a moral and aesthetic justification and should be admitted to the school canon only after careful deliberation and for good and sufficient reasons."[74] While many of his conclusions on the development of children's thinking seem crude in comparison with those of present-day cognitive psychologists, his work spawned the "child-study" movement, a major trend in educational psychology focused on consideration of children's psychological (i.e., cognitive) development; it thus represented an important contribution to the field of educational psychology.

Another scientifically influenced perspective on the importance of music education that differed considerably from that of many other scientifically minded music educators at the turn of the twentieth century stemmed from the writings of John Dewey, perhaps the most highly influential educational philosopher of the era. Dewey was briefly a student of Peirce at Johns Hopkins University, and the *instrumentalist* philosophy he developed in various writings over the course of his lifetime shares much in common with the philosophical perspective we have adopted in this inquiry. Dewey held that truth is best regarded as an instrument used by human beings to solve their problems and that it invariably changes as one's problems change. This view, and his belief in democracy as the most ethical of all political systems, led him to reject authoritarian methods of education and to assert that teaching should center on the needs and interests of individual students (i.e., on each student's unique potential for development). On these bases, he encouraged "learning-by-doing," individualized instruction, and experimentation with educational methods in the public schools. His teaching and his writings had a profound impact on educational practices in the U.S. over the course of his life, contributing a great deal to the "progressive" movement in education.

In his *Psychology* of 1887, Dewey articulated a view of *art* that shares much in common with the Peircian pragmatic view we have explored in this inquiry.

> [T]he end of art is to create that in which the human soul may find itself perfectly reflected. Or as the essential factor in beauty is harmony—harmony with self—we may say that the end of art is to produce a perfectly harmonized self. The various fine arts, architecture, sculpture, painting, music, and poetry, are the successive attempts of the mind adequately to express its own ideal nature, or, more correctly stated, adequately to produce that which will satisfy its own demands for and love of a perfectly harmonious nature, something in which admiration may rest.[75]

Horatio Parker, Osborne McConathy, Edward Bailey Birge, and W. Otto Miessner sought to apply Dewey's philosophy to music education in their music textbooks, *The Progressive Music Series* of 1916. The following passage from their introduction reveals the very different orientation they advocated for music education, one that focused more on the development of the individual student than on the subject of music.

> The general aim of education is to train the child to become a capable, useful, and contented member of society. The development of a fine character and of the desire to be of service to humanity are results that lie uppermost in the minds of the leaders of educational thought. Every school subject is valued in proportion to its contribution to these desirable ends. Music, because of its powerful influence upon the very innermost recesses of our subjective life, because of its wonderfully stimulating effect upon our physical, mental, and spiritual nature, and because of its well-nigh universality of appeal, contributes directly to both of the fundamental purposes of education. By many of the advanced educators of the present day, therefore, music, next to the "three R's," is considered the most important subject in the public school curriculum.[76]

Indeed, Dewey's pragmatic contention that the "end" of music is to effect harmony in the individual was taken by the "progressive" educators influenced by his philosophy to imply that music education should be used primarily as a vehicle of socialization, specifically to orient or shape students' tastes, attitudes, and perspectives in ways appropriate to life in the U.S. in the early twentieth century. Simultaneously, his focus on the efficiency with which each subject was taught—which was rooted in the belief that by teaching students efficiently they would have more time to explore a wide variety of subjects during the school day—tended to take precedence in these music educators' classes. Needless to say, these classes focused very little if at all on understanding the psychosocial origins of the music under study. However, as we shall see, these ideas of Dewey did mesh well with the increasing orientation toward industry emerging in the nation's public forum.

USE OF TECHNOLOGIES

The second trend we identified earlier as emerging in U.S. society around the turn of the twentieth century was the nation's fascination with applying scientific method to the development of various *technologies* for improving the quality of human life. Clearly, the new technological innovations that began to impact music education most strikingly at this time were those of audio recording and radio broadcasting. Following Thomas Edison's invention of the phonograph in 1877, recording technology was gradually perfected. The first phonographs and recordings became commercially available to the general public in 1904, and the introduction of electric, rather than acoustic, technologies greatly improved the quality of sound and led to sales of more of the devices in the mid-1920s.

Whereas teachers had previously been able to introduce their students to the music of the European "masters" only by having them sing the simplest of their works in class (or, rarely, by taking them to a concert), it suddenly became possible for them to introduce students to the composers' more complex symphonic and choral music via recordings. This turn of events gave rise to "music appreciation," a relatively new instructional focus in music education. This approach had as its primary focus teaching students how to listen to and grasp the formal characteristics of the different varieties of art music that were then becoming available on recordings. Frances Elliott Clark, the primary innovator and advocate for music appreciation in the schools, emphasized the importance of educated listening in the Foreword she wrote for *Music Appreciation for Children*, a 1930 publication of the Victor Talking Machine Company, a manufacturer of the new devices.

> Hearing the great masterpieces by means of the Orthophonic Victor recordings is an opening of the gates into toneland, but for intelligent following of the paths in the garden of enchantment . . . much skillful leading, definite direction, investigation, and analysis is needed.[77]

Calvin Brainerd Cady, Clark's colleague, explained the origins of this new approach to music education in the Preface that followed her Foreword.

> The study of music appreciation emanated from the effort to prepare audiences at symphony concerts to listen more intelligently to pure (instrumental) music; to help the people to better understand, and, therefore, to enjoy what they hear.
>
> ... Naturally such study was possible only for the relatively few, and especially for adult minds, because it (1) involved a musical imagination possessed by relatively few concert-goers, and (2) because there were not means for the widespread presentation of music of all characters, pure (instrumental) and vocal.
>
> The perfection of the recording and interpretative capacities of the Victor Talking Machine immensely broadened the scope of the problem and, for the first time in history, made the study universally practical.[78]

Despite having had a highly successful teaching career in the public schools, Clark saw such potential in the Victor Talking Machine that she gave up an offer to become supervisor of high school music programs in Milwaukee, Wisconsin, to assume the directorship of the Educational Department of the Victor company when it was offered her in 1910. She worked for the company for decades, overseeing the production of several instructional texts, arranging for recordings of music for children, and promoting music appreciation at all large meetings and conventions of music educators.

Edward B. Birge, Mabel E. Bray, Osbourne McConathy, and W. Otto Miessner affirmed in their text *The Music Hour* that the new phonography technology represented a great benefit for music educators on the basis that it provided yet another means for "raising the taste" of their students.

> The study of great composers through their simple but characteristic songs, through singing some of the themes from their instrumental compositions which are heard on the phonograph, and through their pictures and brief consideration of some of the important events in their lives, contributes to a deeper interest in the best types of music.[79]

As the various new technologies began to impact the U.S. populace, many citizens expected that they would eventually be living in a more or less fully automated society, one in which they would have to devise creative ways to use their "free time." Some authors thus lauded the new technology both for its value as a means of "cultivating the emotions" while also extolling the value of listening as a salubrious use of students' leisure time outside of school. The reference to music as providing a valuable and pleasurable use of "free time" thus validated the nation's emerging pro-industry worldview in yet another way.

It is a significant fact that the makers of curricula are recognizing more and more the need of training the emotions as well as the intellects of children. Moreover they are concerned with providing pleasurable and safe activities for the use of leisure hours that are constantly increasing as the by-product of labor saving machinery and mass production. By common consent, the expressive and creative arts are coming to be recognized as deserving of greater emphasis in education since they do provide safe emotional outlets and a pleasurable use of leisure time.[80]

Not only was the new recording technology used to teach children how to listen to art music; it was also employed by some music educators as a means of delivering to students instruction in musical performance. Music education historian James Keene has reported that Charles A. Fullerton used recordings produced by the Victor company as vehicles for teaching songs by rote to large numbers of students in rural areas, preparing as many as ten thousand students to sing in festivals in this way.[81]

Meanwhile, the development of the vacuum electron tube by Sir John A. Fleming had made possible the first transmission of speech and music using electromagnetic radio waves in 1904, and by 1920 Pittsburgh's KDKA had begun weekly broadcasts as the nation's first commercial radio station. During the following decade, the Radio Corporation of America (RCA), General Electric, and several other companies began to share their patents on radio technology with each other (for mutual benefit), and hundreds of radio stations were formed and began broadcasting. By 1931, there were thirteen million radio receivers in America—a ratio of one radio to every three homes.[82]

In a very short time the radio itself became a vehicle for music education, as several local stations and the National Broadcasting Company (NBC) began introducing concerts of the "great" music of the European masters and on-air music appreciation courses into their programming schedules. RCA began subsidizing children's radio concerts featuring conductor Walter Damrosch (in the "Music Appreciation Hour") in 1928, and various other corporations began sponsoring programs featuring the nation's major symphony orchestras over the following years. It is important to realize that the radio became a vehicle for unifying the nation psychosocially during these years, as all citizens who could afford one of the new devices spent a significant amount of time listening to "news" of the nation and the world as well as to musical and theatrical productions.

As phonographs became widely available, citizens began purchasing more and more recordings of the music they heard on radio. Sales of recordings were fostered in numerous ways, most typically by advertisements in newspapers and on the radio. However, one of the most unique incentives for citizens to purchase recordings was instigated by the nation's music educators themselves: The "music memory contests," competitions designed by music educators to test their students' recognition of works of art music, began to take hold as a movement in the nation's public schools in the early decades of the century. The contests are thought to have originated in the classes of music educator and historian Edward Bailey Birge, who played sections of masterworks for his school music students in Indianapolis to identify in competition with one another beginning in 1909. By 1920, the contests were spreading throughout the country, becoming more sophisticated as they proliferated; students were expected not only to be able to name each work but to identify the form as well as various other characteristics of the music they heard. As contest dates approached, record dealers kept their stores open extra hours in order that students could use their listening booths to review. A national memory contest was held in 1932 and broadcast nationwide on NBC radio.[83]

While most music education textbook authors maintained the rhetoric of the previous century in explaining the importance of instruction in music to their readers on the basis of its value as a form of *art*, others influenced by the new technology openly acknowledged that their efforts to emphasize the *best* music in their teaching were being undertaken for the purpose of "making children good consumers." Thus, music had gradually come to be regarded by music educators not just as a *product of the human mind* but also as a *marketable product* of art or entertainment.

EMPLOYMENT OF INDUSTRIAL METHODS

The third and equally far-reaching trend we identified as emerging during this era was the nation's growing interest in the use of industrial methods for making the newly developed technologies accessible to everyone. Henry Ford's innovation of the assembly line was applied by industrialists to the manufacture of numerous goods, including the mass production of phonographs and radios. "Quality control" measures were instituted in the factories to assure that all products would be kept to an even standard, and industrialists actively sought to find more efficient ways of producing their products in order to keep their costs low and their output high.

Simultaneously, the methods of industry gradually began to influence various other parts of life in the U.S., including the teaching of music in the nation's schools. Indeed, now that music was regarded, at least to some degree, as a *product*, it is easy to imagine that teachers might come to regard the teaching of music with *efficiency* as the logical next step. Confirming this turn of events in the practices of music education in the early twentieth century, music education historian Jere Humphreys has noted, "Educators were quick to seize upon efficient management techniques used so successfully by industrialists to increase output and reduce waste in the production of manufactured goods."[84]

One way the techniques of industry were translated into the realm of music education was in educators' development of instructional methods whereby students could quickly learn to replicate works of music for concert performance. In order to develop such efficiency, students needed to acquire highly effective sight-reading skills. For many years prior to his death in 1904, Sterrie Weaver, a music supervisor in Westfield, Connecticut, taught his classes to read music using a "scientific" method, introducing each new tone or rhythm by relating it to tones or rhythms that the students had previously learned; he then followed this instruction by administering tests to assess the effectiveness of the teaching methods he had used.[85] Music education historian Edward Bailey Birge commended him for this work in his 1928 historical chronicle of the profession, describing Weaver's efforts as "the main contribution" to the music education profession between 1885 and 1905. Indeed, the practice of testing students to determine the effectiveness of different educational methods has been employed by generations of music educators since that time.[86]

Likewise, Philip C. Hayden, a music supervisor in Keokuk, Iowa, sought to apply scientific methods to the teaching of rhythm, drawing from psychologist Thaddeus L. Bolton's research on the human tendency to group rapidly occurring sounds in clusters (i.e., "chunks") of twos, threes, and fours. Hayden presented demonstrations showing how this knowledge influenced his teaching at meetings of music supervisors beginning in 1905.[87] Furthermore, John Dewey's view, noted earlier, that the "end" of music is to effect harmony in the individual began to influence scores of "progressive" music educators who thereafter regarded the teaching of music primarily as a vehicle of socialization. They combined Dewey's focus on socialization with the emphasis on efficiency in teaching to make the music class a context in which students learned to make music efficiently. Accordingly, the social skills the students learned and the progressive attitudes they acquired in efficiently making musical *performances* as *products* in class served them well as they took on jobs in industry after graduation.

Furthermore, Humphreys has noted that among progressive educators of the early twentieth century the status of a curricular subject was often determined by the efficiency with which it was taught.[88] Consequently, music teachers set out to advance their efficiency in teaching (and thus raise their status among their peers) by establishing minimum *standards* for students' learning and creating *achievement tests* to determine how well their students were meeting those standards. These efforts strikingly reflected the industrialists institution of "quality-control" measures in the factories for the purpose of assuring that all products produced were above a certain caliber or degree of excellence.

Accordingly, in 1892 the Music Department of the National Education Association adopted a resolution in which they set forth specific goals for school music teaching, establishing standards in sight-singing skills, tone quality, intonation and blend, musical taste, and expressive singing. Birge affirmed that this action "seems to have been the first resolution ever framed by a professional school-music body regarding the aims of school music."[89]

The New England Education League began to recognize high school music as a regular, credited course of study in 1902, and by 1906 the College Entrance Examination Board for New England and the Middle Atlantic States began requiring colleges to administer entrance exams in music and to consider credit students had earned in music classes during high school.[90] The idea of educating students to be skilled and knowledgeable producers of music clearly pervaded the era.

While competition between companies in the nation's marketplace increased during the early years of the twentieth century, the nation's music educators began to initiate performance contests between ensembles. Keene affirms that there are only a few references to music competitions in the nineteenth century in the literature of music education history, and that *non*competitive music festivals were a regular occurrence in many communities.[91] However, by 1915 a band contest was launched in Kansas, a contest for choral groups had taken place in Springfield, Missouri by 1917, and by June of 1923 the first national school band contest had been held in Chicago, Illinois. Not only did the contests kindle widespread public enthusiasm for school music programs amongst the populace; they also opened the eyes of instrument manufacturers to the possibilities of the student market. These companies began to realize that their success depended on the existence of a group of consumers sufficiently large to warrant their mass production of instruments, and they began to provide support for instruction in music to students on the elementary and high school levels. Interest in the contests increased greatly over the following decade, state and national organizations were formed for their administration, and the practice of preparing student ensembles for performance in contests has continued as a significant part of music education to the present day, continuing to reflect and reinforce the competitiveness evident in the U.S. musical marketplace. The societal enthusiasm for scientific discovery, technological innovation, and for applying the methods and practices of industry had indeed impacted public-school music education, turning music classes into situations in which students were socialized into the newly industrialized society in which music was becoming yet another *product*.

THE HUMANISTIC PHILOSOPHY OF JAMES MURSELL

The philosophical perspective articulated by James Mursell in his many books and articles on music education can be regarded as something of a reaction to the notion of music as product held by the more "efficient," industry-oriented educators of his time. Mursell (1893–1963) was born in England and attended school in Scotland, England, and Australia before coming to the U.S. to pursue graduate studies at Union Theological Seminary and Harvard University. Educated in philosophy, psychology, and education as well as music, and influenced to some degree by the ideas of John Dewey,

Mursell focused on the *experience* inherent in musical involvement rather than on the production of music itself, steadfastly recommending the study and performance of music for its intrinsic value throughout his career.

> Why should teachers teach, and pupils learn, any given subject? . . . There is only one possible answer. Any particular study is valuable only in so far as a mastery of it enables one to live more richly and completely; to be a stronger, better, happier, more cooperative person; to succeed more fully in the great business of being human. . . . We cannot define the educated man in terms of any list of things he ought to know, and of skills he ought to possess. We can define him only in terms of the life he ought to live. . . . [Knowledge and skills] are worth having and worth mastering only in so far as they enable boys and girls, and men and women, to live stronger, more satisfying, more worthy lives; only in so far as they release human and spiritual quality.[92]

A highly successful teacher of musical skills, Mursell nevertheless inveighed against an undue focus on the technical aspects of music making in music education in his many writings. He repeatedly asserted that "Music exists to serve human values, and to glorify human life,"[93] and he dedicated his 1934 book, *Human Values in Music Education*, to the elucidation of that theme.

> Musicianship founded upon human values will be a valid musicianship. . . . Musicianship is an affair of the mind and the spirit, not of the fingers, or the lips, or the vocal mechanism. . . . The essentials of musicianship are the ability to feel and the ability to understand, rather than technique and facile display.[94]

To demonstrate this point in the various chapters of this book, Mursell explored music as an *individual experience,* as a *social opportunity,* as an agency for *mental growth,* and as a *moral force* before turning his attention to curricular and instructional matters. In his chapter on music as an *individual experience* he asserted that music, in its essence, expresses and embodies emotion, referring the reader to writings on "aesthetics" by Max Schoen, Vernon Lee, and Charles Diserens rather than providing evidence of this himself.[95] Instead, Mursell wrote rhapsodically and at length about the value of music in education, saying that because musical involvement is primarily a matter of spirit, children's singing and instrumental performance should be, above all, a means of emotional experience, expression, and release. Like many of his forebears in the profession, Mursell explored the physical and mental benefits of involvement in music to support his claim, also praising musical involvement as *culturally significant experience* on the basis that the great musical works of history represent emotional interpretations of life.

In exploring music as a *social opportunity* in his next chapter, Mursell noted that whereas music (i.e., a musical practice) was historically a necessary concomitant of work, war, religion, and love, "societal changes" have resulted in its becoming a mere aesthetic luxury. Despite this fact, he observed, music represents a good use of leisure time, as it serves to meet social needs and personal problems created by the growth of routine jobs. However, he also naively asserted that music provides a "social pattern" that cuts across stratified social classes in providing these benefits. This observation by Mursell would seem to indicate either that he was living in a largely culturally homogeneous society or that he did not give attention to cultural differences; indeed, as we observed in Chapter 3 and elsewhere, it is generally the case that persons of different social communities and cultural backgrounds do *not* find value in the same forms of music, due to the cultural particularity of the musical practices they each undertake.

In considering music as an *agency for mental growth*, Mursell did not clearly define this term, though in discussing music in this way he appears to have been referring to three areas of learning: (1) the self knowledge that accrues with the mastery of a skill and the acquisition of knowledge in a particular domain; (2) the increasing breadth of perspective that develops as one discovers the subject of one's study manifested in different ways throughout the world; and (3) the "overcoming of undue repressions and the progressive achievement of the power of free self-expression." He noted that schools place inhibitions upon free physical activity "to a dangerous and needless degree" in requiring students to remain focused on their studies while in attendance, and that musical performance can serve as an important part of the curriculum since it provides students with an avenue for disciplined emotional release.

In his chapter on music as a *moral force*, Mursell observed that morality has both outward and inner aspects. In his view, the outward sign of morality is simply socially well-adjusted behavior, while its inner dimension has to do with the attainment of personal happiness through self-fulfillment. On these bases he asserted that music education could be regarded as a moral force insofar as it serves as an opportunity for creative, social self-expression, making possible the experience of successful achievement in an educational situation and simultaneously supporting each student's social integration. To this end, Mursell noted, teachers "must constantly emphasize process rather than product."[96] In addressing the question of whether music has any intrinsic moral effect on the individual student, Mursell was guarded in his claims. He asserted that musical involvement has moral value because of the rich feelings associated with it; in making music, he wrote, "we create in ourselves attitudes which are so highly constructive and carry over so readily into other departments of life."[97] However, he conceded, such involvement does not necessarily make a person moral.

> [I]t is clear that we must not hope too much from music as a moral force. We cannot expect, for instance, that it will magically transform

a bad man into a good one; or that it is capable alone, of preventing a child from sliding into a criminal career. But . . . when an immoral person is actively interested in music, it means that he is not wholly bad. *This is one of his virtues.* . . . Music favors the kind of attitudes leading to constructive and creative social adjustment and effective self-expression in a social medium.[98]

While Mursell's claims of the moral benefits of musical engagement might seem rather quaint and perhaps ill founded by today's standards, his assertion does not seem entirely invalid when one considers that he was writing in the context of a society in which only certain music was recognized as "good." Indeed, within the bounds of any relatively culturally homogeneous community, an individual's regular, voluntary, and spirited participation in the musical practice of the community could indeed be construed as a *sign* of that person's embrace (or embodiment) of the values of that community. On the basis of the Peircian pragmatic perspective we have set forth in this inquiry, we can see that Mursell's philosophical focus on the benefits accruing to the individual and society through musical participation must have represented a stabilizing force against the more "music as *product*"-oriented movements of his time.

At the same time, Mursell's references to writings in the field of aesthetics, his expressed belief that the essence of music is the expression and embodiment of emotion, and his argument that students' performance should be primarily a means of emotional experience, expression, and release served to strengthen further music educators' consideration of their work as *aesthetic education*, a concept that was to gain even greater importance in the profession later in the twentieth century.

CONCEPTS OF MUSIC IN EDUCATION DURING WORLD WAR II

Following the German invasion of Poland in September of 1939, marking the beginning of World War II in Europe, the concepts of music as *art* and as *product* began to be displaced somewhat in the public schools of the U.S. as music educators began once again to regard musical practices specifically as psychosocially equilibrating behavior in their teaching. Realizing that they could play an important societal role by utilizing music education as a means of contributing to the nation's solidarity, the nation's music educators set aside many of their more artistically oriented goals for the purpose of bolstering the morale of the nation's populace in the face of the growing crisis. This change in their orientation did not stem from a well-considered philosophical or theoretical shift within the profession; rather, it emerged naturally as citizens became increasingly distraught over the war in Europe and fearful that they might be engaged in it.

At the meeting of the MENC Executive Committee in Chicago in October 1940, National MENC President Fowler Smith, Eastern Conference

President Glenn Gildersleeve, and other leaders of the organization made the decision to orient the organization's efforts toward promoting musical engagement as a means of effecting national solidarity and buoying citizens' morale. Notably, the statement of their position on this decision was carefully worded so as not to imply that the profession's long-held concept of music as *art* should be set aside *entirely* in favor of the more culturally unifying and psychologically stabilizing purposes they were promoting.

> In keeping with the spirit of the times, *National Unity Through Music*, or some similar theme should dominate the entire program of the Music Educators National Conference and associated organizations during the current biennium. This does not necessarily involve a special project in itself, nor any particular change in the fundamental aspects, procedures, or concepts having to do with the philosophy or purpose of music education. It does, however, imply special emphasis or focusing on those values which music can contribute during this period of stress and strain. Through the various channels which may be open to the Conference, its organized units, and its individual members, opportunities for such emphasis are automatically provided in the schoolroom, the home, the church, in community affairs, in radio programs—wherever music may have a place, its normal functions are doubly essential now. With some forethought and guidance, these functions may be given added, not to say unique significance.[99]

To emphasize these values, MENC encouraged all music educators to feature American patriotic songs plus any types of songs that might "stimulate loyalty and fidelity to American ideals and principles and allegiance to the American flag" in their classes. At the same time, MENC leaders extended an offer of support to various departments and agencies of the U.S. government, proposing that they coordinate the efforts of MENC, the Music Teachers National Association (MTNA), and the National Association of Schools of Music (NASM) in addressing the national emergency. The government agencies responded by requesting help in building "spiritual values and attitudes of mind" among the nation's populace, acknowledging that the efforts of these organizations would be of great importance.[100]

From our Peircian pragmatic perspective, we can infer that the war must have represented a philosophical difficulty for the nation's music educators, placing them in an awkward position, culturally speaking, when it came to the matter of deciding what music to recommend as repertoire for use in public school classrooms. As we have seen, music educators in the U.S. had until this time maintained a universalizing position on the different forms of music manifested in different world societies, generally regarding them merely as products of culturally different human minds. Indeed, as we have noted, they had tended to acknowledge, but had otherwise generally ignored, the cultural differences evident in the forms of music manifested in the different musical practices undertaken by different world peoples. Now they found themselves in a position in which it appeared that it would be necessary for them to use musical practices for the purpose of unifying the nation psychosocially. Of course, this would have been quite simple had the nation historically embraced a societally central, nationally distinctive form of music throughout its history, as many of the European nations had done. However, as we saw in Chapter 4, the U.S. government has never supported or condoned such a musical practice, instead allowing the nation's constituent cultural communities to undertake their own forms of music for their own unique purposes. Clearly, this situation represented a problem.

On the one hand, music educators couldn't embrace just one form of music in their teaching during the war, as this would conflict with the egalitarian ideals of the nation. On the other hand, they could not continue to promote *all* forms of music in their classes because this might involve promotion of music produced by nations then engaged in war with allies of the U.S. Thus, they recommended for inclusion in the curriculum those forms of music that seemed to be representative of the various communities present in the nation. In this way they were able both to promote the nation's egalitarian ideals *and* to use music for the societal unification and psychological solace of the nation as a whole. At the same time, they would not have to give up the notion of music as *art* that lay at the center of their curricula. In 1941, MENC, MTNA, and NASM collectively pledged to support the *American Unity through Music* program by encouraging the playing and singing of songs that "best embody the spirit and ideals of our U.S." The wording of their public statement illustrates the way in which they resolved the quandary. They recommended:

(1) The fervent and frequent singing of our national and patriotic songs, with full understanding of their meaning both as to word content and as to their significance in relation to the history and future of our country.
(2) The maintenance and enhancement of respect for the rich heritage of music brought to America by various racial groups who are now Americans-all, and whose cultural contributions have helped to make us a powerful and vital nation.
(3) A more extensive knowledge of and appreciation for, and more general use of America's folk and pioneer songs, a vast storehouse of strong, robust music which is inseparably liked with our national growth but which is too little known by our teachers and too little used in our schools.
(4) More attention to the meritorious compositions by American composers, especially the music, both instrumental and vocal, which possesses unique American qualities or characteristics.[101]

However, it seems highly likely that the leaders of these organizations must have become aware that a political alliance had been formed between

the German and Japanese governments and that they were growing fearful of the possibility of "a war between the hemispheres," since they also
recommended that the nation's music teachers introduce in their classes not
only music of the U.S., but also folk songs "reflecting the spirit of neighbor
peoples" in North and South American nations. MENC leaders encouraged
all members of the organization to undertake efforts toward the strengthening of cultural ties between the nations of North and South America, and
they themselves began establishing connections with musicians and educators on both continents. In addition, they established a *Music for Uniting
the Americas* program, which brought South American officials interested
in public-school music education to the U.S. and took representatives of
MENC to various South American countries for the purpose of establishing musical and cultural connections. They explained the purpose behind
these efforts in practical terms.

> Music is an important factor in cementing hemisphere unity between
> North and South America, and *music in the schools* affords a medium
> for *contributing* and *receiving* specific benefits and values which are
> vital to the attainment of friendly interest, mutual respect, and under-
> standing among the peoples of the twenty-one republics.[102]

Thus, not only music of the U.S., but also "music of the Americas" was
included in the repertoire officially regarded as most suitable for study and
performance in the nation's school programs during the war.

Once they resolved the matter of which music to promote, the war
effort became something of a boon to music educators, as it provided
them with a more unified, clearly defined purpose for their work than
they had ever previously known. Indeed, the curricular goals of the past,
such as "raising students' taste" or "cultivating their emotions," seem
to have diminished during the war, as educators' interest in promoting
musical activity as a means of staving off the fears that gripped the nation
began to take precedence. The editorial that appeared in the *Music Educators Journal* in early 1941 confirms the serious purpose music educators saw as motivating their work.

> In the conflicts between the democratic and totalitarian states, as has
> often been pointed out, the leaders of the latter, through their power
> over the forces which influence people, frequently have unquestioned
> and even fanatical support of their followers. Such religious zeal also
> inspired the proponents of democracy, too, in the great crusading days.
> It is no wonder, in these times of conflicting reports and flagrant pro-
> paganda, that the mind of the individual becomes confused. Hence, in
> this situation, a courageous and united faith must come through appeal
> to the hearts, to the emotions, and to the spirit of our people. In this
> appeal, music has a strange, even mysterious unifying power. Taking it

for granted that the people of the Americas are determined to preserve their way of living, let us use the power of music to quicken loyalty and to deepen appreciation of free democracy.

On the vast tidal surge of patriot fervor now swelling to every nook and corner of our country, our people can be united positively and idealistically through music, thus averting the inculcation of base or even beastly thoughts that accompany hate, hysteria, and fear. With music we can help to generate and mobilize the thoughts and feelings which spring from deserved pride in our country. With music we can build and sustain morale. Such building for better citizenship on the part of our entire populace, in and out of training camps, is quite as important as man power, machines, and guns.

. . . Music is of especial value in furnishing our youth a means of dramatizing spiritual values in which they can believe, and for which they will sacrifice, thereby helping them to the realization that they are benefactors, supporters and defenders of a common cause . . . [103]

The passing allusion to the "strange, even mysterious unifying power" of music in this passage would seem to suggest that the authors of the article had either lost sight of the ways music had been used to promote nationalistic solidarity in other nations historically or that they were disinclined to acknowledge them.

Notably, the same editorial featured both a direct acknowledgment of the psychologically balancing or "spiritual" benefits participation in a musical practice can provide, as well as an uncharacteristic admission that the commercial uses of music in the U.S. might obscure them.

As individuals we must not allow our minds to dwell constantly on [negative thoughts concerning the war in Europe] lest we lose mental equilibrium. We need sources of spiritual refreshment and invigoration. . . . And we must remember that, while music may be used for . . . practical and materialistic purposes, . . . without providing a measure of joy and beauty to which these other ends must be subservient, we defeat the very purposes we set out to achieve.

Therefore, first of all, music must create joy, happiness, wholesome attitudes, and inner satisfactions. For these are the conditions which contribute to mental health, and today we need mental health as much as muscle health—and for building this we need the might of music.[104]

This acknowledgment that music had been put to "practical and materialistic purposes" in the public forum of the U.S. not only validates one of the theses presented in this inquiry (i.e., that engagement in a musical practice is essentially psychosocially equilibrating and culturally unifying behavior and that this tends to be obscured in the U.S. public forum due to its commercial uses there), but it also suggests how far the nation had gone toward regarding music primarily as societally peripheral *art* or *entertainment* by the mid-twentieth century.

During the week that followed the bombing of Pearl Harbor on December 7, 1941, the U.S. declared war, first on Japan and then on Italy and Germany. Over the following year, MENC put more energy and resources into the *American Unity through Music* program.

> The *Music Educators National Conference* believes that, as an organization, it can best serve both the immediate and future cause by continuing with stepped-up vigor its projects to generate and fortify unity in and among the Americas. . . . Our principle [*sic*] concern, therefore, will be . . . to tie our professional activities with the vastly important behind-the-lines defense. . . . It is our job to see that our way of life is here for those who come back . . . [and that it is] growing in soundness and practice.[105]

One way MENC stepped up its efforts was by working with the U.S. Office of Education to bring music into the activities of the Victory Corps, a patriotic organization of high school students formed at the time. This organization emphasized the importance of having every student who participated in music work to maintain the morale of the nation, encouraging *singing* as a means of contributing to the patriotic spirit in the schools and in other places. Documents published by the corps advocated that its members hold *bon voyage* concerts for men departing for training camps, welcome-home concerts for groups of soldiers returning on leave, and still other concerts in conjunction with such war-related community activities as Red Cross meetings, bond sales programs, and, remarkably, air-raid drills. In addition, the Victory Corps challenged student performing groups and classes to modify their in-school activities in various specific ways to support the national effort.

> *Choirs* should serve a broader function than that of merely giving recital and concert programs. They can be invaluable as teachers, leaders, and therefore promoters of a community-wide singing movements . . . It is not necessary to forego learning some of the world's great music or to eliminate concerts and recitals, but there must not be exclusive emphasis on public performance as such . . .
>
> *Orchestras and bands* need to examine their functions and practices in the light of enlarging their service, that is, of leading, teaching, and promoting *school-wide singing*. Performing groups, instrumental and vocal, should adopt the policy of including audience participation (singing) as a part of every performance.
>
> *Theory and composition courses* have an unprecedented opportunity to shake off the bonds of formalism and do vital service in encouraging students to write music true to the life of the times . . . Many

students other than those involved in composition classes can be provided with needed emotional release and a challenging medium of expression through writing words for songs and, in many cases, with a little encouragement, both words and melody. Harmonization of melodies thus written offers another challenge to students who, without the incentive of the war, the emotional urge to do something about it, the demand for self-expression—call it what you will—would perhaps never know the fascination afforded in the field of creative music.[106]

In addition to these recommendations, the Victory Corps encouraged high school music departments to add to their curricula courses that might enable those who would be entering the armed services to maintain their own psychological well-being in the field. They advocated an emphasis on instruction not only on singing, but also on teaching students to play pocket instruments like the harmonica and ocarina.[107]

Scattered throughout the world, our armed forces naturally are in many places where the regular musical instruments and music materials are not available or practicable, and for this reason singing and the playing of the informal type of instrument, such as the pocket varieties, are of tremendous assistance—*if* the men know how to play these instruments and if they have a good repertory of songs to play and sing.[108]

A statement appearing in a brochure issued by the Radio Branch of the War Department's Bureau of Public Relations suggests that by about 1943 the nation's involvement in the war may have reached the point at which some U.S. government officials were actually considering implementing a policy of musical nationalism.

Perhaps more important than striving for adult participation would be a long-range program of *music indoctrination through our present school generation.* Band repertoires include, of course, a great deal of music that bespeaks our nation's vigilant concern for the institutions of liberty. Less so the repertoires of orchestra and chorus. It is suggested that the repertoires of orchestra and chorus be added to in this respect.[109]

By 1944 the U.S. was fully engaged in the war in Europe, and the Victory Corps had established a plan for holding victory concerts, admission to which required the purchase of a war bond or stamps. Schools sending reports to MENC documenting such concerts were eligible to receive a special "Music in the Service of Schools at War" citation, and, in turn, J. Henry Morganthau, secretary of the Treasury, telegraphed John C. Kendel, president of MENC, to express gratitude for the organization's "enthusiastic cooperation in our schools at war program."[110]

Incidentally, an interesting glimpse into MENC's efforts to maintain neutrality with respect to the music of different communities on the home front during the war is revealed in the minutes of the organization's National Executive Committee meeting held in March 1944. Amid discussions concerning the location of the 1946 biennial meeting and various other topics, the board discussed the relationship of MENC and the National Catholic Music Educators Association meeting (NCMEA), as well as a proposal by the Negro Music Educators Association (NMEA) to establish an affiliate or auxiliary relationship with the conference. While the board members agreed that MENC should "do everything possible to encourage cooperation with and contribute to the success of" the Catholic organization, representatives of both the Northern and Southern parts of the nation "discussed frankly" the relationship of MENC to NMEA, finally deciding that "the time had not yet arrived for consideration of an arrangement of the kind suggested on a national basis."[111] Agreeing that "the problem" should be handled by the state organizations, the board agreed unanimously that MENC should maintain a cooperative relationship with all "Negro" music educators' organizations and "do everything possible to maintain and extend the present friendly and mutually helpful status."[112] It seems probable that the organization's leaders chose to take this noncommittal position owing to the uncertain status of African-American citizens in several of the Southern states at that time.

AFTER THE WAR

At the conclusion of the war in 1945, rationales for and explanations of music education in the schools once again reflected the profession's embrace of the concept of music as *art*, though an increased awareness of and emphasis on the *community-related* (i.e., psychosocially equilibrating) nature of music making during the war years can also be discerned in the writings by music educators during this period. However, both the *artistic* and *psychosocially equilibrating* conceptions of music began to be attenuated as the steadily emerging notion of music as *product* became yet more societally pervasive over the following years.

The long-standing concept of music as a socially elevating form of *art* was reflected in a brochure revised for release in 1951 by MENC entitled *Outline of a Program for Music Education*. The author of this pamphlet set forth certain "outcomes" of the public-school music education program in terms of what "the generally educated person" should be able to do upon graduation from high school. The last objective articulated in this document confirms the continuing influence on the profession of the concept of music as a form of *art*, while also revealing the influence of the more industrial view of music as *product* then impacting the society.

The generally educated person has good taste. He has learned to make musical choices based upon musical knowledge and skill in listening. He evaluates performances. He distinguishes between music that is merely entertaining and that with more profound content. He is not naive with respect to the functional use of music for commercial purposes nor to the commercial pressures which will be exerted to obtain what money he can spend for music.[113]

At the same time, certain other publications on music education released after the war reveal that music educators' wartime experiences had developed in them a somewhat greater understanding and appreciation for the role of music in community life. Indeed, their expanded awareness of the community-engaging nature of music, or perhaps their greater inclination to acknowledge it openly, is clearly reflected in the music textbooks of this period. Osbourne McConathy, Russell V. Morgan, James Mursell, and the other authors of the school music text *New Music Horizons* of 1949 began their book with the statement "Music education is not merely the teaching of music. It is also the relating of music to human life. . . ."[114] Likewise, Peter W. Dykema, Gladys Pitcher, and J. Lilian Vandevere affirmed in their 1949 textbook series *Music in the Air* that "The general purpose of each book is to increase the love and use of music by providing material which naturally appeals to children, and which makes them desire music as a regular part of their lives."[115] Even the titles of some of the elementary music textbook series of the era manifest educators' greater awareness of the community-related nature of music: The *Together We Sing* series recognizes the important role of music in community in its title and its content, and the *Music for Living* series of 1956 featured books focusing on music in particular communities (e.g., *In Our Town, Now and Long Ago, Near and Far, In Our Country*, and *Around the World*). The notion of community was sufficiently pervasive that MENC was motivated to institute a committee on "School-Community Music Relations and Activities" as part of its "Music Education Advancement Program" in the late 1940s.

However, instructional approaches used in the classroom during this period also clearly bore the influence of the nation's scientific and industrial orientation, and this bent was reflected in the other activities of the profession as well. Music textbooks became more highly organized for pedagogical purposes, describing more systematic approaches to instruction in rhythm and pitch reading, dealing with developmental issues related to the maturation of students' voices, and introducing or describing measures for assessing students' achievement. In addition, members of MENC began a *Journal of Research in Music Education* in 1953; it featured articles on such "scientific" subjects such as "the comparison of alternative methods of sight-reading instruction" and "the relationship of music reading skills to I.Q. scores."[116] Furthermore, when MENC Executive Secretary Vanette

Lawler set out to draft a summary report on "Music Education in the United States" in 1958, she articulated what the leaders of the organization held to be the ten "general objectives" of music education at the time, and two of them are decidedly industry-related. Indeed, Lawler's fourth objective, "Music education aims to *develop good work habits*," and her tenth objective, "Music education in the secondary school affords a foundation for *vocational training*," further affirm the nation's orientation toward industry during this era.[117]

Meanwhile, the advent of television in the 1940s had a powerfully transformative effect on radio broadcasting of the time, and it impacted music education as well. As we noted earlier, the arrival of radio had contributed greatly to making the nation somewhat more homogeneous in worldview. Indeed, many citizens across the nation "tuned in" to the same shows and concerts, and they were influenced by their common content. As television began to draw the U.S. populace away from the radio collectively in the latter part of the decade, revenues from radio advertising declined, and radio stations gradually found it necessary to change their programming to feature fewer live shows and more recorded music. Competition forced them to change the content of their programming to focus on particular forms of music, reflecting the cultural orientation of those smaller segments of the population that found these forms of music to be valuable; individual stations began dedicating their broadcast time to classical or *art* music, rhythm and blues, "top 40," and, beginning in the 1950s, rock and roll.

With radio and television media becoming increasingly influential in U.S. society and, in some measure, creating a new arena in the nation's public forum, a curious process began to evolve by which the music broadcast by the media began to affect the psychosocial balancing of the nation as a whole. Indeed, ever since this time the musicians who have found popularity on television and radio have been those whose music has generally reflected the worldviews of large segments of the nation's populace. Following the account of the effects of musical practices we set forth in Chapter 3, we might note that the music of such individuals is generally "of the nature of *possession*," in that it serves to validate a particular worldview in the public forum. On occasion, musicians representing unique cultural communities or cultural perspectives that have been generally marginalized or that are lying latent in the nation's public forum will "break through" with their music into the public forum to find an audience within the "popular culture" mainstream of American society; they thus *shamanically* transform the society (or, at least, some segment of it) with their unique vision. (We might also note that these individuals often receive great financial rewards for their efforts.) Over time, however, most such musicians gradually lose their distinctive "edge" and are subsumed into the nation's public forum not only because the society itself changes to reflect or allow for the differing worldview manifested in the music they introduced, but also, in many cases, because their changed financial status has contributed to their assimilation into the larger society. In some measure, this process continues to this day, although it is important to note also that there are *many* culturally distinctive communities present in the nation whose music is rarely if ever heard in the nation's public forum. (As we shall see, the stronghold held by one large, culturally homogeneous group over control of these media was to have profound effects on the political stability of the nation during the 1960s.)

Accordingly, a term that has surfaced frequently in the writings of U.S. music educators during the mid-twentieth century is *creativity*, the word being used widely in American society to describe a quality of mind characterized by originality of thought or innovation in a particular field of endeavor, including "music." Authors of elementary music texts began to highlight the importance of creativity in music education during the years following World War II. For instance, Osbourne McConathy, Russell V. Morgan, James L. Mursell, and the other writers contributing to the 1949 music text *New Music Horizons* strongly affirmed the importance of creativity in music education instruction on the basis that it would provide the child with a means of understanding what music *is*.

> *Creative activities* enable the child to give expression to personal musical initiative, and can bring to him a very intimate and revealing insight into the significant values of music itself. Here, as always, the immediate and specific aim is to make music a real, living factor in the lives of children. Music creation or composition, a natural child activity, helps greatly to achieve this purpose. Given encouragement and assistance, children find the experience intriguing and interesting; it can reveal to them in a personal way just what music is and what it means.[118]

Certainly no one can deny that children's experimentation and "play" with musical elements is valuable to their growth. It seems possible, however, that music educators' use of the word *creativity* to describe the performance or composition of music is a reflection of the market-oriented worldview presently shared by many citizens in the nation at large. In our exploration of conceptions of music in ancient Christian communities and during the Colonial era of American history, we noted that the musical practices of *worship* were often associated with *prophecy*; certain music was regarded as "prophetic" because of its personally and societally transformative effects, and the individuals who manifested such music were regarded as recipients of special gifts from God. Then, in discussing the post-Enlightenment conception of music as a form of *art*, we noted that certain musicians (particularly composers) were revered because they were thought to be possessed of "genius," because of the ways their music reflected not only their powerful intellectual capabilities but also their great psychosocial insight; their music profoundly influenced the communities of which they were a part. Twentieth-century music educators' use of the conceptually narrower word *creativity* would seem to be a manifestation of American society's more limited and limiting perspective on the societal importance of music, as the term clearly evokes fewer imaginative possibilities and suggests a much diminished social significance for music than the notions of prophecy and genius. Indeed, musical "creativity" is generally associated with the popular notion of music as a mere entertainment product, a marketable entity that manifests an individual's engagement in innovative thought for profit, rather than suggesting any wider psychosocial or sociopolitical influence.

Considered collectively, the application of scientific methods to describe and quantify the human production and perception of music (as in the work of Seashore and others), the advent of recording and broadcast technologies and their proliferation and in U.S. society, and the emergence of industrial methods of mass production and the influence of these methods on music teaching in the nation's public school classroom during the first half of the twentieth century contributed to an emerging tendency amongst the nation's populace to regard music not just as a form of *art* and not just as a *product of the human mind*, but largely as a *marketable product* produced primarily for the purpose of entertainment. Using the sign diagram derived from Peirce's pragmatic philosophy, we could represent the conception of music as *product* held in some measure by U.S. music educators in the early- to mid-twentieth century as in Figure 5.3.

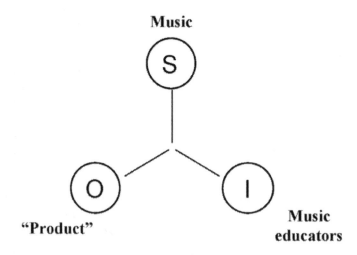

Figure 5.3 The Sign "Music" conceptualized as "Product"; in a Peircian pragmatic view, this represents a near-"meaningless" conception, as it does not adequately account for the human valuing of musical practices.

MUSIC EDUCATION IN A POSTMODERN
ERA: MUSICAL PRACTICES AS . . .

At the beginning of the 1960s, the U.S. was caught in the grip of numerous external and internal cultural tensions that were reflected in the nation's music. Not surprisingly, these tensions also came to impact music education curricula. First of all, the differences that existed between the communist Soviet Union and the capitalist U.S. at the end of World War II became manifest in a "Cold War," a decades-long period of mutual distrust and political tension between the two "superpower" nations and their respective allies. Each side suspected the other of having world control as its primary objective, and each took measures to protect itself from being dominated by the other. On Oct. 4, 1957, the Soviet Union launched "Sputnik," the first radio satellite, into outer space, raising concerns among U.S. citizens that the Soviets were ahead of the nation both technologically and in the control of "space"; this state of affairs stimulated politicians and government officials to advocate stepping up the nation's research efforts in defense and space-related areas. The tension was further exacerbated in 1961, when a group of Cuban exiles trained and equipped by the U.S. government attempted to overthrow Cuban Premier Fidel Castro, a Soviet ally, by invading Cuba near the Bay of Pigs. In addition, a civil war erupted in 1954 between communist and noncommunist groups in the Southeast Asian nation of Vietnam. The U.S. became militarily involved in this conflict early in the 1960s, sending over a million troops to the region to oppose the Soviet-supported communist factions.

The war in Vietnam raised profound internal tensions back in the U.S., where many citizens opposed the nation's military involvement, sparking public demonstrations and stimulating widespread protest movements. The buildup of nuclear weapons by both of the superpower nations raised profound fears amongst the U.S. populace, with the possibility of another world war becoming a matter of primary concern. A second and equally significant source of internal tension stemmed from the long-standing propagation (via broadcast and printed media) of the image of an apparent cultural homogeneity in the nation's public forum, essentially denying the simultaneous marginalization and derogation of citizens of different cultural backgrounds and races by many persons of European descent. The divisions between some European-Americans and citizens of African origin were especially strong, motivating the African-American pastor, the Rev. Dr. Martin Luther King, Jr., to deliver a speech on his dream of a racially undivided nation to a crowd of over 200,000 people in the nation's capital on August 28, 1963. His life was cut short by an assassin on April 5, 1968, confirming the cultural volatility of the era.

Not surprisingly, these events were reflected in transformations in the forms of music embraced by many of the nation's various cultural communities at the time. While those working in the tradition of art music began to stretch the limits of musical meaning with twelve-tone, serialist, electroacoustic, and aleatoric approaches to composition, the presence of jazz and of rock and roll, both of which have their roots in African and European traditions, also began to increase in the public forum. In the realm of popular music, Elvis Presley had incorporated aspects of African and American folk traditions in his unique performances as early as 1953, and he began to draw widespread public attention in 1956. In 1964, the English rock-and-roll band the Beatles arrived in America, evoking a frenzied public response that stemmed largely from the iconoclastic image they projected in their performances; their music reflected a personal freedom and a wide-ranging musical inventiveness uncharacteristic in U.S. society at the time. Five years later, the Woodstock Music and Arts Fair, a weekend concert event held at a dairy farm in upstate New York, attracted an audience of nearly 400,000 to hear performances by musical ensembles from the nation's various "counterculture" communities (as they were then called), many of whom had voiced protests on the nation's civil rights offenses and its involvement in the Vietnam war throughout the decade. In many respects, the new musical practices manifested in these performances *shamanistically* preordained great shifts in worldviews in the nation's public forum, giving vent to political views that had been repressed during the previous decades.

The Soviets' launch of Sputnik impacted the practice of music education in the U.S. in the 1960s, as it raised public concern over whether the nation's public schools were maintaining sufficiently high standards in science- and technology-related areas. The fear of Soviet domination spurred educational theorists to recommend that additional instructional time be devoted to more high-priority subjects and to question whether music education was anything more than a "frill." This turn of events contributed to MENC President Allen P. Britton's decision to focus the organization's 1962 national convention on the theme "The Study of Music as an Academic Discipline," a decision that did not sit well with much of membership, though it did simulate some educators to consider music in different ways. At the same time, the profound political changes taking place in the public forum began to provoke questions about what music—or, more accurately, *whose* music—should be included in the curriculum of the nation's public-school music classes. While most music educators continued to maintain a focus on the "masters" of Western *art* music in their teaching, others were beginning to give more attention to jazz, folk traditions, and different varieties of popular music.

These events and the curricular issues they raised stimulated educators to hold two conferences to discuss the content of music education programs in the mid-1960s. The first of these, the Yale Seminar on Music Education of June 1963, was sponsored by the U.S. Office of Education Cooperative Research Program. The group of participants, comprised largely of university faculty members, sought to examine why public-school music programs had not yielded a more musically knowledgeable and active public, one that preferred the more "substantive" forms of art music to popular music. At the end of twelve days of discussion, they determined that much of the problem stemmed from a lack of communication between those involved with contemporary music and music educators in the schools. In concluding the conference, the participants proposed (among other things) that students should learn to identify musical *structure* through performing, listening to, and discussing music, and that they should focus especially on contemporary works (including jazz and folk music) in their studies. The participants asserted that such an approach would help students to understand and find value in different musical forms. They also advocated the expansion of performance activities, courses for advanced students, the involvement of musicians-in-residence in the schools, and the retraining of teachers.[119]

A rather more pragmatic conclusion was reached by the more diverse group of individuals participating in the Tanglewood Symposium, the decade's second major conference on curricular issues in music education, held at the summer home of the Boston Symphony Orchestra in late July and early August of 1967. As we noted at the beginning of this inquiry, the group participating at Tanglewood was made up of fifty musicians, educators, scientists, philosophers, theologians, heads of labor organizations, representatives from corporations, foundations, communications, and government, and other concerned leaders from throughout the U.S. In their "interpretive report" of the Tanglewood Symposium, Judith Murphy and George Sullivan described the fundamental dilemma the Tanglewood participants saw themselves as facing.

> To enrich the life of the individual is the ostensible purpose of all our technology, all our skills of social organization, all our social and political institutions. The arts must enhance the quality of American life in the years to come.
>
> Music has an undoubted role here. But what, precisely, *is* that role? How can it best be filled? What priorities should guide those responsible for turning a noble purpose into effective action? What, in short, are the values and functions of music in the emerging American society, and how may these potentials be attained?[120]

Murphy and Sullivan's account of the symposium suggests that despite an overt collegiality, the participants at Tanglewood split along ideological lines. One group held the position that even if "great" or serious music is difficult to identify, it *can* be recognized and that the primary curricular objective of music programs in the public schools is to teach students to know and love such exemplary music. This position was represented by Harry Broudy, a professor of educational philosophy from the University of Illinois, who asserted that while *some* contemporary painting, music, and

literature might be notable for its quality, educators should confine themselves to focusing on the great classics plus those selections "of the recent
past about which the critics are reaching some consensus."[121]

Ethnomusicologist David McAllester represented the views of those
opposed to this curricular focus. In his remarks, he denounced the "Music
Establishment" (in which he included himself) for its arrogance in insisting that "only one cultural language be spoken and that the natives on the
other side of the barrier do not, in fact, really have a language at all."[122]
While he tempered his remarks by encouraging those in attendance to
"make the great musical heritage of the middle class and aristocracy accessible to everybody," McAllester ultimately advocated a highly egalitarian
position, one that embraced many different varieties of music.

> There must be real communication, especially in the arts, between all
> sectors of a democratic society if it is to remain healthy. It is our duty to
> seek true musical communication with the great masses of our popula-
> tion. We must also learn the language of the great musical arts which
> we have labeled "base" because they are popular.
>
> When we have learned that any musical expression is "music," we
> hope to be able to reduce the class barriers in our schools and concert
> halls. The resulting enrichment of our music will give it a new vitality
> at all levels, and provide a united voice that can speak, without sham,
> of our democratic ideals.[123]

At the end of the conference, participants affirmed their collective belief
in the importance of the study of music to public education in the U.S., they
called for music to be placed in the core of the school curriculum, and, most
notably, they advocated a change in the curricular focus of the subject, stating
positively that school music programs should be global in scope. They articulated their beliefs in a document titled "The Tanglewood Declaration."

> We Believe that education must now concern itself with the art of
> living, with building personal identity, and with creativity. Since the
> study of music can contribute so much to these ends, WE NOW CALL
> FOR MUSIC TO BE PLACED IN THE CORE OF THE SCHOOL
> CURRICULUM.
>
> The arts afford a continuity with the aesthetic tradition in man's
> history. Music and other fine arts, largely nonverbal in nature, reach
> close to the social, psychological, and physiological roots of man in his
> search for identity and self-realization.
>
> Educators must accept the responsibility for developing opportu-
> nities which meet man's individual needs and the needs of a society
> plagued by the consequence of changing values, alienation, hostility
> between generations, racial and international tensions, and the chal-
> lenges of a new leisure.[124]

More specifically, the participants had agreed on the following points at the conclusion of the symposium.

1. Music serves best when its integrity as an art is maintained.
2. Music of all periods, styles, forms, and cultures belongs in the curriculum. The musical repertory should be expanded to include music of our time in its rich variety, including currently popular teenage music, avant-garde music, American folk music, and the music of other cultures.
3. Schools and colleges should provide adequate time for music in programs ranging from pre-school through adult or continuing education.
4. Instruction in the arts should be a general requirement in the senior high school.
5. Developments in educational technology, educational television, programed [*sic*] instruction, and computer-assisted instruction should be applied to music study and research.
6. Greater emphasis should be placed on helping the individual student to fulfill his needs, goals, and potentials.
7. The music education profession must contribute its skills, proficiencies, and insights toward assisting in the solution of urgent social problems as in the "inner city" or other areas with culturally deprived individuals.
8. Programs of teacher education must be expanded and improved to provide music teachers who are specially equipped to teach high school courses in the history and literature of music, courses in the humanities and related arts, as well as teachers equipped to work with the very young, with adults, with the disadvantaged, and with the emotionally disturbed.[125]

At the conclusion of the symposium, the publication of the "Tanglewood Declaration" by MENC officially opened the music education curriculum in the public schools to include "[m]usic of all periods, styles, forms, and cultures" as indicated in the aforementioned point #2. Publication of this declaration represented a bold, official endorsement of cultural inclusiveness in the curriculum, and following this event, many educators who had not previously done so began to include instruction in the music of different cultural communities in their teaching.

MUSIC EDUCATION AS AESTHETIC EDUCATION

Bennett Reimer's book *A Philosophy of Music Education* represents a major contribution to the philosophy of music education in the U.S., though its conservative orientation seems somewhat remarkable when one considers that it was published just three years after the Tanglewood participants had made their egalitarian recommendation to open the music education curriculum to include music of all periods, styles, forms, and cultures. We will explore Reimer's writings in somewhat greater detail not only because of the complexity of his ideas but also because these ideas have had great influence on music educators in the U.S. for many years and because they still serve as a philosophical basis for the practice of music education in many of the nation's public schools. Indeed, Reimer's philosophy has served as a conceptual foundation for the creation of several textbook series used by the nation's music educators in recent decades, and it has inspired numerous writings and curricular projects in the field.[126] The concept of "music education as aesthetic education," upon which these texts are based, stems in part from his doctoral dissertation "The Common Dimensions of Aesthetic and Religious Experience," for which he drew on the writings of philosophers John Dewey, Leonard Meyer, Susanne Langer, and theologian Paul Tillich, among others. (But, as we have seen, the "aesthetic" notion of music education as a way of "cultivating the feelings" had actually been held by U.S. music educators since Lowell Mason first introduced music into the Boston schools in 1837.) Since it is difficult to understand Reimer's views without first grasping the ideas of the thinkers from whom he derived them, we will first give some attention to their writings. Then we will summarize Reimer's own ideas and consider them in light of the philosophical perspective we have set forth in this inquiry.

In his book *Art as Experience*, philosopher John Dewey observed: "Impulsion forever boosted on its forward way would run its course thoughtless, and dead to emotion . . . The only way it can become aware of its nature and its goal is by obstacles surmounted and means employed."[127] Several twentieth-century philosophers and psychologists have made use of this notion of Dewey's, which has since become known as the "conflict theory of emotions." Specifically, it is the idea that emotion or affect arises in an individual when her or his tendency to respond is arrested or inhibited. In *Emotion and Meaning in Music* (1956) and numerous other publications, Leonard B. Meyer adapted and expanded this idea into a theory of musical meaning.

In this influential book, Meyer argued that music activates emotional tendencies, inhibits them, and provides meaningful and relevant resolutions in much the same way that life experience does. Noting that musical experience differs in many respects from other forms of life experience, he also observed that the two have an essential similarity.

> Both in life and in music the emotions . . . arising have essentially the same stimulus situation: the stimulation of ignorance, [i.e.,] the awareness of the individual's impotence and inability to act where the further course of events is unknown. Because these musical experiences are so very similar to those existing in the drama and in life itself, they are often felt to be particularly powerful and effective.[128]

Meyer observed that much emotional response, though it is habitual and thus seems automatic and natural, is actually *learned*, and he drew a connection from the emotional responses human beings have to life events and the emotional responses they have to musical events, suggesting that a *stylistic genre* in music is essentially a complex system of sound relationships learned and used in common by a group of musicians who make music within that style. Thus, human *musical* expectations are products of learned responses developed in connection with particular musical styles, and they are associated with "the modes of human perception, cognition, and response—the psychological laws of mental life."[129] Meyer noted that while some listeners intellectualize the organization of musical tendencies inherent in a work of music, most are *unconsciously* aware of them. As a result, "the mental tensions and the deliberations involved when a tendency is inhibited are experienced as feeling or affect rather than as conscious cognition."[130]

Meyer observed that within any "stylistic genre," only certain combinations of sounds are allowable, only certain sounds may be used in certain situations, and the music is likely to develop only in certain specified ways. (In fact, Meyer asserted, without such a "style"—or habitually based set of expectations—a composer would be unable to manipulate musical tendencies.) He contended that it is therefore possible to analyze music in terms of its tendencies and inhibitions *within* any particular "style." Drawing from Gestalt psychology, Meyer cited the law of Prægnanz, which states that an individual's psychological organization of any perceived configuration will always be as "good" as the prevailing conditions allow. (These conditions might include the quality of the musical performance or the health and perceptual capabilities of the listener.) Meyer also used as tools the "law of good continuation" (which holds that "a shape or pattern will tend to be continued in its initial mode of operation") and the "principles of completion and closure" (according to which an individual strives for psychological completeness, stability, and rest in all matters of mentation) in order to analyze musical works for their affective power and aesthetic value.

Meyer devoted the second half of *Emotion and Meaning in Music* to explaining particular points of his theory, applying it to musical examples from a variety of "stylistic genres" (most of them drawn from Western art music). However, he also asserted that the basis of his theory (i.e., the conflict theory of emotions) is applicable to the music of different cultural communities around the world. To demonstrate this, Meyer considered four kinds of evidence: (1) statements of composers, performers, theoreticians, and critics that relate musical practice to affect or aesthetic pleasure; (2) statements that relate a specific musical passage to affect or aesthetic pleasure; (3) musical processes in music commonly agreed to be "affective;" and (4) musical examples.

Bennett Reimer found these ideas of Meyer's to be well framed by the conceptions of music and "mind" described by philosopher Susanne K.

Langer in her books *Philosophy in a New Key* and *Feeling and Form*, as well as her various other writings. In these works, Langer sketched a theory of artistic meaning that complements Meyer's theory in certain ways, though the substance of her ideas is, like that of other writers on "art" and music of her time, frequently compromised by a rather flowery locution. At the root of Langer's conception is her belief that *symbol making* is a primary human need. Asserting that human beings have a "need" to give form to the material generated by the mind in dreams (and at other times), and acknowledging that collective rituals represent means by which such material may be symbolically transformed and articulated in community, Langer regarded all forms of art (including music) as varieties of such symbol making. She observed that the field of human communication and meaning is wider than that of mere language, including not only discursive symbols (i.e., such as those of language, which are organized in succession), but also nondiscursive or "presentational" symbols (which one can understand only by grasping the meaning of the whole, as when one considers a work of art or music). In Langer's conception, *science* deals primarily in the realm of discursive knowledge, whereas the function of *art* is to symbolize holistically the "essential pattern of human life" or "central facts of our brief human existence."[131] Furthermore, believing that artworks reflect primarily the *emotions* of their creators, she asserted: "All art is the creation of perceptible forms expressive of human feeling."[132]

Langer regarded music as a rather unusual form of art, noting that it is almost completely nonrepresentative. In striving to explain how music derives its meaning or importance, she asserted that a work of music is a "pattern of sentience—the pattern of life itself, as it is felt and indirectly known . . . [M]usic is 'significant form', and its significance is that of a symbol, a highly articulated sensuous object, which by virtue of its dynamic structure can express the forms of vital experience which language is peculiarly unfit to convey. Feeling, life, motion, and emotion constitute its import."[133] In another formulation, she explained the significance of music in a different but complementary way that seems generally congruent with Meyer's view:

> The tonal structures we call music bear a close logical similarity to the forms of human feeling—forms of growth and attenuation, flowing and stowing, conflict and resolution, speed, arrest, terrific excitement, calm or subtle activation and dreamy lapses—not joy and sorrow perhaps, but the poignancy of either and both—the greatness and brevity and eternal passing of everything vitally felt. Such is the pattern, or logical form, of sentience; and the pattern of music is that same form worked out in pure, measured sound and silence. Music is a tonal analogue of emotive life.[134]

In the next-to-last chapter of his dissertation, Reimer explored the systematic theology of Paul Tillich, finally demonstrating a congruence between the ideas of Dewey, Langer, and Meyer on art and Tillich's liberal concept of religion as the object of "ultimate concern." He concluded his study by demonstrating that the notions of aesthetic experience articulated by the first three thinkers are essentially identical with Tillich's concept of religious experience, and he asserted that the function of great art is thus to provide insights that might be called religious. On this basis he argued that the purpose of arts education in the public schools must be to develop students' comprehension and sensitivity to "greatness" in art.

In his book *A Philosophy of Music Education*, Reimer developed these ideas of Dewey, Meyer, Langer, and Tillich into a philosophical statement he thought useful as basis for the practice of music education in the U.S. In this work, he explained the importance of art, arts education in general (which he termed "aesthetic education"), and music education in particular in the following concise way:

> The major function of art is to make objective, and therefore conceivable, the subjective realm of human responsiveness. Art does this by capturing and presenting in its aesthetic qualities the patterns and forms of human feelingfulness. The major function of aesthetic education is to make accessible the insights into human feelingfulness contained in the aesthetic qualities of things. Aesthetic education, then, can be regarded as the education of feeling.
>
> When music education is regarded as aesthetic education, its major function is the same as that of all aesthetic education. One way of stating this function . . . is [to say] that music education is the education of human feeling, through the development of responsiveness to the aesthetic qualities of sound. The deepest value of music education is the same as the deepest value of all aesthetic education: the enrichment of the quality of people's lives through enriching their insights into the nature of human feeling.[135]

In the final chapters of his book, Reimer asserted that music educators have a dual responsibility: to develop the talents of those who are gifted musically and to develop the aesthetic sensitivity to music of all people "for their own personal benefit, for the benefit of society which needs an active cultural life, . . . [and] for the benefit of the art of music which depends on a continuing supply of sympathetic, sensitive consumers."[136]

Reimer also set forth certain principles of aesthetic education by which a teacher might enable students to realize the "deepest values" of music: First, he wrote, the music used in music education, at all levels and in all activities, should be *good* music (by which he meant "genuinely expressive" music). Second, opportunities must constantly be provided for the expressive power of music to be *felt*. Third, the most important role of music education as aesthetic education is to help children become progressively more sensitive to the elements of music which contain the conditions which can yield insights into human feeling. Finally, the language used by the teacher should be appropriate for the purpose of illuminating the expressive content of music.[137] His book concludes with a discussion on implementation of these goals in the general music program (i.e., nonperformance-based music classes), in the performance program, and in relation to other arts classes.

From the perspective we have established in developing our Peircian pragmatic conception of musical practices in Chapter 3 and in chronicling the historical emergence of the concept of "the aesthetic" in Chapter 4, we can see that each of the writers upon whose ideas Reimer developed his philosophy was trying to explain the value of music in a rational, scientific way, striving to explain the effects of musical practice (generically) on a purely empirical basis and thus to supersede cultural difference, in accordance with the ideals of modernism. However, the conceptions held by each of the theorists upon which Reimer based his philosophy were inadequate to account for the great variety of musical practices manifested throughout the world. As a result, the value of Reimer's philosophy of "music education as aesthetic education" as a basis for the practice of music education in the egalitarian public schools of the U.S. is questionable. In order to demonstrate the weakness in Reimer's philosophy, we will return to address the ideas of two of the thinkers upon whom he based his work.

First of all, Leonard Meyer's theory is *generally* consistent with the Peircian pragmatic conception of music we developed in Chapter 3, most particularly in its recognition that musical meaning is associated with the *habits* of a community. In addition, his observation that music activates emotional tendencies, inhibits them, and provides meaningful resolutions in much the same way that life experience does serves as a credible explanation of the way *some* musical practices (e.g., those of Western classical and romantic music) impact the psyches of those who find them meaningful. However, in applying his theory to the music of different cultural communities around the world, Meyer made the error of reading Western meanings into musical practices to which they are not applicable. As we saw in Chapter 3, the experiences of "tension and resolution" associated with much Western music stem largely from the iconicity of this music with the coherence system of the society of which it is a part. Furthermore, it evidently did not occur to Meyer that he might be inappropriately projecting Western meanings into the statements of the non-Western musicians and others with whom he consulted in developing his theory. Many of his quotations (of this variety) are suspect, while others—particularly those of Westerners "interpreting" non-Western practices—are even more questionable. For this reason (and others), Meyer's theory cannot be regarded as a universally applicable theory of meaning in music, though it likely has applicability to musical practices in a number of (mostly Western) cultural traditions.

For her part, Langer was constrained primarily by the modern Western concept of *art* at the center of her philosophy, restricted by her apparent need to account for different forms of music (i.e., the sound artifacts) as *objects*. In calling music an *art* and asserting that "All art is the creation of perceptible forms expressive of human feeling," she tied herself to a particular cultural tradition, one in which all forms of music are typically considered in the abstract, rather than attending to musical practices as socially situated means of psychosocial equilibration. On the other hand, her observation that "the tonal structures we call 'music' bear a close logical similarity to the forms of human feeling" might be construed as an effort to express her recognition of the iconicity a given form of music has with a particular cultural community's worldview. In her writings, Langer admits to having been influenced by Peirce's philosophy, yet her limited development of this idea suggests that she did not fully grasp the implications of his philosophy for her own inquiries.

Most important, however, is the fact that both of these writers effectively depoliticized the different forms of music they set out to describe, focusing on the *objects* produced in different musical practices rather than acknowledging the varieties of musical practices produced by different cultural communities as important psychosocially equilibrating *behaviors*, each uniquely effective in its own particular cultural contexts and having roots in the collectively held beliefs of a culturally distinctive community.

Thus, we can see from the perspective of the Peircian pragmatic philosophy we have set forth in this inquiry that several aspects of Reimer's philosophy render it inappropriate as a basis for music education in U.S. public schools. First of all, in focusing primarily on the *object* "music," Reimer denied the social importance of active involvement in particular musical practices as important means of psychosocial equilibration. Second, in implying that the quality of music can be objectively determined, rather than recognizing that what the members of one cultural community regard as "good" may not be so regarded by another, Reimer sustained Kant's untenable belief in the existence of subjective universals. Third, and perhaps most importantly, in asserting that all music should be regarded as "expressive," Reimer ethnocentrically suggested that all forms of music should be viewed through the culturally specific lens of Western art music, rather than encouraging students to understand different musical practices (and their resulting artifacts, "musics") on their own terms.[138]

Nevertheless, Reimer's philosophy spawned the creation of numerous textbooks predicated on his conception of music as a form of *art*. Featured prominently in these books were listening lessons designed to raise students' awareness of the formal characteristics of various forms of music. Regrettably, however, lessons based on Reimer's philosophy typically did not involve the next step: substantive exploration of the social contexts and circumstances from which the different forms of music stemmed. Such studies could have demonstrated to students *how* these formal elements reflect the efficaciousness or meaning of particular musical practices in their respective social contexts.

MULTICULTURAL MUSIC EDUCATION

Although "ethnic studies" was recommended for U.S. schools in the first decades of the twentieth century to recognize the cultural contributions to the nation by large immigrant populations, and "intercultural education" was implemented in schools in the 1930s to give second-generation immigrants a sense of pride in their heritages (and renewed following the end of World War II), it was not until the late 1960s that U.S. educators in all subjects began to consider their work as "multicultural."[139] This change became inevitable following passage of the Immigration Act of 1965, when the number of immigrants entering the nation from Europe began to diminish and the presence of new citizens from Hispanic, Asian, and Arabic backgrounds increased markedly. Media coverage of the civil rights movement and the African-American "black power" movement raised public awareness of the nation's diverse ethnicity, and U.S. citizens of Hispanic, Asian, and Native American backgrounds also sought equal recognition in the public forum. The U.S. Congress enacted laws to meet the special needs of schoolchildren whose primary language was not English.

For their part, U.S. music educators had long included the music of "many lands and peoples" in their teaching, but the diversity of musics within the U.S. and their places in the lives of the cultural communities with whom they originated had not been their central curricular concern. Following the Tanglewood Symposium of 1967, MENC sought specifically to realize the symposium's recommendations by reviewing the profession's goals and objectives in the GO Project of 1968–69, forming numerous subcommittees including Music for All Youth, Music Education in the Inner City, and Music of Non-Western Cultures to address concerns emerging from their recognition of the nation's increasing cultural diversity.

The Music of Non-Western Cultures committee was formed specifically "to suggest procedures and prepare materials for use in presenting different musical systems of the world as integral parts of the music education curricula in American elementary and secondary schools, colleges, and universities."[140] In their final report, the committee emphasized that "the world of music consists of many equally logical but different systems" and "music is *not* an international language," and it recommended the creation of multimedia resources and textbooks in world music, changes in teacher education to include instruction in world musics, and involvement of native-culture bearers in schools. Correspondingly, the 1968 national MENC conference included music from different cultural communities around the world and featured instructional sessions intended to help music educators introduce these musics in their teaching, setting a precedent for future conferences. Simultaneously, the *Music Educators Journal* began to feature articles on resources and methods for teaching the musics of different cultural traditions.

But after the U.S. Supreme Court's unanimous 1971 ruling that forced busing of students could be ordered to achieve racial desegregation in schools, students in urban schools, including recent immigrants and especially African-Americans, began to resist school music education, asserting that they found more personal value in the music they experienced outside the classroom.[141] U.S. music educators teaching in urban schools thus found it essential to expand the cultural content of their instruction, and more and more began featuring in their classes music from traditions they had previously included only minimally, including jazz and rock and roll. Barbara Reeder and James Standifer's *Source Book of African and Afro-American Materials for Music Educators* of 1972, containing background information, resource materials, and sample lesson plans, was a milestone publication.

Also in 1972, MENC created a national Minority Concerns Commission to "make a study of minority concerns as they apply to music education in the United States." The commission sought to identify suitable instructional methods and materials to include persons from minority groups in conferences, and to address the need for multicultural music teacher education at all levels. That same year, the National Association of Schools of Music standards indicated that all undergraduate music curricula should provide "a repertory for study that embraces all cultures and historical periods." "Cultural authenticity" became a concern, and the Silver-Burdett Company engaged ethnomusicologists to ensure the authenticity of the music included in their 1978 textbooks.

In 1980, a MENC Commission on Graduate Music Teacher Education recommended that master's degree studies should include "Basic knowledge of music literature, including jazz, popular, ethnic, and non-Western music; An acquaintance with instructional materials for multicultural needs; [and] Techniques for motivating and relating to students of diverse cultures."[142] Where previous issues of the *Music Educators Journal* had largely encouraged teachers to adopt a multicultural perspective on music teaching, articles in the May 1983 special issue asserted that music educators *must* do so, cautioning that they dare not ignore the cultural diversity of U.S. classrooms. The MENC-sponsored Wesleyan Symposium on the Application of Social Anthropology to the Teaching and Learning of Music of 1984 explored practical implications of research on other cultures for the daily instruction of U.S. music teachers.

In 1990, MENC held a Multiculturalism Symposium: Multicultural Approaches to Music Education, focused on the culture and music of African-American, Asian-American, Hispanic-American, and Native American communities in collaboration with the Society for Ethnomusicology, the Smithsonian Institution's Office of Folklife Programs and its own Society for General Music. At the symposium's end, participants adopted a Resolution for Future Directions and Actions affirming that "multicultural approaches to music education" would be incorporated in elementary and secondary schools, in "general, instrumental, and choral music education," that music teachers would "assist students in understanding that there are many different but equally valid forms of musical expression," and that music instruction would include "not only the study of other musics but the relationship of those musics to their respective cultures: further that meaning of music within each culture [would] be sought for its own value."[143]

Following an extended process of national consensus building with concerned educators and other specialists, a Consortium of National Arts Education Associations created and published in 1994 the *National Standards for Arts Education,* a statement of "what every young American should know and be able to do" in four arts disciplines—dance, music, theatre, and the visual arts. With the passage of the Goals 2000: Educate America Act that same year, the arts, including music, were named a core academic subject in K–12 schools, along with English, mathematics, history, civics and government, geography, science, and foreign language, and many states and school districts have since voluntarily adopted the standards or related standards of their own. Content Standard 9 for Music for grades K–4, 5–8, and 9–12 in this document addresses "Understanding music in relation to history and culture" and, on the grades 9–12 advanced level, requires that students "identify and explain the stylistic features of a given musical work that serve to define its aesthetic tradition and its historical or cultural context."[144]

But despite the good intentions motivating all these efforts, numerous criticisms of multicultural music education have been raised over the past four decades, including concerns that teachers too often present the musics of non-Western cultural communities from a perspective largely appropriate only to Western art music; that introducing varieties of music that are *not* intended as art music into school programs can obscure the meanings they hold for the cultural communities from whom they stem; and that the formal teaching methods teachers typically use are antithetical to approaches taken in the cultural contexts in which the music originated (e.g., using notation to teach music from oral traditions).

A number of alternative approaches to implementing multicultural curricula have been proffered over the years, some intended to aid teachers in overcoming such problems. For example, in the 1970s, David Williams recommended a "multi-directional ethnic American approach," according to which "an American child should first discover the relevant musical diversity within his own culture before studying the music of non-American cultures."[145] David Elliott argued in 1990 for a "dynamic multiculturalism" approach, in which "a critical perspective is applied to a broad range of music cultures, creating a [student] community of interest distinguished by a dynamism that compares and contrasts concepts and practices from one music culture to another."[146] Patricia Shehan Campbell noted in 2002 that studying the music of fewer musical traditions in depth is far more beneficial for students than touching briefly on many traditions in school programs.[147]

Notwithstanding the apparent interest in including the music of different cultural traditions in the curriculum and an abundance of supplementary materials to support culturally meaningful instruction, many practicing music teachers in the schools have largely continued to adhere to point #1 in the Tanglewood Declaration, maintaining their focus on the music of different cultures as works of *art* and continuing to practice music education as "aesthetic education." This tacit maintenance of the status quo has all but assured that musics of diverse cultural origins will continue to be considered on the same basis—that is, as *objects* (i.e., sound artifacts) manifesting different *personal* artistic expressions—in U.S. public schools. Thus, in the context of U.S. music education, all musical practices have generally continued to be subsumed into the marginalizing conceptual frameworks of "music as *art*" and "music as product" that have long been dominant in the public forum. As a result, many students—especially those of minority cultural communities—have not found the content of school music classes to be personally relevant. While recent years have seen the publication of scholarship and educational materials that address in some measure the longstanding concerns of minority communities in the U.S.— especially those of racism and "lingering colonialism"[148] and that might reveal their musical practices as dynamic activities having wider social importance,[149] these writings have scarcely begun to influence the practice of music education in the nation's classrooms. Meanwhile, another basis of argument for the inclusion of music in the schools—one that regards music making as *praxis*—has recently been gaining influence.

MUSIC AS *PRAXIS*

In 1991, philosopher Philip Alperson presented a paper entitled "What Should One Expect from a Philosophy of Music Education?" in which he proffered a so-called *praxial* view of music and music education, according to which "[t]he attempt is made . . . to understand [music] in terms of the variety of meaning and values evidenced in actual practice in particular cultures."[150] In using the term *praxial*, Alperson was drawing upon the ancient Greeks' distinction (discussed by Aristotle) between three areas of knowledge: *theoria*, *techne*, and *praxis*. Roughly equivalent to the contemporary English words *theory*, *technique*, and *practice*, *theoria* denoted for the Greeks rational and therefore speculative knowledge of pure, eternal truth, *techne* designated the kind of knowledge required for making, producing, or creating something, and *praxis* signified knowledge that takes into account the sorts of reasoning and critical thinking necessary for getting "right results" for the benefit of people in a given domain or situation. According to the praxial view of music and music education articulated by Alperson, different varieties of musical endeavor are regarded as different *praxes*, and the aesthetic approaches to music are best "placed alongside" the functions that different musical practices serve and have served in different cultural contexts. Notably, Alperson's conception expressly included musics from outside the Western art tradition as appropriate for music education, and it focused attention on the motives and intentions of those who undertake them, as well as "the social, historical, and cultural conditions and forces in which practices of music production arise and have meaning."[151]

Following on Alperson's argument, music education scholars have advanced philosophical statements and critiques based on the notions of *music as praxis* and *music education as praxis*. Two of them—David Elliott and Thomas Regelski—have had considerable influence on music education discourse and practice in the U.S. and elsewhere in recent years, so we will explore their perspectives at some length here in relation to the Peircian pragmatic perspective we have advanced in this inquiry.

In 1995, David Elliott published a book-length work based on his application of the notion of music as praxis, *Music Matters: A New Philosophy of Music Education*.[152] In this book, he critiqued "the aesthetic concept of music" manifested in the writings of such thinkers as James Mursell, Susanne Langer, and, most particularly, Bennett Reimer (whose ideas we explored earlier), concluding that their philosophies are ill-founded, illogical, and not credible, owing largely to their focus on the *object* of music as a form of art, their adherence to the notion of "aesthetic experience" as a special realm of human experience, and their attendant reductive view of "music education as aesthetic education" (i.e., the education of feeling). In seeking to provide a more plausible alternative, Elliott drew conceptions from the writings of philosopher Francis Sparshott, cognitive theorist Daniel Dennett, and psychologist Mihaly Csikszentmihalyi (among others) to form a foundation for his own philosophy.

Borrowing first from Sparshott, Elliott observed that "[w]hat music is, at root, is a human activity" that involves (1) a doer, (2) some kind of doing, (3) something done, and (4) the complete context in which doers do what they do.[153] Noting that the noun *praxis* derives from the Greek verb *prasso*, meaning (among other things) "to do" or "to act purposefully," Elliott adopted the adjective *praxial* to describe his philosophy for the purpose of emphasizing that "music ought to be understood in relation to the meanings and values evidenced in actual music making and music listening in specific contexts rather than on aesthetic principles.[154]

For Elliott, *"musicers"* (i.e., persons who make music) are practitioners of "a diverse human practice" called MUSIC that is manifested in many different ways throughout the world.[155] He laid out his premises for considering the value and significance of MUSIC in human life as follows.

First, the fact that most (if not all) human societies have shown an interest in some form of musicing [i.e., music making] and music listening does not establish the presence of a specific human need for which musical practices are a necessary satisfaction. . . . Second, in considering what tendencies might underpin MUSIC, both common sense and logic suggest that we are under no obligation to identify one overriding tendency. Third, in attempting to explain its significance, we must not lose sight of what is most obvious and curious about MUSIC: that the actions of music making and music listening often give rise to experiences of positive or satisfying affect. Indeed, even a quick glance around the world is enough to show that while some people make music chiefly for money, status, and other tangible rewards, most do not. Most musicers and listeners find the actions of musicing and listening rewarding in themselves.[156]

On these bases, Elliott concluded that the keys to understanding the human valuing of MUSIC (including the valuing of musical works) are likely to be found in "the nature of human consciousness" and the human tendencies that stem from it.

Turning next to the contemporary scholars who informed his thinking, Elliott recounted Daniel Dennett's argument that *consciousness* is a characteristic of the human nervous system that has resulted from the evolution over several millennia of certain biological processes through both natural selection and cultural development.[157] As each individual person is born, grows, and matures, the individual's consciousness develops to form an integrated whole that he or she comes to regard as the *self*. Elliott cited Mihaly Csikszentmihalyi's observation—congruent with Dennett's view—that the self is an *epiphenomenon* (i.e., an occurrence or fact that is "over" or "above" that which can be perceived directly by the senses); in Csikszentmihalyi's view, the *self* is "the result of consciousness becoming aware of itself."[158] According to Elliott, Dennett and Csikszentmihalyi agree that consciousness evolved to meet certain needs of the human organism, and they argue from this point that the attendant central goal of each *self* is to bring order or strength to itself.

Elliott observed that while some life experiences (such as the loss of a loved one) may tend to weaken or bring disorder to the self, undertaking activities that are congruent with the individual's self-goals tends to bring order and strength. Csikszentmihalyi termed the positive affective experience associated with such challenging activities "optimal experience, autotelic experience, or *flow* [italics added]."[159] The enjoyment the individual experiences while engaging in such behaviors, Elliott affirmed, is "the affective concomitant of self-growth."[160]

Csikszentmihalyi and his fellow researchers have observed that the various flow entailing, self-growth-producing activities undertaken by human beings have several characteristics in common. First, flow experiences generally occur in specific kinds of action contexts that involve challenge and challenge-related knowledge (e.g., sports, games, and the arts); notably, the acquisition of knowledge is the key to enjoyment and control in these "mini-worlds of effort." Second, these experiences typically entail the individual's complete focus of concentration. Third, this absorbing concentration tends to be facilitated by pursuits or activities that involve clear goals and feedback within the context of a distinct tradition. Fourth, such experiences typically entail a loss of self-consciousness while one is engaged in the activity. Finally, these consciousness-ordering pursuits are usually undertaken for the enjoyment and order they bring to the self, rather than for external reward. With this foundation, Elliott observed that a consequence of the self-growth that occurs as one meets the challenges that arise in any such action context is *raised self-esteem*, the awareness that one has achieved or come to possess desirable qualities.[161]

Seeking to draw connections to MUSIC from this set of assertions, Elliott argued that the development of skills and the taking on of challenges in both music making and music listening (in all world traditions) are unique and important ways of effecting *flow* and bringing order to consciousness, and that they lead to self-growth, self-knowledge, and raised self-esteem.[162] On the basis of this argument, Elliott concluded that the task of music education must be to develop the musicianship of learners—and thus to effect their self-growth—through progressive musical problem solving in balanced relation to appropriate musical challenges.[163]

Early in his book, Elliott put forth the notion, noted earlier, that *musicers* (i.e., music makers) are practitioners of "a diverse human practice" called MUSIC that is manifested in different ways worldwide. In his view, this practice "has various subpractices, subspecialities, or arts of music that go by such names as jazz, choral music, rock music, and opera."[164] Different musical practices "pivot on" the understandings and efforts shared by *musicers* who are practitioners of that practice. Furthermore, each such practice produces "listenables" that manifest the "shared principles and standards" of those who make them.

> This is how we know Baroque choral singing, bebop jazz improvisation, Balinese *kebyar*, and Korean *kayagûm sanjo* when we hear them: by the stylistic features manifested in the musical sound patterns themselves. Specific musical practices eventuate in distinct musical styles.
>
> A musical *style* is a body of musical products that share certain auditory features in common. These commonalities are explained by the fact that the musicers and listeners of a musical practice share a certain set of musical beliefs, understandings, and preferences in common.[165]

Since MUSIC consists in many different musical practices, Elliott asserted, music educators have a responsibility to teach such practices and thereby to induct children into a variety of different "music cultures" during the time they spend in music education programs.[166]

In the last major section of his book, Elliott returned to his conception of engagement in a musical practice as self-growth-eliciting behavior, and he asserted that music education programs should serve as reflective musical practicums in which children learn to work with one another in solving musical problems. Further, students participating in such practicums may learn "to make music well through deeper understandings of the beliefs (artistic, social, and cultural) that influence music making and listening in different practices," thus realizing the goals of a humanistic education.[167]

From the perspective of the Peircian pragmatic philosophy we have set forth in this inquiry, numerous elements of Elliott's work make it a valuable contribution to music education philosophy. Indeed, his critique of aspects of the conception of "music education as aesthetic education" (which he abbreviates "MEAE") is especially well founded: As he correctly observes, MEAE's apparently central conception of music as an *object* (rather than "musicing" as a human praxis) is culturally limiting, and its focus on "aesthetic perception" (i.e., attention to the formal designs of musical works without consideration of their social meanings) denies the diversity of the myriad varieties of musical practices. In addition, Elliott's effort to locate the origins of "musicing" in human biological processes is laudable, in that—like the pragmatic conception set forth in this inquiry—it moves music education philosophy into the range of an arguably more neutral lens through which the musical practices of different cultural communities may be considered.

However, despite Elliott's assertions in his book that the different musical practices evidenced around the world must be understood in context (and despite the great number of musical practices he has referenced), his discourse focuses almost entirely on musicians and musicianship communities and includes little discussion of the larger cultural communities for whom musical practices have personal and social efficacy. Indeed, his account seems to take musical practices narrowly as musical-worlds-of-their-own (i.e., as more or less strictly musical) and rarely explores any details of the social contexts that call them into being. Additionally, Elliott scarcely considers in his book the radically differing human motivations giving rise to many of the musical practices manifested in different world societies *or* their broader (i.e., not strictly musical) personal and social effects. His scant attention to larger cultural concerns in his book is surprising, since his previous writings on multicultural music education suggested his recognition of the importance of considering different musics in a broader social frame.[168] In his subsequent writings, too, he has acknowledged the need to prepare music students to "engage with the public sphere."[169]

By contrast, the praxial philosophy described by Thomas Regelski is largely in agreement with the Peircian pragmatic perspective on music we have established in this inquiry. Regelski has also challenged aesthetic philosophies of music education in his writings, and he has advocated in their place a praxial philosophy of music and a rationale for music education that would equitably accord all forms of music their pragmatic value "in the total scope of human agency."[170] Although he has written prolifically on the topic for more than a decade, Regelski's 1996 paper, "Prolegomenon to a Praxial Philosophy of Music and Music Education," arguably represents the most complete single exposition of his praxial view to date. For the ancient Greeks, Regelski emphasized, "[p]raxis . . . referred to practical knowledge and activity, usually in connection with human conduct, such as ethical or political actions," and he introduced the additional Greek term *phronesis*—which denotes a capacity for realizing the proper values of rational human conduct in a given situation—to highlight the prudent "reflection in action" that guides any genuine musical praxis toward the good results it is intended to realize. For Regelski, *praxis* implies that one is enjoined to get "right results" with one's music making in particular situations where contextually unique results are called for.

Drawing support from arguments made previously by scholar Ellen Dissanayake, writer of such books as *What Is Art For?* (1988) and *Homo Aestheticus: Where Art Comes from and Why* (1992), Regelski expressed three additional tenets of his praxial view: that music is a "universal human trait," a way by which moments in life are "made special," and a "key means by which life is well-lived."[171] Drawing a line between these three key ideas and any notions that could be misconstrued as having metaphysical or transcendental overtones, he emphasized the importance of understanding music in terms of its pragmatic consequences. In his view, "the goods of music . . . are rooted . . . in the situated and highly specific conditions of the here and now—to current life, the experienced quality of 'good time' between the recently remembered past and the avidly anticipated future."[172] With notions involving the contemplation of music such as those usually associated with aesthetic philosophies thus set aside, Regelski stated an additional tenet of his view, that "a praxial philosophy of music in and through education is concerned to get people into action musically."[173]

According to Regelski, all music should be regarded as "functional" in some way, whether it is a central focus of a given praxis (as it is, for example, at a concert) or is not the central focus (as in, say, advertising). For him, the all-important question is: What is music "good for" in each situation in which it is present? Regelski observed that the greatest percentage of music made in the world is *not* made for concert listening, and he stressed that the traditional aesthetic distinction between "pure music," attended to strictly for its own sake, and "functional music," which serves some other purpose (or praxis), is simply not valid. He noted further that while important "goods" can of course be served without the presence of music, "the Being and Becoming involved with musical practice—its 'making special' of human time and events—is unique and available in no other manner."[174]

Regelski observed that there is a unique set of "process values" present in every musical praxis that is associated with the *qualia* given to sounds by human beings (such as pitch, rhythm/meter, intonation, and so on) by which we come to recognize music as music. The fact that we give attention to these values does not mean, however, that an amateur performance, being less well in tune or having "less-refined" tone than that of the professional, will be any less meaningful for the amateur performer; the "good" associated with the praxis for that individual may be served whether or not these process values are fully achieved. Moreover, it is important to note that the "training" required for an individual to become competent in one musical praxis (say, the "in-tune" performance of Western art music) may be at odds with the requirements of another musical praxis (say, the "microtonal" constructions of the music of another world culture, the uniqueness of which may cause it to be heard by a Western listener as "out-of-tune"). However, he stressed, it is not true that one must be an "insider" of a given praxis to find value in it; all that is required is an informal familiarity with the nature of the activity. Notably, even where one has never been (and never expects to be) involved in its performance, many aspects of a musical praxis can be accessed via listening. Listening, he noted further, is a unique praxis of its own, distinct from the praxis of performing.

Continuing his discussion of musical process-values, Regelski pointed out that these values are assessed as "good" by those persons involved with a particular musical praxis only when they conform to the individual, social, religious, and/or other cultural meanings the praxis is intended to serve. While it is possible to attend to musical process-values without regard for the praxis with which they originated, doing so can neutralize or negate the original intentions of the attendant praxis, as when one treats madrigals as concert music rather than as a means of social interaction (as they were originally intended to be). Still, musical process-values *can* legitimately be separated from a praxis, as when the performers engaged in one praxis "are influenced by" or "borrow from" another.

Regelski argued that it is *intentionality* that defines a praxis as music, and it also establishes the musical process-values involved. Thus, the intention to "make special" certain human ends via music *is* a musical praxis, and the intention determines the way it is actualized musically. Challenging once again the views of those who hold aesthetic views, Regelski reasserted that "music . . . is rarely if ever to be about or for itself," but that it rather "serves a wonderfully complex variety of social and other human 'goods.'"[175] Moreover, he noted, music is not a mere servant in such processes; instead, "means and ends, process and product are inseparable and are jointly conditioned by the intentionality governing the situated context of music making."[176] He pointed out that while some people regard strictly intramusical processes as worth considering and undertaking for their own sake, such intentions are very rare in the world, and are held mostly by trained musicians.

Regelski has explained the difference between his position and Alperson's and what he believes to be Elliott's position with regard to "the aesthetic ideology." In his view, Alperson was not concerned with establishing a universal characteristic of all music, but rather focused on what different forms of music have meant to people in their different cultural contexts, thus including and acknowledging the existence and the cultural significance of "aesthetic experience" to those people who find the concept meaningful. Elliott, on the other hand, evidently replaced the idea of aesthetic experience with Csikszentmihalyi's notion of "flow," and he regarded the aesthetic response "to be a social fabrication or myth."[177] Regelski explained that he personally follows "the pragmatic criterion that the worth or value of a proposition or belief is seen in the actual results that obtain from its use,"[178] noting that belief in aesthetic experience can "produce something like the experience predicted."[179] Like belief in God (whose existence, he stated, cannot be definitely proved any more than it can be disproved), belief in aesthetic experience is associated with "right results" or a musical "good" for some people. However, he stated that he would discourage "the aesthetic motive" for music praxis within the context of education "if only for the pragmatic reason that the covertness and intangibility claimed for aesthetic responding makes it impossible to evaluate either teaching or learning."[180] He thus agreed with Elliott that aesthetic philosophies should no longer be used as a basis for music education curriculum and pedagogy.

Both Elliott and Regelski have striven independently to provide philosophical accounts sufficiently capacious to embrace *all* musical practices, and both thus hold theses about what is *universal* in the various practices undertaken by the world's diverse peoples that they regard collectively as music. But on this point their views differ. In the view of both scholars, "MUSIC" is a "diverse human practice" that is manifested in many different ways in different world cultures.[181] From this point, Elliott puts his attention primarily on musical practices themselves as means to self-growth rather than being concerned with the *effects* those musical practices have for people in the different cultural contexts in which they have arisen or the differing ways in which those people experience and understand them. For Regelski, by contrast, music is (as ethnomusicologist John Blacking proposed) "a universal human trait,"[182] but beyond recognizing music as an invariably social phenomenon, he is a relativist with regard to situated particulars. For Regelski, the social or culture-specific component is the key factor for determining "right results."[183] Regelski's social theory-based philosophy thus seems generally in line with the Peircian pragmatic perspective we have developed in this inquiry, specifically, that the various different practices involving sound undertaken by people of different cultural backgrounds (which some people call music) must be understood in the terms of their respective, unique worldviews.

In the Peircian pragmatic view we have established in this inquiry, Regelski's praxial philosophy thus represents a more important contribution to the literature in philosophy of music education in that it provides a useful compass for attending to "what music is good for" in particular contexts (that is, the personal and social impact of different forms of "real" musical practices) and for predicating the practice of music education on such bases. In this important respect, his philosophical account is closer than Elliott's to both the original Greek notion of praxis as well as closer to Alperson's idea of how this notion might be applied to music education. Notably, it also shares the concern with the context-particular *effects* of musical practices that we have established in this inquiry. From the Peircian pragmatist perspective we have set forth here, we can assert that praxial conceptions of music are satisfactory as a basis for music education in U.S. schools only insofar as they take into account the *effects* of different musical practices in the social, cultural contexts in which they have arisen *and* the unique ways in which people in those contexts experience and understand them. By these measures, Regelski's praxial philosophy hits the mark.

A SUMMATION

Despite having included the music (i.e., the sound artifacts) of more and more cultural communities in their classrooms throughout the history of their profession, U.S. music educators have generally tended to avoid cultural issues, instead largely emphasizing *performance* (i.e., replication) and *scientific* (i.e., technical analysis) approaches in their instruction. In accord with concepts stemming from Western aesthetics since the Enlightenment era, they have also tended to regard all music as artistic manifestations of personal "self-expression," rather than cultivating in their students a historically and culturally grounded understanding of the different musical practices of different cultural communities on their own terms and addressing the question of *how* they provide psychological and social benefit to those who engage with them in the differing cultural contexts in which they have arisen.[184] In certain respects this may have been beneficial for some U.S. citizens, since in focusing on "music" as an object, they have bracketed issues of cultural difference from the public forum, promoting an egalitarian ethos among the nation's citizenry with respect to music. However, in failing to address adequately the unique, *community*-related roots of different musical practices, music educators have contributed to promoting an inappropriately universalizing conception of the widely different cultural forms of music as mere "objects" or "products," and closed out the often differing perspectives of many of the nation's constituent communities from their classrooms. Insofar as they have advanced a universalizing conception of music in their instruction without adequately addressing *how* different musical practices provide psychophysiological and psychosocial benefit to the culturally disparate individuals and communities with whom they have arisen (thus accounting for their social efficacy), *they have contributed to limiting their students' awareness of the importance of musical practices* throughout history, also *thereby undermining the public's recognition of the value of their own subject in the curriculum.*

What has long been needed as a basis for U.S. public-school music curricula is a philosophy that acknowledges what is presently known to be shared among the musical practices undertaken throughout the world, that is sufficiently broad to embrace *on their own terms* the great variety of musical practices undertaken by the nation's (and the world's) different cultural communities, and yet is focused enough to be relevant and accessible to students in the nation's public schools. Estelle Jorgensen observed the great need for such a philosophy in an article she wrote in 1994 on the philosophical foundations of music education.

> [I]f music is to assume a central place in the public schools from elementary to advanced levels of instruction, a political philosophy of music education must be forged—one that speaks to ideas of freedom, democracy, community, and the importance of social values of music. Seeing musical experience as an integral part of life also suggests a radical change in the ways music is taught and learned not only during the preschool and school years, but beyond, through adulthood. While it remains as to how such arguments might be shaped and evaluated, they portend broadly based and alternative visions of music education that are compelling in the present world.[185]

A music education curriculum founded on a Peircian pragmatic conception of different musical practices as culturally unique varieties of "psychosocially equilibrating behavior" (such as we developed in Chapter 3) *and* that takes into account the differing conceptions of music and its effects held by people and communities within (and beyond) the culturally pluralistic, democratic U.S. would seem to meet Jorgensen's requirements and to serve the present needs of the profession. Adopting Elliott's universalizing use of the word *MUSIC* as "a diverse human practice," philosopher Wayne Bowman has pointed toward praxialism's promise in this regard.

> [M]ulticulturalism as a music educational ideal should arise from concern about peoples and oppression and understanding and sharing, rather than upon an interest in knowing MUSIC adequately. And this is so, at least in part, because nobody anywhere can know MUSIC. A concern for the world's musics and cultures must be motivated by a concern for its peoples. I would like to think this is a plausible extension of praxial views.[186]

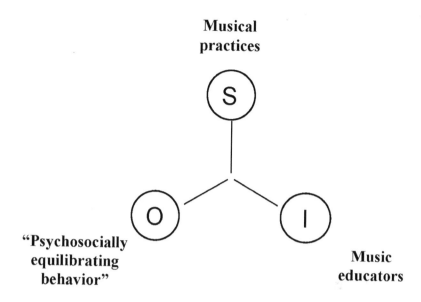

Figure 5.4 The Sign "musical practices" conceptualized as context-specific "psychosocially equilibrating behavior"; a Peircian pragmatic conception.

As we saw in Chapter 3, we could use the sign diagram from Peirce's semiotic to represent as in Figure 5.4 the Peircian pragmatist conception of musical practices we have developed in this inquiry.

We will review Peirce's philosophy and our applications of it in this inquiry and then trace the outline of a music education curriculum based on it in our concluding chapter.

6 Community, Autonomy, and Music Education in the Postmodern United States
Summary and Recommendations

> It is always instructive to ask a relativist how he raises his children.[1]
>
> Annie Dillard

LIVING BY FICTION (1982)

DRAFT: 1

At the beginning of this inquiry we identified two problems presently impacting music education programs in the public schools of the United States: First, we noted that the influx of students from diverse cultural backgrounds and the appearance of music from many different cultural traditions in the public forum has raised a quandary among music educators over what music should be included in the music education curriculum of the nation's public schools. Second, we observed that support for school music classes has been lukewarm and often inconsistent throughout the history of the nation, since the varied, frequently ambiguous, and sometimes changing views held by the nation's citizens concerning the personal and societal importance of music have made its inclusion in the curriculum difficult to justify. We pointed out that, despite the nation's apparent ambivalence concerning music education, music has been an important part of human life throughout history and it is apparent that it remains so for citizens of the U.S. Indeed, as the sounds of music from more and more different traditions have increased in the nation's public forum over the twentieth century, sales of recorded music have risen to a consistently high level. Faced with these quandaries, the nation's music educators have recently been discussing in earnest the philosophical foundations of their profession and debating its purposes, practices, and societal importance. Clearly, if music education is to continue in the public schools of the U.S., the foundations and practices of the profession must be both viable and valuable to the various cultural communities comprising the nation. Conversely, if a majority of the nation's citizens cannot collectively affirm that the inclusion of music in school curricula fulfills an important societal need, its place in the public schools is likely to remain tenuous at best. In recognition of this situation, the following question presented itself to us as being unavoidable:

THIS STILL LEAVES LOTS OF ROOM — GOAL OF MUSED IS INCREASING MUSICIANSHIP, NOT NEC. CULTURE EDUCATION (WHICH IS GREAT BY-PRODUCT).

What is the (societal role) or (social importance) of public school music education in the United States as a postmodern society?

We acknowledged that for any answer to this question to be regarded as worthy of consideration by the profession it would require a strong conceptual base in three areas. First, we noted that, due to the cultural diversity of the U.S., the preconceptions upon which any answer was to be based would need to be grounded in a philosophical foundation adequate for embracing the diverse perspectives of the different cultural communities that comprise the nation. Second, we observed that we would need to establish an understanding of the diverse nature of music as it is manifested in the lives of people of different cultural backgrounds, in order that any recommendations we might make for the future practice of the profession would adequately reflect consideration of the great diversity of human musical practices and beliefs. Third, we acknowledged that we would need to gain a perspective on the premises upon which music education in the U.S. has been based historically, in order that our recommendations would be informed by the profession's past and present tenets. We then set out to accomplish these goals.

ESTABLISHING A PHILOSOPHICAL FOUNDATION -CHAPT. 2

In Chapter 2, we observed that (cultural anthropology) a field of inquiry that arose in Europe during the early nineteenth century, represents the most long-continuing, cooperative effort to come to an empirically verifiable understanding of human beings and their ways of life in different societies, and that its comprehensive inclusion of and accounting for diverse cultural perspectives and practices would seem to render it the most appropriate basis for our inquiry. Recognizing that the different forms of music manifested throughout the world are clearly *cultural* (i.e., group- or community-based) phenomena, we briefly surveyed the development of the concept of *culture* as it has been held historically by cultural anthropologists in order to find a satisfactory foundational conception for our use. We discovered that a gradual shift has occurred among anthropologists over the history of their inquiry, *away* from conceptualizing European society as the pinnacle of cultural development and *toward* recognizing culture as a system of beliefs tacitly held by a community of people who have come to conceptualize Reality in the same unique way largely owing to their having collectively undergone certain struggles in adapting to their shared environment. We found this concept of "culture" to be implicit in the writings of Charles Sanders Peirce, a turn-of-the-century American thinker, whose pragmatic philosophy we adopted as the conceptual foundation of our inquiry.

We found Peirce's pragmatic philosophy particularly well suited for our purposes in this inquiry due to a fundamental premise upon which it is based: Peirce held that *all phenomena are interconnected*. Following from this premise of "synechism," Peirce argued that mind and matter are but different aspects of the same totality, and he recognized that behavioral and conceptual differences among *individual* human beings must stem largely from the differing "habits of mind," or *beliefs*, they have acquired as survival strategies in their respective communities of origin. Attendant to this notion, Peirce regarded *communities* not merely as collectives of discrete minds, but as living *unions* of individual minds, each characterized by the shared, unique, habitualized coping patterns of behavior collectively evolved by its constituent members. Consistent with Peirce's philosophy, we defined a *worldview* as the unique constellation of signs and meanings shared by the members of a community—that is, the *coherence system* manifested in their overall conception of Reality—that distinguishes their ultimate values and beliefs from those of other cultural communities.

From these foundational ideas, Peirce inferred that the *meaning* any perception, action, or thought has for the members of a community must inevitably be related to the *effects* they conceive it to have; that is, as it relates to their collective coping habits. Articulating this notion in what has come to be known as his "pragmatic maxim," Peirce wrote: "Consider what effects, that might conceivably have practical bearings, we conceive the object of our conception to have. Then, our conception of these effects is the whole of our conception of the object."[2] Recognizing that concepts, including the overall conception of Reality itself (or *worldview*), differ among communities, Peirce asserted that the scientific method (i.e., hypothesis-testing by experiment) represents the only effective means for determining ultimate Truth (i.e., Truth beyond the relative truths tacitly recognized by particular communities). However, he also recognized that, because of their culturally rooted nature, even scientifically determined conceptions of Reality could be superseded by further inquiry. He thus adopted a position of *fallibilism*, a point of view that acknowledges that any and all conceptions of Reality are potentially incomplete and thus subject to change, as his own.

Along with his pragmatic philosophy, Peirce developed his *semiotic* as a provisional theory of cognition. Peirce's triadic conception of the *sign* as the fundamental "building block" of cognition (according to which each *sign* entails a triadic relationship between a Sign, Object, and Interpretant), his triadic diagram of the *sign*, and the terminology he developed to describe different *kinds* of signs (e.g., Icon, Index, and Symbol) have been utilized by a number of scholars in recent years for describing systematically both intra- and intercultural meanings. Briefly stated, Peirce held that each Sign or perception that presents itself to one's consciousness is inevitably conceptualized as an Object according to the "habits of mind" of the individual or community (Interpretant) that perceives it. In addition, we noted that any given perception (as a Sign) could be conceived differently (as an Object) according to the "habits of mind" of individuals (embodied Interpretants) who stem from different cultural traditions and who have had different life experiences.

Furthermore, according to Peirce, a given Sign may refer to the Object it denotes in one or more of several ways: owing to a *quality* shared between the two (Peirce termed such a Sign an Icon), due to *contiguity* or a physical connection between them (an Index), or strictly by *convention* (a Symbol). We also noted that Signs are in continuous motion and constantly changing through the process of *semiosis*, which Peirce described as "the action or influence" of signs upon one another, and that the way in which the "habits of mind" of an individual person (Interpretant) conceptualize a Sign as an Object is thus likely to change over time.

In addition, we noted that Peirce's *phenomenology*, which is attendant upon his semiotic, provides a useful vocabulary for describing the ontological relationship one individual has to the culturally distinctive worldview of another. According to Peirce's terminology, a relationship of *Thirdness* of Thirdness describes one who *intellectually understands* another's worldview; *Secondness* of Thirdness implies an individual's *physical connection* or involvement with that worldview; and *Firstness* of Thirdness describes an individual's *emotional resonance* with the community that embodies that worldview. Combinations of these three relationships are also possible, with a relationship of Firstness, Secondness, *and* Thirdness of Thirdness implying ontological unity and thus consistency in worldview.

ESTABLISHING A PRAGMATIC CONCEPTION OF MUSIC ~ CHAPT. 3

In Chapter 3 we explored the ethnocentric, universalizing, and relativizing conceptions of music that have been held in the Western academic forum during the nineteenth and twentieth centuries, demonstrating the inadequacy of each as a foundation for present and future music curricula in the U.S. public schools. We first noted the nonuniversality of *music* as a concept, and we decided to use the anthropological construct *musical practices* to denote the disparate behaviors involving sound production purposefully undertaken in different cultural communities (i.e., those that are typically conceptualized by Europeans and Americans as "musical"), and the term *music* to denote the sound artifacts produced in such practices. We then noted that *ethnocentric* views tend to be held by persons who assume that the practices of the cultural communities to which they personally belong (such as their own musical practices) are superior to all others; *universalist* views are held by persons having an interest in comparing and observing aspects that seem to be shared in common among the practices of different cultural communities; and *relativist* views are held by those who insist that the practices of different cultural communities must be understood in terms of their inherent cultural uniqueness.

At the conclusion of this analysis, we considered writings on music by scholars in clinical psychiatry, ethnomusicology, and cultural anthropology for the purpose of developing our own Peircian *pragmatic* conception of music in *traditional* societies, which resolves the dilemmas to which the ethnocentric, universalist, and relativist conceptions give rise. Specifically, we concluded on the basis of this research that, stemming from their powerful psychophysiological and psychosocial *effects*, the musical practices of different cultural communities represent a diverse cluster of community-specific ritualized behaviors involving sound, each of which serves those persons who meaningfully participate in it as a means of *psychophysiological, psychosocial, and/or sociopolitical equilibration* relative to the worldview—or ordered conception of Reality—they tacitly share. We noted further that the musical practices undertaken by the members of a particular community tend to have one of two effects on the worldview they collectively embody: Musical practices that are of the nature of *possession* have the effect of validating a community's existing worldview, whereas musical practices that are of the nature of *shamanism* have the effect of manifesting or giving rise to culturally contrary beliefs and conceptions lying latent in the collective psyche of the community, and they are thus often transformative of the community's worldview.

We then observed that in *traditional* societies (i.e., those characterized by cultural homogeneity) the musical practices collectively undertaken by the members of the community typically have the effect of unifying them psychosocially and of concomitantly serving as a means of psychosocial equilibration with the "religious" worldview—or conception of Reality— they collectively embody. Similarly, we saw that in some *culturally pluralistic, state* societies, a particular musical practice is supported by the state's leaders and may be tacitly valued by citizens for its validation or acceptable transformation of the worldview they regard as being most amenable to the state's continued stability. However, we also noted that *theatre* has emerged to serve this purpose in some culturally pluralistic societies, displacing musical practice as the primary ritual form of the state, largely because a single musical practice generally has no capacity for manifesting a worldview that is acceptable to all of the cultural communities comprising the society. Theatre, in contrast with most traditional musical practices, has the innovative capacity to give voice to different cultural views, effectively representing the worldviews of the communities that comprise the state and reconciling them in a manner that is consistent with the authority structure of the state. Further, we saw that disparate, culturally unique musical practices typically continue in complex pluralistic societies to support the psychosocial equilibration and internal unity of their constituent communities.

We observed further that, in culturally pluralistic state societies, citizens regularly come into contact with musical practices and musics different from their own, and that the ontological relationship an individual has to a music that manifests a worldview different from her or his own can take many different forms. We utilized Peirce's phenomenological terminology to demonstrate this more specifically, showing that an individual might not be able to relate to the music of another cultural community at all, or that he or she might engage with it strictly *intellectually* (i.e., on the level of *Thirdness*), participate in it *physically* (i.e., on the level of *Secondness*), or engage with it *emotionally* (i.e., on the level of *Firstness*). We noted that an individual's involvement on all three of these levels *simultaneously* would reflect that person's *ontological unity* or *identity* with the worldview manifested in the music.

At the conclusion of Chapter 3, we further substantiated our Peircian pragmatic conception by demonstrating how any musical practice or instance of music—as a sound artifact of a community's psychosocial equilibration—can be recognized or "read" as a multidimensional *sign* of the worldview of those from whom it stems. Specifically, we saw that a given cultural form of music can be heard as *iconic* of (or qualitatively isomorphic with), *indexical* of (or physically connected with), and *symbolic* of (or related by convention to) the worldview of those with whom it originated. We also noted that musical practices are sometimes mistaken for *merely* symbolic behavior, but that social conflicts sometimes arise when people are confronted with music different from that in which their own worldview is embodied, thus demonstrating the great personal and cultural importance music often has for human beings. Finally, we observed that the iconic, indexical, and symbolic aspects of a particular music are sometimes exploited in culturally pluralistic societies for the purpose of manipulating psychologically members of the cultural community whose worldview it manifests, as in radio and television advertising.

ESTABLISHING A HISTORICAL PERSPECTIVE ON MUSIC IN THE U.S.

We observed in Chapter 4 that certain historical and social factors have contributed to obscuring awareness of the cultural rootedness and thus the personal, collective, and societal importance of the musical practices of different cultures among citizens of the U.S. First of all, we saw that unlike traditional societies the U.S. maintains a *separation of religion and state*, and, as a result of this, the nation has no single, shared vocabulary for describing subjective matters of the psyche (as traditional societies typically do); discussion of such matters has thus largely been suspended from the nation's public forum. As a result, nearly all public discussion of musical practices (particularly in the nation's mass media) has historically tended toward describing the externally observable, formal aspects of particular instances of different musics themselves (i.e., the mere "sound artifacts"), rather than accounting for the *effects* that different musical practices have on the psyches of individual human beings and the communities with which they originated.

In addition, unlike many other culturally pluralistic state societies, the U.S. has sanctioned *no official political worldview other than democracy itself*, and the organization of the nation around principles of democracy has rendered the nation quite unlike some other culturally pluralistic, state societies which have embraced or adopted a unique tradition of music as their own. A national music has historically been embraced by the totalitarian governments of certain nations (such as the former Soviet Union and the now defunct Nazi Germany) generally to the mandatory exclusion of other cultural forms of music. Other nations presently having more socialistically oriented, democratic governments (such as the UK, Italy, Germany) have historically embraced and supported nationally distinctive forms of music among their citizens as well, although they have not been so restrictive. The nations in both of these groups have historically upheld a culturally distinctive tradition of music primarily as a means of effecting national unity and identity. We noted that government support for music and other arts has been far greater in those nations than in the U.S., the government of which has never officially endorsed a particular form of music and has provided comparatively little financial support for musical endeavors throughout its history. Instead, the nation's constituent cultural communities have been free to continue pursuing their own respective musical practices, the great diversity of which has reflected the nation's complex cultural composition.

Finally, in place of an official religion or worldview, *the U.S. gradually came to adopt democratic capitalism as its social system.* This turn of events had three major effects on the nation, each of which has contributed to diminishing citizens' association of musical practices with community and thus attenuated their conscious recognition of its effects as societally important, psychosocially equilibrating behavior. First, the nation's efforts at developing a more complete scientific understanding of the physical universe have increasingly challenged for many citizens the validity of the "religious" conceptions of Reality embodied in and described by the nation's different cultural communities, thus promoting a general ambivalence (or superficiality) with respect to worldview among many members of the population. The cultural variability of the U.S. populace is manifested in the fluidity of citizens' membership in particular communities as well as in the diversity of musical practices they undertake. As an effect of the nation's having passed laws sanctioning religious and cultural liberty, the respective connections between ethnicity, cultural orientation, and musical practice have become much less clearly defined in the U.S. than they have been historically in other nations, thus obscuring the conceptual connection between particular practices and particular cultural communities in the minds of the nation's citizens.

Second, the economic success of capitalist democracy and the scientific, technological bent of the nation has significantly raised the standard of living among the nation's citizens, diminishing the *necessity* for them to be connected integrally with the cultural community of their origins (or, for that matter, any particular community) for physical survival. Because many citizens of the U.S. do not feel that they need to maintain attachments to a particular community to assure their continued physical well-being (as persons living in many other world societies do feel), they have come to regard their presence and participation in the musical rituals of a culturally distinctive community (such as those of a temple, a church, or other such institution) as optional, not essential. Thus, the connections between community and musical practice have been further obscured.

Third, scientific inquiry and the subsequent capitalist promotion of technology in one broad area of application—specifically, that of audio and video broadcasting and recording—have made it unnecessary for people to be *physically present* in community to experience many of the psychophysiologically and psychosocially equilibrating effects of musical engagement. Indeed, it is now possible for citizens to gain many of the benefits of musical participation simply by listening to a recording of their "favorite" performers or by tuning their radios, televisions, or computers to transmissions of music that are generally validating of their personally held worldview, thus making them members of "virtual" (or geographically diffused) communities. Many such citizens now select the music they listen to or participate in strictly on the basis that it suits their personal "taste," rather than consciously recognizing the cultural associations it tacitly entails. As a result, the conceptual connections between musical practice and community—and thus worldview—have become still further obscured in the U.S.

Collectively, these historical events have contributed to obscuring for U.S. citizens how different musical practices have had and continue to have importantly beneficial effects for those who undertake them and thus for the nation as a whole. We observed, however, that due to the dominant influence the nation's media have grown to have on the consciousness of many citizens during the twentieth century, the leaders of media corporations are now in a unique position to assure that the commercial conception of "music as entertainment" will predominate in the nation's public forum. As these corporations have promoted the musical practices of different cultural communities as mere "entertainment" (and as purely *symbolic* phenomena) to the nation's citizens, providing little or no insight into the greater meanings they have for those who undertake them (i.e., their effectiveness at contributing to psychosocial balance among people of like mind because of their iconic, indexical, and symbolic relationships with a shared worldview), they have effectively curtailed most public discussion of the different culturally unique conceptions of Reality that inhere in different musics. Finally, as these corporations have come to promote certain musical practices *and not others* in the nation's mass media, they have assured that the distinctive conceptions of music held by the various culturally disparate communities comprising the nation's populace will not pose a challenge to notions of "music as entertainment" from which the corporations stand to benefit financially.

At the conclusion of Chapter 4, we observed that music education has also taken different forms in different types of societies throughout history. We observed that in *traditional societies* (i.e., those characterized by cultural homogeneity) certain culturally unique musical practices typically serve as vehicles for the psychosocial equilibration of individuals and the community in ways that validate the worldview collectively shared by that community. In these traditional societies, a form of music education has typically served as the means by which the elders of the society instill in their young the skills necessary for them to participate in and contribute to the community's unique musical practices. Similarly, we observed that in *culturally pluralistic state societies* in which the state government tacitly embraces or actively enforces a common worldview, a certain musical practice has typically served as a vehicle for the psychological equilibration of individuals and the community in a way that validates the worldview held by the government. The state's leaders typically support music education for the purpose of instilling in their youth a musical practice that will socialize them in a manner consistent with the worldview they collectively believe to be optimal.

Given this background, we noted that we might expect to find that much of the music education undertaken in the U.S.—a culturally pluralistic, democratic capitalist nation in which matters of cultural difference are largely bracketed from the public forum—to be regarded by citizens collectively as the responsibility of the churches, temples, and other institutions established and maintained by the culturally distinct communities coexisting within the society. However, we saw that since the inception of the discipline in the early nineteenth century, much of the music education undertaken in the U.S. has *not* been carried out primarily by the nation's constituent "religious" or culturally unique institutions, but has instead been implemented in the nation's state-supported, ostensibly culturally neutral public schools and universities. Thus, we asked the question: On what basis (or bases) has music education been included in the public schools of the U.S. historically?

ESTABLISHING A HISTORICAL PERSPECTIVE   CHAPT. 5
ON MUSIC EDUCATION IN THE U.S.

We reviewed in Chapter 5 the justifications and explanations that have been voiced in support of music education over the history of the nation and considered the historical forces that prompted their composition and thus influenced their content. We discovered that, prior to the advent of the U.S. as a nation, persons living in the various culturally distinct communities of North America generally conceptualized participation in the musical practices they respectively undertook (most typically as part of their collective "religious" practices) as important means of psychosocial equilibration in community.

For persons belonging to the North American Colonial communities that originated in the various Christian religious traditions of Europe, the musical practices regarded as societally important were regarded as (i.e., were *signs* of) worship and many communities predicated them on their understanding of the characterizations of worship practices that they found in the Holy Bible, the collection of sacred writings of the Christian religion. The members of each community tacitly regarded the form of music education they carried out as an important means of instilling in their young the skills necessary for them to participate in their own culturally distinctive musical practices. However, members of many of the different cultural communities disagreed with and even disparaged the approaches to worship and the attendant musical practices undertaken by other communities then living in North America.

We also noted that, though little recorded information remains, available evidence suggests that culturally distinctive, if less formal forms of music education were being undertaken during the same era among the communities of Native Americans who had lived on the continent long before the arrival of the colonists, and among the African people the colonists brought with them to North America as slaves. In each community that sustained a socially central musical practice, a form of music education served as a means of socializing children into the culturally unique, socially harmonizing traditions and the distinctive beliefs of that community.

However, we saw that a confluence of forces contributed to changing community-held conceptions of societally important music during the late eighteenth century. We noted that the U.S. was formed as a nation at this time, during a period of European history that historians now call the "Enlightenment" era. The Enlightenment began as an intellectual movement in France that emphasized above all the application of human reason (rather than religious revelation) to understanding the universe and to improving the human condition. The Enlightenment philosophers' confidence that reason could solve all human problems was also reflected in their writings in the area of *aesthetics*, a field of inquiry that emerged and attained some prominence during the latter part of the eighteenth century. The reifying conception of music (i.e., the notion of a musical "work" as an *object* of beauty) in those writings has continued to carry considerable influence in the public forum of the U.S. up to contemporary times. Indeed, the tendency of those European intellectuals to focus on the mere *artifacts* or *objects* of music (and to bracket them from the public forum) rather than accounting in a more satisfactory way for the important psychophysiological, psychosocial, and sociopolitical *effects* of musical *practices* in particular communities came to have far-reaching effects on both concepts of music and on music education in the U.S.

We saw that with the gradual emergence of a middle class in European societies, many composers and other musicians came to attain financial independence from church and court. The music they created reflected their greater freedom in worldview, with large-scale musical performances of opera, oratorio, and other "secular" works progressively taking a more prominent role in their output. Simultaneously captivating central European citizens for the first time during this era was the modern notion of "genius"—as a gift of nature at work within the human imagination. Musicians (primarily composers) possessed of "genius" were thought not merely to have extraordinary intellectual ability, but also to have a profound or prophetic quality of mind that manifested itself in the emotionally, societally stirring products of their labors, which were, in turn, assessed as by the European populace of the eighteenth and nineteenth centuries as works of great *art* or "masterpieces."

In a sense, it was not unreasonable at all for these Europeans to bestow such high approbation on the composers of their age, since the music of such composers as Wolfgang Amadeus Mozart and Ludwig van Beethoven contributed greatly to validating the new ordered and reason-based conceptions of Reality idealized—and in some measure manifested—in the minds of the citizens of central European communities who participated in them. Those who attended performances of the newly emerging "art music" of the time no doubt experienced a profound psychosocial validation of the new, rationalistic and ordered worldviews then animating European society, since such order was embodied in the formal characteristics of the music they revered. At the same time, the newly emerging works of "art music" could be heard with a degree of psychological remove, considered intellectually as "unique expressions of the Absolute" and as separated or bracketed from former cultural associations (unlike the music of the church or state, which required both participation and doctrinal or ideological commitment), thus reflecting the rationalistic conception of Reality that was emerging at the time in yet another way. However, some contemporary scholars have argued that at least some of the veneration accorded these "genius" composers and their works was actually propagated within the ranks of the composers themselves, who naturally stood to gain a great deal from such public acclaim. In any event, the praise bestowed on them seems to have stemmed as much from the characteristics of the rationalist *zeitgeist* they shared with their supporters—and from what "musical" freedom (i.e., freedom in worldview) meant to them—as from qualities inherent in their music.

Meanwhile in the American colonies, the influence of Enlightenment thought, combined with an evangelistic religious movement known as the Great Awakening and a new societal penchant for the rewards of foreign trade to advance a spirit of religious toleration among the culturally disparate populace, gradually moving the colonies toward enacting laws disestablishing religion as they became states of the new republic. A new work ethic began to emerge as citizens realized they could acquire greater influence and respectability in their communities by imitating the gentry—persons who held higher social standing than themselves owing largely to the sizable coffers they had brought with them from Europe—by buying luxury items, many of them imported, that had previously been beyond their reach. As a result, trade with other nations and between the states increased. As the new nation moved toward the development of an industrial, trade-based economy, the colonies' earlier, more religiously based forms of social organization were thus displaced.

Concurrently, affluent persons of European descent living in the U.S. were becoming enthralled with the culturally liberated "art music" of the European composers, and they began to undertake and promote the performance of this new music in their own towns. Individuals who had formerly attended the singing schools (which, as we noted earlier, had been formed expressly for the purpose of improving the quality of singing in churches) found themselves drawn toward participation in the newly forming singing societies, which were dedicated primarily to performing the new, more culturally assimilative "art music" of the "geniuses" of Europe. Symphony orchestras and conservatories appeared on the American scene soon after this time, all of them founded on the Enlightenment conception of music as an elevating form of "art."

From our present historical perspective, we saw that the philosophers of the Enlightenment made a valuable contribution in liberating citizens of the U.S. (and, over time, the European nations) from the confines of culturally oppressive churches and autocratic state governments, but their failure to account adequately for the place of musical *practices* in their conceptions of the new reason-based societies they envisioned eventually led to a societal ambivalence about music. Persons with strong emotional ties to the church retained the view that all societally important musical practices were those that took place in worship (and they were put off by others' "artistic" conceptions), while those caught up in the new, more rationalistic conception of Reality came to regard the products of all musical practices (i.e., music) as works of art, even subsequently reinterpreting the music of the past that had been incorporated in religious worship as manifestations of "artistic" expression. Within this latter group, some idolized the works of the "genius" composers of Europe as the apotheosis of "art," while others held more egalitarian perspectives, accepting different works of "art music" on their own terms while continuing to value also the sacred and folk musics of their respective historical traditions. Reflected in the ideas of this latter group and emerging tacitly in the society in general was one of the most revolutionary ideas of the age: the modern concept of *art* or "the realm of the aesthetic" as a *hypothetically neutral mental space* in which differences and new assimilative conceptions could be considered intellectually, and according to which conflicts arising from cultural differences would be bracketed or provisionally set aside in the nation's public forum.

Personally convinced of the value of vocal music as an intellectually elevating form of *art*, as an important form of physical activity (due to the exercise of the lungs and voice that singing entails), and as a way of cultivating the feelings by providing a means of training them, public figures like William Channing Woodbridge and Lowell Mason championed the inclusion of vocal music as a subject of study in the schools of Boston in the early nineteenth century. Their efforts eventually resulted in the introduction of vocal and instrumental music courses into public schools throughout the U.S. The public statements and writings proffered by the nation's early public-school music educators and others who supported the inclusion of music classes in the schools at the time reveal the universalizing (but often reifying) views they held toward all music, although examinations of the music textbooks they used reveals that—not surprisingly—they included in their teaching only those forms of music that were generally held to be "good" by the members of their own society (and were thus generally validating of their own worldview). Having predicated their efforts in some measure on the conception of music as an elevating form of *art* advanced by the philosophers of the eighteenth century, and thus accounting for cultural differences among composers and communities under the rubric of "the aesthetic" (yet giving little or no attention to forms of music outside the realm of European and American sacred, folk, and art traditions), they thus laid the foundation for the culturally rooted curricular quandaries that have dogged public-school music education to the present day and have led to its perpetually tenuous status in the curriculum. The notion that instruction in vocal music "cultivates the feelings" provided the basis, held throughout most of the history of U.S. public-school music, for regarding music education as a form of aesthetic education.

In the last years of the nineteenth century and the early years of the twentieth, the Enlightenment conception of different forms of music as works of *art* (i.e., an individual's *personal* expression) continued to guide the work of U.S. music educators, and many maintained their focus on the works of the "great masters" of Europe, giving them prominence in their teaching as the epitome of musical excellence. Simultaneously, some music educators began to be influenced by the increasingly scientific and industrial orientation taken to all phenomena in the public forum, and they gradually came to conceptualize music more and more as a *product* of the human mind. Researchers like G. Stanley Hall sought to account for the emergence of musical ability in human developmental psychology, and, later, Carl Seashore and Jacob Kwalwasser sought to locate musical ability in certain human aptitudes or skills; their work and that of their followers served as a foundation for teaching music (i.e., music making) on the basis of its importance as an inherent and cultivable human propensity.

In addition, the nation's growing interest in developing technologies out of recent scientific discoveries as well as its ever-increasing interest in commerce led to the invention and mass production of recording and broadcast technologies. As radios and gramophones or, later, "record players" became widely available, music gradually came to be regarded not only as a *product of the human mind*, but also as a *marketable product* of entertainment, though much of the previous era's rhetoric on music as a form of *art* was maintained in justifications voiced for the inclusion of music in the schools. However, the nation's industrial and materialistic orientation with regard to music was reflected in the music-teaching methods that came to be employed in the public schools, as music educators used recordings, programmed learning methods, performance and memory contests, and musical achievement tests to support their instruction on the music of the "great masters" (i.e., the "geniuses") of Europe and others. Faced with the continuing existence of musical traditions of Christian religious communities, the presence of various "artistic" forms of music, and the growing prevalence of popular songs and jazz on recordings in the mid-twentieth century, citizens of the U.S. began to apply more widely the notion of *genres* or *styles* to the sound artifacts of different cultural practices, thus gradually separating forms of music having widely differing cultural origins into relatively discrete, culturally neutral mental categories. The societal predilection toward regarding music as *product* was interrupted during World War II, at which time music educators returned briefly to treating musical practices as culturally rooted means of effecting the psychosocial balance and unity of the nation as a broad community, but music educators' more scientist and, perhaps, more economically grounded orientation toward music was resumed once again at the conclusion of the war.

With publication of the Tanglewood Declaration following the symposium of the same name in 1967, the music education curriculum in the public schools was officially opened to include "[m]usic of all periods, styles, forms, and cultures."[3] Publication of this declaration represented a bold, public endorsement of cultural inclusiveness in music education curricula by the profession, but, sadly, many of those who promoted it did not emphasize teaching the musical practices undertaken by different cultural communities on their own terms. Despite a growing interest in "multicultural" music education, U.S. music educators largely maintained their conception of all musical creations as works of *art*. The influence of Bennett Reimer's 1970 book, *A Philosophy of Music Education*, on the content of elementary music textbooks helped to assure that the concept of "music education as aesthetic education"[4] would remain foundational in the profession. Thus, the differing forms of music of different cultural communities continued to be considered on the same basis—that is, as *objects* manifesting different *personal* artistic expressions, each to be appreciated for the emotions it evoked—in the U.S. public forum for many years. Indeed, as "multicultural" music educators have included the musics (i.e., the sound artifacts) of more and more cultural communities in their curricula over the years, most have kept the general focus of their instruction on music making (i.e., the reproduction and creation of sound artifacts) and on the technical analysis of different forms of music, rather than acknowledging and exploring the culturally disparate origins of different musical practices in the psychosocial equilibration of the communities and individuals who undertake them.

As the growing presence of non-Western cultural communities in the U.S. has brought to light the cultural relativity of the reifying conception of "music as an art object" that has come to predominate in the U.S. public forum, some music educators have begun to challenge the approaches to music education taken by their historical forebears. Adopting the notion of *praxis* described by the ancient Greek philosopher Aristotle, they have recommended a *praxial* approach to music education. In such an approach, philosopher Philip Alperson explained, "[t]he attempt is made . . . to understand [music] in terms of the variety of meaning and values evidenced in actual practice in particular cultures."[5] Extending from this idea, music education philosopher David Elliott advanced the idea that the development of skills and the taking on of challenges in both music making and music listening (in all world traditions) are unique and important ways of bringing order to consciousness, and he asserted that they lead to self-growth, self-knowledge, and raised self-esteem.[6] Therefore, in his view, the task of music education is to develop the musicianship of learners—and thus to effect their self-growth—through progressive musical problem solving in balanced relation to appropriate musical challenges.[7] Music education philosopher Thomas Regelski followed Aristotle's notion of praxis more closely in his writings, recognizing that different intentions and "functions" motivate different musical practices and that attention must be given to what they are "good for" in their respective contexts. Regelski argued for the inclusion of music education in schools on the bases that music is a "universal human trait," that musical practice is a way by which moments in life are "made special,"[8] and that "the Being and Becoming involved with musical practice . . . is unique and available in no other manner."[9] Accordingly, he wrote, "a praxial philosophy of music in and through education is concerned to get people into action musically."[10] In their use of the ancient Greek notion of praxis, these philosophers have made a great contribution to American music education, helping to extricate the field from the reifying and universalizing notions of the aesthetic philosophers of the Enlightenment and their followers. From the perspective of the Peircian pragmatist account we have set forth in this inquiry, we asserted that praxial conceptions of music are satisfactory as a basis for music education in U.S. schools only insofar as they take into account the *effects* of different musical practices in the social, cultural contexts in which they have arisen *and* the unique ways in which people in those contexts experience and understand them. Regelski's praxial philosophy does both.

We concluded that although music educators have included the music of increasing numbers of cultural communities in their teaching since the advent of public-school music education in the early nineteenth century, they have generally stayed away from exploring cultural issues, instead emphasizing *performance* (i.e., replication) and *scientific* (i.e., technical analysis) approaches in their teaching. In line with "aesthetic conceptions," they have generally regarded all music as artistic manifestations of personal "self-expression" instead of helping students to see *how* different musical practices provide personal and social benefit to those who engage with them in the differing, culturally unique contexts in which they have arisen. But by not addressing the *community*-related roots of different musical practices, music educators have contributed to promoting an inappropriately universalizing conception of the widely different cultural forms of music as mere "objects" or "products" and obscured from consideration in their classes the distinctive views and experiences of music held by many of the nation's constituent communities. To the degree that they have advanced a universalizing conception of music in their instruction without adequately helping their students to see *how* different musical practices provide psychophysiological and psychosocial benefit to the culturally disparate individuals and communities with whom they have arisen (and thus accounting for their social efficacy), they have contributed to limiting their students' awareness of the importance of musical practices throughout history, and have consequently undermined the public's recognition of the value of their own subject in the curriculum. This brings us to a modified version of our original question:

> Should music education continue to be included in the public schools of the U.S. in the emerging postmodern era, and if so, on what basis? (More precisely, *can* music education be included in the nation's public schools in a way that is consistent with the democratic principles on which the nation was founded *and* at the same time be substantively meaningful and important to its constituent citizens and communities, and if so, *on what basis* might its inclusion be regarded as educationally sound and societally important?)

On the basis of the philosophical and historical perspective we have established in this inquiry, we can answer this question in the affirmative, asserting that music education should indeed be included in U.S. public schools *both* as a means of promoting the psychophysiological and psychosocial health of the nation's citizens collectively, *and* as a means of fostering understanding among people of different cultural communities comprising the nation. Furthermore, music education should adopt a semiotic theoretical foundation, whereby students can come to understand the musical practices manifested in U.S. society (and beyond) *on their own terms* and come to experience them as dynamic means of psychophysiological, psychosocial, and/or sociopolitical equilibration (i.e., for individuals and communities).

CURRICULAR GOALS

In order to address the two problems described at the beginning of this inquiry, it seems advisable that U.S. public-school music educators should now expand their teaching to attend to the tremendous variety of musical practices manifested in the nation (and throughout the world), working specifically to raise students' awareness and understanding of their personal, societal, and political *effects*, and the way those effects are conceptualized in the culturally diverse communities in which they are undertaken. In order to accomplish this, it would seem appropriate for music educators to adopt the following three curricular goals as the basis of their instruction. (Note that these goals are stated as intended outcomes of a K–12 education; this assertion is in no way meant to imply that all of these goals should be addressed throughout the entire curriculum.)

1. Introduce students to the full musical dimension of human life, helping them to experience and understand different musical practices as dynamic *psychophysiologically, psychosocially,* and *sociopolitically equilibrating behaviors*, each having efficacy for particular individuals and/or communities in particular contexts at particular points in time.
2. Enable students to see how the personal, social, and political effects of engagement in particular musical practices influence the social and political balance of the nation, how awareness of these effects has tended to be obscured in the public forum over the history of the U.S., and how they are often exploited commercially and politically, owing largely to the nation's democratic capitalist political orientation.
3. Empower students with skills to engage in the musical practices of more than one cultural tradition—including the multifaceted and evolving tradition of Western art music—for the purpose of supporting *their own* psychosocial equilibration and that of others. As possible, prepare them to engage with the musical practices of different cultural communities in different historical eras for the purpose of enabling them to grasp experientially how different individuals and communities have experienced and presently experience them as meaningful.

To conclude this inquiry, we will explore each of these curricular goals more fully and discuss instructional concerns. Finally, we will consider ways in which the nation's universities might best prepare public school teachers to teach to meet these goals.

Curricular Goal #1

Introduce students to the full musical dimension of human life, helping them to experience and understand different musical practices as dynamic *psychophysiologically, psychosocially, and sociopolitically equilibrating behaviors*, each having efficacy for particular individuals and/or communities in particular contexts at particular points in time.

Three objectives stem from this curricular goal. The first or primary objective is for music educators to nurture students' development as educated listeners, helping them to hear, engage physically with, and understand different musical practices as having psychological and/or social efficacy in the particular contexts in which they are undertaken. As we have seen, all musical practices are situated in particular cultural contexts and reflect particular social coherence systems. Insofar as the factors that contribute to its personal, social, and political meanings can be discerned, the music (i.e., the sound artifact) produced in any musical practice can thus be experienced and "read" as a multidimensional *sign* of psychosocial equilibration, relative to a particular worldview at a particular point in time. Once this is recognized, it is but a short step to realizing that semiotic exploration of different musical practices and musics can serve to illuminate worldviews (i.e., the patterns of cognition or characteristics of the coherence systems) held by culturally different peoples throughout human history, providing windows into the ways individuals and communities have ordered their worlds mentally and come to terms with them personally and socially at different times and in different places.

However, as we have seen, it is important to realize that, because of their origins in culturally different traditions, not all musical practices work to effect psychosocial equilibration in the same way. Understanding what makes each musical practice effective (or not effective) in a particular social context is vitally important if students are to grasp fully the diversity and value of musical practices in human life. The Peircian pragmatic perspective and the semiotic vocabulary we acquired in Chapters 2 and 3 could be used as a basis for music instruction by music teachers and students in schools, since, as we saw in Chapter 3, Peircian pragmatism and semiotic provide effective (if provisional) means for discussing such concerns. Specifically, they serve as a means by which the music made in a given musical practice can be identified as *iconic* of the worldview of those persons who find it meaningful in its original sense (owing to its isomorphic relationship with their cultural coherence system), *indexical* of their worldview (owing to the physical relationships that inhere between the music, themselves, and their environment), and *symbolic* of their worldview (owing to its employment of conventional *signs* native to a distinctive cultural community). Furthermore, students may experience and describe their experiences with different musical practices as being on the levels of Thirdness (i.e., intellectual), Secondness (i.e., physical), and perhaps (but not necessarily) Firstness (i.e., emotional), as they undertake performance of them in their classes.

Some readers may argue that such an approach is impracticable, as many public-school teachers do not have the cultural and historical background to address the meanings of all musics, especially those outside their own personal fields of experience. From our Peircian pragmatic perspective, however, we can see that it is important for teachers to introduce in their classes only those musics that they can teach *meaningfully*—that is, with an understanding of the *effects* they have or have had historically in the social contexts in which they have emerged.

A second, related objective stemming from this curricular goal must be to help students recognize musical practices as *dynamic* means of psychosocial equilibration; that is, that each is undertaken *in relation to* the unique conception of Reality *embodied by an individual or community at a particular time.* In Chapter 2 we encountered Peirce's notion that Signs—and our conceptions of them as Objects—are continuously in motion and constantly changing. We noted that signs change through the process of *semiosis*, which Peirce described as the "action, or influence"[11] of signs upon one another. We used the visual representation in Figure 2.3 (reproduced below as Figure 6.1) to illustrate how any given perception (as a Sign) may be conceptualized differently (as an Object) by a single, continually changing individual (an Interpretant) over the course of that individual's lifetime.

We saw that upon a person's first conscious perception of and involvement with a particular music or practice (as the Sign), he or she may regard it as *new information*, as it has much new data to yield. However, as that individual encounters and reflects on the same music or musical practice over a period of time, meeting it perhaps in a variety of social contexts, the sign may be said to become more *meaningful* (i.e., more well-understood and more well-integrated into her or his habitual patterns of belief), while yielding less and less new *information* with each encounter (illustrated here by I_1, I_2, I_3 . . . I_x). This description accounts for the life experiences any individual might have with a musical practice that is "of the nature of

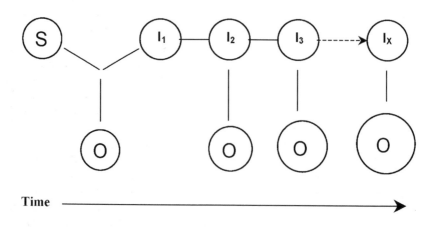

Time ⟶

Figure 6.1   Changes in the Interpretant over time, resulting in changes in the conception of the Sign as Object.

possession" (i.e., psychophysiologically validating of her or his present or past conception of Reality).

However, it is important for our purposes here to note that as an individual *person* (or *community*) changes and grows over time, that person (or community) may come to engage with a new and different music (or musics). As we have seen, such changes invariably manifest themselves in a culture-specific way. That is, the observable effect of such *shamanic* change depends on the culturally particular beliefs and practices of that individual or community. As we saw in Chapter 3, the Chopi people of Mozambique collectively experienced cultural transformation through participating in the evolving *ngodo* in the central musical practice of their village. Correspondingly, some U.S. citizens whose psychological equilibration is effected via recordings of a particular popular music tradition may find themselves "growing tired of *that* song," and "liking a *new* one" better, thus accounting for their continuing interest in purchasing new musical recordings. Incidentally, we might note that whether an individual experiences a music that is new to her or him as shamanically "prophetic" and thus transformative or expanding of worldview—*or* merely as a satisfying reinforcement of what he or she already subconsciously "knows"—varies from individual to individual. The possibility also exists that the individual may regard a new form of music he or she encounters as a mere novelty (i.e., possibly entertaining, but not importantly meaningful) or as "noise" (i.e., not at all revelatory of an appropriate or satisfying conception of Reality). Indeed, as we saw in Chapter 3, Peirce's semiotic accounts for an individual's potential level of engagement with a particular music as being largely determined by her or his present "habits of mind."

A third, related objective stemming from this curricular goal is perhaps the most important: Music courses, if taught pragmatically (that is, enabling students to experience and understand the music of different communities in terms of how they were originally intended), should have the effect of encouraging insight and tolerance among the nation's populace, providing students with skills, experiences, and knowledge to listen to and engage *meaningfully*—i.e., with culturally and historically informed understanding—with musical practices previously outside their respective realms of experience. Indeed, perhaps the greatest effect of studying the semiotic bases (and thus the psychological effectiveness) of different musics is that such study can provide students with windows into the worldviews of other people and communities, thereby fostering greater understanding between culturally disparate peoples. Historically, one of the pragmatic goals of a liberal arts education has been to foster tolerance and understanding among disparate peoples by helping them to understand one another. As music educators enable students to grasp differences among cultural communities as they are manifested in music, they will be helping to cultivate civility among their students and thus among the nation's populace.

Curricular Goal #2

Enable students to see how the personal, social, and political effects of engagement in particular musical practices influence the social and political balance of the nation, how awareness of these effects has tended to be obscured in the public forum over the history of the U.S., and how they are often exploited commercially and politically, owing largely to the nation's democratic capitalist political orientation.

Three objectives stem from Goal #2. First of all, students must be helped to see how certain historical factors, some of them stemming from the nation's democratic capitalist and individualist political orientation, have had the effect of reifying, marginalizing, and—in some measure—trivializing the musical practices of different communities manifested in the U.S. public forum. We saw in Chapter 4 that several historical factors—the advent of music notation by the church in the ninth century, the emergence of music publishing in France around the turn of the sixteenth century, the institution of music copyright laws in Europe in the late eighteenth century, the constitutional separation of church and state in the U.S. at about the same time, the nation's lack of a defined worldview apart from democracy (and the emergence of its attendant capitalist economic system), the development of broadcast and recording technologies, and the popular media's propagation of a "product" mentality toward music—have all contributed to promoting a societal conception of music as "object," obscuring from the consciousness of the general public in some measure the important effects musical practices have for those who undertake them.

The nation's popular mass media have further contributed to this obfuscation by portraying different community-related conceptions of music in the public forum of the U.S. in professedly ironic, but often actually negative, ways rather than giving them serious credence as potentially valid cultural perspectives.[12] As we noted in Chapter 4, the religious practices and the beliefs of culturally distinctive communities are often portrayed by the mass media as odd, rather than as legitimate manifestations of unique conceptions of Reality. Likewise, "art music" has received mixed portrayals in the nation's popular media, sometimes being characterized as elitist owing largely to the historical association of the concept *art* with the music of the European aristocracies of the seventeenth and eighteenth centuries and subsequently adopted by the upper classes of the U.S.; at other times the notion of different forms of music as unique forms of *art* has been characterized as legitimate. At the same time, musical practices undertaken in *entertainment* contexts have been given mixed portrayals, sometimes being represented as "art music" (and thus taken seriously in some way), while at other times characterized as socially insignificant behavior undertaken simply for amusement. Such mixed characterizations may have prevented the nation's populace from grasping the social efficacy of all musical practices.

Because of this societal ambivalence concerning music, teachers must help students to recognize the various physical forms of music sold in the public forum of the U.S. (e.g., as printed music, CDs, MP3s) as "sound artifacts" that have roots in community-particular, personally and socially important, psychosocially effective practices. Indeed, as we have seen, the reifying notion of "music as product" advanced by the nation's mass media has adversely affected music education, supporting the trivializing notion of music as societally unimportant behavior and thus raised questions about its importance in education. Furthermore, as we have already noted, the societal predilection of U.S. media to focus on the *individual person* undertaking the musical practice rather than on the worldview manifested in the music or on the actual or virtual community of people to whom it is meaningful has tended also to reduce public awareness of the sociopolitical significance of many musical practices.

So, a second objective stemming from this goal must be to help students grasp how, despite these societal hindrances to recognizing their effectiveness and societal importance, the musical practices undertaken in the nation continue to provide psychosocial benefit to those who engage in them. Indeed, those undertaken in churches, synagogues, temples, and in informal communities, clubs, concert halls, homes, or even on the street all contribute to validating and sometimes transforming the worldviews of the persons who actively or even passively engage with them. Musical practices may be as simple as casually singing or playing together *or* as concerted and sophisticated as a semiotically dense, music-filled worship service undertaken expressly for meditational, culturally grounding purposes. In any case, they often contribute to bringing together and validating the identities of the individuals who earnestly participate in them.

Thus, a third objective stemming from this goal must be to help students see how musical practices influence the social and political balance of communities and the nation (and thus the world) in various ways. As we noted in Chapter 4, citizens' engagement with some musical practices (and not others) has significant influence in U.S. society, since it contributes to supporting their sense of identity. Furthermore, the music put forth as *entertainment* in the nation's public forum—via radio, television, and other media—manifests worldviews that reflect the beliefs of large segments of the population. Indeed, as we noted in Chapter 4, advertisers and others in the public forum regularly exploit the psychosocially validating effects of music for commercially and politically coercive purposes. This is one of the costs of living in a capitalist democracy, a society in which one's worldview is relatively "free" or unconstrained. But because of this state of affairs, students must be helped to think critically and act defensively with respect to their engagement with music, learning to recognize how it is often used for purposes of manipulation in the nation's public forum.

Curricular Goal #3

> Empower students with skills to engage in the musical practices of more than one cultural tradition—including the multifaceted and evolving tradition of Western art music—for the purpose of supporting *their own* psychosocial equilibration and that of others. As possible, prepare them to engage with the musical practices of different cultural communities in different historical eras for the purpose of enabling them to grasp experientially how different individuals and communities have experienced and presently experience them as meaningful.

On the basis of the argument we have presented in this inquiry, some readers might be inclined to think that, due to its cultural particularity and potential political volatility, active involvement in performance of *all* musical practices (i.e., Secondness of Thirdness) should be curtailed in the public schools and that the intellectual study of music (i.e., Thirdness of Thirdness) should be the only goal (if any). Some may even hold the opinion that any music education should be the responsibility of the various different cultural communities comprising the nation. On the contrary, eliminating performance-based public-school music education programs on this (or any other) basis would be a serious mistake, and it is important to understand why.

Over the past several years, researchers in early childhood education have come to a greater appreciation and understanding of the important role a child's engagement with a musical practice can play in her or his development of a "coherence system" (worldview) and to realize that this involvement tends to support the cognitive skill development of young children in various areas. For example, the benefits of children's participation in a musical practice are reflected in their acquisition of reading skills and related proficiencies. Early childhood educators who are familiar with this research usually incorporate varieties of music that are consistent with coherence systems that tend to predominate in the U.S. public forum in their teaching, since such engagement provides reinforcement for the children's learning. Not only are they socialized musically into this coherence system, but their development of reading skills and other proficiencies is enhanced.[13] This use of music in education has received tacit corroboration from specialists in music therapy who have found that when they engage patients who have suffered strokes or brain damage through accidents of various sorts in a musical practice (especially singing) in conjunction with speech therapy, the patients have greater success in relearning language skills than those who are not so musically engaged.

Furthermore, other researchers have found that certain musical practices serve as effective means of restoring the *emotional* balance of patients undergoing various sorts of physical and psychological traumas (e.g., patients with cancer and other terminal illnesses). They have suggested that these efforts are successful because musical engagement provides a means by which the patient's personal identity is validated or "balanced" (i.e., psychophysiologically equilibrated) according to their personal musical background, and that such engagement contributes to reducing patients' anxiety.[14] It seems evident, based on our earlier observations, that when U.S. citizens "turn on the radio," "play a recording," or, better, sing or play an instrument during periods of emotional hardship, their actions are motivated by their tacit, perhaps subconscious recognition of the psychological solace or validation—via affirmation of worldview—that such a musical practice is likely to provide. Indeed, a person's engagement with a particular music at such difficult times can be highly therapeutic, providing psychological validation for the individual owing to her or his long engagement with that form of music and with a community that engages with it.[15]

In addition, the distinguished neurologist Oliver Sacks has observed the importance of engaging in a musical practice (i.e., such as listening, movement, or active participation in performing) as a means of establishing a coherence structure for persons with severe perceptual and cognitive disorders. For example, Sacks described the case of a patient afflicted as an infant with meningitis, which brought about lifelong mental retardation, impulsiveness, seizures, and spasticity and for whom the only thing that made life tolerable was involvement in some form of musical practice. When Martin sang, Sacks explained, "all that was defective or pathological [in him] fell away, and one saw only absorption and animation, wholeness and health."[16]

Sacks has also described the cases of several patients who contracted a sleeping sickness (*encephalitis lethargica*) during an epidemic that followed World War I that rendered the individuals afflicted with it largely immobile for decades. Many of the patients were given up as hopeless until Sacks administered L-DOPA, a drug revolutionary for its time, which had an "awakening" effect on them. While working with these recently "reanimated" patients, Sacks discovered that some of them would become additionally responsive and find relief from some of their other constricting mental and physical symptoms via participation in a musical practice (even if just by listening). Sacks affirmed that the psychophysiological efficacy of a musical practice as a stabilizing, structuring force in many such circumstances is incontrovertible and that the matter thus merits further inquiry.

> The power of music, narrative and drama is one of the greatest practical and theoretical importance . . . We see how the retarded, unable to perform fairly simple tasks involving perhaps four or five movements or procedures in sequence, can do these perfectly if they work to music—the sequence of movements they cannot hold as schemes being perfectly holdable as music, i.e., embedded in music. The same may be seen, very dramatically, in patients with severe frontal lobe damage and apraxia—an inability to *do* things, to retain the simplest motor sequences and programmes, even to walk, despite perfectly preserved

intelligence in other ways. This procedural defect, or motor idiocy, as one might call it, which completely defeats any ordinary system of rehabilitative instruction, vanishes at once if music is the instructor . . .

What we see, fundamentally, is the power of music to organise—and to do this efficaciously (as well as joyfully!), when abstract or schematic forms of organisations fail. Indeed it is especially dramatic, as one would expect, precisely when no other form of organisation will work. Thus music, or any other form of narrative, is essential when working with the retarded or apraxic—schooling or therapy for them must be centred on music or something equivalent.[17]

Indeed, it seems apparent that an individual's involvement in a musical practice can positively impact her or his psychophysiological balance as well as enhance certain brain and body functions in ways not yet understood.[18] For this reason alone it would be inappropriate to discontinue music education in the nation's public schools.

We have seen in this inquiry that every music is rooted in and semiotically manifests a particular coherence system or worldview. Furthermore, we have just seen that a person's engagement in a particular musical tradition may be a vital part of her or his cognitive development in—or healthy rehabilitation into—that coherence system or worldview. Recognition of these two points raises the following question: Owing to the egalitarian premises upon which the U.S. was founded, the inherent cultural rootedness of musical practices, *and* the cultural diversity of the U.S. populace, into *which* tradition (or traditions) of music (i.e., which cultural coherence system) should students be introduced in U.S. public schools? This question is a modified version of the question of curriculum content with which we began this inquiry, and we are now ready to suggest an answer, although our answer will be, of necessity, rather complex.

First of all, owing to the tremendous benefit that participation in a musical practice can provide not only in terms of the learning of language and other skills, but also for their importance in effecting psychophysiological and psychosocial equilibration, it seems apparent that every child *should* be inculcated into a musical tradition consistent with the worldview or cultural coherence system embraced by the community of which he or she is a part. The worldview upon which the organization of much of the music in the public forum of the U.S. has historically been grounded has its origins in the Semitic religious traditions (especially Judaism and Christianity) that have predominated in Europe. As we saw in Chapter 3, this worldview is manifested not only in the religious practices of the communities that have historically prevailed in the U.S. but also in the language that is widely used in the nation's public forum (i.e., English), in the nation's orientation toward social "progress," in the forms of music that have attained prominence historically in the nation's public forum, and in a variety of other cultural dimensions. Since children living in the U.S. must learn to survive in the nation's public forum as it now stands, it would seem appropriate for them to be inculcated into the coherence system historically embodied in the music that has predominated in Western society, in order to support their cognitive development in other areas *as well as* to allow them to share common musical meanings with their fellow students.

This is not merely a matter of "taste," nor is it a suggestion that the coherence system (or systems) manifested in the nation's music is somehow superior to others. It is strictly a practical matter of giving the child skills to engage with a form (or forms) of music that will contribute to her or his successful cognitive development and socialization in the U.S. public forum as it now stands. Since it is not necessarily the case that students will be involved in or receive instruction in a musical practice in their homes, it is incumbent upon the public schools to provide *some* such form of instruction. The logical choice of musical traditions with which to begin such instruction are those that have predominated historically in the nation's public forum.

Some readers, particularly those from nations and cultural and religious communities in which radically different forms of musical practice are undertaken, may protest that this recommendation is inappropriately biased or exclusionary and thus inappropriate for the nation's public schools. However, it is important for those readers to realize that the forms of music that have predominated and presently predominate in the mainstream of U.S. society do not represent a single culturally unique tradition, but instead represent a sort of aural palimpsest, the "audible surface" of which has changed a great deal since the nation's inception and is continuing to evolve. Indeed, a survey of the so-called canon of Western "art music"—as well as the nation's popular musics—reveals their "shamanic" transformations over time, reflecting the perpetually shifting emergence of different worldviews in the public forum throughout history, as different cultural communities have attained greater influence in U.S. society.

In fact, the tradition of European "art music" emerging around the time of the American Revolution has evolved—has been *shamanically* transformed—a great deal over the years of the nation's existence, reflecting the influence of the nation's constituent cultural communities. This is clearly evident in the confluence of European and African musical traditions manifested (differently) in the American jazz of John Coltrane and George Gershwin's *Porgy and Bess*; the influence of European art music, African-rooted jazz, Latin rhythms, and Jewish musical traditions melded together in the symphonies, theatrical shows, and other music of Leonard Bernstein; and the unfolding of Asian cyclical approaches to musical organization within European parameters in the music of Philip Glass, David Conte, and others, to give but a very few examples.

Furthermore, readers concerned that such an approach is inappropriately indoctrinatory might also reflect on the experience of children raised in families who have emigrated from countries in which English is *not* the most widely spoken language; that is, children of families in which a different language is spoken at home. Children who have grown up in homes where a "foreign" language is regularly spoken by the primary caregivers (e.g., the parents or grandparents), while they are simultaneously learning the English language in school and other contexts, typically develop the ability to "anthropologize" (i.e., to identify common aspects of the disparate cultural systems manifested in the two languages in which they are expected to participate). It is something of an axiom that children raised in bilingual surroundings typically manifest greater facility at learning other languages later in life. Indeed, children can be remarkably successful at adapting to more than one coherence system, essentially learning to "play by different rules" in different sociocultural contexts. Since, as we saw in Chapter 3, both languages and musical traditions are isomorphic with a particular cultural coherence system or worldview, children may likewise learn to grasp the meanings of more than one musical tradition early in their lives—one at home and one at school.

This is *not* to say, however, that *many* musical traditions should be introduced into the school music program in the early grades. Indeed, if a teacher were to introduce many different systems (introducing, say, Carnatic music of India, Capoeira music of Brazil, medicine songs of a Navaho tribe, plus still other unique cultural forms) to children in the early elementary grades, the likelihood is that few or none of them would "make sense"—or be *meaningful*, in a pragmatic sense—to the child, and he or she would be unlikely to find them relevant to any of her or his other learning. Something like this is what may, in fact, be occurring in those public-school music programs in which teachers have acquired a superficial familiarity with the music of a number of different traditions and are including them in their teaching, but lack the experiential knowledge to give adequate attention to the cultural origins and thus address the *meanings* of the music they are including in instruction. Thus, focusing *primarily* on the popular, folk, and art music that has historically been present—and continues to be present—in the U.S. while introducing a limited amount of music from cultural traditions not generally heard (or heard very little) in the nation's public forum would be more appropriate, especially if the *other* musics are reflective of the diverse cultural backgrounds of the students in the class and meaningful connections are drawn for the students to grasp how this is so. Featuring music from the diverse cultural heritages of students in class would be particularly advisable, especially in the secondary grades, if the teacher has the necessary background to present each one meaningfully (i.e., with knowledge of its pragmatic efficacy for those who usually engage with it).

The second objective stemming from Curricular Goal #3 entails an expanded approach to music education in the nation's schools that might be best termed *informed performance* of different musical traditions. This approach would involve gradually broadening the content area over the course of a K–12 education to include student involvement in some of the distinctive musical practices undertaken by different communities—particularly those represented in the heritages of the students present in the school—while simultaneously helping students to experience and understand the personal and social import or efficacy of each on its own terms.

Some readers may object that this curricular approach is potentially dangerous, in that by encouraging students to experience and explore the musical traditions of communities different from their own, they may be encouraged to leave their own traditions (i.e., those of their own cultural communities) and adopt the traditions of others. In response, we might note that it is quite possible for teachers and students to maintain their respective cultural orientations while actively undertaking and exploring the musical traditions of others for the purpose of understanding them intellectually and experientially. It is a commonplace of educational practice that students learn best *by being actively engaged*—i.e., by undertaking actual practices—rather than passively listening or observing. In public-school music classes, this would mean that secondary-school students would have an opportunity to undertake different forms of music as "scientists" or "actors"—actively participating without necessarily becoming emotionally committed to the worldview manifested in any one of them. As we noted in the discussion in which we applied Peirce's phenomenology to musical practices, it is quite possible for a student to understand a given music *intellectually* (on the level of Thirdness) and be *physically* involved in the musical practice as a performer (on the level of Secondness), without necessarily committing to it *emotionally* (on the level of Firstness). Certainly, a student's emotional commitment to a particular cultural worldview is the concern of the student, the student's parents, and of their respective cultural communities, and *not* the concern of the public schools. However, as we noted earlier, *fostering understanding* among students of different backgrounds *is* a responsibility of educators in public schools.

Notably, this instructional approach does not negate the worldviews of any communities present in the U.S. (including those of the nation's conservative religious communities), which are often uniquely reflected in their own musical practices. Instead, it acknowledges and affirms the worldview manifested in every form of music as a potentially valid and beneficent "way of knowing," simultaneously providing a means by which students may come to recognize our shared characteristics as human beings as well as our differences.

Once students have gained an understanding of different musical practices as psychosocially equilibrating behaviors for the members of communities, they will also be able to grasp the notion of composers and improvisers as the *shamans* of particular cultural traditions. As U.S. society continues to evolve culturally, technologically, and in myriad other ways, students must be given opportunity and encouraged to undertake musical practices of their own, stemming from their own sociocultural circumstances, and thus effecting their own personal psychosocial equilibration in the cultural contexts in which they live.

Adoption and implementation of these three curricular objectives will result in an informed populace, one that recognizes different musical practices as societally important (and thus values music education), yet observes cultural differences and encourages freedom with respect to worldview, consistent with the First Amendment to the U.S. Constitution.

UNIVERSITY PREPARATION OF PUBLIC-SCHOOL MUSIC TEACHERS

Implementation in the public schools of a pragmatism-based curriculum such as the one just described would require that preparatory programs for teachers in the nation's universities be somewhat modified from their present forms. Before we consider the nature of such modifications, we should have an understanding of the content of music teacher preparation programs at present.

In many universities, the undergraduate degree programs designed to prepare music educators now require five years to complete. Besides the liberal arts core required of bachelor's degree students in all areas of study (generally involving two years of coursework in the sciences, social sciences, and humanities), music education majors typically take classes in applied music (in which they focus on developing mastery in performance on an instrument or voice), music theory (typically including a series of courses in ear-training and sight-singing plus the same for keyboard), music history and musicology (focusing primarily on the history of Western art music), and ensemble participation (usually choir, orchestra, or band). In addition, they complete courses in conducting (vocal or instrumental), an ongoing course in "concert music" (or another noncredit course designed to promote students' attendance at concerts and thus raise their familiarity with different modes of performance), plus "methods" courses (focusing on instructional techniques unique to elementary music classes or secondary choir, orchestra, or band classes)[19] and courses in education (typically including studies in the sociology and psychology of education).

Furthermore, recent years have seen the addition to the music education undergraduate program of an ethnomusicology-based course in "world music" (typically only one such course), the introduction of one or more courses focusing on computer applications in music (or the modification of existing courses to include the use of such technologies), and the expansion of existing courses to deal with issues concerning "special" learners in the schools (i.e., students challenged by various disabilities). At or near the conclusion of this program the student is required to undertake an extended practicum: a period of "student teaching" in a public school under the supervision of a master teacher (typically lasting for one or two terms).

Given this demanding and lengthy program of study, the student majoring in music education usually has *no* time left for elective courses, although the possibility does exist in a number of colleges and universities for the student to participate in some form of non-Western music ensemble; many music education majors elect *not* to do so.

In most universities, the various classes in schools of music are more or less independent of each other, the curriculum having historically drawn its coherence largely from university instructors' shared use of the "canonized" repertoire of Western art music. Several schools, however, have instituted a parallel curriculum in which *jazz* has served as the primary focus, spawning the creation of courses in jazz theory, history, and applied music, plus ensembles (jazz bands and choirs). In many such schools, music education majors may elect to participate in a jazz program once they demonstrate adequate proficiency in the core courses of the Western art music curriculum (though such courses typically represent an addition to their existing program of study). More recently, some university schools of music have introduced ensemble-based courses in Caribbean steel drum, Javanese gamelan, African drumming, and other non-Western areas of performance, though instruction on the music theory and cultural circumstances surrounding these ensembles is often limited, and, as we have just noted, many music education students do not choose to participate in these "other" ensembles.[20]

Owing to the numerous demands on students' time inherent in teacher preparation programs as they stand, university faculty members are understandably reluctant even to consider adding further courses to the curriculum. However, given the tremendous influx of students from a wide variety of different cultural traditions into the U.S. and the continuing difficulty music educators have had in justifying the inclusion of their classes in the public schools (i.e., the issues with which we began this inquiry), some change would certainly seem to be in order. As we have seen, the long-standing societal focus on different varieties of music as forms of *art* has led students in music classes to focus increasingly on preparing performances and recordings as *products*. However, a shift in the emphasis of existing courses to address directly the psychosocial efficacy of music, that is, to illuminate *different musical practices* as dynamic *psychosocially equilibrating behaviors* undertaken by *individuals in communities*, could ultimately serve to demonstrate more clearly the importance of both music and music education to fledgling music educators. Their teaching would be informed by this understanding, and not only would they have a greater sense of their role as agents of psychological health and intercultural understanding in a multicultural society, but they would be able to impart this understanding to their students. (Notably, aside from public television and radio, which maintain a similarly nonpartisan position on the musical practices of different cultural communities, no social agency besides public-school music education is in a position or has the capacity to foster such intercultural understanding with regard to music.)

Specifically, it would seem appropriate to begin this shift by modifying *existing* courses in music history and musicology to adopt a more global approach, one in which semiotic analysis of different musical practices is used to help students understand how they have effected psychosocial equilibration in their respective social contexts, and, perhaps more importantly, how the musical practices of different cultural communities of the present manifest such effects. Once nascent public-school teachers are enabled to grasp (i.e., to *hear* and *experience*) how the musical practices of particular communities reflect their respective worldviews, they will be able to provide such experiences for their students, thus sharing with them a "common set of stories" concerning the heritages of the persons who comprise the nation and revealing to them the importance of the different musical practices undertaken presently and historically in the nation's "soundscape." To support these studies, it would also seem advisable for music-education majors to undertake coursework in the related areas of history, anthropology, sociology, comparative literature, and cultural studies as "background" studies while completing their liberal arts core courses.

At the same time, *ensemble* classes might be regarded as opportunities for exploring experientially the musical practices of different communities manifested in the society surrounding the university as well as those from more distant places.[21] Collaborative inquiry and teaching between music faculty members—musicology instructors, applied music teachers, and ensemble directors—would seem to be an ideal means of addressing both the intellectual and affective dimensions of musical practices manifested in different historical eras and cultural contexts. Other courses might also be redirected in this way, with greater emphasis placed on student composition (or improvisation) as students come to recognize the value and importance of undertaking musical creation as "shamans," and thus work to benefit listeners in their own cultural circumstances.

Finally, we might note that such a pragmatism-based curriculum opens up new research horizons for students undertaking graduate studies in music education. Graduate students might begin to focus more specifically on the psychophysiological, psychosocial, and sociopolitical *effects* of musical practices undertaken in particular cultural contexts. The explication of Peirce's semiotic terminology introduced in Chapter 2 of this inquiry might provide a useful (if provisional) common vocabulary for the undertaking of such interdisciplinary and intercultural studies, as demonstrated in Chapter 3. All of these research areas hold great promise for strengthening the future practice of music education in the egalitarian public schools of the U.S.

CONCLUDING REMARKS

Through involvement in pragmatism-based curricula in music, students will acquire experience and understanding of how the musical practices undertaken in different communities have served historically—and continue to serve—as important means of psychophysiological and psychosocial equilibration in those communities. They will come to engage with these musical practices and understand them *on their own terms*, thereby gaining intercultural knowledge and potentially developing greater interpersonal understanding. Simultaneously, semiotics-informed instruction in music will enable students to become more conscious of—and thus less vulnerable to—manipulation methods of media advertisers and others who use the music of particular communities for economically or politically coercive purposes. Most importantly, students will come to understand the value and importance of undertaking a musical practice of their own—and will be empowered to do so. The ultimate effect of adopting a Peircian pragmatism-based approach to music education is potentially a more musically informed and psychosocially astute citizenry—and, thus, a democratic society made more stable. In addition, this form of music education will enable citizens of the U.S. to recognize more clearly and consistently the personal and societal value of different musical practices and the importance of music study in the nation's public schools.

The recommendations set forth here provide a foundation for the development of curricula in music education that are both culturally inclusive and societally relevant; they resolve many of the present problems of music education curricular content stemming from the nation's ever-evolving cultural diversity, while also affirming the vital importance of music education in the public schools. Still, as with all philosophical viewpoints, the perspective presented here may need to be revised as further relevant information is brought to light. It seems quite probable that other scholars in music education will provide such corrective balance when they read and critique this inquiry.[22]

In any case, we can affirm on the basis of the Peircian pragmatist account presented in this inquiry that if the place of music education is to be strengthened in the public schools of the U.S., it must enable students to recognize the different musical practices undertaken throughout the world as culturally important means of effecting psychosocial equilibration, it must foster understanding between different individuals and communities by helping students to understand the intracultural *effects* of different musical practices on their own terms, and, above all, it must encourage and enable students to undertake a musical practice of their own as a means of effecting their own personal, psychological, and social balance with the ultimate psychophysical Reality of which we are all a part.

Notes

NOTES TO CHAPTER 1

1. Walt Whitman, "Preface 1855—First Edition," in *Leaves of Grass: Comprehensive Readers' Edition*, ed. Harold W. Blodgett and Sculley Bradley (New York: New York University Press, 1965), 709.
2. Robert A. Choate, ed., Documentary Report of *The Tanglewood Symposium: Music in American Society* (Washington, DC: Music Educators National Conference, 1968), Section 1. [The pages of this document are not numbered.]
3. Ibid., Section 2.
4. Some European settlers also brought with them onto the continent Black people from Africa as slaves.
5. U.S. Bureau of the Census, *American FactFinder 2000*, Fact Sheet, http://factfinder.census.gov/servlet/SAFFFacts?_submenuId=factsheet_1&_sse=on (accessed on June 11, 2006). Specifically, the 281,421,906 population count is 75.1 percent White, 12.5 Hispanic or Latino, 12.3 percent Black or African American, 3.7 percent Asian, Native Hawaiian, or Pacific Islander, and 0.9 percent American Indian and Alaska Native.
6. Ibid., 11.
7. See Mircea Eliade, ed., *Encyclopedia of Religion* (New York: Macmillan, 1987), s.v. "Music and Religion," by Ter Ellingson.
8. See Judith and Alton Becker, "A Musical Icon: Power and Meaning in Javanese Gamelan Music," chap. in *The Sign in Music and Literature*, ed. Wendy Stainer (Austin, TX: University of Texas Press, 1981), 203–15.
9. See Alan P. Merriam, *The Anthropology of Music* (Chicago: IL: Northwestern University Press, 1964), 82–83.
10. Personal experience of the author.
11. Bennett Reimer, *A Philosophy of Music Education*, 2nd ed. (Englewood Cliffs, NJ: Prentice Hall, 1989), and *A Philosophy of Music Education: Advancing the Vision*, 3rd ed. (Englewood Cliffs, NJ: Prentice Hall, 2002).
12. David Elliott, *Music Matters: A New Philosophy of Music Education* (Oxford, England: Oxford University Press, 1995).
13. Estelle Jorgenson, founding ed., *Philosophy of Music Education Review* (Bloomington, IN: Indiana University Press, 1990–) and Thomas Regelski, founding ed., *Action, Criticism, and Theory for Music Education* (2002–), accessible online at http://act.maydaygroup.org/.
14. 2008 Year-End Shipment Statistics on U.S. Recorded Music. Recording Industry Association of America, http://www.riaa.com/keystatistics.php (accessed April 21, 2009).

15. The conception of *worldview* to be used in this book will be developed more fully in Chapter 2.
16. See, for example, Jean-François Lyotard, *The Postmodern Condition: A Report on Knowledge*, trans. Geoffrey Bennington and Brian Massumi (Minneapolis: University of Minnesota Press, 1984). [Originally published in France in 1979.]
17. This notion will be explored more fully in Chapter 2.

NOTES TO CHAPTER 2

1. Albert Einstein, quoted in *Island in Space: Prospectus for a New Idea*, ed. Pamela J. Peck (Vancouver, British Columbia: United Nations Association Canada, 1986), 59.
2. Edward B. Tylor, *Primitive Culture*, 5th ed. (London: S. Murray, 1929), 1.
3. Rodney Needham, *Belief, Language, and Experience* (Chicago: University of Chicago Press, 1972), 180.
4. Lucien Lévy-Bruhl, *How Natives Think.*, trans. Lilian A Clave (London: George Allen and Unwin, 1926), 77.
5. Lucien Lévy-Bruhl, *The Notebooks on Primitive Mentality*, trans. Peter Rivière (Oxford, England: Basil Blackwell and Mott, 1975), 101. [Originally published in 1949.]
6. Franz Boas, "The Limitations of the Comparative Method of Anthropology," in *Race, Language and Culture* (New York: The Free Press, 1896), 280.
7. Claude Levi-Strauss, *Structural Anthropology*, trans. Claire Jacobson and Booke Grundfest Schoepf (New York: Basic Books, 1963), 207. [Originally published in 1958.]
8. Specifically, Levi-Strauss concluded that the "meaning" of the Oedipus myth is that "the overrating of blood relations is to the underrating of blood relations as the attempt to escape autochthony is to the impossibility to succeed in it." Claude Levi-Strauss, *Structural Anthropology*, 216.
9. Ward Goodenough, quoted in Clifford Geertz, *The Interpretation of Cultures* (New York: Basic Books, 1973), 11.
10. Clifford Geertz, *The Interpretation of Cultures* (New York: Basic Books, 1973), 18.
11. Ibid., 5.
12. Ibid., 27.
13. Ibid., 30.
14. See Ferdinand de Saussure, *Course in General Linguistics*, ed. C. Balley and A. Sechehaye, in collaboration with A. Riedlinger; trans. Roy Harris (Chicago: Open Court, 1972), 81/117. [Originally published in 1915.]
15. Charles Sanders Peirce, unpublished manuscript (MS949), quoted by Michael L. Raposa, *Peirce's Philosophy of Religion*; Peirce Studies, no. 5; ed. Kenneth Laine Ketner (Bloomington, IN: Indiana University Press, 1989), 41.
16. Peirce grudgingly acknowledged having recognized a possible connection between his philosophical perspectives and those of Buddhist Asia: "I may mention, for the benefit of those who are curious in studying mental biographies, that I was born and raised in the neighbourhood of Concord—I mean in Cambridge—at the time when Emerson, Hedge, and their friends were disseminating the ideas that they had caught from Schelling, and Schelling from Plotinus, from Boehm, or from God knows what minds stricken with the monstrous mysticism of the East. But the atmosphere of Cambridge held many an antiseptic against Concord transcendentalism; and I am not

conscious of having contracted any of that virus. Nevertheless, it is probable that some cultured bacilli, some benignant form of the disease was implanted in my soul, unawares, and that now, after long incubation, it comes to the surface, modified by mathematical conceptions and by training in physical investigations." Peirce, *Collected Papers*, 6.102.

17. Many Christians also believe in the eventual resurrection of the bodies of the faithful. Such beliefs contrast greatly with various Hindu and Buddhist traditions which conceptualize death as an "eclipse of individual awareness in the light of total awareness," followed in some cases by reincarnation as another embodiment of universal spirit. See, for example, Huston Smith, *The Religions of Man*. (New York: Perennial Library of Harper and Row, 1958), 130–31.

18. Vincent Colapietro, *Peirce's Approach to the Self: A Semiotic Perspective on Human Subjectivity* (Albany, New York: State University of New York Press, 1989), 78.

19. Peirce acknowledged similarity of his synechistic conception with that of Hegel's "absolute mind"—with some important reservations. See Peirce, *Collected Papers* 5.436 and 6.305.

20. Peirce, *Collected Papers*, 6:158.

21. Ibid., 6.268.

22. Ibid., 5.400.

23. Ibid., 6.228.

24. Ibid., 5.417.

25. Ibid.

26. Ibid., 5.394.

27. Herbert P. Ginsburg and Sylvia Opper, *Piaget's Theory of Intellectual Development*, 3rd ed. (Englewood Cliffs, NJ: Prentice Hall, 1988), 221–33.

28. Peirce, *Collected Papers*, 5.189.

29. Ibid., 5.181.

30. Ibid., 1.545.

31. Colapietro, *Peirce's Approach to the Self*, 78.

32. Peirce, *Collected Papers*, 1.545.

33. Peirce, unpublished manuscript (MS 498), quoted by Colapietro, *Peirce's Approach to the Self*, 104.

34. Peirce, *Collected Papers*, 5.400.

35. Ibid., 1.343.

36. Ibid., 5:421.

37. The discourses from which these related terms stem are as follows: As we have already noted, *culture* is the central defining term of one branch of anthropology, generally termed cultural anthropology or ethnoanthropology, and as such it has been defined in a variety of related ways by a number of theorists. *Ideology* is a central term from the discipline of political science. A historical study of the usage of the term *ideology* is presented in Terrence N. Tice, "Ideology Old and New: Historical-Analytical Background for Use of the Concept 'Ideology' in Scholarly Discourse, with Systematic Bibliography" (PhD diss., University of Michigan, 1970). *Habitus* is Pierre Bourdieu's Latinization of the word *habit* defined as "the universalizing mediation which causes an individual agent's practices, without either explicit reason or signifying intent, to be nonetheless 'sensible' and 'reasonable.'" Bourdieu introduced and used the term in *Outline of a Theory of Practice*, trans. Richard Nice (Cambridge, England: Cambridge University Press, 1972), 79. *Cosmology* has traditionally been used to designate the metaphysical branch of philosophy, specifically in the discussion of questions concerning the origin, nature, and structure of the universe. *Paradigm* is the

term used by Thomas Kuhn in *The Structure of Scientific Revolutions* (Chicago: University of Chicago Press, 1962) to refer to a model of reality from which springs a particular internally coherent tradition of scientific research. *Tacit dimension*, a term referring to implicitly shared and thus not-discussed aspects of human experience, was introduced by Michael Polanyi in *The Tacit Dimension* (London: Routledge, 1967). *Myth* or *cultural myth* is a concept developed by Claude Levi-Strauss in "The Structural Study of Myth," *Structural Anthropology*, 1963).

38. Peirce, *Collected Papers*, 6.3.
39. Ibid., 5.384.
40. Ibid., 5.387.
41. Ibid., 5.408–9. (Regrettably, Peirce was not always consistent in using capital and small letters to aid the reader in grasping his distinction between reality—as a partial, relative human conception of Reality—and true Reality—the way things actually are.)
42. Ibid., 5.401.
43. Ibid., 5.402.
44. Peirce, "Review of William James *Principles of Psychology*," *Nation* 53 (1891), 32, in Justus Buchler, *The Philosophy of Peirce: Selected Writings* (New York: Harcourt, Brace and Co., 1940), 305.
45. Peirce, *Collected Papers*, 1.171.
46. Ibid., 1.55.
47. Peirce's term for what philosophers commonly call phenomenology was *phaneroscopy*, and his full definition is as follows: "Phaneroscopy is the description of the *phaneron*; and by the *phaneron* I mean the collective total of all that is in any way or in any sense present to the mind, quite regardless of whether it corresponds to any real thing or not." Peirce, *Collected Papers*, 1.284.
48. Ibid., 1.378.
49. Michael Shapiro, *The Sense of Grammar: Language as Semiotic* (Bloomington, IN: Indiana University Press, 1983), 28–32.
50. Peirce used the word *sign* to designate the sign relationship—that is, the complete triad of *Sign, Object, and Interpretant* and to refer to a single sensory perception as a constituent part of the triadic sign relationship. He also occasionally used the term *Representamen* in place of the word *Sign* in this latter sense, perhaps to help prevent confusion on the part of the reader. Regrettably, he was not consistent in this usage.
51. Peirce, *Collected Papers*, 6.522.
52. Ibid., 5.395.
53. See Ferdinand de Saussure, *Course in General Linguistics* (New York: McGraw-Hill, 1959), and Claude Levi-Strauss, "The Scope of Anthropology," *Current Anthropology* 7 (1966): 112–23.
54. Paul Ricoeur, *The Philosophy of Paul Ricoeur*, edited by C.E. Reagan and D. Stewart (Boston: Beacon Press, 1978), 110.
55. Peirce, *Collected Papers*, 2.353
56. Peirce, *Collected Papers*, 1.355.
57. Peirce's tenfold classification of signs includes the following: a Qualisign, an Iconic Sinsign, a Rhematic Indexical Sinsign, a Dicent Sinsign, an Iconic Legisign, a Rhematic Indexical Legisign, a Dicent Indexical Legisign, a Rhematic Symbol or Symbolic Rheme, a Dicent Symbol or ordinary Proposition, and an Argument. For further explanation of these sign classes, see Peirce, *Collected Papers*, 2.254–64.
58. Ibid., 2.247.
59. Ibid., 2.248.

60. E. Valentine Daniel, *Fluid Signs* (Berkeley, CA: University of California Press, 1984), 39–40.
61. Ibid., 5.484.
62. Peirce would regard the concept to which the word is given as a Legisign.
63. The subdivision of Immediate Interpretants was described only tentatively by Peirce, and thus will not be addressed further here. The Dynamic Interpretant is described in the main body of the preceding text. The Final Interpretant he divided into the Gratific—the standard or norm by which qualities are evaluated; the Practical—which directs conduct and is thus ethical; or the Pragmatistic—which produces "self-control." The Final Interpretant is also further divided into a Rheme—a quality which might be embodied in a possibly existing object; a Dicent—which proposes some information about an existent; or an Argument—which is interpreted by its Final Interpretant as a law, rule, or principle. For further information see Peirce, *Collected Papers*, 5.475–89.
64. Note that all of this takes place on the level of Thirdness. At the level of Secondness, the actual physical body of the individual does not substantially change. (For example, the physical attributes of a person of Caucasian American or Northern European descent would not change to match that of a Black African person, despite the fact that cultural unity between two such persons exists as a possibility.)
65. Colapietro, *Peirce's Approach to the Self*, 104.

NOTES TO CHAPTER 3

1. Ronald W. Clark, *Einstein: The Life and Times* (New York: World Publishing Co., 1971), 243.
2. Scholars' differing interests in conceptualizing music formally (structurally) or in terms of how it is used (socially) are particularly apparent in their accounts.
3. Guido Adler, *Umfang, Methode und Ziel der Musikwissenshaft* (1885), quoted in Alan Merriam, "Definitions of 'Comparative Musicology' and 'Ethnomusicology': An Historical-Theoretical Perspective," *Ethnomusicology* 21 (May, 1977), 199.
4. Alexander J. Ellis, "On the Musical Scales of Various Nations," *Journal of the Society of Arts* 33 (1885), 485–527.
5. S. F. Nadel, "The Origins of Music," in *Readings in Ethnomusicology*, ed. David McAllester (New York: Johnson Reprint Corporation, 1971), 279.
6. Ernest Newman, "Herbert Spencer and the Origin of Music," chap. in *Musical Studies* (London: Ballantyne, Hanson, & Co., 1905), 212.
7. Nadel, "Origins of Music," 281–82.
8. Erich Moritz von Hornbostel, "Lecture before the Local Branch of the International Musical Society in Vienna, March 24, 1905," in *Hornbostel Opera Omnia*, vol. 1, ed. Klaus P. Wachsmann, Dieter Christiensen, and Hans-Peter Reinecke (The Hague: Martinus Nijhoff, 1975), 270.
9. Curt Sachs, *The Wellsprings of Music*, ed. by Jaap Kunst (The Hague: Martinus Nijhoff, 1962), 15.
10. Alan Merriam, "Definitions of 'Comparative Musicology' and 'Ethnomusicology': An Historical-Theoretical Perspective," *Ethnomusicology* 21 (May, 1977), 197.
11. Charles Seeger, *Studies in Musicology 1935–1975* (Berkeley, CA: University of California Press, 1977), 115–17.
12. Mantle Hood, *The Ethnomusicologist*, 2d ed. (Kent, Ohio: Kent State University Press, 1982), 343–46. [Originally published in 1971.]

13. Alan Merriam, *The Anthropology of Music* (Chicago: Northwestern University Press, 1964), 53.

14. Steven Feld, *Sound and Sentiment: Birds, Weeping, Poetics and Song in Kaluli Expression* (Philadelphia: University of Pennsylvania Press, 1982), 3.

15. Feld, *Sound and Sentiment*, 45.

16. Christopher Small has suggested that the verb "musicking" should be used in place of the noun "music" to place emphasis on the activity rather than the resulting product. See Christopher Small, *Musicking: The Meanings of Performing and Listening*. (Hanover, New Hampshire: Wesleyan University Press, 1998), 1–18.

17. Use of the term "musical practice" in this inquiry is consistent with sociomusicologist Kurt Blaukopf's usage. Blaukopf wrote: "[T]he word *practice* should not be taken in the narrow sense of referring only to 'what is actually heard.' It should be extended to include all musical acts and omissions, as well as observable behavior patterns." See Kurt Blaukopf, *Musical Life in a Changing Society: Aspects of Music Sociology*, trans. David Marinelli (Portland, OR: Amadeus Press, 1992), 5. [Originally published in German in 1982.]

18. See, for example, Steven Feld, "Linguistics and Ethnomusicology," *Ethnomusicology* 18 (1974), 197 on music and language; R. Keeling, ed., *Women in North American Indian Music: Six Essays* (Bloomington, IN: Indiana University Press, 1989) on music and gender; and Bruno Nettl, *The Western Impact on World Music: Change, Adaptation, and Survival* (New York: Schirmer Books, 1985) on the influence of Western musical practices on various cultural communities.

19. Bruno Nettl, "Recent Directions in Ethnomusicology," in *Ethnomusicology: An Introduction*, ed. Helen Myers (London: Macmillan Press, 1992), 392–93.

20. John Blacking has clarified this point, explaining that while the possibility exists that a species-specific "musical intelligence" exists, it cannot be defined in strictly acoustical terms. In some measure, this notion will be more fully developed in the latter half of this chapter. See John Blacking, "The Biology of Music-Making," in *Ethnomusicology: An Introduction*, ed. Helen Meyers (London: Macmillan Press, 1992), 310–11.

21. Peirce, *Collected Papers*, 5.384.

22. Ibid., 5.402.

23. David P. McAllester , "Some Thoughts on 'Universals' in World Music," *Ethnomusicology* 15 (September, 1971), 379–80.

24. Klaus P. Wachsmann, "Universal Perspectives in Music," *Ethnomusicology* 15 (September, 1971), 383.

25. George List, "On the Non-Universality of Music Perspectives," *Ethnomusicology* 15 (September, 1971), 402.

26. However, it must be noted that while all of the persons comprising a given cultural community who collectively participate in musical practices may typically conceptualize these activities in *generally* the same way, it is unlikely that they will conceptualize them in *exactly* the same way. To some degree, the conceptions held by members of a given cultural community will inevitably be *somewhat* different, as they are all unique individuals with *somewhat* dissimilar backgrounds. Thus, we might say more precisely that the conceptions of musical practices held by the members of a given cultural community all generally *overlap* one another in meaning, while the conceptions of that same "musical practice" held by persons of other cultural communities are likely to be dissimilar.

27. Nevertheless, it is important to note that a particular musical practice that originated in one cultural community may be adopted by the members of

another community who find it to be meaningful in a sense different from its original meanings. Witness the growth of Javanese gamelan ensembles and Caribbean steel drum bands in U.S. communities in which the individuals participating in them have little or no interest in the social meanings the gamelan or steel drum had or has to those with whom it originated, but may simply share in common an enjoyment of the *qualities* of the sounds produced by the instruments, an interest in making music with them, and a desire for the camaraderie of others who also enjoy them. Such groups typically develop *their own* collectively shared meanings, which changes the nature of the gamelan or steel drum ensembles as musical practices.

28. See, for example, Bruno Nettl, "On the Question of Musical Universals," *The World of Music* 19 (1977), 5.
29. Judith Becker, "Aesthetics in Late 20th Century Scholarship," *The World of Music* 26 (1983), 74–75.
30. Gilbert Rouget, *Music and Trance: A Theory of the Relations between Music and Possession*, trans. Brunhile Biebuyck in collaboration with the author (Chicago: University of Chicago Press, 1985), 205.
31. Jalal ad-Din Rumi, *Fihi ma fihi*, cited and trans. by William C. Chittick in *The Sufi Path of Love: The Spiritual Teachings of Rumi* (Albany, New York: State University of New York Press, 1983), 25.
32. Toshihiko Izutsu and Toyo Izutsu, *The Theory of Beauty in the Classical Aesthetics of Japan* (The Hague: Martinus Nijhoff, 1981), 26–34.
33. Kenneth J. DeWoskin. *A Song for One or Two: Music and the Concept of Art in Early China* (Ann Arbor, Michigan: Center for Chinese Studies, University of Michigan, 1982), 31–39.
34. See the Holy Bible. Study of the Old Testament reveals that musical activity permeated the lives of the early Hebrews to the point that its cessation came to signify misery or desolation for them. (See especially Jeremiah 25:10 and Ezekiel. 26:13.) The texts of the Psalms, the sacred songs of the Holy Bible, have been set to music perhaps more than any other set of texts, and they have been used almost continuously in both Jewish and Christian worship. In the New Testament, worship and music are continually associated, and musical practices are sometimes regarded as prayer. (See especially First Corinthians 14:15, Ephesians 5:19, and Colossians 3:16.) Note that the statement above is not meant to imply that *all* Jewish and Christian groups involve musical practices in their worship; not all such groups do.
35. Personal experience of the writer in visiting a Pentecostal worship service.
36. Peirce, *Collected Papers*, 5.189.
37. For example, philosopher Susanne Langer explored the relationship between "music" and ritual in her writings, and her views subsequently influenced music education scholar Bennett Reimer in his development of a philosophy of music education for the U.S. We will see the influence of Langer on Reimer's music education philosophy in Chapter 5.
38. Eugene G. d'Aquili and Charles D. Laughlin, Jr., "The Neurobiology of Myth and Ritual," in *The Spectrum of Ritual: A Biogenetic Structural Analysis*, ed. Eugene G. d'Aquili, Charles D. Laughlin, Jr., and John McManus (New York: Columbia University Press, 1979), 156.
39. Ibid.
40. In a separate article, d'Aquili cites various studies done on the effects of repetitive or rhythmic emanation of signals among various animal behaviors that generate a high degree of arousal of the limbic system of the brain. See Eugene d'Aquili, "Human Ceremonial Ritual and the Modulation of Aggression," *Zygon* 20 (March, 1985), 22.
41. d'Aquili and Laughlin, "Neurobiology of Myth and Ritual," 162.

42. Ibid., 159.
43. Ibid., 170.
44. Ibid.
45. Barbara Lex, "The Neurobiology of Ritual Trance," in *The Spectrum of Ritual: A Biogenetic Structural Analysis*, ed. Eugene G. d'Aquili, Charles D. Laughlin, Jr., and John McManus (New York: Columbia University Press, 1979), 117.
46. Lex based her model of neural functioning on a model originated in the theoretical works of W. R. Hess, which emphasizes the interconnectedness and inseparability of various components of the nervous system more than some more recent models of brain operation. See Walter R. Hess, *On the Relations between Psychic and Vegetative Functions* (Zurich, Switzerland: G. Thieme, 1925).
47. Theories of the past that have attributed certain kinds of thinking (e.g., musical) to *particular* cerebral hemispheres of the human brain (as in "left brain/right brain" theory) have been shown to be something of an oversimplification, partly due to the great variability in brain activity during the same activities among individuals of different cultural communities. However, individuals representing a particular cultural community do tend to exhibit relatively homogeneous patterns of hemispheric dominance in response to the same stimuli. We will return to this notion later in this chapter. See Tadanobu Tsunoda, *The Japanese Brain: Uniqueness and Universality*, trans. Yoshinori Oiwa (Tokyo: Taishukan Publishng Co., 1985).
48. In a separate article, d'Aquili has presented a compelling argument that one of the principal, concomitant effects of human rituals is the decreasing or eliminating of intragroup aggression. See d'Aquili, "Human Ceremonial Ritual and the Modulation of Aggression," 21–30.
49. Lex, "The Neurobiology of Ritual Trance," 144.
50. Gilbert Rouget, *Music and Trance: A Theory of the Relations between Music and Possession*, trans. Brunhilde Biebuyck in collaboration with the author (Chicago: University of Chicago Press, 1985), 45.
51. Rouget also identifies and discusses various other "methods" used by different cultural communities for extricating an individual from these "demons." Discussion of these forms has been omitted here for purposes of brevity and clarity. See Ibid., 133–66.
52. Ibid., 65.
53. Rouget acknowledges and consistently returns to the conceptual difference in terminology concerning music throughout his chapter on "Music and Trance among the Greeks." It is important to note that the behaviors we have termed musical practices in this inquiry are not given the name *music* by Plato in his writings. Rouget carefully identifies each instance when Plato is actually discussing dance or another "thing of the Muses." However, Rouget himself gives centrality to the sound of music as the "trigger" of trance. For his most important clarifying statements, see Rouget, *Music and Trance*, 202 and 206–7.
54. Ibid., 201–2.
55. Ibid., 203–4.
56. Ibid., 193–201.
57. Ibid., 205.
58. Ibid., 206.
59. Felicitas Goodman has made just such an argument for the historical interrelationship of gesture and speech in religious ritual, describing the interrelationship of the two in ritual as our "genetic endowment." See Felicitas D. Goodman, *Ecstasy, Ritual, and Alternate Reality: Religion in a Pluralistic World* (Bloomington, IN: Indiana University Press, 1982), 10–16.

60. Ibid., 132.
61. Ibid., 129.
62. Claude Levi-Strauss, quoted by Rouget, *Music and Trance*, 131.
63. Jacques Attali, *Noise: The Political Economy of Music*, trans. Brian Massumi (Minneapolis: University of Minnesota Press, 1985), 11.
64. Ibid., 10.
65. Hugh Tracey, *Chopi Musicians*, 2nd ed. (London: Oxford University Press for the International African Institute, 1970).
66. Christopher Small, *Music—Society—Education: A Radical Examination of the Prophetic Function of Music in Eastern, Western, and African Cultures with Its Impact on Society and Its Use in Education*, 2nd ed. (London: John Calder, 1980), 56.
67. Hugh Tracey, quoted by Christopher Small, ibid.
68. These categories may indeed be applicable to the musical movements of communities within culturally pluralistic, state societies as well. While many examples could be cited from popular culture in the U.S., certainly the apparently eternal value some individuals find in the operettas of Gilbert and Sullivan and the more recently, societally subversive power of the hip hop rap of Eminem suggest that they could be considered as distinct examples of possession and shamanic rituals, respectively.
69. This too may describe musical movements in culturally pluralistic, state societies—especially large-scale mass movements. Certainly the young Elvis Presley and the Beatles can be said to have had magical, shamanic effects upon those who were captivated by the "new worlds" they respectively pre-ordained for U.S. popular culture. By contrast, it would seem that the impassioned performances of today's Elvis impersonators might be best regarded as manifesting their possession by the spirit of the deceased "King." Similarly, since their first cataclysmic appearance, much of the Beatles' music and thought has been assimilated into the "collective mind" of European and American popular culture and is now performed by "possessed" others.
70. The qualities we are identifying in different musical practices as being "of the nature of possession" or "of shamanism" have been recognized in works of art by others. Philosopher Friedrich Nietzsche, for instance, drew a similar, but not identical, distinction between the calm, conformational rationality of Apollo and the transformative passion of Dionysus manifested in works of art in *The Birth of Tragedy*, his 1872 treatise on Greek tragedy. See Friedrich Nietzsche, *The Birth of Tragedy*, trans. Francis Golffing (New York: Anchor Press/Doubleday, 1956). [Originally published in 1872.]
71. Victor Turner, *From Ritual to Theatre: The Human Seriousness of Play* (New York: Performing Arts Journal Publications, 1982), 10.
72. Victor Turner, *The Ritual Process: Structure and Anti-Structure* (Chicago: Aldine Publishing Co., 1969), 94.
73. Ibid., 96.
74. Ibid.
75. Ibid., 127.
76. Ibid., 128.
77. Ibid., 112.
78. However, while this *effect* might be described as "psychophysiological" by a pragmatist, it will, when consciously acknowledged, be invariably described by an individual in vocabulary unique to her or his own cultural community.
79. Of course, the possibility also exists that those who are dominant in the existing society may effectively silence those in whom the new "vision" is emerging, but in many such situations the very effort to stifle the new vision is enough to ensure its eventual emergence.

80. John Blacking, *How Musical Is Man?* (London: Faber & Faber, 1976), 101.
81. Roy Rappaport, "The Obvious Aspects of Ritual," chap. in *Ecology, Meaning, Religion* (Berkeley, CA: North Atlantic Books, 1979), 178.
82. Peirce, *Collected Papers*, 5.421. Since Peirce acknowledges here and elsewhere that not *all* human thought is of the nature of language, we must recognize that his use of the word *saying* in this instance was something of a concession to the limitations of the English language in describing mentation.
83. In his words: "The feeling of believing is a more or less sure indication of there being established in our nature some habit which will determine our actions." Peirce, *Collected Papers*, 5.371.
84. See, for example, Simon Frith, "Towards an Aesthetic of Popular Music," in *Music and Society: The Politics of Composition, Performance, and Reception*, ed. Richard Leppert and Susan McClary (Cambridge, England: Cambridge University Press, 1987), 133–49, and Daniel Cavicchi, *Tramps Like Us: Music and Meaning among Springsteen Fans* (New York: Oxford University Press, 1998).
85. Victor Turner, *From Ritual to Theatre: The Human Seriousness of Play* (New York: Performing Arts Journal Publications, 1982), 13.
86. William Morgan and Per Brask, "Towards a Conceptual Understanding of the Transformation from Ritual to Theatre," *Anthropologica* 30 (1988), 197.
87. Henry Raynor has mentioned that during the emergence of opera (which, incidentally, followed the Protestant Reformation and Counter-Reformation), "the Renaissance men of culture" responsible for opera's early development predicated the form of this new musical practice on their belief that Greek theatre had included a considerable amount of music; he also cites historical evidence to support their belief. Thus, it can be asserted that a new musical practice did indeed accompany theatre as it was developed during the gradual emergence of statehood in both early Greece and in the Italian renaissance. See Henry Raynor, "The Beginnings of Opera," chap. in *A Social History of Music* (New York: Schocken Books, 1972), 156.
88. A given form of music typically manifests the worldview of only one cultural community because it can only "make sense" or be fully coherent if it somehow iconically manifests the community members' shared coherence system. This point will be explored in greater detail in the last section of this chapter.
89. Remarkably, in contemporary pluralistic societies, a particular music is sometimes adopted by a listener or community of listeners as "theirs," rather than emerging more directly from an existing need within a preexisting community. Nevertheless, the effect is the same: Validation of worldview via participation in the musical practice.
90. Henry Raynor, *A Social History of Music* (New York: Schocken Books, 1972), 133.
91. John Kifner, "Khomeini Bans Broadcast Music, Saying It Corrupts Iranian Youth," *New York Times*, July 24, 1979, sec. A, pp. 1, 6.
92. Andrei Zhdanov, "Statute of the Union of Soviet Writers (1934)," quoted by Monroe Beardsley in *Aesthetics from Classical Greece to the Present* (Tuscaloosa, AL: University of Alabama Press, 1966), 360.
93. Adolf Hitler, "Aims and Tasks of the New Government (Speech of March 23, 1933)," *The Speeches of Adolph Hitler*, ed. and trans. Norman H. Baynes (New York: Howard Fertig, 1969), 568.
94. Peirce, *Collected Papers*, 1.284.
95. E. Valentine Daniel, *Fluid Signs* (Berkeley, CA: University California Press, 1984), 39–40.

96. Peirce, *Collected Papers*, 2.247.
97. Judith and Alton Becker, "A Musical Icon: Power and Meaning in Javanese Gamelan Music," in *The Sign in Music and Literature*, ed. Wendy Stainer (Austin, TX: University of Texas Press, 1981), 206.
98. Ibid.
99. Ibid, 209.
100. Ibid., 208.
101. Ibid., 210.
102. Christopher Small, "Performance as Ritual: Sketch for an Enquiry into the True Nature of a Symphony Concert." In *Lost in Music: Culture, Style and the Musical Event* (London: Routledge & Kegan Paul, 1987), 19.
103. Ibid., 16.
104. Ibid., 17.
105. Holy Bible, Psalms 62:12.
106. Ibid., Romans 5:1–5.
107. Small, "Performance as Ritual," 17–18.
108. Peirce, *Collected Papers*, 2.248.
109. See Holy Bible, Joshua 6:4–20.
110. Feld, *Sound and Sentiment*, 171–74.
111. Notably, the recent development of electronic synthesizers has all but completely obliterated the indexical connection between the instrumental *timbres* of "music" with the indexically grounded worldview of the people who originally produced it for listeners in European and U.S. popular culture.
112. Jon Parales, "On Rap, Symbolism and Fear," *New York Times*, February 2, 1992, sec. 2, p. 1.
113. It also must be noted, however, that Tsunoda's investigations have suggested that the patterns of brain function that he has identified as being uniquely Japanese are shaped largely or entirely by the Japanese language. The question of which came first (i.e., the patterns of Japanese brain function, the Japanese language, or even Japanese music) may be as irresolvable as the proverbial "chicken and egg" conundrum. For further details on the research of both Kikuchi and Tsunoda, see Tadanobu Tsunoda, *The Japanese Brain: Uniqueness and Universality*, trans. Yoshinori Oiwa (Tokyo: Taishukan Publishing Co., 1985), iii–vii and 111.
114. Peirce, *Collected Papers*, 2.249.
115. We should note, however, that some Native American tribes do assign names to members on the basis of iconicity between the symbolic meaning of the words and a particularly unique and outstanding characteristic of the person (e.g., "Black Elk" and "Running Bear"). Peirce would regard such names as dicent symbols. See Peirce, *Collected Papers*, 2.262.
116. For example, Feld has noted that the sound preferences evident in the practices of the Kaluli involve a great deal of interlocking, overlapping, and alternation. The Kaluli metaphor for this variable layering of sound is *dulugu ganalan*, which Feld translates as "liftupoversound," and it stems from the natural and variable dynamic layering they perceive in the sounds of birds, insects, waterfalls, and other entities heard in the rainforest where they live. As certain sounds and patterns of sounds become louder than others, they can be said to "lift up over" the other sounds. In Feld's words, "In the forest, sounds constantly shift figure and ground; examples of continually staggered alternations and overlaps, at times sounding completely interlocked and seamless, are abundant. For the Kaluli this is the naturally coherent organizing model for soundmaking, whether human, animal, or environmental: a constant textural densification constructed from "liftupoversounds." See

Steven Feld, "Sound Structure as Social Structure," *Ethnomusicology* 28 (September, 1984), 392.

117. One student visiting the U.S. from India, upon hearing a Beethoven symphony for the first time, was heard to exclaim, "Good *raga*s!" (personal anecdote shared by an associate of the writer). Readers not familiar with the terminology of Indian classical "music" should know that the word *raga* translates roughly into English as a "mode" or series of notes associated with a particular emotion or mood, and used as a basis for improvisation. The student's comment reveals that he was responding favorably to Beethoven's music on the basis of criteria rooted in his own worldview.

118. Igor Stravinsky, quoted by Boris Mikhailovich Yarustovsky, foreword to *Rite of Spring: Full Score*, by Igor Stravinsky (New York: Dover Publications, 1989), viii.

119. Igor Stravinsky, *Conversations*, quoted in Truman Campbell Bullard, "The First Performance of Igor Stravinsky's Rite of Spring" (PhD diss., Eastman School of Music of the University of Rochester, 1971), 156.

120. See, for example, Jann Pasler, "*Pelleas* and Power: Forces Behind the Reception of Debussy's Opera," *19th-Century Music* 10 (Spring 1987), 244–64.

121. See Clyde Haberman, "Old Agonies Revive: Israeli Philharmonic to Perform Wagner," *New York Times*, December 16, 1991, p. A1.

———. "Barenboim Defends Decision but Passions on Wagner Are High," *New York Times*, December 17, 1991, p. C15.

———. "Israel Philharmonic Puts Off Wagner Concert," *New York Times*, December 23, 1991, pp. C11–12.

122. Despite the prevalence of this practice, some debate continues about its effectiveness. See, for example, M. P. Gardner, "Mood States and Consumer Behavior: A Critical Review," *Journal of Consumer Behavior* 12 (1985), 281–97, or John J. Wheatley and George Brooker, "Music and Spokesperson Effects on Recall and Cognitive Response to a Radio Advertisement," in *Attention, Affect, and Attitude in Response to Advertising*, ed. Eddie M. Clark, Timothy C. Brock, and David W. Stewart (Hillsdale, NJ: Lawrence Erlbaum Associates, 1994), 189–204.

123. See "Marines Blast Heavy Metal at Iraqi Troops," *Atlanta Constitution*, February 21, 1991, p. A6.

124. Edna Gundersen, "Rock's Roar Soars over Gulf war," *USA Today*, January 28, 1991, p. D2.

NOTES TO CHAPTER 4

1. John Philpot Curran, "Speech on the Right of Election of Lord Mayor of the City of Dublin" (1790) in *The Speeches of the Celebrated Irish Orators Phillips, Curran, and Grattan*, ed. Charles Phillips (Boston: Patrick Donahoe, 1857), 192.

2. While democracy may have had its origins in ancient Greece, the religious, scientific, social, and economic circumstances of its establishment in Athens as well as the actual political system itself differed substantially from the democratic form of government instituted in the U.S. during the eighteenth century. The Athenians themselves eventually abandoned their version of democracy for other forms of government.

3. It must also be noted that while the U.S. may have been the first to adopt democracy, scientific progress, and capitalist economics as defining principles, other nations that have since adopted some or all of them have arguably sustained them more effectively and beneficently than the U.S. has done.

4. Jean-Jacques Rousseau, *The Social Contract* and *Discourse on the Origin of Inequality*, ed. Lester G. Crocker (New York: Washington Square Press, 1967), 22. [Originally published in 1762.]

5. This statement is not meant to suggest that some secular or nonofficially sanctioned musical practices (e.g., folk traditions and other secular forms) were not also being undertaken separate from the central rituals of the church. However, in our Peircian pragmatic perspective such musical practices are not considered historically important unless they connote a worldview significantly different from that manifested in that society's central rituals. While some of the musical practices that took place outside of the church served to satirize or comment on it, most such activity did not represent a substantive political difference from that generally held in the existing social order. During an eleven-year period in England (beginning in 1642), when Puritan hostility was directed expressly toward church music, many church organs were moved to inns and taverns where they were used for entertainment, thus sustaining the extant English musical traditions in secular contexts. See Henry Raynor, *A Social History of Music* (New York: Schocken Books, 1972), 243.

6. Ibid., 169.

7. Cited by Henry Raynor, *A Social History of Music*, 284–85. Regarding Handel's awareness that the presentation of a secular oratorio such as *Messiah* would shock and be deemed inappropriate by London society, see also Paul Henry Lang, *George Frideric Handel* (W. W. Norton & Co., 1966), 334–35.

8. Reebee Garofalo, "Understanding Mega-Events: If We Are the World, Then How Do We Change It?" In *Rockin' the Boat: Mass Music and Mass Movements*, edited by Reebee Garofalo (Boston: South End Press, 1992), 21.

9. Augustine also saw music in worship as well suited for "weaker minds," to make them more receptive to the teachings of the church. See Augustine, "From *De Musica*" in *Contemplating Music: Source Readings in the Aesthetics of Music*, vol. 2, ed. Ruth Katz and Carl Dahlhaus (Stuyvesant, NY: Pendragon Press, 1987), 10–33.

10. Marsilio Ficino, "From *Opera Omnia*" (1476) in ibid., vol. 1, 91.

11. Johannes Kepler, "From *Harmonia Mundi*," in *Contemplating Music*, vol. 1, ed. Katz and Dahlhaus (Stuyvesant, NY: Pendragon Press, 1987), 127. Kepler was not the first to claim a correspondence between planetary movements and music, as the doctrine of ethos held in ancient Greece also associated music with planetary motion.

12. Ibid., 129.

13. See, for example, Carl Dahlhaus, *Esthetics of Music*, trans. William W. Austin (Cambridge, England: Cambridge University Press, 1982) [originally published in German in 1962] and Terry Eagleton, *The Ideology of the Aesthetic* (Oxford, England: Basil Blackwell, 1990).

14. David Hume, "Of the Standard of Taste," in *Art and Philosophy: Readings in Aesthetics*, ed. W. E. Kennick (New York: St. Martin's Press, 1979), 488. [Originally published in 1777.]

15. Ibid., 488.

16. Ibid., 497.

17. We can see that Kant's views in this area are similar to those of Peirce, who in fact was influenced greatly by Kant's philosophy.

18. Immanuel Kant, *Critique of Judgement*, trans. J. H. Bernard, 2d ed. (London: Macmillan, 1914), 64. [Originally published in 1790.]

19. About Kant's resolute adherence to notions of universality (implicit in most religious worldviews), historian Carl Dahlhaus has noted, "Esthetics, even

for the cautious Kant, is tinged with Utopia." See Carl Dahlhaus, *Esthetics of Music*, 9.

20. From the standpoint of many scholars of music history today, this claim seems particularly outrageous, since such historical luminaries of music as Mozart and Beethoven were Hegel's contemporaries.

21. Furthermore, musical practices are more inherently communal than the other "arts" included in Hegel's classification, in that they often involve physical participation. A contemporary *Aesthetik* much closer to our Peircian pragmatic view in all these respects is that of the other philosopher in the University at Berlin, the esteemed theologian Friedrich Schleiermacher (1768–1834). [Personal communication with Schleiermacher scholar and translator Terrence N. Tice.]

22. In fact, we might point out that Kant's and Hegel's viewpoints coincide roughly with the "ethnocentric" and "universalist" perspectives we explored in Chapter 3. We should also note that the "relativist" perspective was not really a possibility for Enlightenment philosophers, as they were operating at that time on the largely tacit assumption that European society represented the peak of cultural development, and they saw it as their task to create a grand, universal "philosophy of everything."

23. In Peirce's terms, this describes the distinction between two possible relationships to the same "musical event" (as a sign). A person who experiences a given musical practice (i.e., the human behavior) as validating and confirming her or his own conception of Reality or worldview would feel it to be a Thirdness, Secondness, and Firstness of Thirdness, while one who regards a given instance of music (i.e., a sound artifact) only as an *object* (i.e., with relative detachment) would be experiencing it on the level of Secondness.

24. Definition from the *New Grove Dictionary of Music and Musicians*. See Stanley Sadie, ed., *New Grove Dictionary of Music and Musicians*, vol. 1 (London: Macmillan Publishers, 1980), 646.

25. The concept of "art music," or a notion akin to it, has emerged in other parts of the world as well, including India and China, and, to this day, the practice of composing "art music" continues to be taken up in disparate nations influenced by European traditions. For example, musicologist Olabode Omojola has reported that the conceptions of music as an integral part of a social or ritual event predominated in Nigeria prior to the arrival of European missionaries in the middle of the nineteenth century, when Nigerian art music first began to emerge. Notably, the composition of Nigerian "art music," which manifests the fusion of elements of traditional Nigerian music with European traditions, has been undertaken mostly by native Nigerians. See Olabode F. Omojola, "Contemporary Art Music in Nigeria: An Introductory Note on the Works of Ayo Bankole," *Africa* 64 (Fall, 1994): 533–43.

26. Johann Wolfgang von Goethe, "Über Wahrheit und Wahrscheinlichkeit" ["On Truth and Probability in Works of Art"] (1798), *Goethe's Literary Essays*, ed. and trans. J. E. Spingarn (New York: Harcourt, 1921), 54.

27. Ernst Theodor Amadeus Hoffmann, "Beethoven's Instrumental Music" (1813) in Oliver Strunk, ed., *Source Readings in Music History* (New York: W. W. Norton, 1950), 775.

28. Wilhelm Heinrich Wackenroder, "Phantasien über die Kunst" ["Musings on Art"] (1799), quoted by Oskar Walzel in *German Romanticism*, trans. A. E. Lussky (New York: G. P. Putnam's Sons, 1932), 122–23.

29. Johann Wolfgang von Goethe, "April 18, 1827," *Conversations with Eckermann*, trans. John Oxenford (San Francisco: North Point Press, 1984), 159. [Originally published in 1850.]

30. Arthur Schopenhauer, *The World as Will and Idea*, vol. 1 (London: Routledge & Kegan Paul, 1950), 239. [Originally published in 1883.]
31. Ibid., 1:335.
32. Ibid., 1:336.
33. Note that these philosophers may not have been responsible for consigning music and art to the periphery of society, but rather may have been accounting in their writings for their relative societal diminishment at the time.
34. Carl Dahlhaus, *Esthetics of Music*, vii.
35. Terry Eagleton, *The Ideology of the Aesthetic* (Oxford, England: Basil Blackwell, 1990), 8–9.
36. Ibid., 368.
37. Charles Burney, *A General History of Music* (New York: Harcourt, Brace, & Co., 1935), 21. [Originally published in 1789.]
38. For example, the New England Separatists and Puritans came to North America to escape persecution by the Church of England in the early seventeenth century, only to establish the Massachusetts Bay Colony as a theocracy of their own; they made attendance at their churches mandatory for all members of the community, and they required church membership for all who wished to vote or hold office. The Congregationalist religion of this community was later established in Connecticut and New Hampshire as well. In 1625, Dutch settlers founded the middle Atlantic colony of New Netherland on the faith of their Reformed church, though the area was later seized by the British, who enforced conformity with the Church of England there. Pennsylvania, New York, and Delaware established Lutheranism, the middle Atlantic region included communities of Presbyterians and Methodists, and Maryland was originally settled by a family of English Roman Catholics. By contrast, the Church of England itself was established as the religion of the southern states of Virginia, North Carolina, South Carolina, and Georgia, where all settlers were required to support it by paying taxes. While most of the new communities in the "new world" of North America were Christian denominations, a group of Jewish settlers also arrived in the Dutch settlement of New Netherland in 1654, beginning a historically important religious contrariety. Of course, the Native Americans and African people brought as slaves to North America held distinctive religions that were uniquely their own. A more careful tracing of the intricate history of the different European churches represented in the early American colonies may be found in Anson Phelps Stokes and Leo Pfeffer, *Church and State in the United States*, revised edition (New York: Harper and Row, 1964). [Originally published in four volumes in 1950.]
39. Spain was granted control of French territories west of the Mississippi.
40. Among the most influential ministers of the Great Awakening were Congregationalist Jonathan Edwards in New England, Presbyterian Gilbert Tennant in the mid-Atlantic region, and visiting British evangelist George Whitefield, who traveled throughout the colonies.
41. George Brown Tindall, *America: A Narrative History*, vol. 1 (New York: W. W. Norton, 1984), 127.
42. Anson Phelps Stokes and Leo Pfeffer are among the historians who regard the development of foreign trade as contributing to the emerging doctrine of religious freedom in the U.S. See Stokes and Pfeffer, *Church and State in the United States*, 28–29.
43. See, for example, Christopher Clark, *The Roots of Rural Capitalism: Western Massachusetts, 1780–1860* (Ithaca, New York: Cornell University Press, 1990) and James A. Henretta, *The Origins of American Capitalism: Selected Essays* (Boston: Northeastern University Press, 1991).

44. See, for example, Winifred Barr Rothenberg, *From Market-Places to a Market Economy: The Transformation of Rural Massachusetts, 1750–1850* (Chicago: University of Chicago Press, 1992).

45. This explanation for the emergence of capitalism around the time of the American revolution has been supported by the research of historian Richard Buel, Jr., who has shown that when luxury goods became less widely available for a time following the war, Connecticut farmers worked less hard and their crops surpluses disappeared. See Richard Buel, Jr., "Samson Shorn: The Impact of the Revolutionary War on Estimates of the Republic's Strength," in Ronald Hoffman and Peter J. Albert, eds., *Arms and Independence: The Military Character of the American Revolution* (Charlottesville, VA: University Press of Virginia, 1984), 157–60.

46. Stokes and Pfeffer, *Church and State in the United States*, 28–29.

47. See James Madison to Thomas Jefferson, Jan. 22, 1786, in William T. Hutchison et al., eds., *The Papers of James Madison*, vol. VIII (Chicago: University of Chicago Press, 1973), 474. Cited in Rhys Isaac, *The Transformation of Virginia 1740–1790* (Chapel Hill, NC: University of North Carolina Press, 1982), 284.

48. The states of Connecticut, New Hampshire, and Massachusetts retained their established churches well into the 19th century, albeit on a relatively circumscribed basis. The era of established churches in the U.S. did not end until the disestablishment of the Congregational Church in Massachusetts in 1833.

49. See Leonard W. Levy, *The Establishment Clause: Religion and the First Amendment* (Chapel Hill, NC: University of North Carolina Press, 1994), 93.

50. First Amendment to the U.S. Constitution.

51. Robert Cord, *Separation of Church and State: Historical Fact and Current Fiction* (New York: Lambeth Press, 1982), 15.

52. Ibid.

53. James Madison, "Memorial and Remonstrance Against Religious Assessments" (1785), reprinted in Arlin M. Adams and Charles J. Emmerich, *A Nation Dedicated to Religious Liberty: The Constitutional Heritage of the Religion Clauses* (Philadelphia: University of Pennsylvania Press, 1990), 104.

54. Thomas Jefferson, "Freedom of Religion at the University of Virginia," in Saul K. Padover, ed., *The Complete Jefferson* (New York: Duell, Sloan & Pierce, 1943), 958.

55. However, it must be noted that while the bracketing of religious differences— or differences in worldview—from the public forum was indeed the stated intent of the bill's authors, these European immigrants and their descendants in fact tacitly denied these privileges to many of the non-European peoples then populating the new nation—such as the African peoples brought as slaves to North America and the various tribes of Native Americans—precisely on the basis of their racial and cultural difference. Indeed, these peoples were often not allowed to "coexist peacefully," as their distinctive worldviews were frequently denied, derogated, and in some cases all but destroyed by those of European descent. Societal reparations for these wrongdoings continue to this day.

56. Again, we must note that this was not the case for many of those then living in the U.S. who were not of European descent and whose musical practices were discouraged or silenced. Nevertheless, some populations, such as those of African descent, undertook musical practices of their own when they could, borrowing sounds, formal aspects, and religious stories from their

European "owners" and integrating these with their own traditions, thus manifesting new musical practices such as spirituals and gospel traditions. From a Peircian pragmatic perspective, the resulting forms of music may be regarded as *signs* of their efforts at psychosocial equilibration.

57. The various religious practices (e.g. prayer and meditation), the telling of creation-myth stories, and the enactment of traditional community stories are but a few of the other means of psychosocial equilibration commonly employed in culturally homogeneous communities. However, none of these typically involves as much active physical participation as do musical practices.

58. Again, this statement is made with the caveat that it does not include those peoples who were not allowed to participate on the basis of racial or cultural difference. Fortunately, this situation has been—and is continuing to be—rectified, as various laws have been enacted to promote racial and cultural inclusiveness.

59. Alexis de Tocqueville, the celebrated early nineteenth-century French aristocrat and commentator on life in the new, democratic society of the United States, observed that the new democratic nation was already tending toward the use of abstract language, thereby obscuring important details and encouraging superficiality, when he visited America in 1831. He wrote: "This abundance of abstract terms in the language of democracy, used the whole time without reference to any particular facts, both widens the scope of thought and clouds it. They make expression quicker but conceptions less clear. However, in matters of language democracies prefer obscurity to hard work." (Of course, this statement also reveals Tocqueville's own cultural bias.) See Alexis de Tocqueville, *Democracy in America,* 13th ed., trans. George Lawrence, ed. J. P. Mayer (New York: Harper & Row, 1969), 482. [Originally published in 1850.]

60. Indeed, the modern science of psychology only began to emerge in the mid-nineteenth century, and it has not been until quite recently that researchers have begun considering the beneficial effects of musical practices on the human psyche.

61. In relation to this point, Jane Rasmussen has written a fascinating study of the attitudes held by clergy and laypersons on musical practices undertaken in the Episcopal churches of the U.S. between 1804 and 1859. Specifically, Rasmussen reports that the *concerned* clergy sought to have their congregations singing reverently, while musicians "saw the Church service as a vehicle for their own advancement as 'entertainers.'" See Jane Rasmussen, *Musical Taste as a Religious Question in Nineteenth-Century America* (Lewiston, NY: Edwin Mellen Press, 1986), xv.

62. For example, the Taliban, a fundamentalist Islamic militia group, imposed their version of Islamic law on the city of Kabul, Afghanistan, in December of 1996, seeking to prevent citizens from participating in *any* musical practice. More alarmingly, Malaysian nationals performing American jazz in Kuala Lumpur in February 1997 were executed for ideological insubordination (i.e., for their differences in worldview). On the Taliban conflict, see Michael A. Lev, "Artists Lament Taliban's Ban on Music," *Chicago Tribune,* 3 December 1996, sec. 1, p. 1. British Broadcasting Company World Service, a news program carried by affiliates of U.S. National Public Radio, reported the Kuala Lumpur incident in February, 1997.

63. Anthony Barresi is the scholar who has done the greatest amount of synoptic historical work in this area, and his writings have served as the main source for this brief summary.

64. George Washington, "Letter to Rev. Joseph Willard, March 22, 1781," in J. C. Fitzpatrick, ed., *Writings of George Washington from the Original*

Manuscript, 1745–1799, Vol. 21, December 22, 1780–April 26, 1781 (Washington, DC: United States Government Printing Office, 1937), 352; quoted in Fannie Taylor and Anthony Barresi, *The Arts at a New Frontier: The National Endowment for the Arts* (New York: Plenum Press, 1984), 6.

65. Ibid. No such federally funded center existed in Washington, DC, until the late 1960s, when the Kennedy Center for the Performing Arts was erected, but again, no cultural or political agenda beyond democracy itself was evident in its establishment.

66. The U.S. Military and Naval Academy bands were not instituted until the early nineteenth century, and the Army and Navy bands not until World War I. While the music performed by these ensembles naturally had its roots in European traditions of music, no expressed political agenda was included in their charters. See Ibid., 7.

67. Of course, it must be recognized that prior to the advent of recording technology Western sacred and art music were the only forms of music that were collected, as they were the only forms that were written down. Still, one could argue that since folk music and popular music were not then considered important enough to warrant such treatment, some cultural bias was evident.

68. Taylor and Barresi, *The Arts at a New Frontier*, 9.

69. Employment statistics for the U.S. population during the "Great Depression" (1929–34) can be found in Samuel Eliot Morison, *Oxford History of the American People* (New York: Oxford University Press, 1965), 944. Statistics on musicians' employment during the same era can be found in W. F. McDonald, *Federal Relief Administration and the Arts* (Columbus, OH: Ohio University Press, 1969), 587.

70. It could be argued that the U.S. Congress's adoption of the song "The Star-Spangled Banner" as the nation's "national anthem" during this era was effected for purposes of unifying the nation's collective worldview. Notably, the 1931 adoption has stirred controversy intermittently ever since it was first proposed. See George J. Svejda, *History of the Star-Spangled Banner from 1814 to the Present* (Washington, DC, Division of History, Office of Archeology and Historic Preservation, 1969).

71. Taylor and Barresi, *The Arts at a New Frontier*, 9. Notably, a Federal Theatre Project established at the same time received severe criticism in congressional hearings held shortly after its inception, when various legislators asserted that communist themes were present in the dramatic works presented by the project and that members of its leadership were avowed Communists. The Federal Theatre Project met with an early demise, largely in response to the nation's perception of a growing Soviet threat. Apparently no such issues were raised about the Federal Music Project, suggesting that the nation's legislators either held musical practices to be politically benign or that they placed more confidence in the political allegiance of the administrators of the Federal Music Project.

72. Taylor and Barresi, *The Arts at a New Frontier*, 11.

73. In an address given prior to the establishment of the NEA, President John F. Kennedy stated, "I see little of more importance to the future of our country and our civilization than full recognition of the place of the artist . . ." Quoted by Livingston Biddle in *Our Government and the Arts* (New York: ACA Books, 1988), 31.

74. Ibid., 411.

75. The disparate nature of the statements made by various legislators about federal funding for the arts is perhaps reflective of the American public's degree of confusion on the purpose of the NEA and its intended benefits for U.S. society.

76. Of course, we must qualify this statement by noting that many of the musical practices undertaken by several of the nation's constituent non-European peoples were suppressed outright and tacitly excluded from consideration in the public forum until recent years for reasons having to do with the racism, cultural bias, and political dominance of the original European settlers and their descendants.

77. Nevertheless, many instances of such societally changing (or shamanistic) music have eventually had a substantial transformative effect on the nation as a whole. David King Dunaway's 1981 biography of folksinger Pete Seeger, *How Can I Keep from Singing?* provides a chronicle of music and American politics through the so-called McCarthy era of the 1950s. In recent history, however, governmental involvement has occurred only at times when the artwork or lyrics on widely distributed recordings or the performers themselves have demonstrated or described such violent or base behavior that a significantly sized group of citizens has taken the matter to the courts. In all known cases the individuals involved have been protected by the First Amendment, though in some instances the ordeal has been painful and exoneration has taken a long time. On Pete Seeger and the civil rights movement, see David King Dunaway, *How Can I Keep From Singing?* (New York: McGraw-Hill, 1981). On the social outcries raised in response to the music of various "rock and roll" performers, see Linda Martin and Kerry Segrave, *Anti-Rock: The Opposition to Rock and Roll* (Hamden, CT: Archon Books, 1988).

78. Hughes, Robert. "Pulling the Fuse on Culture," *Time*, 7 August 1995 [NEA survey cited in "Comparing Commitments" (inserted box)], 61.

79. Admittedly, however, those nations which provide greater state support for music than does the U.S. tend to be more overtly socialistic than laissez-faire capitalistic in their political orientation.

80. Attendant to this, various protests have been raised in recent years about the proportion of funding allocated for prisons as opposed to public education. See, for example, Patrick Healy and Peter Schmidt, "Public Colleges Expect Tough Competition in Annual Fight for State Appropriations," *Chronicle of Higher Education*, 10 January 1997, sec. A, pp. 29–30.

81. Presumably assessing the "greatness" of a work by the degree to which it has psychosocially profound effects on a great number of culturally related people, the aristocratic Tocqueville too observed that in a democracy few works are likely to have far-reaching effects. While his comments on the matter were made in reference to the various "arts," the following statement of his about painting seems generally applicable to music as well. He wrote: "Aristocracies produce a few great pictures, democracies a multitude of little ones." See Tocqueville, *Democracy in America*, 468.

82. Social researcher Francis Fukuyama has pointed out that despite the effects of the nation's scientific orientation toward undermining the credibility of religious conceptions of Reality, religious *belief* has continued to be stronger in the U.S. than in many other state societies precisely because no religion was established by the state. See Francis Fukuyama, *Trust: The Social Virtues and the Creation of Prosperity* (New York: The Free Press, 1995), 288–89.

83. Indeed, while a 1987 Gallup poll revealed that 94 percent of U.S. citizens openly acknowledge that they believe in God or a "supreme being," a 1988 poll showed that 44 percent did not attend church or synagogue. Nevertheless, of those in the latter group, 30 percent said religion was very important to their lives and 77 percent said that they occasionally prayed. See George Gallup, *Religion in America,* Report No. 259 (April 1987), and *The Unchurched American . . . 10 Years Later* (1988), Princeton Religion Research Center.

84. The prayerful chant practices undertaken in Catholic monasteries and Buddhist temples, the prayerful intonation and singing done in Jewish temples, and the hymns sung in most Christian churches are among the numerous examples that could be cited.

85. The appropriation of some forms of secular "rock and roll" by contemporary Christian youth groups in recent years has amounted to something of a multiple irony, culturally speaking. While their lyrics are typically Bible-centered (or are at least Bible-sentimental) and the basic tonal and temporal organization of the music has its origins in the traditions of the early Christian church (like that of much contemporary American pop), the rhythms and melodic variants of which much of the music is constructed stem from African tribal traditions and various other subsequent influences. Most if not all contemporary Christian youth music is directly derived from American pop and set with semi-biblical lyrics. It seems likely that some of the "composers" of this tradition may be consciously using this practice to attract outsiders to "the faith." A brief discussion of the appropriation of mainstream popular music genres by Christian popular music groups can be found in Nicholas Dawidoff, "No Sex, No Drugs, but Rock and Roll (Kind Of)," *New York Times Magazine* (5 February, 1995), 40–44, 66–72.

86. At the same time, many Israelis tend to ignore persons of culturally indeterminate backgrounds (such as tourists), in most cases mentally exempting them from such concerns.

87. Notably, not *all* cultural communities living in the U.S. welcome the participation of outsiders in their most sacred rites. For example, Mormons, certain Native American tribes, and most if not all inner-city youth gangs are generally ill disposed to allowing outsiders access to certain of their most sacrosanct social activities and rituals.

88. Of course, it must be recognized that it is now often difficult to draw a clear line between "virtual" *versus* "actual" community membership. Many individuals who were once *virtual* members of a given community (e.g., as "fans" of a particular artist) have gradually become *actual* members of a physically associated community. In many cases, the distinctive origins of "possessed" listeners have gradually been obscured as they have adopted the manners of speech, dress, and social custom associated with their adopted culture and its concomitant worldview. Prime examples of this are the "Deadheads" (i.e., long-standing aficionados of the 1960's rock band The Grateful Dead) and "Gangsta Rappers" (devotees of rap music, which has its origins in the practices of inner-city youth gangs). Still, speech, dress, and social custom are not always necessarily evidence of a *complete* "conversion" from one worldview to another (i.e., on the levels of Thirdness, Secondness, *and* Firstness); despite outward signs, true emotional commitment (i.e., Firstness) is never certain.

89. This has reached its apogee with the invention of the portable, solitary listing device (e.g., the Apple iPod®). Such devices permit a person to be *physically* present in one cultural context (i.e., on the level of Secondness) while simultaneously experiencing a "virtual" psychosocial union (i.e., on the levels of Firstness and Thirdness) with a physically absent community.

90. Conductor Daniel Barenboim created a public stir when he protested the broadcast of music in public places such as shops, restaurants, and hotels for the purpose of manipulating human thoughts and emotions. See Kathryn Westcott, "Barenboim Hits Out at 'Sound of Musak,'" *BBC News Online*, 7 April 2006, http://news.bbc.co.uk/2/hi/entertainment/4883612.stm (accessed June 11, 2006).

91. It should be clear by now that just because a person is able to *recognize* a specific musical practice as stemming from a particular cultural community (i.e., on the level of Thirdness) does not necessarily imply that that person *experiences* that music as substantively meaningful in the way that a person embodying the worldview of that group would do (i.e., on the levels of Thirdness, Secondness, *and* Firstness).

92. So-called *karaoke* clubs (i.e., nightclubs in which patrons have an opportunity to sing popular songs to pre-recorded accompaniments) have offset this somewhat, although some of the performances undertaken in them derive at least appeal from the comic inability of patrons to successfully replicate the performances of the artists who recorded the songs originally. Ironically, the apparently "perfect" performances of many contemporary musicians that *karaoke* patrons are attempting to replicate are actually "products" created by "multiple take" recordings and sophisticated electronic editing in recording studios.

93. As we noted in Chapter 3, music is often used in radio and television advertisements as a cultural association device to entice customers to buy a given product. Hearing certain music reinforces potential customers' sense of unity with the attractive, culturally distinctive group with which the music is associated, thus goading them to buy the product.

94. A prime example of this is the 1994 album *Chant*, a recording of the Benedictine monks of the monastery of Santo Domingo de Silos. Music scholar Katherine Bergeron has written a provocative essay in which she suggests that the success of the *Chant* recording stems from its reflection of the "unreal" state of suspension between sacred and secular realities in which many citizens of modern societies now find themselves. See Katherine Bergeron, "The Virtual Sacred: Finding God at Tower Records," *The New Republic* 212 (February 27, 1995), 29–34.

95. The chanting of monks has long been a favorite ironic device employed on television comedy shows. Paradoxically, advertisers have used various sacred forms of music (e.g., chant and hymns) in television commercials for computer software, automobiles, and the sports television network ESPN for the purpose of appealing to a "sense of spirituality" to make their products seem more respectable. See James Martin, "Contemplation in Action," *America* 172 (April 8, 1995), 21.

96. Paul Simon made precisely such a claim when challenged about the inclusion of South African musicians on his 1986 *Graceland* record album. In Simon's words, "I didn't say 'I'd love to bridge cultures somewhere in the world, and mmm . . . where? Maybe South Africa.' No, I just fell in love with the music and wanted to play . . . My view is instinctually cultural. Looking at things culturally, as I did with *Graceland* . . . there's a political implication, but essentially I come at the world from a cultural sociological point of view, and [my critics] want to define the world politically." McNeil Lehrer Report, Public Broadcasting System, February 25, 1987. Quoted by Louise Meintjes, "Paul Simon's *Graceland*, South Africa, and the Mediation of Musical Meaning," *Ethnomusicology* 34 (Winter 1990), 39.

97. For example, during the "Year of Tibet" in 1991, groups of Tibetan monks living in exile in India toured the U.S. presenting demonstrations of their chanting and other religious practices. They made these presentations and sold recordings of their chant for the purpose of raising awareness among U.S. citizens of their political plight *and* to raise money to support their monasteries.

98. We should note that this argument has indeed been used, although more typically by those purveyors of music judged by certain segments of the U.S. population to be profane and societally deleterious.

99. Francis Fukuyama, *Trust: The Social Virtues and the Creation of Prosperity* (New York: The Free Press, 1996), 316.

100. Clearly, only those having socially "separate" or isolated lifestyles, such as the various Amish communities of Pennsylvania and Ohio, are likely to be more or less completely unaffected by these media.

101. For example, Christians are admonished to be *in* the world but not *of* the world. Certain doctrines and practices of "nonattachment" serve much the same purpose for Buddhists.

102. Herman and Chomsky cite as an example the meagerness of the U.S. mass media's coverage of an Indonesian invasion of East Timor beginning in 1975, in which the U.S. government bore considerable responsibility for the human slaughter. They assert that the reason this war received such scant coverage in U.S. news media was because the multinational corporations owning the U.S. media companies held major interests in Timorian oil and elected to keep the American public in the dark to avoid domestic protest. See Edward S. Herman and Noam Chomsky, *Manufacturing Consent: The Political Economy of the Mass Media* (New York: Pantheon Books, 1988), 33, and also the 1993 film of Canadian Filmmakers Mark Achbar and Peter Wintonick, *Manufacturing Consent: Noam Chomsky and the Media,* which was followed by a book of the same title (Montréal, QC: Black Rose Books, 1994).

103. Admittedly, such influences as public television stations, public radio stations, and especially quality music education programs in the nation's public school are among the countervailing forces presently existing in U.S. society.

104. Of course, as Alan Merriam and others have noted, societal conceptions of "musicians" do differ widely among and within the world's various cultural communities. Among his many observations on the ambiguous status of musicians when considered cross-culturally, Merriam wrote, "Musicians may form a special class or caste, they may or may not be regarded as professionals, their role may be ascribed or achieved, their status may be high or low or a combination of both." See Alan Merriam, "Social Behavior: The Musician," chap. in *The Anthropology of Music* (Chicago: Northwestern University Press, 1964), 123.

105. In fact, many of the students now entering the nation's universities to study music clearly have hopes of acquiring the performance skills necessary for them to become "entertainers" and possibly "stars," rather than seeking to become self-aware artists, shamans, or psychosocial equilibrators of their communities. [Personal experience of the writer.]

106. In the view of journalism and film scholar Paul Wilkes, the reason that religious leaders' views tend to be misrepresented by the media stems from two problems: First, many reporters lack sufficient and appropriate education to enable them to report accurately and fairly on religious matters, so they often miss the cultural and doctrinal subtleties among different religious speakers. Second, their editors are often seeking religious scandals in order to create alluring headlines and hold the accurate representation of religious leaders' views to be a secondary, less profitable interest. Thus, on those occasions when religious leaders' perspectives *are* represented in the mass media, they often come off as mere superstitious idiosyncrasies. See Paul Wilkes, "Why People of God Don't Talk to the Press," *Columbia Journalism Review* 31 (September/October, 1992), 54–55.

107. Despite the fact that the National Association of Schools of Music (NASM) now requires the inclusion of courses in world music and ethnomusicology

for all schools seeking their accreditation, many university faculty members remain uncommitted to including them in their curricula.

108. By this account, the incredible diversity and simplicity of much of the music that now predominates in the U.S. public forum can be regarded as an indication of the cultural fragmentation of the society at present.

109. Specifically, European music was suppressed in Japan from the early seventeenth century until 1873, following the beginning of the Meiji Restoration in 1868. See Ury Eppstein, *The Beginnings of Western Music in Meiji Era Japan* (Lewiston, NY: Edwin Mellen Press, 1994).

110. Information provided to the writer by a graduate student from England studying music education in a U.S. university.

111. In the case of some of the religious traditions presently existing in the U.S., however, such instruction has been minimal. As we shall see in the next chapter, the main reason that many of the nation's Christian denominations discontinued their own forms of education in music likely stemmed from the fact that the programs introduced into the public schools served the church's purposes of skill development quite adequately, primarily because so many church musicians took jobs in the public schools.

NOTES TO CHAPTER 5

1. Robert M. Pirsig, "Afterward" to *Zen and the Art of Motorcycle Maintenance: An Inquiry into Values* (New York: William Morrow and Co., 1984), 413.

2. The survey presented in this chapter is not intended as a thoroughgoing history, but is rather a review of representative statements, viewed through the lens of Peircian pragmatist philosophy, compiled for the purpose of determining where certain factors have caused the practice of music education to deviate from pragmatist norms.

3. *The Bay Psalm Book; being a facsimile reprint of the first edition, printed by Stephen Daye at Cambridge, in New England in 1640, with an introduction by Wilberforce Eames* (New York: New England Society, 1903) [unnumbered prefatory pages].

4. Cotton Mather, *The Accomplished Singer* (Boston, MA: Printed by B. Green, For S. Gerrish, at his shop in Cornhill, 1721). Cited in *Music in Boston*, ed. John C. Swan (Boston: Trustees of the Public Library of the City of Boston, 1977), 10–11.

5. Specifically, we might note that the music the Puritans made while musically engaged in their worship services *iconically* manifested the Christian coherence system (in the ways we explored in Chapter 3), it *indexically* incorporated the sounds of their voices, and it included the linguistic *symbols* inherent in the *psalms*—or song texts—found in the translation of the Bible ordered by James I of England and completed in 1611.

6. See, for example, Holy Bible, Jeremiah 25:10 and Ezekiel 26:13.

7. See 1 Samuel 10:5 and 2 Kings 3:15.

8. 1 Samuel 16:15–16, 23.

9. See Exodus 13:21.

10. 2 Chronicles 5:13–14.

11. See Matthew 26:30.

12. Ephesians 5:15–19.

13. Martin Luther, *Formula Missae et Communionis* (1523), *Opera Latina*, VII, 16f. Quoted by Walter E. Buszin, in "Luther on Music," *The Musical Quarterly* 32 (January 1946), 94.

14. Martin Luther, quoted in Friedrich Blume, *Protestant Church Music* (London: Victor Gollancz, 1975), 10.
15. Martin Luther, *Luther's Works,* Volume 53, "Liturgy and Hymns." Edited by Ulrich S. Leupold (Philadelphia: Fortress Press, 1965), 324.
16. Notably, many Protestant church musicians have followed Luther's example, appropriating for use in their own worship forms of music from other, radically differing religious traditions throughout their history, thus denying the culturally distinctive form and substance of different forms of music. This practice of the Protestants represents one of the main reasons the relationship between music and worldview has been confused in Western scholarship.
17. Martin Luther, *Letter to the Aldermen and Cities of Germany to Erect and Maintain Christian Schools* (1524). Quoted by Walter E. Buszin, "Luther on Music," *The Musical Quarterly* 32 (January 1946), 92.
18. John Calvin, *Institutio* (1536), cited in Thomas Young, *The Metrical Psalms and Paraphrases* (London: A. & C. Black, 1909), 16–17.
19. Martin Luther, quoted by Andrew Wilson-Dickson in *The Story of Christian Music* (Oxford, England: Lion Publishing, 1992), 65.
20. John Calvin, quoted by Joseph Haroutunian and Louise Smith, "Chapter VIII: Ethics and the Common Life," in *Calvin: Commentaries,* vol. XXIII, The Library of Christian Classics (Philadelphia: The Westminster Press, 1958), 355.
21. Robert F. Hayburn, *Papal Legislation on Sacred Music: 95 A.D. to 1977 A.D.* (Collegeville, MN: The Liturgical Press, 1979), 27.
22. Congregational music making remained almost nonexistent in the Roman Catholic Church until November 22, 1903, when Pope Pius X issued the *Motu Proprio,* which reinstituted congregational singing. Remarkably, the pope also recommended at this time that *schola cantorum* (i.e., musical training schools) be established in the principal churches, and many such schools were started in smaller churches and county parishes as well.
23. The "fasola" method of music reading, a method of assigning syllables ("fa, sol, la, and mi") to the pitches of the musical scale in order to facilitate their recognition in music reading and their manipulation in musical performance, is traditionally thought to have it origins in the method created by Italian monk and music theorist Guido d'Arezzo in the eleventh century. Such methods are now generally termed *solfeggio* or *solfège.*
24. Cotton Mather, *Singing of Psalms a Gospel Ordinance* (1647). Cited in Percy Scholes, *The Puritans in Music* (London: Oxford University Press, 1934), 265.
25. Thomas Mace, *Musick's Monument,* cited in Albert Edward Bailey, *The Gospel in Hymns* (New York: Scribner's, 1950), 88.
26. Thomas Walter, *The Grounds and Rules of Musick Explained* (Boston, MA: J. Franklin for S. Garrish, 1721), 4.
27. Rev. Thomas Symmes, quoted in H. Wiley Hitchcock, *Music in the United States,* 3rd ed. (Englewood Cliffs, NJ: Prentice Hall, 1988), 7.
28. Percy Scholes, *The Puritans and Music in England and New England* (London: Oxford University Press, 1934), 51.
29. Many traditional, historical musicologists do not accept DiNora's sociological perspective, but her account is not out of step with recent postmodern trends in that discipline.
30. Jean Starobinski, "The Age of Genius," *Unesco Courier* 44 (July 1991), 18–21.
31. Count Ferdinand Waldstein, quoted in Tia DeNora, *Beethoven and the Construction of Genius* (Berkeley, CA: University of California Press, 1995), 84.

32. Tia DeNora, *Beethoven and the Construction of Genius*, 84–85.
33. Ibid., 13.
34. Otto Erich Deutsch, *Mozart: A Documentary Biography* (Stanford, CA: Stanford University Press, 1965), 290. Quoted by Tia DeNora in *Beethoven and the Construction of Genius*, 13.
35. This point notwithstanding, it is doubtful that any artists conceived themselves as "neutral" as they sought to conceive and render Reality in a personal and special way.
36. "Rubric Preceding Psalms and Hymns," *New American Prayer Book*, 1798. Cited in Jane Rasmussen, *Musical Taste as a Religious Question in Nineteenth-Century America* (Lewiston, NY: Edwin Mellen Press, 1986), xvii.
37. "Pastoral Letter, 1856." Cited in Jane Rasmussen, *Musical Taste as a Religious Question*, xix.
38. Simeon Pease Cheney, *The American Singing Book* (Boston: White, Smith, and Company, 1879), 2.
39. The separation between the music of the church and music of the Enlightenment was not at all clear in the conservatory movement. For example, the Oberlin College Conservatory of Music in the U.S. represents one conservatory that grew out of a Christian educational institution and maintained its church affiliation.
40. George Peabody, quoted by Ray Edwin Robinson, "A History of the Peabody Conservatory of Music" (DMusEd diss., Indiana University, 1969), 7.
41. Baltimore *American*, September 25, 1872. Cited by Robinson, "A History of the Peabody Conservatory," 112.
42. George Peabody, founding letter; in Robinson, "A History of the Peabody Conservatory," 139.
43. Robinson, "A History of the Peabody Conservatory," 87–88.
44. Letter from Lucien H. Southard to Charles Eaton, chairman of the Committee on the Academy, April 20, 1871. Archives of the Peabody Institute, Baltimore. Cited by Robinson, "A History of the Peabody Conservatory," 174.
45. Robinson, "A History of the Peabody Conservatory," 5–6.
46. William Channing Woodbridge, *A Lecture on Vocal Music as a Branch of Common Education. Delivered in the Representatives Hall, Boston, August 24, 1830, before the American Institute of Instruction* (Boston: Hilliard, Gray, Little, and Wilkins, 1831), 6.
47. Music education historian Howard Ellis has demonstrated that "Mason's relationship to the *Manual* is that of an editor rather than an author, and . . . the *Manual* is not essentially Pestalozzian in nature." For an exploration of this matter of historical controversy, see Howard Ellis, "Lowell Mason and the *Manual of the Boston Academy of Music*," *Journal of Research in Music Education* 3 (Spring 1955), 3–10.
48. Quoted in Edward Bailey Birge, *History of Public School Music in the United States* (Reston, VA: Music Educators National Conference, 1988), 41, 47. [Originally published in 1928.]
49. It is important to note that music instruction had been featured in the schools of Boston (and other cities) prior to this decision of the Boston School Board, but prior to this time it had not been included as a regular subject in the curriculum.
50. George B. Loomis, "Preface" to *The Progressive Glee and Chorus Book* (New York: Ivison, Blakeman, Taylor & Co., 1878) [unnumbered prefatory pages].
51. Notably, his list also included Marschner, Abt, Franz, Kreutzer, Curschmann, Barnby, Hatton, and Farmer, composers whose works have not sustained such public reverence over the ensuing centuries.

52. Luther Orlando Emerson and W. S. Tilden, "Preface" to *The Hour of Singing: A Book for High Schools, Seminaries, and the Social Choir* (Boston: Oliver Ditson & Co., 1871) [unnumbered prefatory pages].
53. Henry Southwick Perkins, H. J. Danforth, and E. V. DeGraff, "Preface" to *The Song Wave: Designed for Schools, Teachers' Institutes, Musical Conventions, and the Home Circle* (New York: D. Appleton and Company, 1883) [unnumbered prefatory pages].
54. Caryl Florio, ed., "Preface" to *Children's Hymn, with Tunes* (New York: Biglow & Main, 1885), 3–4.
55. Frederick H. Ripley and Thomas Tapper, "Preface and Directions," in *Natural Course in Music: Music Reader Number Five* (New York: American Book Company, 1895), 3.
56. Frederic A. Lyman, "Preface" to *The Normal Music Course in the Schoolroom: A Practical Exposition of the Normal Music Course* (Boston: Silver, Burdett and Company, 1896), v.
57. Ibid., 167.
58. Eleanor Smith, *The Modern Music Series: The Fourth Book of Vocal Music* (Boston: Silver, Burdett & Co., 1905): iii.
59. James Edward Houlihan, "The Music Educators National Conference in American Education," PhD dissertation, Boston University, 1961, 49–57. Houlihan's dissertation provides the most complete historical account of this organization's first half-century.
60. Houlihan, "The Music Educators National Conference," 50.
61. Osborne McConathy, "High School Music," *Journal of Proceedings of the Third Annual Meeting of the Music Supervisors National Conference* (St. Cloud, MN, 1910), 70–78. Cited in Houlihan, "The Music Educators National Conference," 85.
62. Will Earhart, Notes of MSNC Planning Committee Meeting on Century of Progress Exposition, Subcommittee on Values and Objectives, October 10, 1931.
63. Frederic A. Lyman, *The Normal Music Course in the Schoolroom: A Practical Exposition of the Normal Music Course* (Boston: Silver, Burdett and Company, 1896), 160.
64. Robert Foresman, *Fifth Book of Songs* (New York: American Book Company, 1926), 4.
65. Robert Foresman, *Manual to Accompany Books of Songs* (New York: American Book Company, 1925), 11.
66. Robert Foresman, *Manual to Accompany a Child's Book of Songs* (New York: American Book Company, 1930), 2.
67. Leo R. Lewis, "International Music Society," *Volume of Proceedings of the Music Teachers National Association* (Hartford, CT: The Association, 1911), 240.
68. Eleanor Smith, *The Modern Music Series: The Fourth Book of Vocal Music* (New York: Silver, Burdett & Co., 1905), iv.
69. Karl Gehrkens, quoted by E. B. Birge in "The Music Supervisors Conference," *Music Supervisors Journal* 18 (March, 1932), 19.
70. Robert Foresman, *First Book of Songs* (New York: American Book Company, 1925), 4.
71. Osbourne McConathy, John W. Beattie, and Russell V. Morgan, *Music of Many Lands and Peoples* (New York: Silver, Burdett and Company, 1932), iii.
72. James Edward Houlihan, "The Music Educators National Conference," 71–73.
73. G. Stanley Hall, "The Psychology of Music and the Light It Throws upon Musical Education," *National Education Association Journal of Proceedings and Addresses* (1908), 849.

74. Ibid., 853.
75. John Dewey, *Psychology* (1887). In *The Early Works of John Dewey, 1882–1898* (Carbondale, IL: Southern Illinois University Press, 1967), 274.
76. Horatio Parker, Osborne McConathy, Edward Bailey Birge, and W. Otto Miessner, *The Progressive Music Series* (Boston: Silver, Burdett, & Co., 1916), 9.
77. Frances Elliott Clark, Foreword to *Music Appreciation for Children* (Camden, NJ: RCA-Victor Company, 1930), 9.
78. Calvin Brainerd Cady, Preface to *Music Appreciation for Children* (Camden, NJ: RCA-Victor Company, 1930), 10–11.
79. Edward B. Birge, Mabel E. Bray, Osbourne McConathy, and W. Otto Miessner, *The Music Hour* (Silver, Burdett, & Co., 1931), 3.
80. Ibid., 6–7.
81. James A. Keene, *A History of Music Education in the United States* (Hanover, NH: University Press of New England, 1982), 257.
82. Ibid., 260.
83. Ibid., 263–68.
84. Jere Humphreys, "Applications of Science: The Age of Standardization and Efficiency in Music Education," *Bulletin of Historical Research in Music Education* 9 (January 1988), 6. Jere Humphreys has done the most incisive historical research on the early applications of the scientific method to music education to date, and this article of his has served as a main source for this brief account.
85. Edward Bailey Birge, *History of Public School Music in the United States* (Washington, DC: Music Educators National Conference, 1966), 113. Cited in Humphreys, "Applications of Science," 4.
86. Birge, *History of Public School Music*, 128–31. Cited in Humphreys, "Applications of Science," 4.
87. Humphreys has reported that Bolton's research played an important role in the 1907 Keokuk, Iowa, meeting that led to the founding of the Music Supervisors National Conference, later MENC. See Jere T. Humphreys, "Thaddeus Bolton and the First Dissertation in Music Education," *Journal of Research in Music Education* 38 (Summer 1990), 143.
88. Humphreys, "Applications of Science," 8.
89. Birge, *History of Public School Music*, 234–35. Cited in Humphreys, "Applications of Science," 11.
90. Birge, *History of Public School Music*, 168.
91. Keene, *A History of Music Education*, 294.
92. James Mursell, *Human Values in Music Education* (New York: Silver, Burdett and Company, 1934), 4.
93. Ibid., 8.
94. Ibid., 9.
95. Max Schoen, "The Æsthetic Attitude in Music," *Psychological Monographs*, 39 (1928), 169–70. Vernon Lee, *Music and Its Lovers* (George Allen and Unwin, 1932), Chapter 3. Charles Diserens, "Reactions to Musical Stimuli" *Psychological Bulletin* 20 (1932), 173–99.
96. Mursell, *Human Values in Music Education*, 152.
97. Ibid., 162–63.
98. Ibid., 163–64.
99. 1940 Executive Committee of MENC—Joint Meeting with Presidents of Sectional Conferences and Auxiliary Organizations, "Minutes," Chicago, October 18–20, 1940.
100. Houlihan, "The Music Educators National Conference," 149.
101. Fowler Smith, Richard W. Grant, et al., "American Unity through Music," *Music Educators Journal* 27 (March–April 1941): 10.

102. Ibid., 12.
103. Ibid., 10.
104. Ibid., 13.
105. Music Educators National Conference, Editorial, *Music Educators Journal* 29 (September–October 1942), 19.
106. ˙Music Educators National Conference, "Music in the Victory Corps," *Music Educators Journal* 29 (May–June 1943), 14.
107. Another means by which the psychological stability and ideological solidarity of the armed services was maintained overseas during the World War II was via the presentation of musical and variety show performances "in the field" by the United Service Organization (USO). This organization, which is supported by citizens' financial contributions and volunteers, was founded on February 4, 1941, specifically for the purpose of providing social, recreational, welfare, and spiritual services to U.S. citizens serving in the armed forces. The USO has presented programs featuring music to military service personnel serving overseas in numerous conflicts in which the nation has been engaged since that time.
108. Music Educators National Conference, "Music in the Victory Corps," 15.
109. Radio Branch, Bureau of Public Relations, War Department, *Music in the National Effort* (United States Government Printing Office), n.d. [ca. 1943], 2.
110. J. Henry Morganthau, Secretary of the Treasury, telegram to John C. Kendel, president of MENC, August 18, 1944.
111. MENC National Executive Committee, *Minutes*, March 1944.
112. Ibid.
113. Music Educators National Conference, *Outline of a Program for Music Education* (Washington, DC: Music Educators National Conference, 1951). [The pages of this pamphlet are not numbered.]
114. Osbourne McConathy, Russell V. Morgan, James L. Mursell, Marshall Bartholomew, Mabel E. Bray, W. Otto Miessner, and Edward Bailey Birge, *New Music Horizons* (New York: Silver Burdett Company, 1949), ii.
115. Peter W. Dykema, Gladys Pitcher, and J. Lilian Vandevere, *Music in the Air*. Teacher's Manual (Boston: C. C. Birchard & Co., 1949), 394.
116. Doris Hutton, "A Comparative Study of Two Methods of Teaching Sight Singing in the Fourth Grade," *Journal of Research in Music Education* 1 (Fall 1953), 119–26.
    Harry A. King, "A Study of the Relationship of Music Reading and I.Q. Scores," *Journal of Research in Music Education* 2 (Spring 1954), 35–37.
117. Vanette Lawler, *Music Education in the United States—Present Status, Prospects and Future: A Report Prepared for the International Society for Music Education* (Washington, DC: Music Educators National Conference, 1958), 4–5.
118. Osbourne McConathy, Russell V. Morgan, James L. Mursell, Marshall Bartholomew, Mabel E. Bray, W. Otto Miessner, and Edward Bailey Birge, *New Music Horizons* (New York: Silver Burdett Company, 1949), iv.
119. Harold Arberg and Claude V. Palisca, "Implications of the Government Sponsored Yale Seminar in Music Education," *College Music Symposium* 4 (1964), 113–24. See also Claude V. Palisca *Music in Our Schools: A Search for Improvement*, report of the Yale Seminar on Music Education. Washington, DC: United States Department of Health, Education, and Welfare, Office of Education, OE-33033, bulletin 1964, no. 28.
120. Judith Murphy and George Sullivan, *Music in American Society: An Interpretive Report of the Tanglewood Symposium* (Washington, DC: Music Educators National Conference, 1968), 2.

121. Harry S. Broudy, quoted by Murphy and Sullivan, *Music in American Society*, 11.
122. David McAllester, quoted by Murphy and Sullivan, *Music in American Society*, 11.
123. Murphy and Sullivan, *The Tanglewood Symposium*, 11–12.
124. Ibid., 56.
125. Ibid.
126. Perhaps the music textbook series featuring the most extensive development of Reimer's ideas is the special "Centennial Edition" of *Silver Burdett Music*. See Elizabeth Crook, Bennett Reimer, David S. Walker, et al., *Silver Burdett Music*, centennial edition (Morristown, NJ: Silver, Burdett & Co., 1985).
127. John Dewey, *Art as Experience* (New York: Perigee Books/G. P. Putnam's Sons, 1980), 59. [Originally published in 1934.]
128. Leonard Meyer, *Emotion and Meaning in Music* (Chicago: University of Chicago Press, 1956), 28.
129. Ibid., 30.
130. Ibid., 31.
131. Susanne Langer, *Philosophy in a New Key* (New York: New American Library, 1948), 211.
132. Susanne Langer, *Problems of Art* (New York: Charles Scribner's Sons, 1957), 80.
133. Susanne Langer, *Feeling and Form* (New York: Charles Scribner's Sons, 1953), 31–32.
134. Ibid., 27.
135. Bennett Reimer, *A Philosophy of Music Education* (Englewood Cliffs, NJ: Prentice Hall, 1970), 39.
136. Ibid., 112.
137. Ibid., 40–41.
138. Notably, Reimer has attempted to redeem his theory by addressing these criticisms and those of others (especially David Elliott) in subsequent editions of his book (1989 and 2002) with variable success.
139. Terese M. Volk has most thoroughly researched multiculturalism in U.S. music education, and her book *Music, Education, and Multiculturalism* (New York: Oxford University Press, 1998) has served as a main source for this brief account.
140. Music Educators National Conference GO Project—Committee 18, "Final report—1969." MENC Historical Center Music Library, University of Maryland.
141. James Standifer, quoted in Volk, *Music, Education, and Multiculturalism*, 94.
142. Chuck Ball et al., "Report of the MENC Commission on Graduate Music Teacher Education," *Music Educators Journal* 67 (October 1980), 48.
143. "Symposium Resolution for Future Directions and Actions," in William M. Anderson, *Teaching Music with a Multicultural Approach* (Reston, VA: Music Educators National Conference, 1991), 90.
144. Consortium of National Arts Education Associations, *National Standards for Arts Education* (Reston, VA: Music Educators National Conference, 1994), 63.
145. David Williams, "SWRL Music Program: Ethnic Song Selection and Distribution," Report #SWRL-TN-3-72–28 (Los Alamitos, CA: Southwest Regional Laboratory for Educational Research and Development, September 6, 1972) (ERIC document ED109040).
146. David J. Elliott, "Toward a Multicultural Concept of Arts Education, "*Journal of Aesthetic Education* 24 (Spring 1990), 163–64.

147. Patricia Shehan Campbell, "Music Education in a Time of Cultural Transformation," *Music Educators Journal* 89 (September 2002), 31.
148. Deborah Bradley, "Music Education, Multiculturalism, and Anti-Racism: 'Can We Talk?'" *Action, Criticism, and Theory for Music Education* 5 (December 2006), 2–31.
149. A relatively new series of books (with accompanying CD recordings) edited by Patricia Shehan Campbell and Bonnie C. Wade is a notable step forward in this regard, as are essays collected by Carlos Xavier Rodriguez in a relatively new book on popular music and music education. See Bonnie C. Wade, *Thinking Musically: Experiencing Music, Expressing Culture* (Global Music Series, 1) (New York: Oxford University Press, 2003) and Carlos Xavier Rodriguez, *Bridging the Gap: Popular Music and Music Education* (Reston, VA: Music Educators National Conference, 2004).
150. Philip Alperson, "What Should One Expect from a Philosophy of Music Education?" *Journal of Aesthetic Education* 25 (Fall 1991), 233.
151. Alperson, "What Should One Expect," 236.
152. Since Elliott's exposition of his philosophy is lengthy and complex, only those aspects of his work that seem most essential and pertinent to our present discussion are described here.
153. Elliott, *Music Matters*, 39–40.
154. Ibid., 14.
155. Elliott's use of the term *MUSIC* is similar to the term *musical practice* we have adopted in this inquiry, with the exception that (as we noted in Chapter 3) our concepts *musical practice* and *music* are not intended to denote cultural universals but rather reflect our acknowledged provisional application of the Western concept *music* to different cultural practices, a distinction that Elliott did not make.
156. Ibid., 109.
157. Dennett set forth this argument in Daniel C. Dennett, *Consciousness Explained* (Boston: Little, Brown & Co., 1991).
158. Mihalyi Csikszentmihalyi and Isabella Csikszentmihalyi, eds., *Optimal Experience: Psychological Studies of Flow in Consciousness* (Cambridge, England: Cambridge University Press, 1988), 20. Quoted in Elliott, *Music Matters*, 112.
159. Mihalyi Csikszentmihalyi has described his notion of *flow* and his research on autotelic experiences in a manner accessible to nonspecialized readers in *Flow: The Psychology of Optimal Experience* (New York: Harper & Row, 1990) and subsequent books.
160. Elliott, *Music Matters*, 114.
161. Ibid., 116–18.
162. Ibid., 121.
163. Ibid., 122.
164. Ibid., 43.
165. Ibid., 44.
166. Ibid., 135.
167. Ibid., 293.
168. See David J. Elliott, "Music as Culture: Toward a Multicultural Concept of Arts Education," *Journal of Aesthetic Education* 24 (Spring 1990), 149–51.
169. See David J. Elliott, "Music for Citizenship: A Commentary on Paul Woodford's *Democracy and Music Education: Liberalism, Ethics, and the Politics of Practice*," *Action, Criticism, and Theory for Music Education* 7 (January 2008), 55.
170. Thomas A. Regelski, "Taking the 'Art' of Music for Granted: A Critical Sociology of the Aesthetic Philosophy of Music," in *Critical Reflections on Music Education: Proceedings of the Second International Symposium on*

the Philosophy of Music Education, June 12–16, 1994, ed. Lee R. Bartel and David J. Elliott (Toronto: Canadian Music Education Research Centre, University of Toronto, 1996), 27.

171. Thomas A. Regelski, "Prolegomenon to a Praxial Philosophy of Music and Music Education," *Musiikkikasvatus: The Finnish Journal of Music Education* 1 (1996), 25. [Note: This article was reprinted in *Canadian Music Educator* 38 (Spring 1997), 43–51.]
172. Ibid., 26.
173. Ibid.
174. Ibid., 27.
175. Ibid., 32.
176. Ibid.
177. Ibid., 33.
178. Ibid.
179. Ibid., 34.
180. Ibid.
181. Elliott, *Music Matters,* 43.
182. Regelski, "Prolegomenon to a Praxial Philosophy of Music Education," 25.
183. It should be noted that the "cultural relativist" nature of Regelski's position has become clearer in his writings since 1996. See especially Thomas A. Regelski, "Musical Values and the Value of Music Education," *Philosophy of Music Education Review* 10 (Spring 2002), 49–55, and "Social Theory, and Music and Music Education as Praxis," *Action, Criticism, and Theory for Music Education* 3 (December 2004), 2–52.
184. In defense of U.S. music educators, it is important to note that the universalizing bias of their past methods of musical instruction stems largely from the pervasiveness of the ideals of modernism in the nation's public forum, and not necessarily from any intentional closed-mindedness on their part.
185. Estelle Jorgensen, "Justifying Instruction in American Public Schools: An Historical Perspective," *Bulletin of the Council for Research in Music Education* 120 (Spring 1994), 31.
186. Wayne Bowman, "The Limits and Grounds of Musical Praxialism," in *Praxial Music Education,* ed. David J. Elliott (New York: Oxford University Press, 2005), 74.

NOTES TO CHAPTER 6

1. Annie Dillard, *Living by Fiction* (New York: Harper & Row, 1982), 132.
2. Peirce, *Collected Papers,* 5.402.
3. Robert A. Choate, ed., *Documentary Report of the Tanglewood Symposium: Music in American Society.* (Washington, DC: Music Educators National Conference, 1968), Section 1. [The pages of this document are not numbered.]
4. Bennett Reimer, *A Philosophy of Music Education* (Englewood Cliffs, NJ: 1970), 10, 51.
5. Philip Alperson, "What Should One Expect from a Philosophy of Music Education?" *Journal of Aesthetic Education* 25 (Fall 1991), 233.
6. David Elliott, *Music Matters: A New Philosophy of Music Education* (New York: Oxford University Press, 1995), 121.
7. Ibid., 122.
8. Thomas Regelski, "Prolegomenon to a Praxial Philosophy of Music and Music Education," *Musiikkikasvatus: The Finnish Journal of Music Education* 1 (1996), 25.
9. Ibid. 27.

10. Ibid.
11. Peirce, *Collected Papers*, 5.484.
12. As we noted in Chapter 4, it is important to remember that the popular mass media companies have not necessarily portrayed different cultural forms of music in these ways with malicious intent. However, their historical downplaying of cultural differences has contributed to maximizing their earnings.
13. For example, see Linda Louise Kelley, "A Combined Experimental and Descriptive Study of the Effect of Music on Reading and Language," PhD dissertation, University of Pennsylvania, 1981, and Richard R. Bentley, *Music and Language Reading: The Third International Symposium on Music in Medicine, Education, and Therapy for the Handicapped* (New York: University Press of America, 1985). Also of note is Aniruddh D. Patel, *Music, Language, and the Brain.*(New York: Oxford University Press, 2007).
14. See, for example, Lucanne Magill Bailey, "The Use of Songs in Music Therapy with Cancer Patients and Their Families," *Music Therapy: The Journal of the American Association for Music Therapy* 4 (1984), 5–17, and Jodi Levine-Gross and Robert Swartz, "The Effects of Music Therapy on Anxiety in Chronically Ill Patients," *Music Therapy: The Journal of the American Association for Music Therapy* 2 (1982), 43–52.
15. Other articles in *Music Therapy: The Journal of the American Association for Music Therapy* provide additional examples of ways in which musical practices contribute to human psychophysiological balance. Professionals in this field have used musical practices as therapy with persons exhibiting mental retardation, autism, physical disabilities, behavior disorders, emotional disturbances, and various sorts of mental illness, and also with geriatric patients suffering with various sorts of disorders.
16. Oliver Sacks, *The Man Who Mistook His Wife For A Hat and Other Clinical Tales* (New York: Touchstone/Simon & Schuster, 1998), 192. [Originally published in 1970.]
17. Ibid., 185–86.
18. For example, cognition researcher Frances Rauscher and her colleagues identified some surprising effects associated with listening to a particular form of music, and her research has stirred considerable controversy among music educators in the U.S. Specifically, Rauscher found that students who listened to a recording of W. A. Mozart's *Sonata for Two Pianos* (K448) for ten minutes prior to taking a test designed to measure their spatial reasoning skills (i.e., in paper cutting and folding) performed significantly better than students who had listened to other forms of music or to no music at all. While Rauscher's results have met with a good deal of skepticism (primarily because of the popular media's subsequent promotion of the absurd notion that "listening to Mozart makes children smarter"), it seems possible that listening to Mozart's music may have had the effect of attuning the brains of those preparing to take the test to a coherence system (or pattern of neural firings in the brain) consistent with the form of logic required for success in the tests. In fact, a subsequent study using electroencephalographic recordings demonstrated common patterns of neural activity in the children's brains while listening to Mozart's music and during the exam. Based on the perspectives we have set forth in this inquiry, it might be appropriate for researchers to consider in future studies both the ethnic and cultural background of the students whose results were so markedly improved. Incidentally, veteran music education researcher Rudolph E. Radocy has tendered a critique of Rauscher's studies that gives qualified support to her conclusions. See Frances Rauscher, Gordon L. Shaw, and Katherine N. Ky, "Listening

to Mozart Enhances Spatial-Temporal Reasoning: Towards a Neurophysiological Basis," *Neuroscience Letters* 185 (1995), 44–47, and J. Sarnthein, A. vonStein, P. Rappelsberger, H. Petsche, F. H. Rauscher, and G. L. Shaw, "Persistent Patterns of Brain Activity: An EEG Coherence Study of the Positive Effect of Music on Spatial-Temporal Reasoning," *Neurological Research* (1997), 19, 107–16. See also Rudolph E. Radocy, "Music Doesn't Make You Smarter . . . But It Doesn't Hurt," *Kodály Envoy* (Winter 1998), 44–46.

19. We should note also that general music classes are becoming more prevalent in the nation's secondary schools, and that courses dealing with instructional methods appropriate to them are presently being introduced into the nation's public university schools of music.

20. We may infer that the introduction of these diverse music classes—many of which represent some of the nation's culturally distinctive constituent populations—without a connecting curricular philosophy addressing their social roots may have contributed to attenuating students' concern with the social efficacy of the musical practices of different cultural communities.

21. Jazz programs were added to the curricula of university and public-school music programs when a critical mass of people expressed displeasure at its exclusion. It would seem appropriate for schools of music to consider including programs featuring other musical practice traditions *before* such a critical mass makes their inclusion an absolute necessity.

22. It is, after all, important to keep in mind Peirce's admonition that all conceptions should be held provisionally. He wrote, "The scientific spirit requires a man to be at all times ready to dump his whole cartload of beliefs, the moment experience is against them." Peirce, *Collected Papers*, 1.55.

References

U. S. GOVERNMENT DOCUMENTS AND PUBLICATIONS

Constitution of the United States of America.

Palisca, Claude V. *Music in Our Schools: A Search for Improvement*. Report of the Yale Seminar on Music Education. Washington, DC: United States Department of Health, Education, and Welfare, Office of Education, OE-33033, bulletin 1964, no. 28.

Radio Branch, Bureau of Public Relations, War Department. *Music in the National Effort*. Washington, DC: United States Government Printing Office. No date [ca. 1943], 2.

Svejda, George J. *History of the Star-Spangled Banner from 1814 to the Present* (Washington, DC, Division of History, Office of Archeology and Historic Preservation, 1969).

United States. Bureau of the Census, *Statistical Abstract of the United States: 1994*, 114th ed. (Washington, DC, 1994).

BOOKS AND PAMPHLETS

Achbar, Mark, ed. *Manufacturing Consent: Noam Chomsky and the Media*. Montréal, QC: Black Rose Books, 1994.

Adams, Arlin M., and Charles J. Emmerich. *A Nation Dedicated to Religious Liberty: The Constitutional Heritage of the Religion Clauses*. Philadelphia: University of Pennsylvania Press, 1990.

Anderson, William M. *Teaching Music with a Multicultural Approach*. Reston: VA: Music Educators National Conference, 1991.

Attali, Jacques. *Noise: The Political Economy of Music*. Translated by Brian Massumi. Minneapolis: University of Minnesota Press, 1985.

Bailey, Albert Edward. *The Gospel in Hymns*. New York: Scribner's, 1950.

Ball, Chuck, Jerrold Ross, Harry R. Mamlin, Gary Martin, D. Edward Brookhart, and Bette Y. Cox. "Report of the MENC Commission on Graduate Music Teacher Education," *Music Educators Journal* 67 (October 1980), 46–53, 66–68.

Baumgarten, Alexander. *Aesthetica*. Hildesheim, Germany: G. Olms, 1961. [Originally published in 1750.]

Bay Psalm Book; being a facsimile reprint of the first edition, printed by Stephen Daye at Cambridge, in New England in 1640, with an introduction by Wilberforce Eames. New York: New England Society, 1903.

Beardsley, Monroe. *Aesthetics from Classical Greece to the Present*. Tuscaloosa, Alabama: University of Alabama Press, 1966.

Bentley, Richard R. *Music and Language Reading: The Third International Symposium on Music in Medicine, Education, and Therapy for the Handicapped*. New York: University Press of America, 1985.

Biddle, Livingston. *Our Government and the Arts*. New York: ACA Books, 1988.

Birge, Edward Bailey. *History of Public School Music in the United States*. Augmented reprint ed. Reston, VA: Music Educators National Conference, 1984. [Originally published in 1928.]

Birge, Edward B., Mabel E. Bray, Osbourne McConathy, and W. Otto Miessner. *The Music Hour*. New York: Silver, Burdett, & Co., 1931.

Blacking, John. *How Musical Is Man?* Seattle: University of Washington Press, 1973.

Blaukopf, Kurt. *Musical Life in a Changing Society: Aspects of Music Sociology*. Translated by David Marinelli. Portland, OR: Amadeus Press. [Originally published in German in 1982.]

Blume, Friedrich. *Protestant Church Music*. London: Victor Gollancz, 1975.

Bourdieu, Pierre. *Distinction: A Social Critique of the Judgment of Taste*. Translated by Richard Nice. Cambridge, MA: Harvard University Press, 1984.

Buchler, Justus, ed. *The Philosophy of Peirce: Selected Writings*. New York: Harcourt, Brace and Co., 1940.

Bullard, Truman Campbell. "The First Performance of Igor Stravinsky's Rite of Spring." PhD diss., Eastman School of Music of the University of Rochester, 1971.

Burney, Charles. *A General History of Music*. New York: Harcourt, Brace & Co., 1935. [Originally published in 1789.]

Cavicchi, Daniel. *Tramps Like Us: Music and Meaning Among Springsteen Fans*. New York: Oxford University Press, 1998.

Cheney, Simeon Pease. *The American Singing Book*. Boston: White, Smith, and Company, 1879.

Chittick, William C. *The Sufi Path of Love: The Spiritual Teachings of Rumi*. Albany, New York: State University of New York Press, 1983.

Choate, Robert A., ed. *Documentary Report of the Tanglewood Symposium: Music in American Society*. Washington, DC: Music Educators National Conference, 1968.

Clark, Christopher. *The Roots of Rural Capitalism: Western Massachusetts, 1780–1860*. Ithaca, NY: Cornell University Press, 1990.

Clark, Frances Elliott, ed. *Music Appreciation for Children*. Camden, NJ: RCA Victor Company, 1930.

Clark, Ronald W. *Einstein: The Life and Times*. New York: World Publishing Co., 1971.

Colapietro, Vincent. *Peirce's Approach to the Self: A Semiotic Perspective on Human Subjectivity*. Albany, NY: State University of New York Press, 1989.

Consortium of National Arts Education Associations. *National Standards for Arts Education*. Reston, VA: Music Educators National Conference, 1994.

Cord, Robert. *Separation of Church and State: Historical Fact and Current Fiction*. New York: Lambeth Press, 1982.

Courtis, Stewart Appleton. *The Courtis Standard Research Tests: Recognition of Characteristic Rhythms*. Detroit, MI: S. A. Courtis, no date (ca. 1920).

———. *The Courtis Standard Research Tests: Recognition of Mood from Melody*. Detroit, MI: S. A. Courtis, No date (ca. 1920).

Crook, Elizabeth, Bennett Reimer, David S. Walker, et al. *Silver Burdett Music*. Centennial edition. Morristown, NJ: Silver, Burdett & Co., 1985.

Csikszentmihalyi, Mihalyi. *Flow: The Psychology of Optimal Experience*. New York: Harper & Row, 1990.

Csikszentmihalyi, Mihalyi, and Isabella Csikszentmihalyi, eds. *Optimal Experience: Psychological Studies of Flow in Consciousness*. Cambridge, England: Cambridge University Press, 1988.

Dahlhaus, Carl. *Esthetics of Music*. Translated by William W. Austin. Cambridge, England: Cambridge University Press, 1982. [Originally published in German in 1962.]

Daniel, E. Valentine. *Fluid Signs*. Berkeley: University of California Press, 1984.

d'Aquili, Eugene G., Charles D. Laughlin, Jr., and John McManus, eds. *The Spectrum of Ritual: A Biogenetic Structural Analysis*. New York: Columbia University Press, 1979.

Dennett, Daniel C. *Consciousness Explained*. Boston: Little, Brown & Co., 1991.

DeNora, Tia. *Beethoven and the Construction of Genius*. Berkeley: University of California Press, 1995.

———. *Music in Everyday Life*. Cambridge, England: Cambridge University Press, 2000.

Deutsch, Otto Erich. *Mozart: A Documentary Biography*. Stanford, CA: Stanford University Press, 1965.

Dewey, John. *Art as Experience*. New York: Perigree/G. P. Putnam's Sons, 1980. [First published in 1934.]

———. *The Early Works of John Dewey, 1892–1898*. Carbondale:, IL: Southern Illinois University Press, 1967.

DeWoskin, Kenneth J. *A Song for One or Two: Music and the Concept of Art in Early China*. Ann Arbor, MI: Center for Chinese Studies, University of Michigan, 1982.

Dillard, Annie. *Living by Fiction*. New York: Harper & Row, 1982.

Dissanayake, Ellen. *What Is Art For?* Seattle: University of Washington Press, 1988.

———. *Homo Aestheticus: Where Art Comes from and Why*. New York: Free Press, 1992.

Dunaway, David King. *How Can I Keep From Singing?* New York: McGraw-Hill, 1981.

Dykema, Peter W., Gladys Pitcher, and J. Lilian Vandevere, *Music in the Air*. Teacher's Manual. Boston: C. C. Birchard & Co., 1949.

Eagleton, Terry. *The Ideology of the Aesthetic*. Oxford, England: Basil Blackwell, 1990.

Edelman, Gerald M. *Neural Darwinism: The Theory of Neuronal Group Selection*. New York: Basic Books, 1987.

Eliade, Mircea, ed. *Encyclopedia of Religion*. New York: Macmillan, 1987.

Elliott, David. *Music Matters: A New Philosophy of Music Education*. Oxford, England: Oxford University Press, 1995.

Emerson, Luther Orlando, and W. S. Tilden. *The Hour of Singing: A Book for High Schools, Seminaries, and the Social Choir*. Boston: Oliver Ditson & Co., 1871.

Eppstein, Ury. *The Beginnings of Western Music in Meiji Era Japan*. Lewiston, New York: Edwin Mellen Press, 1994.

Feld, Steven. *Sound and Sentiment: Birds, Weeping, Poetics and Song in Kaluli Expression*. Philadelphia: University of Pennsylvania Press, 1982.

Florio, Caryl, ed. *Children's Hymn, with Tunes*. New York: Biglow & Main, 1885.

Foresman, Robert. *First Book of Songs*. New York: American Book Company, 1925.

———. *Manual to Accompany Books of Songs*. New York: American Book Company, 1925.

———. *Fifth Book of Song.* New York: American Book Company, 1926.

———. *Manual to Accompany a Child's Book of Songs.* New York: American Book Company, 1930.

Fukuyama, Francis. *Trust: The Social Virtues and the Creation of Prosperity.* New York: The Free Press, 1995.

Gallup, George. *Religion in America,* Report No. 259. Princeton, NJ: Princeton Religion Research Center, 1987.

———. *The Unchurched American . . . 10 Years Later.* Princeton, NJ: Princeton Religion Research Center, 1988.

Garofalo, Reebee, ed. *Rockin' the Boat: Mass Music and Mass Movements.* Boston: South End Press, 1992.

Geertz, Clifford. *The Interpretation of Cultures.* New York: Basic Books, 1973.

Ginsburg, Herbert P., and Sylvia Opper. *Piaget's Theory of Intellectual Development.* 3d ed. Englewood Cliffs, NJ: Prentice Hall, 1988.

Goethe, Johann Wolfgang von. *Goethe's Literary Essays.* Translated and edited by J. E. Spingarn. New York: Harcourt, 1921.

Goodman, Felicitas D. *Ecstasy, Ritual, and Alternate Reality: Religion in a Pluralistic World.* Bloomington, IN: Indiana University Press, 1982.

Hayburn, Robert F. *Papal Legislation on Sacred Music: 95 A.D. to 1977 A.D.* Collegeville, MN: The Liturgical Press, 1979.

Hegel, Georg Wilhelm Friedrich. *Introductory Lectures on Aesthetics.* Translated by Bernard Bosanquet. Edited by Michael Inwood. London: Penguin Books, 1993. [Originally published in 1886.]

———. *Aesthetics: Lectures on Fine Art,* 2 vols. Translated by T. M. Knox. Oxford: Clarendon Press, 1975. [Originally published in 1835 and 1838.]

Henretta, James A. *The Origins of American Capitalism: Selected Essays.* Boston: Northeastern University Press, 1991.

Herman, Edward S., and Noam Chomsky. *Manufacturing Consent: The Political Economy of the Mass Media.* New York: Pantheon Books, 1988.

Hess, Walter R. *On the Relations between Psychic and Vegetative Functions.* Zurich: G. Thieme, 1925.

Hitchcock, H. Wiley. *Music in the United States: A Historical Introduction,* 3d ed. Englewood Cliffs, NJ: Prentice Hall, 1988.

Hitler, Adolf. *The Speeches of Adolph Hitler.* Translated and edited by Norman H. Baynes. New York: Howard Fertig, 1969.

Hobbes, Thomas. *Leviathan.* New York: Liberal Arts Press, 1958. [Originally published in 1651.]

Hood, Mantle. *The Ethnomusicologist,* 2d ed. Kent, OH: Kent State University Press, 1982. [Originally published in 1971.]

Hornbostel, Erich Moritz von. *Hornbostel Opera Omnia,* vol. 1. Edited by Klaus P. Wachsmann, Dieter Christiensen, and Hans-Peter Reinecke. The Hague: Martinus Nijhoff, 1975.

Houlihan, James Edward. "The Music Educators National Conference in American Education." PhD dissertation, Boston University, 1961.

Isaac, Rhys. *The Transformation of Virginia 1740–1790.* Chapel Hill, NC: University of North Carolina Press, 1982.

Izutsu, Toshihiko, and Toyo Izutsu. *The Theory of Beauty in the Classical Aesthetics of Japan.* The Hague: Martinus Nijhoff, 1981.

Jakobson, Roman, and Morris Halle. *Fundamentals of Language.* The Hague: Mouton, 1956.

Jefferson, Thomas. *The Complete Jefferson.* Edited by Saul K. Padover. New York: Duell, Sloan & Pierce, 1943.

Kant, Immanuel. *Critique of Judgement,* 2d ed. Translated by J. H. Bernard. London: Macmillan, 1914. [Originally published in 1790.]

Katz, Ruth, and Carl Dahlhaus, eds. *Contemplating Music: Source Readings in the Aesthetics of Music,* 4 vols. Stuyvesant, NY: Pendragon Press, 1987.

Keeling, Richard, ed. *Women in North American Indian Music: Six Essays.* Bloomington, IN: Indiana University Press, 1989.

Keene, James A. *A History of Music Education in the United States.* Hanover, NH: University Press of New England, 1982.

Kuhn, Thomas. *The Structure of Scientific Revolutions.* Chicago: University of Chicago Press, 1962.

Kwalwasser, Jacob, and Peter W. Dykema. *K-D Music Tests: Manual of Directions.* New York: Carl Fischer, 1930.

Kwalwasser, Jacob, and G. M. Ruch. *Kwalwasser-Ruch Test of Musical Accomplishment.* Iowa City, IA: Extension Division of the State University of Iowa, 1924.

Lang, Paul Henry. *George Frideric Handel.* W. W. Norton & Co., 1966.

Langer, Suzanne. *Philosophy in a New Key.* New York: New American Library, 1948.

———. *Feeling and Form.* New York: Charles Scribner's Sons, 1957.

———. *Problems of Art.* New York: Charles Scribner's Sons, 1957.

Lawler, Vanette. *Music Education in the United States—Present Status, Prospects and Future: A Report Prepared for the International Society for Music Education.* Washington, DC: Music Educators National Conference, 1958.

Lee, Vernon. *Music and Its Lovers.* George Allen & Unwin, 1932.

Leppert, Richard, and Susan McClary, eds. *Music and Society: The Politics of Composition, Performance, and Reception.* Cambridge, England: Cambridge University Press, 1987.

Levi-Strauss, Claude. *Structural Anthropology.* Translated by Claire Jacobson and Booke Grundfest Schoepf. New York: Basic Books, 1963. [Originally published in 1958.]

Levy, Leonard W. *The Establishment Clause: Religion and the First Amendment.* Chapel Hill, NC: University of North Carolina Press, 1994.

Lévy-Bruhl, Lucien. *How Natives Think.* Translated by Lilian A Clave. London: George Allen & Unwin, 1926.

———. *The Notebooks on Primitive Mentality.* Translated by Peter Rivière. Oxford, England: Basil Blackwell & Mott, 1975. [Originally published in 1949.]

Locke, John. *Essay Concerning Human Understanding.* Oxford, England: Clarendon Press, 1924. [Originally published in 1689.]

Loomis, George B. *The Progressive Glee and Chorus Book.* New York: Ivison, Blakeman, Taylor & Co., 1878.

Luther, Martin. *Luther's Works,* Vol, 53, Liturgy and Hymns. Edited by Ulrich S. Leupold. Philadelphia: Fortress Press, 1965.

Lyman, Frederic A. *The Normal Music Course in the Schoolroom: A Practical Exposition of the Normal Music Course.* Boston: Silver, Burdett & Co., 1896.

Lyotard, Jean-François. *The Postmodern Condition: A Report on Knowledge.* Translated by Geoffrey Bennington and Brian Massumi. Minneapolis: University of Minnesota Press, 1984. [Originally published in France in 1979.]

Martin, Linda, and Kerry Segrave. *Anti-Rock: The Opposition to Rock and Roll.* Hamden, CT: Archon Books, 1988.

Mason, Lowell. *Manual of the Boston Academy of Music, for Instruction in the Elements of Vocal Music on the System of Pestalozzi.* Boston: Carter, Hendee, & Co., 1834.

McAllester, David, ed. *Readings in Ethnomusicology.* New York: Johnson Reprint Corporation, 1971.

McConathy, Osbourne, John W. Beattie, and Russell V. Morgan. *Music of Many Lands and Peoples.* New York: Silver, Burdett & Co., 1932.

————. *American Music Horizons*. New York: Silver Burdett & Co., 1951.

McConathy, Osbourne, Russell V. Morgan, James L. Mursell, Marshall Bartholomew, Mabel E. Bray, et al. *New Music Horizons*. New York: Silver Burdett & Company, 1949.

McDonald, W. F. *Federal Relief Administration and the Arts*. Columbus, OH: Ohio University Press, 1969.

Merriam, Alan. *The Anthropology of Music*. Chicago: Northwestern University Press, 1964.

Meyer, Leonard B. *Emotion and Meaning in Music*. Chicago: University of Chicago Press, 1956.

Morison, Samuel Eliot. *Oxford History of the American People*. New York: Oxford University Press, 1965.

Murphy, Judith, and George Sullivan, *Music in American Society: An Interpretive Report of the Tanglewood Symposium*. Washington, DC: Music Educators National Conference, 1968.

Mursell, James. *Human Values in Music Education*. New York: Silver, Burdett & Co., 1934.

Mursell, James L., Gladys Tipton, et al., *Music for Living*. Elementary music textbook series. Morristown, NJ: Silver Burdett & Co., 1956.

Music Educators National Conference. *Outline of a Program for Music Education*. Washington, DC: Music Educators National Conference, 1951.

Music Educators National Conference GO Project—Committee 18. Final report. MENC Historical Center Music Library, University of Maryland, 1969.

Needham, Rodney. *Belief, Language, and Experience*. Chicago: University of Chicago Press, 1972.

Nettl, Bruno. *The Western Impact on World Music: Change, Adaptation, and Survival*. New York: Schirmer Books, 1985.

Newman, Ernest. *Musical Studies*. London: Ballantyne, Hanson, & Co., 1905.

Nietzsche, Friedrich. *The Birth of Tragedy*. Translated by Francis Golffing. New York: Anchor Press/Doubleday, 1956. [Originally published in 1872.]

Parker, Horatio, Osborne McConathy, Edward Bailey Birge, and W. Otto Miessner. *The Progressive Music Series*. Boston: Silver, Burdett & Co., 1916.

Patel, Aniruddh D. *Music, Language, and the Brain*. New York: Oxford University Press, 2007.

Peirce, Charles Sanders. *Collected Papers of Charles Sanders Peirce*, Vols. I–VI. Edited by Charles Hartshorne and Paul Weiss. Cambridge, MA: Harvard University Press, 1931–35.

————. *Collected Papers of Charles Sanders Peirce*, Vols. VII–VIII. Edited by A. Burks. Cambridge, MA: Harvard University Press, 1958.

Perkins, Henry Southwick, H. J. Danforth, and E. V. DeGraff. *The Song Wave: Designed for Schools, Teachers' Institutes, Musical Conventions, and the Home Circle*. New York: D. Appleton and Company, 1883.

Pirsig, Robert M. *Zen and the Art of Motorcycle Maintenance: An Inquiry into Values*. New York: William Morrow & Co., 1984.

Polanyi, Michael. *The Tacit Dimension*. London: Routledge, 1967.

RCA-Victor Company. *Music Appreciation for Children*. Camden, NJ: RCA-Victor Company, 1930.

Raposa, Michael L. *Peirce's Philosophy of Religion*. Peirce Studies, no. 5. Edited by Kenneth Laine Ketner. Bloomington, IN: Indiana University Press, 1989.

Rappaport, Roy. *Ecology, Meaning, Religion*. Berkeley, CA: North Atlantic Books, 1979.

Rasmussen, Jane. *Musical Taste as a Religious Question in Nineteenth-Century America*. Lewiston, NY: Edwin Mellen Press, 1986.

Raynor, Henry. *A Social History of Music*. New York: Schocken Books, 1972.

Reimer, Bennett. *A Philosophy of Music Education*. Englewood Cliffs, NJ: Prentice Hall, 1970.

———. "The Common Dimensions of Aesthetic and Religious Experience." EdD diss., University of Illinois, 1963.

———. *A Philosophy of Music Education*, 2nd ed. Englewood Cliffs, NJ: Prentice Hall, 1989.

———. *A Philosophy of Music Education: Advancing the Vision*, 3rd ed. Englewood Cliffs, NJ: Prentice Hall, 2002.

Ricoeur, Paul. *The Philosophy of Paul Ricoeur*. Edited by C. E. Reagan and D. Stewart. Boston: Beacon Press, 1978.

Ripley, Frederick H., and Thomas Tapper. *Natural Course in Music: Music Reader Number Five*. New York: American Book Company, 1895.

Robinson, Ray Edwin. "A History of the Peabody Conservatory of Music." DMusEd. diss., Indiana University, 1969.

Rodriguez, Carlos Xavier, ed. *Bridging the Gap: Popular Music and Music Education*. Reston: VA: Music Educators National Conference, 2004.

Rothenberg, Winifred Barr. *From Market-Places to a Market Economy: The Transformation of Rural Massachusetts, 1750–1850*. Chicago: University of Chicago Press, 1992.

Rouget, Gilbert. *Music and Trance: A Theory of the Relations between Music and Possession*. Translated by Brunhilde Biebuyck in collaboration with the author. Chicago: University of Chicago Press, 1985.

Rousseau, Jean-Jacques. *Discourse on the Origin of Inequality* and *The Social Contract*. Edited by Lester G. Crocker. New York: Washington Square Press, 1967. [Originally published in 1754 and 1762, respectively.]

Sachs, Curt. *The Wellsprings of Music*. Edited by Jaap Kunst. The Hague: Martinus Nijhoff: 1962.

Sacks, Oliver. *Awakenings*. Expanded ed. New York: HarperCollins, 1990. [Originally published in 1973.]

———. *The Man Who Mistook His Wife for a Hat and Other Clinical Tales*. New York: Touchstone/Simon & Schuster, 1998. [Originally published in 1970.]

Sadie, Stanley, ed. *New Grove Dictionary of Music and Musicians*. London: Macmillan Publishers, 1980.

Saussure, Ferdinand de. *Course in General Linguistics*. Edited by C. Balley and A. Sechehaye in collaboration with A. Riedlinger. Translated by Roy Harris. Chicago: Open Court, 1972. [Originally published in 1915.]

Scholes, Percy. *The Puritans and Music in England and New England*. London: Oxford University Press, 1934.

Schopenhauer, Arthur. *The World as Will and Idea*, 3 vols. London: Routledge & Kegan Paul, 1950. [Originally published in 1883.]

Seashore, Carl E. *Manual of Instructions and Interpretations for the Measures of Musical Talent*. New York: Columbia Phonograph Company, 1919.

Seeger, Charles. *Studies in Musicology 1935–1975*. Berkeley, CA: University of California Press, 1977.

Shapiro, Michael. *The Sense of Grammar: Language as Semiotic*. Bloomington, IN: Indiana University Press, 1983.

Small, Christopher. *Music—Society—Education: A Radical Examination of the Prophetic Function of Music in Eastern, Western, and African Cultures with Its Impact on Society and Its Use in Education*, 2nd ed. London: John Calder, 1980.

———. *Musicking: The Meanings of Performing and Listening*. Hanover, NH: Wesleyan University Press, 1998.

Smith, Adam. *An Inquiry into the Nature and Causes of the Wealth of Nations*. Oxford, England: Oxford University Press, 1976. [Originally published in 1776.]

Smith, Eleanor. *The Modern Music Series: The Fourth Book of Vocal Music.* New York: Silver, Burdett & Co., 1905.

Smith, Huston. *The Religions of Man.* New York: Perennial Library of Harper and Row, 1958.

Standifer, James A., and Barbara Reeder. *Source Book of African and African-American Materials for Music Educators.* Reston, VA: Music Educators National Conference, 1972.

Stokes, Anson Phelps, and Leo Pfeffer. *Church and State in the United States.* Revised ed. New York: Harper & Row, 1964. [Originally published in four volumes in 1950.]

Stravinsky, Igor, and Robert Craft. *Conversations.* New York: Doubleday, 1959.

Swan, John C., ed. *Music in Boston.* Boston: Trustees of the Public Library of the City of Boston, 1977.

Taylor, Fannie, and Anthony Barresi. *The Arts at a New Frontier: The National Endowment for the Arts.* New York: Plenum Press, 1984.

Tice, Terrence N. "Ideology Old and New: Historical-Analytical Background for Use of the Concept 'Ideology' in Scholarly Discourse, with Systematic Bibliography." PhD diss., University of Michigan, 1970.

Tindall, George Brown. *America: A Narrative History,* 2 vols. New York: W. W. Norton, 1984.

Tocqueville, Alexis de. *Democracy in America,* 13th ed. Translated by George Lawrence. Edited by J. P. Mayer. New York: Harper & Row, 1969. [Originally published in 1850.]

Tracey, Hugh. *Chopi Musicians,* 2nd ed. London: Oxford University Press for the International African Institute, 1970.

Tsunoda, Tadanobu. *The Japanese Brain: Uniqueness and Universality.* Translated by Yoshinori Oiwa. Tokyo: Taishukan Publishing Co., 1985.

Turner, Victor. *The Ritual Process: Structure and Anti-Structure.* Chicago: Aldine Publishing Co., 1969.

———. *From Ritual to Theatre: The Human Seriousness of Play.* New York: Performing Arts Journal Publications, 1982.

Tylor, Edward B. *Primitive Culture,* 5th ed. London: S. Murray, 1929.

Volk, Terese M. *Music, Education, and Multiculturalism: Foundations and Principles.* New York: Oxford University Press, 1998.

Wade, Bonnie C. *Thinking Musically: Experiencing Music, Expressing Culture* (Global Music Series 1). New York: Oxford University Press, 2003.

Walter, Thomas *The Grounds and Rules of Music Explained.* Boston: J. Franklin for S. Garrish, 1721.

Weber, William. *The Rise of Musical Classics in Eighteenth-Century England.* Oxford, England: Clarendon/Oxford University Press, 1992.

Whitman, Walt. *Leaves of Grass: Comprehensive Readers' Edition.* Edited by Harold W. Blodgett and Sculley Bradley. New York: New York University Press, 1965.

Wilson-Dickson, Andrew. *The Story of Christian Music.* Minneapolis, MN: Fortress Press, 1996.

Wolfe, Irving, Beatrice Perham Krone, and Margaret Fullerton. *Together We Sing.* New York: Follett Publishing Co., 1956.

Woodbridge, William Channing. *A Lecture on Vocal Music as a Branch of Common Education. Delivered in the Representatives Hall, Boston, August 24, 1830, before the American Institute of Instruction.* Boston: Hilliard, Gray, Little, & Wilkins, 1831.

Young, Thomas. *The Metrical Psalms and Paraphrases.* London: A. & C. Black, 1909.

ARTICLES AND LETTERS

Alperson, Philip. "What Should One Expect from a Philosophy of Music Education?" *Journal of Aesthetic Education* 25 (Fall 1991): 215–42.

Arberg, Harold, and Claude V. Palisca. "Implications of the Government Sponsored Yale Seminar in Music Education." *College Music Symposium* 4 (1964): 113–24.

Augustine. "From *De Musica*." In *Contemplating Music: Source Readings in the Aesthetics of Music*, vol. 2. Edited by Ruth Katz and Carl Dahlhaus, 10–33. Stuyvesant, NY: Pendragon Press, 1987.

Bailey, Lucanne Magill. "The Use of Songs in Music Therapy with Cancer Patients and Their Families." *Music Therapy: The Journal of the American Association for Music Therapy* 4 (1984), 5–17.

Barresi, Anthony L. "The Role of the Federal Government in Support of the Arts and Music Education." *Journal of Research in Music Education* 29 (Winter 1981): 245–56.

Becker, Judith. "Aesthetics in Late 20th Century Scholarship." *The World of Music* 25 (1983): 65–77.

Becker, Judith, and Alton Becker. "A Musical Icon: Power and Meaning in Javanese Gamelan Music." In *The Sign in Music and Literature*, ed. Wendy Stainer, 203–15. Austin, TX: University of Texas Press, 1981.

Bergeron, Katherine. "The Virtual Sacred: Finding God at Tower Records." *The New Republic* 212 (February 27, 1995): 29–34.

Birge, Edward Bailey. "The Music Supervisors Conference." *Music Supervisors Journal* 18 (March, 1932), 19.

Blacking, John. "The Biology of Music-Making." In *Ethnomusicology: An Introduction*, ed. Helen Meyers, 301–14. London: Macmillan Press, 1992.

Boas, Franz. "The Limitations of the Comparative Method of Anthropology (1896)." In *Race, Language, and Culture*, 270 80. New York: The Free Press, 1940.

Bowman, Wayne. "The Limits and Grounds of Musical Praxialism." In *Praxial Music Education*, ed. David J. Elliott, 52–78. New York: Oxford University Press, 2005.

Bradley, Deborah. "Music education, Multiculturalism, and Anti-Racism: 'Can We Talk?'" *Action, Criticism, and Theory for Music Education* 5 (December 2006): 2–31.

Buel, Richard, Jr. "Samson Shorn: The Impact of the Revolutionary War on Estimates of the Republic's Strength." In *Arms and Independence: The Military Character of the American Revolution*, ed. Ronald Hoffman and Peter J. Albert, 157–60. Charlottesville, VA: University Press of Virginia, 1984.

Buszin, Walter E. "Luther on Music." *Musical Quarterly* 32 (January 1946): 80–97.

Campbell, Patricia Shehan. "Music, Education, and Community in a Multicultural Society." In *Cross Currents: Setting an Agenda for Music Education in Community Culture*, State of the Arts Series No. 2, ed. Marie McCarthy. College Park, MD: University of Maryland, 1995, 4–33.

———. "Music Education in a Time of Cultural Transformation." *Music Educators Journal* 89 (September 2002), 27–32, 54.

Curran, John Philpot. "Speech on the Right of Election of Lord Mayor of the City of Dublin (1790)." In *The Speeches of the Celebrated Irish Orators Phillips, Curran, and Grattan*, ed. Charles Phillips. Boston: Patrick Donahoe, 1857.

d'Aquili, Eugene. "Human Ceremonial Ritual and the Modulation of Aggression." *Zygon* 20 (March, 1985): 21–30.

Dawidoff, Nicholas. "No Sex, No Drugs, but Rock and Roll (Kind Of)." *New York Times Magazine*, 5 February 1995, 40–44, 66–72.

Diserens, Charles. "Reactions to Musical Stimuli." *Psychological Bulletin* 20 (1932): 173–99.

Earhart, Will. Notes of MSNC Planning Committee Meeting on Century of Progress Exposition, Subcommittee on Values and Objectives, October 10, 1931.

Eliade, Mircea, ed. *Encyclopedia of Religion*. New York: Macmillan, 1987. S.v. "Music and Religion," by Ter Ellingson.

Elliott, David J. "Music as Culture: Toward a Multicultural Concept of Arts Education." *Journal of Aesthetic Education* 24 (Spring 1990): 147–66.

———. "Toward a Multicultural Concept of Arts Education, "*Journal of Aesthetic Education* 24 (Spring 1990): 163–64.

———. "Music for Citizenship: A Commentary on Paul Woodford's *Democracy and Music Education: Liberalism, Ethics, and the Politics of Practice.*" *Action, Criticism, and Theory for Music Education* 7 (January 2008): 45–73.

Ellis, Alexander J. "On the Musical Scales of Various Nations." *Journal of the Society of Arts* 33 (1885): 485–527.

Ellis, Howard. "Lowell Mason and the *Manual of the Boston Academy of Music.*" *Journal of Research in Music Education* 3 (Spring 1955): 3–10.

Feld, Steven. "Linguistics and Ethnomusicology." *Ethnomusicology* 18 (May 1974): 197–217.

———. "Sound Structure as Social Structure." *Ethnomusicology* 28 (September, 1984): 383–409.

Ficino, Marsilio. "From *Opera Omnia*"(1476). In *Contemplating Music: Source Readings in the Aesthetics of Music*, vol. 1. Edited by Ruth Katz and Carl Dahlhaus, 78–93. Stuyvesant, NY: Pendragon Press, 1987.

Frith, Simon. "Towards an Aesthetic of Popular Music." In *Music and Society: The Politics of Composition, Performance, and Reception*, ed. Richard Leppert and Susan McClary, 133–49. Cambridge, England: Cambridge University Press, 1987.

Gardner, M. P. "Mood States and Consumer Behavior: A Critical Review." *Journal of Consumer Behavior* 12 (1985): 281–97.

Goethe, Johann Wolfgang von. "April 18, 1827." In *Conversations with Eckermann*, Translated by John Oxenford. San Francisco: North Point Press, 1984. [Originally published in 1850.]

Gundersen, Edna. "Rock's Roar Soars over Gulf War." *USA Today*, 28 January 1991, D2.

Haberman, Clyde. "Old Agonies Revive: Israeli Philharmonic to Perform Wagner." *New York Times*, 16 December 1991, A1.

———. "Barenboim Defends Decision but Passions on Wagner Are High." *New York Times*, 17 December 1991, C15.

———. "Israel Philharmonic Puts Off Wagner Concert." *New York Times*, 23 December 1991, C11–12.

Hall, G. Stanley. "The Psychology of Music and the Light It Throws upon Musical Education." *National Education Association Journal of Proceedings and Addresses* (1908): 849.

Haroutunian, Joseph, and Louise Smith. "Chapter VIII: Ethics and the Common Life." In *Calvin: Commentaries*, vol. XXIII, the Library of Christian Classics. Philadelphia: The Westminster Press, 1958.

Healy, Patrick, and Peter Schmidt. "Public Colleges Expect Tough Competition in Annual Fight for State Appropriations." *Chronicle of Higher Education* 10 (January 1997): A29–30.

Hoffmann, Ernst Theodor Amadeus. "Beethoven's Instrumental Music (1813)." In *Source Readings in Music History*, ed. Oliver Strunk, 775–97. New York: W. W. Norton, 1950.

Hughes, Robert. "Pulling the Fuse on Culture." *Time* 7 August 1995, 60-68. [NEA survey cited in "Comparing Commitments" (Inserted box).]

Hume, David. "Of the Standard of Taste." In *Art and Philosophy: Readings in Aesthetics*, ed. W. E. Kennick, 486–500. New York: St. Martin's Press, 1979.

Humphreys, Jere. "Applications of Science: The Age of Standardization and Efficiency in Music Education." *Bulletin of Historical Research in Music Education* 9 (January 1988): 1–21.

———. "Thaddeus Bolton and the First Dissertation in Music Education." *Journal of Research in Music Education* 38 (Summer 1990): 138–48.

Hutton, Doris. "A Comparative Study of Two Methods of Teaching Sight Singing in the Fourth Grade." *Journal of Research in Music Education* 1 (Fall 1953): 119–26.

Jorgensen, Estelle. "Justifying Instruction in American Public Schools: An Historical Perspective." *Bulletin of the Council for Research in Music Education* 120 (Spring 1994): 17–31.

Jorgensen, Estelle, ed. *Philosophy of Music Education Review* (Bloomington, IN: Indiana University Press, 1990–).

Kelley, Linda Louise. "A Combined Experimental and Descriptive Study of the Effect of Music on Reading and Language." PhD dissertation, University of Pennsylvania, 1981.

Kepler, Johannes. "From *Harmonia Mundi*." In *Contemplating Music: Source Readings in the Aesthetics of Music*, vol. 1. Edited by Ruth Katz and Carl Dahlhaus, 111–40. Stuyvesant, NY: Pendragon Press, 1987.

Kifner, John. "Khomeini Bans Broadcast Music, Saying It Corrupts Iranian Youth." *New York Times*, 24 July 1979, A1, 6.

King, Harry A. "A Study of the Relationship of Music Reading and I.Q. Scores." *Journal of Research in Music Education* 2 (Spring 1954): 35–37.

Lev, Michael A. "Artists Lament Taliban's Ban on Music." *Chicago Tribune*, 3 December 1996, sec. 1, 1.

Levine-Gross, Jodi, and Robert Swartz. "The Effects of Music Therapy on Anxiety in Chronically Ill Patients." *Music Therapy: The Journal of the American Association for Music Therapy* 2 (1982): 43–52.

Levi-Strauss, Claude. "The Structural Study of Myth." In *Structural Anthropology*, 202–28. Translated by Claire Jacobson. New York: Basic Books, 1963. [Originally published in French in 1958.]

———. "The Scope of Anthropology." *Current Anthropology* 7 (1966): 112–23.

Lewis, Leo R. "International Music Society." *Volume of Proceedings of the Music Teachers National Association*. Hartford, CT: Music Teachers National Association, 1911.

Lex, Barbara. "The Neurobiology of Ritual Trance." In *The Spectrum of Ritual: A Biogenetic Structural Analysis*, ed. Eugene G. d'Aquili, Charles D. Laughlin, Jr., and John McManus, 117–51. New York: Columbia University Press, 1979.

List, George. "On the Non-Universality of Music Perspectives." *Ethnomusicology* 15 (September, 1971): 399–402.

Madison, James. "James Madison to Thomas Jefferson, Jan. 22, 1786." In *The Papers of James Madison*, vol. VIII. William T. Hutchison et al., eds. Chicago: University of Chicago Press, 1973, 474.

———. "Memorial and Remonstrance against Religious Assessments (1785)." Quoted in Arlin M. Adams and Charles J. Emmerich, *A Nation Dedicated to Religious Liberty: The Constitutional Heritage of the Religion Clauses*, 104. Philadelphia: University of Pennsylvania Press, 1990.

"Marines Blast Heavy Metal at Iraqi Troops." *Atlanta Constitution*, February 21, 1991, p. A6.

Martin, James. "Contemplation in Action." *America* 172 (April 8, 1995): 21.

McAllester, David P. "Some Thoughts on 'Universals' in World Music." *Ethnomusicology* 15 (September, 1971): 379–80.

McConathy, Osborne. "High School Music." *Journal of Proceedings of the Third Annual Meeting of the Music Supervisors National Conference.* St. Cloud, MN, 1910), 70–78.

Meintjes, Louise. "Paul Simon's *Graceland*, South Africa, and the Mediation of Musical Meaning." *Ethnomusicology* 34 (Winter 1990): 37–73.

Merriam, Alan. "Definitions of 'Comparative Musicology' and 'Ethnomusicology': An Historical-Theoretical Perspective." *Ethnomusicology* 21 (May 1977): 189–204.

Morgan, William, and Per Brask. "Towards a Conceptual Understanding of the Transformation from Ritual to Theatre." *Anthropologica* 30 (1988): 175–202.

Morganthau, J. Henry. Secretary of the Treasury, Telegram to John C. Kendel, President of MENC, August 18, 1944.

Music Educators National Conference, "Editorial." *Music Educators Journal* 29 (September-October 1942): 13.

———. "Music in the Victory Corps." *Music Educators Journal* 29 (May-June 1943): 13-16.

Music Educators National Conference National Executive Committee. Minutes, March 1944.

Music Educators National Conference Executive Committee, Joint Meeting with Presidents of Sectional Conferences and Auxiliary Organizations, "Minutes," Chicago, October 18–20, 1940.

Nadel, S. F. "The Origins of Music." *Musical Quarterly* 16 (1930): 531–46.

Nettl, Bruno. "On the Question of Musical Universals." *The World of Music* 19 (1977): 2–7.

———. "Recent Directions in Ethnomusicology." In *Ethnomusicology: An Introduction,* ed. Helen Myers, 375–99. London: Macmillan Press, 1992.

Omojola, Olabode F. "Contemporary Art Music in Nigeria: An Introductory Note on the Works of Ayo Bankole." *Africa* 64 (Fall, 1994): 533–43.

Parales, Jon. "On Rap, Symbolism and Fear." *New York Times,* February 2, 1992, sec. 2, 1.

Pasler, Jann. "*Pelleas* and Power: Forces Behind the Reception of Debussy's Opera." *19th-Century Music* 10 (Spring 1987): 244–64.

Radocy, Rudolph E. "Music Doesn't Make You Smarter . . . But It Doesn't Hurt." *Kodály Envoy* (Winter 1998): 44–46.

Rauscher, Frances, Gordon L. Shaw, and Katherine N. Ky. "Listening to Mozart Enhances Spatial-Temporal Reasoning: Towards a Neurophysiological Basis." *Neuroscience Letters* 185 (1995): 44–47.

Recording Industry Association of America, "2008 Year-End Shipment Statistics on U.S. Recorded Music." http://www.riaa.com/keystatistics.php (accessed April 21, 2009).

Regelski, Thomas A. "Prolegomenon to a Praxial Philosophy of Music and Music Education." *Musiikkikasvatus: The Finnish Journal of Music Education* 1 (1996): 23–38.

———. "Taking the 'Art' of Music for Granted: A Critical Sociology of the Aesthetic Philosophy of Music." In *Critical Reflections on Music Education: Proceedings of the Second International Symposium on the Philosophy of Music Education,* June 12–16, 1994, ed. Lee R. Bartel and David J. Elliott. Toronto: Canadian Music Education Research Centre, University of Toronto, 1996, 23–58.

———. "Musical Values and the Value of Music Education." *Philosophy of Music Education Review* 10 (Spring 2002): 49–55.

———. "Social Theory, and Music and Music Education as Praxis." *Action, Criticism, and Theory for Music Education* 3 (December 2004): 2–52.

Sarnthein, J., A., vonStein, P., Rappelsberger, H. Petsche, F. H. Rauscher, et al. "Persistent Patterns of Brain Activity: An EEG Coherence Study of the Positive Effect of Music on Spatial-Temporal Reasoning." *Neurological Research* (1997): 19, 107–16.

Schoen, Max. "The Æsthetic Attitude in Music." *Psychological Monographs* 39 (1928): 169–70.

Small, Christopher. "Performance as Ritual: Sketch for an Enquiry into the True Nature of a Symphony Concert." In *Lost in Music: Culture, Style and the Musical Event*, ed. Avron Levine White, 19–46. London: Routledge & Kegan Paul, 1987.

Smith, Fowler, Richard W. Grant, et al. "American Unity Through Music." *Music Educators Journal* 27 (March–April 1941): 9–12.

Starobinski, Jean. "The Age of Genius." *Unesco Courier* 44 (July 1991): 18–21.

Wachsmann, Klaus P. "Universal Perspectives in Music." *Ethnomusicology* 15 (September 1971): 381–84.

Wackenroder, Wilhelm Heinrich. "Phantasien über die Kunst (1799)" ["Musings on Art"]. Quoted by Oskar Walzel in *German Romanticism*. Translated by A. E. Lussky, 122–23. New York: G. P. Putnam's Sons, 1932.

Washington, George. "Letter to Rev. Joseph Willard, March 22, 1781." In *Writings of George Washington from the Original Manuscript, 1745–1799*, Vol. 21, ed. J. C. Fitzpatrick. Washington, DC: United States Government Printing Office, 1937.

Westcott, Kathryn. "Barenboim Hits Out at 'Sound of Musak.'" *BBC News Online*, April 7, 2006. http://news.bbc.co.uk/2/hi/entertainment/4883612.stm (accessed June 11, 2006).

Wheatley, John J., and George Brooker. "Music and Spokesperson Effects on Recall and Cognitive Response to a Radio Advertisement." In *Attention, Affect, and Attitude in Response to Advertising*, ed. Eddie M. Clark, Timothy C. Brock, and David W. Stewart, 189–204. Hillsdale, NJ: Lawrence Erlbaum Associates, 1994.

Wilkes, Paul. "Why People of God Don't Talk to the Press." *Columbia Journalism Review* 31 (September/October, 1992): 54–55.

Williams, David. "SWRL Music Program: Ethnic Song Selection and Distribution." Report #SWRL-TN-3-72-28. Los Alamitos, CA: Southwest Regional Laboratory for Educational Research and Development, September 6, 1972 (ERIC document ED109040).

Yarustovsky, Boris Mikhailovich. Foreword to *Rite of Spring: Full Score* by Igor Stravinsky. New York: Dover Publications, 1989.

Index

cultural / ontological relationships, 39–41, 92–94, 251, 253,
265, 275; as experience, 125n23;
148n88, 148n89, 149n91
Seeger, Charles, 47
Seeger, Pete 143n77
semiosis, 38–39, 251, 266
semiotic: as basis of music education
curricula, 263–267 passim,
278–279; Geertz's concept of
culture as, 19–20; musical,
95–110; Peirce's theory, 31–39,
250–251; representations of universalist and relativist concepts
of music, 52–54; representation
of pragmatist concept of musical
practice, 83
separation of religion and state,
136–142 passim, 253, 268
shakuhachi, 106
shamanism, 71–72, 75–79, 81–90 passim, 155, 178, 220, 224, 252,
267, 273
sign: interplay and transformation
(semiosis), 38–39, 251, 266;
Peirce's concept of, 31–36,
250–251
Sign (Representamen): as an aspect of a
sign, defined, 33–36, 250–251;
effects of, 40–41; music as,
51–56; 95–110, 253; ontological relationship of individuals
with respect to, 39–42, 251; in
semiosis, 38–39, 266; tenfold
classification, 37n57; types of,
36–38, 251
Simon, Paul, 150n96
singing societies, 182, 259
Singing Society of Stoughton, Massachusetts, 182
slavery, 10, 130n38, 136n55, 172, 176,
257
sleeping sickness, 271
Small, Christopher, 50n16, 77, 98–101,
155
Smith, Adam, 114, 135, 152
Smith, Eleanor, 192, 195
Smith, Fowler, 211
Smithsonian Institution, 141, 235
social drama, 79–80, 88, 107
societies, state: defining characteristics,
66; differences between U.S. and
other, 137, 253–254; formation
of, 113, 115; music education in,

156–157, 256; musical practices
in, 78n68, 78n69, 88–94, 252–
256; religious belief in, 145n82
societies, traditional: defining characteristics, 66; music education in,
156–157, 256; musical practices
in, 66–88, 252, 256; religious
belief in, 87
Society for Ethnomusicology, 61, 235
Society for General Music, 235
Society for Regular Singing, 174
sociology of music, 154
sociopolitical effects of music and
ritual, 79–82
Southard, Lucien H., 185–186
Soviet Union, 92, 140, 157, 223–224
speech therapy, 270
Spain, 131n39, 171
Sparshott, Francis, 238
Sputnick, 223–224
stage drama, 88
standards: learning, 207, 224; music
curricula, 235; *See also National
Standards for Arts Education*
Standifer, James, 235
Star Spangled Banner, 142n70
steel drum, Carribean, 2, 62n27, 277
stock market crash of 1929, 142
Stravinsky, Igor, 107–108
stroke, 270
structuralism, 18
student teaching, 276
Stumpf, Carl, 46
subjective universal, 121–122, 125,
180, 195, 233
subjective vocabulary, 139–140, 144
Sufis, Sufism, 4, 63, 87
Sullivan, George, 225
Sweden, 144, 171
symbol: defined, 37, 43, 250–251;
music as 104–110, 253, 265
symphony concert, 99, 101, 204
synechism: and brainwave topography,
104; defined, 22–28, 250; and
fallibilism, 31; and Hegel's concept of "absolute mind," 23n19;
and musical practices, 59; and
d'Aquili and Laughlin's concept
of ritual; and Peirce's phenomenal categories, 31–32
synthesizer 103n111

T

Taliban, 141n62